The Rainbow after the Storm

The Rainbow
after the Storm

*Marriage Equality and Social Change
in the U.S.*

MICHAEL J. ROSENFELD

Fiona:
With much appreciation for all
your help over The years.
— Michael

OXFORD
UNIVERSITY PRESS

OXFORD
UNIVERSITY PRESS

Oxford University Press is a department of the University of Oxford. It furthers the University's objective of excellence in research, scholarship, and education by publishing worldwide. Oxford is a registered trade mark of Oxford University Press in the UK and certain other countries.

Published in the United States of America by Oxford University Press
198 Madison Avenue, New York, NY 10016, United States of America.

Library of Congress Control Number: 2021941345
ISBN 978–0–19–760044–3 (pbk.)
ISBN 978–0–19–760043–6 (hbk.)

DOI: 10.1093/oso/9780197600436.001.0001

1 3 5 7 9 8 6 4 2

Paperback printed by LSC communications, United States of America
Hardback printed by Bridgeport National Bindery, Inc., United States of America

Contents

PART IV: THE BROADER IMPLICATIONS OF
MARRIAGE EQUALITY

Preface

This book project traveled a long and winding road to get here. More than a decade ago I published a paper about same-sex couples and their children. As most academic papers do, my paper disappeared in the ether and I moved on to other research interests. A few years later some other scholars wrote a critique of my paper about children and parents, and I responded in the same journal. Again, hardly anyone outside of the people involved paid attention.

At some point I received an email from someone in the public who was a stranger to me, explaining that the critics of my work were being called as witnesses by the state of Michigan in a federal case to determine the constitutionality of Michigan's ban on same-sex marriage. The emailer wanted to know what I was going to do about this, and I remember thinking *There is nothing for me to do*. The federal courts in Michigan are well outside my narrow sphere of influence. I was then and still am a sociologist living in San Francisco.

No sooner had I dismissed the email than lawyers for the plaintiffs, having found my name (as an object of criticism) on the CVs of one of the state's witnesses, called me to appear as an expert witness in the case. The case, *DeBoer v. Snyder*, turned out by chance to be an important case in the buildup to the U.S. Supreme Court's *Obergefell v. Hodges* decision that made marriage equality the law of the U.S.

I ended up being able to play a small role in an important legal and social change. Other people have spent years fighting for marriage equality, including plaintiffs who exposed themselves to harassment and defeat and years of bitter disappointments. I try to do justice in this book to some of the people who poured years of their lives into the cause of marriage equality.

After *DeBoer* and *Obergefell*, I started to wonder how marriage equality came to be accepted in the U.S. so seemingly quickly. I started to do research about public opinion, social movements, and the law. I became curious about why so little had been written about the role of social science in making social change. This manuscript had a slow gestation. I am deeply grateful for the faith that Oxford University Press's James Cook showed in me, and in the patience he showed for earlier, much rougher versions of this text.

One of the lessons of this book is that gay and lesbian people coming out of the closet had a profound impact on their friends and family and managed to shift an entire nation's view of gay rights. When I think of the power of face-to-face political interaction, I am always reminded of my mother, Susan, the community activist. I have a lot of sharp childhood memories of walking through the apartment building complex where I grew up in Washington Heights in Manhattan, holding a clipboard with both hands while my mother knocked on several hundred apartment doors, talking to the other tenants about this or that political candidate. Over the course of a few years, every elected official in my neighborhood was replaced by people whom my mother and her friends chose. I did not understand as a child that my mother had outsized influence or why. My mother never talked up her own accomplishments. There were gender and generational dimensions to her modesty. By the time I was old enough to appreciate what she had done, she had already passed away. I would like to think that my mother, a dedicated believer in social change, would enjoy this book. Mom, this one is for you.

I owe a debt of gratitude to my father, Mordecai, the retired lawyer and essay writer. My father always has believed in the value of justice. He also has a great ear for written language and a deep disdain (instilled in him during elementary school in Brooklyn in the 1930s and early 1940s) for grammatical offenses, such as the split infinitive. My father read this manuscript several times, fixed sentences, and eliminated a host of unnecessary commas. I hope that he sees the final product as one that is worthy of his many thoughtful contributions.

Permission to reuse material I previously published is gratefully acknowledged: "Moving a Mountain: The Extraordinary Trajectory of Same-Sex Marriage Approval in the U.S.," *Socius* 3 (2017):1–22, with research assistance from Taylor Orth and Jacob Reidhead and feedback from Kate Weisshaar, Anna Boch, Taylor Orth, Emily Carian, and Jacob Reidhead; "Revisiting the Data from the New Family Structure Study: Taking Family Instability into Account," *Sociological Science* 2 (2015):478–501; and finally thanks to the Population Association of America for permission to reuse material from "Nontraditional Families and Childhood Progress through School," *Demography* 47.3 (2010):755–775.

Feedback (sometimes over several versions) on various chapters of this book has been gratefully received from Vivian Levy, Soomin Kim, Taylor Orth, Anna Boch, Emma Tsurkov, Ingrid Nelson, Kenny Dinitz, Meghan Warner, Amanda Mireles, Amy Johnson, Amy Casselman Hontalas, Alisa

Feldman, Terresa Eun, Emma Williams-Baron, and the Stanford graduate family workshop. My fifteen-year-old daughter, Omara, advised me to simplify the text and clarify the figures. My wife, Vivian, and son, Raúl, made the same suggestions, but more insistently and in more detail.

My old friend Bruno Navasky read the manuscript and sent me twelve pages of notes. My graduate school buddy Chad Broughton read the manuscript and marked up every page. I gratefully acknowledge research assistance on the Christian Right from Emma Tsurkov and Fiona Kelliher. Sonia Hausen took time off from more important projects to read this entire manuscript and help me improve the logical order of a disparate set of historical arguments.

I am a cisgender straight White man married to a woman. I occupy a variety of privileged statuses. Being a professor at Stanford University imbues me with one kind of privilege that is especially salient outside of academia. When I was testifying in federal court in the *DeBoer* case, it did not escape my awareness that some of the deference afforded to me was perhaps due to my privilege, as opposed to my accomplishments. With all endowments, one must simply hope to do the best one can with whatever advantages or challenges one has.

As I am not a lawyer, I have been especially reliant on advice and correction from the following lawyers who were willing to read the entire manuscript: Kenneth Mogill of the *DeBoer v. Snyder* legal team, Emma Tsurkov, and of course my father. Doug McAdam shared his deep wisdom about social movement theories. Reviewers from Oxford University Press provided wonderful (and, in the early versions, stern) feedback and taught me many important things. In short, I have received a great deal of help and specific advice from many smart people in researching and revising this manuscript. Any remaining flaws are entirely my own.

1

Introduction

In the early 2000s, U.S. public opinion was strongly against same-sex marriage. Proponents of marriage equality had lost thirty state referenda in a row. The Republican Party was winning national campaigns on the back of public opposition to gay rights. Same-sex marriage in the U.S. seemed a hopeless cause. Even within the gay rights movement, many smart people thought that marriage equality was unachievable in the U.S. and that devoting energy and money to fighting for same-sex marriage was wasting precious resources.[1]

And yet, under the surface, rapid change was taking place. American attitudes toward gay rights (the right to marry, the right to serve in the military, the right to make a public speech, the right to teach, the right to be free of workplace discrimination, the right to adopt children, among many other rights) were undergoing an unprecedented transformation. It seemed that almost overnight, same-sex marriage was the law in the U.S., delivered by a 5–4 Supreme Court decision in *Obergefell v. Hodges* (2015). This book tells the story of the rapid liberalization of attitudes toward gay rights that made same-sex marriage U.S. law sooner than almost anyone thought possible.

In 1988, only 11.6% of Americans thought same-sex couples should have the right to marry. There are few attitudes in American public life that have less than 12% support.[2] A politician with less than 12% support of voters would probably be urged by leaders of their own party to resign. In the thirty years from 1988 to 2018, American support for same-sex marriage rose from 11.6 to 68.1%. How did attitudes about same-sex marriage change so much? Most public opinions are stable over time.[3] Against this background of mostly stable public opinion, American attitudes toward gay rights have been rapid changing outliers. Social scientists and the general public have understood that the change in attitudes toward gay rights was unusual, but it has not previously been clear exactly *how* unusual it was. Public opinion toward same-sex marriage in the U.S. has in fact changed more than any other American public opinion in recorded history. This liberalization of American attitudes toward gay rights has been revolutionary. Revolutionary change requires explanation.

The Rainbow after the Storm. Michael J. Rosenfeld, Oxford University Press. © Oxford University Press 2022.
DOI: 10.1093/oso/9780197600436.003.0001

There are several possible explanations for why American attitudes toward gays and lesbians changed so much. The most important explanation by far is that gays and lesbians coming out of the closet influenced their friends, their coworkers, their neighbors, and their families. But if being out of the closet (i.e., being open and honest about one's real identity) was enough to dispel prejudice all by itself, there would be a whole lot less prejudice in the world than there is. Being out of the closet by itself was not enough; there is more to the story than that. There are circumstances and characteristics particular to gays and lesbians in the U.S. that help explain why gay rights have progressed so much but why abortion rights, women's rights, and racial justice are all stalled in the U.S. In this book I explore some of the reasons marriage equality and gay rights have undergone such unusual and transformational change, and I attempt to determine which of the principles of gay rights liberalization could be applied to other causes.

Most histories of the gay rights movement are told from the perspective of the gay rights leaders and their social movement organizations. The reader will find some stories of that type in this book. Where possible, however, I try to rely on a different kind of social science: the study of populations derived from censuses and nationally representative attitude surveys. Sometimes the nationally representative data can yield insights that would be missed if one studied only movement leaders and their organizations.

For instance, the leaders of the gay rights social movement organizations in the U.S. were often surprisingly indifferent or hostile to the cause of marriage equality, which is one reason studies of gay rights that center movement leaders tend to miss the revolutionary importance of marriage equality. Faderman's (2015) classic history of the gay rights revolution in the U.S., seen through the eyes of movement leaders, treats marriage equality as an afterthought. Hirshman's (2012; see especially 237–241) classic history of the gay rights revolution in the U.S., published just before the triumph of marriage equality, treats marriage equality as wrongheaded and destined to fail.

Once same-sex couples in the U.S. had the option to legally marry, it was clear they were much more interested in marriage than many gay rights movement leaders and scholars of social movements expected them to be. Gay rights can look quite different from the perspective of the broad population compared to the perspectives of activists and movement leaders. Marriage equality is underappreciated among social movement scholars and activists, but there is no social movement in the past thirty years in the U.S. that has been more transformational.

The Power of Interpersonal Contact

Whereas some gay rights activists and leaders were at least partly out of the closet in 1960s and 1970s, the broad population of American gays and lesbians did not come out until decades later. How do we know this? *Newsweek* magazine sponsored a series of surveys beginning in 1985 asking Americans if they had friends, family members, or coworkers who they knew to be gay or lesbian. The surveys illuminate the time line of *when* gays and lesbians actually came out in the U.S. in numbers large enough to make a difference. Gays and lesbians first came out of the closet in large numbers in the 1990s. The 1990s is also when American attitudes toward gay rights took a sharp and historic liberalizing turn.[4]

Analyzing survey data from different sources, I show that gays and lesbians coming out seems to have *caused* Americans to view gay rights more positively. When Americans were asked why they had changed their mind about gay rights, their most common answer by far was knowing someone gay or lesbian. Scholars and activists have long assumed that interaction between gay and straight Americans might diminish antigay prejudice. I endeavor in this book to document the bias-diminishing effect of contact between gay and straight Americans in some new ways.

The finding that contact between gay and straight Americans has diminished antigay prejudice in a profound way is supported by a classic theory of interpersonal relations, intergroup contact theory (Allport 1954), which was developed to explain why integration between Blacks and Whites would lead to diminished racial prejudice in post–World War II America. With painful historical irony, racial prejudice has proven to be more resilient in the U.S. than mid-century scholars like Gordon Allport expected it to be. Interpersonal contact turns out to be more effective at dispelling bias against sexual minorities than it is at dispelling bias against other kinds of minorities.

One of the great advantages that gays and lesbians have, compared to some other minority groups, is that gays and lesbians come from every type of family, every background, and every region of the U.S. Gay people enter adulthood without the kind of disadvantages and segregation from the American mainstream that other minorities face. There are upper-class White gay people and working-class White gay people, and there are Black gay people of every social class, and gay people in every community in between. There are gay people in San Francisco and New York, of course, and there are gay people in evangelical Christian communities in the Bible Belt of the central and southern U.S. Once gays and lesbians in all these communities had come out of the closet in substantial numbers, Americans who were predisposed to oppose gay rights had to come to grips with the reality that gay and lesbian people were their neighbors, and they always had been.

Unlike the case for racial minorities, homosexuality is at least partly concealable. One cannot tell who is gay or lesbian by looking at them across the room. When a straight person meets a gay or lesbian person, they do not immediately view them through a biased lens. The concealability of homosexuality allows gays and lesbians to come out to people who already know and trust them and makes it easier for gays and lesbians to interact with others on a basis of equal status.

Let's say you have been working at a company for a few years. Sally from Accounting is one of the people in this company who checks your quarterly reports. On several occasions, Sally caught errors that saved you from embarrassment. You have never given Sally much thought, other than that she seems like a reasonable person and is good at her job. Then one day at the company picnic, you meet Sally's partner, Nancy, and you realize that Sally is in a same-sex relationship. Sally and Nancy, it turns out, have been living together for years. Sally may be the first out-of-the-closet gay or lesbian person you have ever met, as far as you know. From the perspective of intergroup contact theory, the crucial fact is that you were able to form an appreciation of Sally before you knew that she was a lesbian. Time goes by. Some years later you hear a conservative politician claiming that gays and lesbians are dangerous, abnormal, and sick, and you think *That does not sound like Sally at all.* The conservative politician's claims lack credibility because they do not square with your personal experience.

Now imagine that someone close to you, someone you really love, perhaps your own child, turns out to be gay. For Americans with a close family member who is gay or lesbian, it is difficult *not* to support gay rights, though there are still families who disown their gay children or seek out discredited therapies to try to convert their gay relative to heterosexuality. Having a gay or lesbian family member was and continues to be an especially strong predictor of support for marriage equality.

Person-to-person, one-to-one interactions between gay and heterosexual Americans are the primary engines of social change that led to marriage equality. Person-to-person interaction can change individual people, and by changing individual people can change public opinion nationally, and by changing public opinion, can change the world.

Social Change and the Courts

The liberalization of American public opinion did not, by itself, make marriage equality the law in the U.S. Majority public support for marriage equality was necessary but certainly not sufficient for marriage equality to be achieved. The federal and state courts were the venue where most of the important gains in the marriage equality movement were made, up to and including the decisive *Obergefell v. Hodges* (2015) decision. Because the courts have been the primary route to the policy achievement of marriage equality in the U.S., same-sex marriage's complicated pathway through the courts is an important thread in this book.

I tell the stories of some of the key plaintiffs[5] who sued the government for the right to marry. Some of the early plaintiffs in the 1970s, such as Jack Baker and Michael McConnell, lost in court, lost all their appeals, and were unable to have their marriage legally recognized in the U.S. until decades later. In the 1990s, same-sex marriage plaintiffs sometimes won in court, but public opinion was so hostile that statewide referenda prevented these couples from being able to legally marry. In the 2000s, marriage equality was beginning to have enough support to allow positive court decisions for marriage equality to survive a political backlash.

The courts were not only the institution where marriage equality was realized; the courts also adjudicated debates between scholars who opposed and scholars who approved of same-sex marriage. Trials are the way the legal system tests the validity of evidence; they bring two conflicting views of the data and the truth into confrontation with a theoretically neutral arbiter, the judge, ruling on the veracity and credibility of both sides.

In the broad case law history of same-sex marriage in the U.S., there were three trials. The first of these, *Baehr v. Miike* (1996), took place in a state court in Hawaii. The second, *Perry v. Schwarzenegger* (2010), took place in U.S. District Court in San Francisco. The third, *DeBoer v. Snyder* (2014), took place in U.S. District Court in Detroit.[6] I served as an expert witness in the *DeBoer v. Snyder* trial on behalf of plaintiffs April DeBoer and Jayne Rowse, who were suing for the right to marry.

Social Science and Antigay Theories on Trial

In all three same-sex marriage trials, scholars who supported and scholars who opposed same-sex marriage testified and were cross-examined. Not only was social science about same-sex couples on trial, but the opponents of same-sex marriage also attacked the integrity of the core institutions of social science, so social science itself was on trial. In all three trials, the judges resoundingly rejected the arguments of scholars opposed to same-sex marriage.

Social scientists usually have little direct influence on public opinion. The academic journal *Demography*, for example, the official flagship journal of the Population Association of America (an association made up of sociologists, economists, demographers, and other scholars), has a print circulation of fewer than three thousand copies. *Demography* happens to be one of the most influential journals in the social sciences, but that does not mean it has much influence outside of the small group of scholars who read it. The newsletter of the Christian Right group Focus on the Family had a circulation of 2.5 million, so naturally whatever Focus on the Family claimed about social science and gay families was going to be more influential to the public than results of research presented in *Demography*.

I published a paper in 2010 in *Demography* about children raised by same-sex couples, using U.S. census data; my paper showed that these children were making good progress through school. Many other scholars published similar findings. A social science consensus developed that children raised by same-sex couples were at no substantial disadvantage. This consensus was endorsed by many national professional organizations of social scientists and doctors.[7] Yet this scholarly consensus was largely invisible to the public.

In the public square, the slow and careful voices of science and social science can be easily drowned out by the much louder and more self-assured voices that spread propaganda. Within the courtroom, however, expertise, research, and science often still prevail while propaganda fares less well. Social science institutions and experts have been very influential in the court victories for marriage equality, and especially influential in the trials. The three same-sex marriage trials helped to turn a social science consensus about the health of children raised by same-sex couples into a national policy of marriage equality.

Before American attitudes about gay rights had started to liberalize in the 1990s, gay and lesbian people had been politically buried under three important falsehoods. One falsehood was that gay and lesbian people were pathological, i.e., sick and abnormal. A result of the falsehood of pathology was that gays and lesbians were seen as not fit to serve in positions of responsibility or trust. A second falsehood was that gays and lesbians were predatory and dangerous, especially to children.[8] A third falsehood declared that homosexuality was an unnatural state of confusion that could be corrected with conversion therapy that would restore apparent homosexuals to a stable, happy, heterosexual state.

The 1950s were the darkest era of gay life in the U.S. All three basic falsehoods were believed to be true and were promoted by the U.S. government, by professional organizations of researchers, and by lawyers and doctors. The three were false, but they were not *known* to be false. It took researchers decades to overturn belief in the three falsehoods within academic and professional circles and to marginalize the scholars who clung to the falsehoods after they had been debunked.

Over decades, social science helped to change the political and legal context for gay people in the U.S. in ways that made it possible for them eventually to come out of the closet with some expectation of safety. Their coming out of the closet generated a historic liberalization of American attitudes toward gay rights. When the majority of Americans had come to have a positive view of gay rights, policy changes on gay rights became possible. When social science reached a consensus about the health of children raised by same-sex couples, this consensus, combined with a rapidly liberalizing public opinion on gay rights, made favorable trial court decisions much more likely.

The Time Line

Figure 1.1 shows the percentage of American adults who said that sex between two adults of the same sex was *not* always wrong,[9] as opposed to those who said gay sex *was* always wrong. Fewer than 30% of American adults thought gay sex was all right in any circumstances in the 1970s and 1980s and as late as 1991. By 2018, approval of gay sex had risen to 68%. Thinking that gay sex *is* always wrong is strongly associated with social distance from gay people and an intolerance of gay rights. Conversely, people who think that gay sex is *not* always wrong are dramatically more likely to think that gay people should have formal rights. The percentage of Americans who supported marriage equality followed a similar but even faster liberalizing

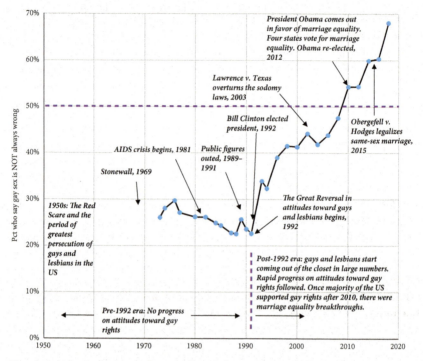

Figure 1.1 Attitudes toward gay rights and progress toward marriage equality.
Source: Weighted data from the General Social Survey, 1973–2018.

time trend (see Figure 8.3). The data on attitudes toward marriage equality do not extend as far back in time, so here we start with the most general and longest time series: the General Social Survey (GSS)'s data on tolerance of gay sex.

Figure 1.1 divides American attitudes toward gay rights in the U.S. into three periods. The first, prior to 1992, corresponds to an era when American attitudes were universally hostile toward gay people and gay rights. In the pre-1992 era, there is no evidence that anything that happened in gay rights activism or in American culture made any headway in undermining widespread intolerance for gay people. American tolerance for gay rights reached a low in 1991. Most histories of gay rights social movements in the U.S. center the 1969 Stonewall riots and the gay rights radicalism of the early 1970s.[10] Stonewall and the 1960s-influenced gay rights radicalism of the Gay Liberation Front (GLF) were certainly important; however the liberalization of attitudes toward gay rights did not begin until a whole generation after

Stonewall, so the timing of this important social change forces us to examine the 1990s more carefully.

While Stonewall and the radicals of the GLF left enduring marks on the gay rights movement and on gay people's self-perceptions, the liberalization of American attitudes took place a generation later, in the 1990s and 2000s. A less radical cast of characters drove attitudinal change in the 1990s. Bill Clinton, a centrist Democrat, introduced gay rights into policy debates in 1992. Ellen DeGeneres, a TV star with a modest, generous, and middle-America nice persona came out of the closet in 1997. Gay couples who wanted the very bourgeois goals of marriage and parenthood helped heterosexual Americans see that gay people and straight people were not as different as they had previously thought.

Gay rights activism in the pre-1992 era was important, but not because it directly influenced American public opinion. Gay rights activism helped gay people envision a better future for themselves. Meanwhile, in academic circles research was increasingly showing that gay people were normal and that homosexuality was a healthy manifestation of human sexuality. This new research started with Alfred Kinsey in the 1940s and Evelyn Hooker in the 1950s. By the 1970s, social science was developing a viable understanding of gay people, same-sex couples, and their children.

Social science studies of gays and lesbians, like the gay activism of the pre-1992 era, had little immediate effect on American attitudes toward gay rights. Instead, gay activism and social science both contributed to a slow change in the openness of what social movement scholars call the "political opportunity structure" of the U.S. political system toward gay rights.[11] The political opportunity structure explains how open (or hostile and repressive) the political system is toward a specific group. Over time the U.S. political system became dramatically less hostile and more open to gay rights claims, and the number of influential elected officials who were allies of gay rights grew. As the U.S. political opportunity structure opened up toward gay people and gay rights, gay people experienced a wider set of opportunities to organize and mobilize.

Starting in the 1970s and 1980s, some U.S. states (influenced in part by social science) decriminalized sodomy. Local police forces reduced their focus on arresting and harassing gay men and started finding other targets. By the 1990s, U.S. popular culture was depicting gays and lesbians in more favorable and less prejudicial ways.

Over time, the political opportunity structure opened enough so that in the 1990s gays and lesbians could come out of the closet in large numbers and directly influence their family, friends, and neighbors. The great reversal in American attitudes toward gay people and gay rights began in 1992, according to the attitude data in Figure 1.1. The great liberalization in American attitudes toward gay rights has been described before, but the *reasons* for the sudden and historically significant reversal have remained elusive.

Since the early 1990s is the turning point at which a historically important shift in attitudes toward gay rights took place, it makes sense to examine the events of that time that could plausibly have influenced closeted gays and lesbians to come out. The brief and controversial reign of *OutWeek* magazine in 1989–1991 was one factor. *OutWeek* represented a radical political view and outed several prominent gay public figures who were leading closeted gay lives.[12] The outing of public people seemed to change the attitudes of less public people to come out of the closet themselves, which was exactly the result that the radicals at *OutWeek* were hoping to achieve.

A second important factor that emerges from the data is the 1992 presidential campaign of Bill Clinton. Part of his campaign platform was to allow gays and lesbians to serve openly in the U.S. military. Clinton did not achieve that goal, and after the Don't Ask, Don't Tell policy was implemented in 1994, the situation for gays and lesbians in the military actually worsened. For this reason, Clinton is not fondly remembered by gay rights activists. What many have overlooked, however, is that his pro-gay-rights rhetoric on the campaign trail seemed to shift the views of many Americans who had never thought about gay rights before.[13]

The third period of American attitudes toward gay rights began around 2010, when support for gay rights and gay people crossed the majority threshold (50%) for the first time. Support specifically for marriage equality crossed the 50% threshold around 2012 (see Figures 6.1 and 9.2). Once there was majority support for gay rights and for marriage equality, state bans against same-sex marriage started falling like dominoes. Old arguments against gay rights and marriage equality that once had been convincing lost their political credibility.

In politics, context is everything. By "context" I mean the context of the time line, with respect to the national support for gay rights. When Clinton was speaking out in favor of gay rights in 1992, he was presenting a view that was completely novel to most Americans. It was more difficult, more politically risky, and also more consequential to be in favor of gay rights in

1992 than it was to be in favor of marriage equality in 2012, when 50% of Americans already favored marriage equality, as President Barack Obama was.[14] Obama is reasonably hailed as a historic champion of gay rights, and Clinton is more often vilified in gay rights circles. Yet in the context of what was politically possible at the different times and with the advantage of hindsight and data, Clinton may have been more responsible for advancing gay rights than Obama was.

Context is also vital in understating social change. In attempting to tell the story of how marriage equality went from impossible and unimaginable to the law of the U.S. in just a few decades, I will rely on the three stages of American attitudes illustrated in Figure 1.1. In the pre-1992 era, I will focus on the ways in which grassroots activism, social science, and political elites helped to nudge open the doors of the political opportunity structure to make it safer for gays and lesbians to come out of the closet.

For the post-1992 period, I will emphasize the way that emergence from the closet helped gays and lesbians influence the attitudes of their friends, family, and coworkers. The background of changing American support for marriage equality and the growing social science consensus in favor of gay rights were two important factors that made it possible for judges, beginning in the 1990s, to decide cases in favor of marriage equality and gay rights. Once American attitudes approached majority support for gay rights and for marriage equality in the 2000s, judicial decisions in favor of marriage equality followed.

Beginning with same-sex civil unions in Vermont in July 2000, and the first marriages of same-sex couples in Massachusetts in May 2004, Americans were seeing same-sex couples making fundamental commitments of love and devotion, with the state's stamp of approval. The political value of public expressions of love and commitment between same-sex partners was tremendous.

For the third period, the post-2010 period, I will describe the way the new majority public support for marriage equality and a social science consensus about same-sex couples (which had been growing for several decades) was translated into a national policy of marriage equality. Marriage equality led, in turn, to an expansion of gay rights in other realms, such as the right to be free from workplace discrimination. The rising approval of gay rights and of marriage equality after 1992 was the freight train that made possible all subsequent gay rights and marriage equality gains in the U.S. The change in attitudes toward gay rights turns out to be a most unusual kind of change, so this attitudinal change deserves special scrutiny.

In the post-2010 period, with marriage equality and gay rights enjoying public approval and steadily increasing support, both movements accumulated victories at a breakneck pace. Barriers to gay, lesbian, and transgender equality that had stood firm for decades were cast aside so quickly that it was difficult to keep up with the changes.

Marriage equality went from crossing the majority approval threshold in 2012 to being U.S. law in 2015, a mere three years later. Marriage equality was able to advance from approval to nationwide policy so quickly because of a simple advantage: it cost straight people nothing. No one *lost* their right to marry when same-sex couples *gained* the right to marry. No one had to pay higher taxes to realize same-sex marriage. Marriage equality is an example of what social movement scholars refer to as a nondisplacing social change.[15] Social movements that do not attempt to displace anyone else's rights have a much greater chance of succeeding. As one judge wrote, "There are enough marriage licenses to go around for everyone."[16]

A dramatic and durable liberalization in public opinion about gay rights made marriage equality viable in the courts. The causal arrow works in the other way as well, but not as dramatically and not as durably. Gay rights victories in the courts probably yielded short-term gains in public approval of marriage equality.[17] As court decisions are only newsworthy for a short time, the public memory of any particular court decision fades and eventually is forgotten. In contrast, one does not forget that one's best friend or one's child is gay, which is why interpersonal contact with gay and lesbian people is the more durable and more powerful engine of public opinion change. First-person experience is the most important teacher there is.

An Overview of the Argument

Figure 1.2 depicts an overview of how marriage equality came to be not only policy but a popular policy in the U.S. The main motor of change was gay and lesbian people coming out of the closet, liberalizing the attitudes of their friends and families toward gay rights. In Figure 1.2, the arrow between gay people coming out of the closet and the liberalization of popular attitudes is the thickest line because this is the relationship for which the evidence is strongest.

Before gays and lesbians could come out of the closet, there had to be change in the political opportunity structure. Police harassment had to

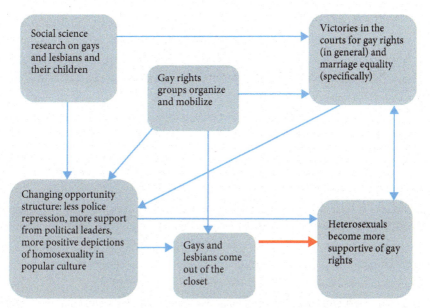

Figure 1.2 Schematic view of social change toward marriage equality.

dissipate, mass culture had to become less prejudicial toward homosexuality, and some mainstream political leaders had to advance gay rights issues. Social science had an independent effect both on the political opportunity structure and also on the outcome of gay rights judicial decisions. Gay rights groups helped to open the political opportunity structure through advocacy and lawsuits.

Mobilization for and against Gay Rights

I do not have much to say in this book about the inner workings of the gay rights groups in the U.S., for several reasons. First, others have written better accounts of the gay rights groups in the marriage equality era than I possibly could.[18] Second, I focus on marriage equality, which was a goal that many of the gay rights groups were hostile to, for both practical and ideological reasons. Third, the gay rights groups were almost always quite small in terms of activists and funds compared to the vast anti-gay-rights groups from the Christian Right. Until very recently gay rights groups were always opposed by larger, stronger, richer anti-gay-rights groups with better political access.

Figure 1.3 shows that the anti-gay-rights groups of the Christian Right were outraising the gay rights groups in 1990 by about 10 to 1.[19] By 2013, the advantage of the anti-gay-rights groups was closer to 3 to 1, but the anti-gay-rights groups still had the advantage at the national level, and they had deeper pockets. Despite this, there were local campaigns where the pro-gay-rights groups outspent their adversaries, especially after 2010. Figure 1.3 simply suggests that in terms of resources the gay rights groups were usually at a disadvantage.

Figure 1.3 probably understates the national cash advantage of the anti-gay-rights groups, because the Catholic Church, the Church of Latter Day Saints, and the Republican Party are not counted among those groups; however, they all devoted vast resources to fighting gay rights, and they had no counterparts on the pro-gay-rights side.[20] Despite being small compared to their opponents, the gay rights groups did win important battles and helped to shape the course of gay rights in the U.S. Their relatively modest size and power simply means that they did not determine the outcome of gay rights politics in the U.S. by themselves.

Same-sex couples comprise about 2.5% of all couples in the U.S. Self-identified lesbian and gay adults together constitute about 2.5% of all

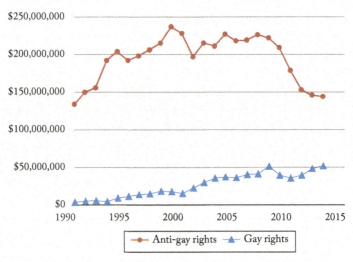

Figure 1.3 Gay rights groups in the U.S. close the national funding gap but remain far behind. Funding of leading gay rights and anti-gay-rights organizations in 2015 dollars.

Source: Rosenfeld (2017), using data from the National Center for Charitable Statistics (2016).

American adults, and bisexuals comprise another approximately 2.5%. Therefore, lesbian, gay, and bisexual adults combined account for about 5% of all adults in the U.S.[21] Thus, no matter how one counts them, people with the most direct interest in gay rights are a small minority of Americans.

As the gay rights groups were dwarfed in spending by anti-gay-rights groups, so too have gay and lesbian people been outnumbered by the social groups in the U.S. most inclined to oppose gay rights. Compared to the small number of gay and lesbian adults in the U.S., conservative Christian adults are much more numerous: 29% of American adults are biblical literalists, believing that the Bible is the actual word of God and is to be taken literally, word for word.[22] Biblical literalism is one of the central pillars of the Christian Right worldview[23] and is a strong predictor of individual opposition to gay rights. The Bible, both Old Testament and New, contains passages that have been read as injunctions against homosexuality.[24] Biblical literalists outnumber gay, lesbian, and bisexual adults by 6 to 1 in the U.S.

Social change is incredibly difficult to make. It is especially difficult for small minority groups to make social change when their opponents outnumber them, outspend them, and have better political access. Public opinion on social issues tends to be stable over time, so it is difficult to move public opinion even a little. On contested public policy issues, each side has resources and mobilized supporters. Whenever one side pushes, the other side pushes back. Whatever resources the gay rights movement had (in terms of money, institutional support, and committed supporters), its opponents in the Christian Right had more.

The victory of marriage equality in the U.S. is therefore a surprising victory for a multitude of reasons. If someone had told you in 1996, when President Clinton signed the Defense of Marriage Act banning the U.S. government's recognition of same-sex marriages,[25] that same-sex marriage would be the law of the land in the U.S. twenty years later, you might not have believed them. The story of marriage equality is a complicated story, and also an iconic twenty-first-century American social change story with ramifications for a wide variety of other social movements.

I try to explain the marriage equality story in this book using all the different kinds of data available, including opinion survey data, census data, historical analyses, and interviews. The 1950s and 1960s in the U.S. predate any national polling on gay rights issues, so I rely on other kinds of sources to describe the slow progress of gay rights in those decades. All the interviews are with supporters of gay rights. My view of the opponents of gay rights is unfortunately limited to their public statements, their published work, and their testimony in court. Readers hoping for insight into the interior logic of the opponents of gay rights will have to look elsewhere.[26]

In evaluating the story of how marriage equality was won in the U.S., readers should keep in mind that hardly anyone (except marriage equality pioneer Evan Wolfson, who had been traveling across the U.S. doing his Paul Revere imitation, telling groups that "marriage is coming") predicted that same-sex marriage would become law in the U.S. as quickly as it did.

The Institution of Marriage and Its Critics

Marriage is a fundamental institution that confers status and rights. In U.S. law there are more than a thousand benefits available exclusively to married people.[27] These include inheritance rights and parenting rights. Having the right to marry does not obligate one to marry, and hetero-sexual couples in the U.S. and Europe increasingly are choosing informal arrangements other than marriage. Whether or not couples choose to marry, having the *right* to marry is a privilege of full adult citizenship. Not having the right to marry implies one is a second-class citizen or worse. In U.S. law, even prisoners, people who have lost most of their rights, may marry.[28] Preventing adults from marrying is a form of social distancing that stigmatizes them and subjects them and their children to further indignities.

As long as same-sex couples were ineligible for marriage in the U.S., gays and lesbians were second-class citizens in the eyes of the law. Despite the benefits of marriage, many gay rights activists opposed marriage equality on the ideological grounds that marriage equality was an assimilationist and bourgeois goal useful only to White middle-class gay people, and that mar-riage equality would worsen the situation of queer people who did not want to marry, an argument made most famously by Paula Ettelbrick (1989). Even after marriage equality was achieved in the U.S., Martin Duberman (2018) offered a similar kind of critique of marriage equality from the Left of the gay rights movement.[29] In Duberman's view, marriage equality was a betrayal of the idealistic and radical principles of the gay rights movement that emerged from the Stonewall riots in 1969.

The gay rights radicals (including Duberman, Ettelbrick, and Nancy Polikoff) who opposed marriage equality wanted to transform the world and they wanted to replace existing institutions like marriage with new family forms like civil unions. The gay rights liberals (such as Wolfson and Thomas Stoddard) who believed in and fought for marriage equality wanted gays and lesbians to be able to marry so that they could have equal rights and equal status with their heterosexual neighbors.

The radicals had a skeptical view of marriage shaped by feminism and by utopian social movements of the 1960s. Gay rights social movement groups of the 1970s, 1980s, and 1990s that were influenced by 1960s radicalism were often hostile to marriage equality as a goal. As a result of the ideological division in gay rights groups over marriage, plaintiffs in the key marriage equality cases I describe were not always able to count on support from gay rights social movement organizations.

The gay rights radicals opposed to marriage equality and the gay rights liberals who fought for marriage equality both had valid reasons for their beliefs. In addition to the unresolvable ideological differences, there was an empirical question that divided the radicals and the liberals. The radicals claimed that marriage equality would hurt queer people who did not want to marry. The liberals claimed that marriage equality would help queer people whether or not they wanted to marry. The empirical evidence strongly suggests that all manner of gay rights became more popular at the same time as marriage equality was becoming the fastest liberalizing attitude in American public opinion history. The data suggest that advocates like Wolfson and Stoddard were right to see marriage equality as a gateway to queer inclusion, visibility, and respect.[30] The marriage equality movement lowered the stigmas against and raised the standing of all queer people, whether or not they wanted to marry. Marriage equality has been broadly and surprisingly transformational.

Stoddard was executive director of Lambda Legal in New York from 1986 to 1992, and he was the author of the 1986 bill in New York City that protected gay people from discrimination in employment and housing. In a famous debate with Paula Ettelbrick, he wrote:

[M]arriage is . . . the political issue that most fully tests the dedication of people who are not gay to full equality for gay people, and also the issue most likely to lead ultimately to a world free from discrimination against lesbians and gay men. Marriage is much more than a relationship sanctioned by law. It is the centerpiece of our entire social structure. (Stoddard 1989: 12)

Stoddard died young of AIDS in 1997, so he never got to see the marriage equality movement begin to succeed in the way he predicted it would.

Organization of the Book

Chapters 2–4 build a scaffold of history, politics, court cases, and culture relevant to gay rights in the U.S. from the 1950s to the end of the 1980s, when American public opinion and popular culture were both overwhelmingly hostile to gay rights. We cannot understand how marriage equality was achieved without understanding some of the history of gay rights struggles and defeats that preceded marriage equality. In order to understand why so few American gays and lesbians were out of the closet before 1990, we need to explore the various barriers they faced.

Chapters 5 and 6 cover cultural and historical events and two key court cases, *Romer v. Evans* (1996) and *Baehr v. Miike* (1996), when the rapidly liberalizing political climate on gay rights in the U.S. was beginning to yield more gay-friendly results in the courts. The *Romer* and *Baehr* decisions both established important precedents for how seriously future American judges were going to have to consider gay rights questions.

Chapters 7 and 8 present the core arguments of this book and represent new approaches to social change and gay rights in the U.S. Chapter 7 shows, using data from several sources, how gay and lesbian people came out of the closet in the 1990s and changed the minds of millions of Americans to become more supportive of gay rights. Chapter 8 documents the uniqueness of this attitude change, especially the historically unprecedented liberalization of American attitudes toward marriage equality. Using a variety of data sets, that chapter shows how Americans' growing appreciation for marriage equality led to greater appreciation for all kinds of queer rights, including transgender rights.

Chapters 9 and 10 describe political and legal events related to marriage equality from 2000 to 2013. By 2010 marriage equality was nearing majority support in the U.S., so marriage equality outcomes in the courts were accordingly more favorable. The *Lawrence v. Texas* (2003) and *U.S. v. Windsor* (2013) Supreme Court decisions wiped out barriers to gay rights, and together led to a whirlwind of activity in the states that would result in just a few short years in a national policy of marriage equality.

Chapter 11 introduces April DeBoer, Jayne Rowse, and their children, who are key protagonists for the final chapters, which cover the period when marriage equality went from being just out of reach to being the law of the entire U.S. Chapter 12 covers research about same-sex couples and their children that ended up being featured in the *DeBoer v. Snyder* same-sex marriage trial. Chapter 13 describes the *DeBoer v. Snyder* trial in detail. *DeBoer v. Snyder* was one of the cases consolidated into *Obergefell v. Hodges*, the decisive U.S. Supreme Court decision on marriage equality, described (along with its impact on April, Jayne, and their children) in chapter 14. While chapters 7 and 8 are the intellectual core of this book, the DeBoer and Rowse family story is the moral core. This is a book about populations and attitudes at the aggregate national level, but it is also a book about individual people, including gay rights pioneers, social scientists, and plaintiffs who sought the right to marry.

When defending her state's same-sex marriage ban in federal court in 2014, Michigan's representative described the ban as "the will of the people"[31] because in 2004 voters had decided, by 59 to 41%, to insert the same-sex marriage ban into Michigan's constitution. Notwithstanding the fact that ten years later marriage equality had majority support in Michigan and in most of the rest of the U.S., Judge Bernard Friedman's decision in *DeBoer v. Snyder* rebuked the state's representatives for having "lost sight of what this case is truly about: people. No court record of this proceeding could ever fully convey the personal sacrifice of these two plaintiffs who seek to ensure that the state may no longer impair the rights of their children and the thousands of others now being raised by same-sex couples."[32]

The decisive marriage equality victory in *Obergefell v. Hodges* followed directly from the trial victory in *DeBoer v. Snyder* and from a series of other cases that were decided in favor of marriage equality across the U.S. leading up to 2015.

Once we bring the story of marriage equality in the U.S. to its denouement in this text, it will be natural to take stock of the broader implications of the movement. Every case study needs to consider the question of generalizability. What are the lessons of the marriage equality movement for other social movements? Why has marriage been so much more popular among same-sex couples than left-wing critics expected it to be? Does coming out of the closet have broader application for other disadvantaged or stigmatized groups? Women who have had abortions are one obvious closeted minority; women who have been victims of sexual assault and harassment are another. I take up the questions of generalizability in four brief final chapters.

A Note on Terminology

I rely in this book on analyses, including some based on prior academic journal publications of mine, using a variety of social science data sets. I will introduce the different data sets as they appear. Terms from law and from social science are defined (sometimes in the notes) at first use. I use the terms "same-sex marriage" and "marriage equality" interchangeably to denote a legal regime in which same-sex couples have the same legal rights and benefits from marriage as heterosexual couples. The language of non-traditional sexual identities in the U.S. has diversified over time, from homosexual, to gay and lesbian, to queer. Rather than superimpose today's terminology on the past, I try to use the language that was used by people in their own times.

PART I
GAY RIGHTS AND THE ANTECEDENTS OF MARRIAGE EQUALITY 1950S–1990

2

The 1950s and 1960s

If hundreds of thousands of gay people coming out of the closet was all that was required to move public opinion, why did it not happen decades before the 1990s? Gay rights leaders of the 1960s and 1970s were not shy about urging their friends to declare their homosexuality, but most gay people in the U.S. remained in the closet because it was simply not safe to come out.

Our actions are always constrained by the world around us, by what some scholars refer to as the political opportunity structure.[1] Injustice is common, but the political opportunity for successful rebellion is rare. Among the structural constraints that kept gay people in the closet were persecution by the police, sodomy laws (criminalizing anal and oral sex) that supported the persecution of gay people by the police, antigay public opinion, and antigay social norms that were reflected in the popular culture.

All of the cultural, legal, and political constraints to gay equality in the U.S. had to be diminished substantially before gays and lesbians had the opportunity to come out of the closet. And the structural constraints to gay equality did decline from the 1950s to the 1990s, so that eventually gay people felt it was safe enough to come out. But in the 1950s, all of the legal, cultural, and political barriers to gay equality were at their highest.

In the 1950s the marriage equality movement in the U.S. was still decades away. The few gay people in the U.S. who were out of the closet were persecuted. Early gay rights organizations of the 1950s were small, beleaguered, and embattled. It is important to recognize how dark the climate was for gay rights in law and in popular culture in the U.S. in the 1950s, so that the rapid successes of the 2000s can be put into proper perspective. Even social changes that seem to occur all at once (as the gay rights gains of the 2010s seemed to do) usually have decades of antecedents when progress was slow.

The Rainbow after the Storm. Michael J. Rosenfeld, Oxford University Press. © Oxford University Press 2022.
DOI: 10.1093/oso/9780197600436.003.0002

Cold War Politics and Persecutions

Laws and political actors define the boundaries of the opportunity structure. In the 1950s and for several decades after, the American legal system persecuted gay people, which meant that anyone the police identified as gay or lesbian was vulnerable to arrest, conviction, and the loss of their job and apartment.

The closet that gay people and gay characters had to live in was fortified by the 1950s anticommunist Red Scare in the U.S. The Red Scare was the U.S. domestic manifestation of the worldwide Cold War struggle between the U.S. and its allies and client states on one side, and the Soviet Union and its allies and client states on the other side. The 1950s Red Scare campaign against Americans who had ever had ties (real, alleged, or imagined) to the Communist Party went hand in hand with a similar campaign against gays and lesbians. Like Americans who were alleged to have ties to the Communist Party, gays and lesbians were closeted minorities, upon whom any vilification could be heaped and about whom any fearful story could be spread.

The Cold War forged a durable alliance between anticommunism and the Christian Right in America.[2] Such an alliance was explicitly sought by J. Edgar Hoover, the long-term director of the U.S. Federal Bureau of Investigation.[3] The Soviet Union was officially atheistic and persecuted religious groups, so it was natural for religious groups in the U.S. to ally themselves with anticommunism. To mobilize the power of the U.S. state to persecute homosexuals, the Christian Right simply needed to suggest that homosexuality was a communist plot to undermine the moral fiber of the U.S., an argument that Hoover and the FBI were all too willing to accept and act on.

President Dwight D. Eisenhower issued executive orders in the 1950s that prohibited gays and lesbians from getting security clearance and from working for the federal government. These executive orders were outgrowths of the antihomosexual paranoia of the Red Scare era;[4] they were not rescinded until the Clinton presidency in the 1990s.[5] The ban on homosexuals serving in government was justified on the grounds that homosexuals could not be trusted, as they were potentially subject to blackmail. Ironically, it was only the government's ban on gays and lesbians serving openly that made blackmail against gays and lesbians in government service possible. Among the Americans who have been convicted of treason or of spying for a foreign power, none is known to have done so to protect a closeted gay identity.[6]

An additional irony of the Red Scare campaign against gays and lesbians is that Hoover, enthusiastic leader of the U.S. government campaigns against alleged communists and supposed homosexuals, may have been himself a gay man. Hoover was especially paranoid about rumors that he was gay.[7]

The restrictive 1952 McCarran-Walter Immigration and Nationality Act barred homosexuals from immigrating to the U.S. based on two provisions. The first provision stipulated that anyone who had been "convicted of a crime of moral turpitude" (understood to include homosexuality and sodomy) was prevented from immigrating. It affected only potential immigrants who had a conviction on their record. The second provision stipulated that people could be blocked from immigrating to the U.S. for "psychopathology," which was understood by the U.S. Immigration and Naturalization Service to include homosexuality since the American Psychiatric Association defined homosexuality as pathological at the time.[8]

The police persecution of gays and lesbians in the U.S. during the height of the Cold War in the 1950s and 1960s was relentless and devastating. Thousands of people, especially gay men, were arrested, punished, imprisoned, and stripped of their jobs, their housing, and their rights. Some were sent to psychiatric hospitals to undergo lobotomies, castration, or electroshock treatment.[9]

The Homophile Groups

In 1950, in the face of ferocious antigay state repression, Harry Hay founded the Mattachine Society, a secretive homosexual men's advocacy group in Los Angeles. As a card-carrying communist, however, Hay brought extra scrutiny from local authorities, and soon he was forced out of the leadership. An offshoot of the Mattachine Society published the magazine *ONE*, whose first issue, published in January 1953, featured Mattachine pioneer Dale Jennings's personal history of being followed, entrapped, and arrested by the Los Angeles Police.[10]

Around the same time that Jennings was arrested in L.A. Bayard Rustin, a brilliant and charismatic advocate for nonviolent social change, was arrested a few miles away in Pasadena, California. Rustin was arrested for having sex in the back seat of a car with two men he picked up late one night after giving a speech on world peace. Rustin would serve sixty days in jail for the offense. He had been incarcerated before, for refusing to cooperate with the military draft during World War II. After the war he had become a celebrated speaker and a leader of the pacifist left-wing group Fellowship of Reconciliation. The news of Rustin's arrest for lewd vagrancy in Pasadena led his old friends in the Fellowship to cut him loose, so he was not only stigmatized and incarcerated but also unemployed and isolated.[11]

Rustin would go on to be a mentor to Martin Luther King Jr. and help plan the historic Civil Rights March on Washington in 1963. Rustin was influential in both the civil rights and antiwar movements, but his prior association with communism and his lifelong homosexuality made him always an outsider, always vulnerable to being outed and discredited. The FBI kept Rustin under close surveillance for much of his activist life.

In San Francisco in 1955 Del Martin and Phyllis Lyon (who had been a couple for a few years already) formed the Daughters of Bilitis with six other women. The Daughters of Bilitis was one of the first lesbian rights groups in the U.S. They started publishing the magazine *The Ladder* by sending free copies to about a hundred people they knew, hoping some of the recipients would send in one dollar for a full-year subscription. The second issue of the magazine reported on a 1956 police raid on a lesbian bar in San Francisco known as Kelly's, in which thirty-six women were arrested and all but four pled guilty to "frequenting a house of ill repute." *The Ladder*'s advice to readers was simple: Don't plead guilty.

In its early years *The Ladder* contained regular advice about what to do when arrested by the police, reassurances to nervous readers that the subscription list would remain secret, and book reviews, essays, poetry, fiction (sometimes suggestive but never lewd), and letters from curious subscribers. There were also listings of events and meetings, most of which took place in San Francisco, where the Daughters of Bilitis was based and where *The Ladder* was published. Over time, news of events from other places started to trickle in.

Eventually *The Ladder* found its way to a select group of readers across the U.S. Readers' letters published in the magazine in the 1950s were a mix of amazement and gratitude that such a publication could exist, and fear that neighbors or roommates might find out what it was about. Some readers in small towns wrote to the editor desperate to be introduced to other readers in their area, but the editors, fearful that the information might fall into the wrong hands, refused to share its mailing list with anyone.[12]

The October 1954 issue of *ONE* magazine had a lead article describing the Postal Service's rules on obscenity as a way of explaining to readers why some of their submissions had not made it into print.[13] The article clarified that matchmaking ads were not allowed; descriptions of gay relationships that too strongly intimated that sex had taken place were impermissible; and graphic representation of the naked male form was of course also not permitted.

The postmaster of Los Angeles had decided that *ONE*'s special issue on the First Amendment and obscenity law was *itself* obscene due to a slightly bawdy poem and an ad for a homophile magazine from Switzerland. The postmaster denied *ONE* the right to be delivered through the mail. Readers realized that something was wrong when their issues never arrived. *ONE*'s attorney Eric Julber sued, lost, and then appealed. The case would go all the way to the U.S. Supreme Court.[14]

Although the Mattachine Society and the Daughters of Bilitis were tiny organizations in the 1950s with obscure names meant to hide the groups' identities, the absence of other voices advocating for gay rights in the 1950s made these groups a historically important vanguard. Both planted organizational seeds that would sprout later. They won some small victories that would be more fully exploited by their organizational descendants. Activists involved with the two organizations would go on to create other, larger organizations.

It is important to remember the Mattachine Society and the Daughters of Bilitis for the perspective they give to more recent progress in the U.S. on gay rights. The gay rights gains of the post-2010 era in the U.S. cannot be fully appreciated without understanding how many obstacles the 1950s homophile organizations faced, how much hostility gay people faced, and how hard it was for the gay rights vanguard of the 1950s to survive.

The Hays Code and the Closet in Popular Culture

To my knowledge, there is no public opinion data on gay rights issues in the U.S. from the 1950s and the 1960s. Opinion polling was in its infancy, and gay rights issues were not on the agendas of the main political parties and their national candidates. To understand the views of gay people and gay rights we need to look elsewhere, such as to Hollywood movies from the era and the depictions of gay people that were allowed.

Those depictions in the 1950s and 1960s were fundamentally negative and deeply prejudicial, reflecting American elites' fear of and hostility toward both communists and homosexuals. Censorship of positive depictions of gay characters in the movies was one method of ensuring that public opinion would be hostile to gay people and to gay rights.

In the 1950s and for several decades before, Hollywood strictly enforced rules about what could be shown on screen.[15] One difference between the everyday closet and the Hollywood closet was that the rules of the Hollywood closet were printed and distributed. They came to be known as the Hays Code, for William Hays, the chairman of the Motion Picture Producers and Distributors of America from 1922 to 1945.

Under the Hays Code crime was never to be shown in a favorable light, and methods of crime were never explained so as not to inspire imitation. Criminals could never be shown as heroes. The Code treated homosexuality as similar to crime because sex between two adults of the same sex was criminal in all or most of the U.S. during the time the Code was in effect. The Hays Code had a specific set of rules about the treatment of homosexuality in the movies:

In the case of impure love,[16] the love which society has always regarded as wrong and which has been banned by divine law, the following are important:

1. Impure love must **not** be presented as **attractive** and **beautiful**.
2. It must **not** be the subject of **comedy** or **farce**, or treated as material for **laughter**.[17]
3. It must **not** be presented in such a way as **to arouse passion** or morbid curiosity on the part of the audience.
4. It must **not** be made to seem **right and permissible**.
5. In general, it must **not** be **detailed** in method and manner. (Motion Picture Association of America, Inc. 1955: 14; emphasis in original)

According to Vito Russo's (1987) classic history of the Hays Code and its effect on gay themes and gay and lesbian people, only fleeting and negative depictions of gay and lesbian characters were allowed in American movies. Consider the unmistakably stereotypical gay inflections of the murderous villains in Alfred Hitchcock's *Rope* (1948), a movie in which two handsome young men murder their former schoolmate just to see if they can get away with it, and then invite the dead schoolmate's friends and family to a dinner party where the dead man lies in a chest in the middle of the room. *Strangers on a Train* is a Hitchcock (1951) movie based on a novel by closeted lesbian Patricia Highsmith, featuring a pathological, devious, and gay-appearing

Bruno, who asks Guy (a stranger Bruno meets on a train) to kill Bruno's father, while Bruno volunteers to kill Guy's wife so he can be free of her. Since neither Bruno nor Guy has any connection to the other's family, Bruno's theory is, they will both get away with murder.

Biographical movies about people who were gay or lesbian in real life were forced by the Hollywood censors to describe those characters as heterosexual. According to Russo (1987), everyone involved in Hollywood, including gay actors and gay directors, thought this erasure of gay and lesbian biographies was appropriate and necessary. U.S. distribution of foreign movies cut out the gay characters, or else the movie was simply not distributed in the U.S. The Hays Code also governed the off-screen behavior of Hollywood public figures in a way that ruled out same-sex relationships or any innuendo of same-sex attraction.

In Joseph Mankiewicz's (1959) film *Suddenly, Last Summer* the main character, Catherine Holly, played by Elizabeth Taylor, is institutionalized in an insane asylum because she carries a terrible secret: her cousin Sebastian had used her to procure young men for him. What Sebastian did with the young men was alluded to but never spoken of directly, because in the 1950s there was no way to describe homosexuality directly in American movies. Sebastian's murder by an angry crowd, serving as a kind of cinematic moral judgment against him, was retold by Catherine at the end of the movie. *Suddenly, Last Summer* had a screenplay by Gore Vidal, based on a play by Tennessee Williams. Two gay men thus wrote the homophobic story.

The Hays Code was relaxed in the 1960s, and unofficial censorship took the place of official censorship in American movies. In the unofficial censorship of the 1960s gay villains were occasionally seen and described, but gay heroes were still absent. Russo (1987) explains that gay characters were allowed in American movies in the 1960s, as long as they killed themselves from shame in the end. In the 1960s and 1970s, Hollywood actors, both gay and straight, were unwilling to play gay characters for fear they would be typecast in those roles and their careers ruined as a result.

The Detective, directed by Douglas Gordon (1968) and starring Frank Sinatra as the honest and world-weary New York detective, contains several classic negative Hollywood tropes about homosexuality. The trailer for the movie declares, "You are Joe Leland, detective, prowling a city sick with violence, full of junkies, prostitutes, and perverts." In the opening scene a man is found dead and mutilated, his genitals and fingers cut off. The coroner declares the dead man to be homosexual and to have been the victim of a lover's spat. "This is the way *they* settle it," the coroner declares. Halfway through the movie, Detective Leland finds the dead man's former roommate, a whining, desperate, and delusional gay man, and coerces him to plead guilty to the murder. The roommate is convicted and electrocuted. At the end of the movie, Leland discovers that the man was innocent: a closeted gay man with a wife had committed the murder and then killed himself, leaving a tape-recorded confession. In confession the real murderer claims, "I was more ashamed of being a homosexual than of being a murderer." The movie depicts homosexuals as desperate, delusional, murderous, self-hating, and suicidal. Popular culture of the U.S. in the 1950s and 1960s painted gay people in a uniformly negative way.

The Effects of the Closet

Youth from racial and religious minorities generally live with at least one parent from the same minority group who is likely to feel identity solidarity with their children. But gay, lesbian, and queer youth generally have hetero-sexual parents who do not share and may not sympathize with their children's sexual minority identity.

In the past, many gay and lesbian youth grew up not knowing anyone else who was gay or lesbian and seeing no positive images in the popular culture. In addition to lacking identity solidary with their parents, they had difficulty finding gay adults to serve as role models. A fundamental aspect of the closet was isolation of gay people from each other. In the absence of identifiable real-life gay role models, the cultural depictions of gays and lesbians took on a special importance. Everyone is affected by the way popular culture portrays their particular group. Gays and lesbians were *especially* affected by popular culture portrayals of homosexuality because real-life homosexuals were hidden from view. Negative depictions of gays and lesbians in pop-ular media were a powerful constraint hardening public opinion against gay rights and narrowing the political opportunity structure for how gay people and gay rights groups could organize.

Russo's (1987) classic text describes the Hollywood closet as one of the chief threats to the lives and safety and political future of gays and lesbians in the U.S. Russo is especially critical of gay Hollywood writers and directors who wrote homophobic and misogynistic work in order to disguise and shield themselves from the potentially ruinous charge of homosexuality.

One of the most painful aspects of the closet was the way that it made some gay and lesbian people hate themselves. A corollary to the self-hate that was nurtured by the closet was the disgust that closeted gay and lesbian people would sometimes find themselves heaping on out-of-the-closet gay and lesbian people to distance themselves from the idea that they themselves might be gay or lesbian.[18]

Everyone needs a community. For isolated gay youth, having a community was essential to survival. In his memoir, Cleve Jones (2016), who would later become assistant to San Francisco gay politician Harvey Milk, and then a formidable gay rights activist in his own right, recalled that as a gay youth he didn't fit in anywhere. He was bullied by his schoolmates and rejected by his parents. Young Cleve was planning to kill himself, and then one day in the early 1970s, he saw a small article in *Time* magazine about gay rights activists in San Francisco, and he realized that his community existed somewhere. He flushed the pills that he had been saving for his suicide down the toilet and moved to San Francisco.

Without examples in movies or media of successful and respected out-of-the-closet gay or lesbian adults, it was incredibly difficult and dangerous for young people to form a plan to come out. Once people committed to being in the closet, the deceptions and deceits piled up, making it more difficult to come out later. People who were social pioneers, as a very few out-of-the-closet gay activists were in the 1950s, faced a bleak environment with oceans of hostility and little support.

Small Steps toward a More Open American Popular Culture

The Hays Code forced movies to be uniformly negative toward homosexuality and uniformly positive toward organized religion.[19] It was abandoned in the 1960s and replaced in 1968 with a rating system: G (suitable for General audiences), M (for Mature audiences, which later became PG for Parental Guidance), and R (Restricted).

The fever of the Red Scare began to break when the anticommunist demagogue Joe McCarthy was censured in the U.S. Senate in 1954. Senator McCarthy died three years later. The political winds in the U.S. were beginning to shift.

In 1957, Captain William Hanrahan of the San Francisco Police Department walked into City Lights bookstore, arrested the store clerk, and issued a warrant for the store owner and City Lights publisher, Lawrence Ferlinghetti, for publishing the gritty and raw poem *Howl* by Allen Ginsberg (1956), which Hanrahan had judged to be obscene. *Howl* contained descriptions of sex, both heterosexual and homosexual. In the 1957 obscenity trial, Judge Clayton Horn, noting that *Howl* had been well received by serious literary critics, acquitted Ferlinghetti. Judge Horn relied on a recent decision from the U.S. Supreme Court, *Roth v. U.S.* (1957).[20]

The *Roth* decision upheld several obscenity convictions, but also established the precedent that the whole work had to be taken into consideration before it could be judged to be obscene. *Roth* was potentially beneficial for movies or written work that had artistic merit despite objectionable scenes.[21] Obscenity in the law had generally meant work that was pornographic, whose only aim was to arouse the viewer. Now books or films that had artistic merit started to be judged as immune from obscenity charges on free speech grounds.

In 1958 the U.S. Supreme Court granted the appeal of *ONE,* the gay magazine whose circulation through the mail had been blocked by the postmaster of Los Angeles on the grounds that the magazine was obscene. The postmaster's judgment had been upheld in Federal District Court and in the Ninth Circuit Court of Appeals. Much to everyone's surprise, the Supreme Court unanimously decided to reverse the lower court rulings without hearing oral arguments from either side. In *ONE, Incorporated v. Olesen, Postmaster of Los Angeles* (1958) the Court offered no explanation other than a one-sentence citation to their previous *Roth* decision. *ONE v. Olesen* forced the Postal Service to deliver *ONE,* and thereby expanded First Amendment protections to material with gay themes. Few Americans in 1958 knew anything about the *ONE v. Olesen* decision. The *New York Times* ran a brief story buried on page 35 that alluded to the magazine's victory without mentioning the magazine by name.[22] But for the editors and the small set of readers of *ONE* and *The Ladder, ONE v. Olesen* was a much-celebrated landmark victory.

U.S. Supreme Court decisions set precedent across the U.S. The *Roth* decision broadened the permissible descriptions of sexuality, including same-sex sexuality, and shielded work with artistic merit from the potential charge of obscenity. *ONE* magazine, *The Ladder,* and Ginsberg's epic *Howl* were among the first beneficiaries of the new openness. As American popular culture started to see glimmers of a broader diversity of treatments of sexuality and human relationships, ideas about gay rights became easier to circulate and easier for Americans to find.

Alfred Kinsey and the Revolution of Sexology

The persecution of gay people in the U.S. in the 1950s and 1960s involved many different local criminal codes that varied from place to place but usually involved some variation of solicitation and lewd behavior. At the root of the legal persecution of gays and lesbians was the criminal ban on gay sex, or sodomy. Before the political opportunity structure could be made more open to gay rights claims, sodomy laws and other structural impediments to gay equality had to be overturned. Before the sodomy laws could be overturned, the antigay laws had to lose some of their legitimacy. Some elites in the U.S. had to be persuaded that the laws and impediments to gay rights were unfair and unreasonable. One way that social change can be made, slowly, is through research that upends previous understandings.

In the 1940s, Indiana University biology and entomology professor Alfred Kinsey was leading a research team interviewing more than twelve thousand Americans about their sexual histories. Kinsey had made his career as a scientist studying the gall wasp, but he found that the ignorance of his students about human sexuality, his own curiosity, and the lack of available scholarly resources on the subject were calling him to study human sexuality.[23]

Kinsey and his research team published two monumental reports, *Sexual Behavior in the Human Male* (Kinsey, Pomeroy, and Martin 1948) and *Sexual Behavior in the Human Female* (Kinsey et al. 1953). Both studies were widely read and impacted the public in a way that few social science research efforts ever have. Kinsey's reports on human sexuality brought him fame, status, and controversy. Christian Right leaders were appalled at his nonjudgmental attitude about the sexual diversity he found. Hoover's FBI investigated (as potentially un-American) Kinsey's Institute for Sex Research and put pressure on his funders.

Kinsey used his fame and status to try to make American policy less punitive toward homosexuality. Among his findings were that American men had more same-sex sexual contact, especially in adolescence, than had previously been imagined. Thirty-seven percent of American men had had at least one orgasm with another male, and 10% were more or less exclusively homosexual (a frequently cited but almost certainly overstated figure).[24] Kinsey described human sexual desire and experience not as a dichotomy (straight vs. gay) but as a continuum on a 7-point scale, with the value 0 representing pure heterosexuality, the value 6 representing pure homosexuality, and the values in between representing different degrees of bisexuality. Kinsey's research outed Americans as less exclusively heterosexual than they had imagined themselves to be. His quantification of same-sex sexual experience helped to normalize homosexuality.

Sodomy Laws and the American Law Institute

Kinsey was not only a researcher; he was an activist as well. In the midst of a firestorm of publicity around his two big books on human sexuality and the enormous pressures he was subjected to by investigations and moralistic backlash, he was an outspoken opponent of laws criminalizing sodomy. Kinsey died young, in 1956, but his campaign against sodomy laws helped lead to a fundamental policy change.

In 1960, all fifty U.S. States and the District of Columbia had laws in place that criminalized sodomy. In practice, when the sodomy laws were enforced (or threatened to be enforced), the targets were usually gay men. The arbitrariness of the enforcement was one of the reasons the influential American Law Institute (1955: 278) proposed in 1955 and adopted in 1962 a change in its model penal code that decriminalized consensual sodomy between adults in private, noting, "[C]apricious selection of a very few cases for prosecution . . . serve[s] primarily the interest of blackmailers." The ALI argued that sodomy is nearly impossible for the authorities to observe and that private sexual behavior between consenting adults posed no threat to the community. The lawyers, judges, and professors in the ALI had read the Kinsey reports and absorbed their lessons. Kinsey had testified persuasively before a commission in Illinois that was considering recommending the decriminalization of sodomy.[25] In 1961, Illinois followed his advice and that of the ALI and decriminalized sodomy.

Sodomy laws had a purpose: to place all gays and lesbians under the presumption of illegality. If gay sex was a crime, then gays' and lesbians' routine intimate behavior was criminal, and people who were presumptively criminal could be reasonably denied all sorts of rights and privileges. In a regime in which gays and lesbians were presumptively criminals, they had much to fear from coming out of the closet.

It took more than forty years after the ALI's model penal code for state legislatures and the courts to decriminalize sodomy in all fifty states. Progress was slow at first. Only two states (Illinois and Connecticut) decriminalized sodomy in the 1960s. Another twenty states followed in the 1970s, but then in 1986 the U.S. Supreme Court interrupted several decades of progress by upholding Georgia's sodomy law in *Bowers v. Hardwick*. The path toward overturning the sodomy laws was long and difficult but necessary in opening the political opportunity structure for gays and lesbians in the U.S. The process started, albeit slowly, with Kinsey's research in the 1940s and the ALI's work in the 1950s.

Frank Kameny's Activism

Frank Kameny is another influential person from the dark and gloomy 1950s era of gay rights in the U.S. In 1956, Kameny, a U.S. Army veteran, was arrested in a public bathroom by undercover police in San Francisco's "Sex Detail" who were looking through a ventilation grate, devoting themselves, as police in many cities did, to arresting men who propositioned each other. Kameny pled guilty and paid a $50 fine and served six months' probation. After six months, his conviction (but not his arrest) was expunged from the public record.

A year later, in 1957, thirty-two-year-old Kameny, who held a PhD from Harvard, took a new job with the U.S. Army Map Service. Although he did not know it at the time, the U.S. Government had a strict policy of excluding gays and lesbians from employment. When the Army found out about Kameny's 1956 arrest, he was fired from his job and blacklisted, which prevented him from having any government employment.[26] In the 1950s, most people who were fired from government jobs (or were denied employment in the first place) for being gay or lesbian never complained, because the social stigma was so severe, and there was no remedy: the FBI was persecuting gays and lesbians everywhere they could find them.

Kameny was in a difficult situation after his firing. However, he had worked on a mortar team in the infantry in World War II in Europe, so he knew something about digging in, and he knew about long campaigns. Without any institutional support, he decided to fight back. Kameny formally appealed his firing with the Civil Service Commission, but his appeal was denied. He then filed suit in federal court, where his case was dismissed. He appealed to the D.C. Circuit Court of Appeals, where his appeal was again dismissed. He asked his lawyer to appeal to the U.S. Supreme Court. Instead, his lawyer gave him a pamphlet explaining Supreme Court procedure and told Kameny to write to the Court himself, which he did. In his petition asking the U.S. Supreme Court to hear his appeal, Kameny (1960) wrote:

> Petitioner has, by this discharge, and by this department been branded, publicly and (if they are not reversed) permanently, by the majesty of the United Sates Government, as a dishonest person, and as an immoral person, neither of which he is. . . .
>
> The regulation indicates, as ground for a decision of unsuitability, "immoral conduct," not further specified. But what is immoral conduct? Petitioner asserts, flatly, unequivocally, and absolutely uncompromisingly, that homosexuality, whether by mere inclination or by overt act, is not only not immoral, but that for those choosing voluntarily to engage in homosexual acts, such acts are moral in a real and positive sense, and are good, right, and desirable, socially and personally.

In 1961, the Court responded to Kameny's petition the same way they respond to 98% of all petitions: they refused it.[27] Kameny had lost at every stage, and he never worked a regular job again.

Without a job, Kameny devoted himself to activism. He founded the Washington, D.C. branch of the Mattachine Society, and he helped to found the D.C. branch of the American Civil Liberties Union. At the first meeting of the D.C. Mattachine Society in 1961, local police were present because the FBI had already started spying on the group.[28] Despite not having legal training, Kameny advocated for scores of gay and lesbian government workers who needed legal advice but could not find or could not afford a lawyer. He became a one-man gay rights advocacy movement.

Lessons of the 1950s and the 1960s

The main lesson I want to convey with this curated version of gay rights in the 1950s and 1960s is how dire the situation was for gay people in the U.S. in this era. Every arm of the state, from the local police to the state hospitals, the federal government, and the courts, was fiercely hostile to their interests. The view of homosexuality among the majority of doctors, scholars, and therapists was hardly any better. Even in places like San Francisco and Los Angeles, now meccas of gay America, there were only small communities of gay and lesbian people who knew each other to be gay and lesbian and who associated with each other on that basis. People in these small homophile communities lived in fear of the police, for good reason. The closet was the only remotely safe place for gay and lesbian Americans, and the closet itself was not safe.

To the extent that there was progress on gay rights in the 1950s and 1960s, it was progress of a type that would not fully pay dividends until decades later. The Hays Code was relaxed and then replaced in the 1960s, but mainstream American movies and television did not begin to show gay characters in a positive light until the 1990s. Kinsey's work on human sexuality helped convince the reformist ALI to recommend in 1962 that sodomy between consenting adults in private be decriminalized in all U.S. states. The process of decriminalization was not completed until 2003. Illinois decriminalized sodomy in 1961 only because no one in the state legislature had read the bill.[29]

The victory of *ONE* magazine in *ONE v Olesen* was important to its readers and to the Mattachine Society and a few of the other small homophile groups who would have known what *ONE* magazine was, but Court's decision was little known outside of those small circles. Given the Court's one-sentence explanation, there was scant opportunity for later courts to cite *ONE v. Olesen* as a precedent. The Supreme Court issued its first decision that gave a reasoned explanation for a defense of gay rights decades later, in 1996, in *Romer v. Evans*. Kameny was fired from his government job in 1957. The Eisenhower executive orders that prevented gays and lesbians from working for the government were not overturned until the Clinton administration in the 1990s.

In the context of political opportunity structure theory, I view gay rights activism in the 1950s and 1960s as akin to a small light that can be a guide in the darkness. Neither Kameny's activism nor the ALI's model penal code nor the organizing by the Mattachine Society or the Daughters of Bilitis made much measurable difference to gay people in the U.S. in the short term, but all were guide posts to others over the course of decades. It is difficult for people to organize in the darkness. With a minimum of guidance and direction, they can at least know which direction to head toward and can organize each other accordingly. In dark times, political opportunities can be expanded in small ways that can have at least the chance of making a difference in the long term. One has to be stubborn to be an activist when the gains from activism are all beyond the visible horizon. Fortunately, Frank Kameny was famous for his stubbornness.

3

Antecedents of Marriage Equality in the 1970s

Stonewall and Gay Power

In many classic histories of gay rights in the U.S., the Stonewall riots have pride of place as the most important single event.[1] The Stonewall riots are reasonably viewed as the turning point in gay rights history, the moment when gay activists and queer people started to fight back publicly against a system that was oppressing them.

In the timeline of U.S. public opinion, however, the early 1990s are when attitudes started liberalizing toward gay rights, so 1969 (the year of the Stonewall riots) is a generation too early to be the central event (see Figure 1.1). My view of marriage equality and gay rights history is organized around the timeline of the public's acceptance of gay rights. Since the Stonewall riots had no measurable effect on public opinion, my focus here is not so much on the events of the Stonewall riots themselves but rather on what the Stonewall riots led to. The Stonewall riots led directly to a tradition of Pride parades that started slowly in the 1970s and grew a thousandfold over the subsequent fifty years. What started out as five thousand marchers and onlookers in a few cities in 1970 has evolved into millions of people worldwide participating in Pride parades every year.

The Stonewall Inn in New York's Greenwich Village was a dim and dingy Mafia-run bar that lacked a liquor license and had no running water. Because serving drinks to gay people was illegal in New York in the 1960s,[2] the bar was run by the Genovese Mafia family and was used to paying off the local police. The regular patrons of the Stonewall were young gay men, drag queens, trans people, and their mostly young male partners and friends.

On the night of June 27, 1969, police showed up at the Stonewall for a surprise raid. Traditionally, police did not need much force to control a crowd at a gay bar, as patrons were often terrified of arrest and exposure. On this night, however, the young gay men were not so easily intimidated. After carting

The Rainbow after the Storm. Michael J. Rosenfeld, Oxford University Press. © Oxford University Press 2022.
DOI: 10.1093/oso/9780197600436.003.0003

away a few patrons, the remaining police were quickly outnumbered by the patrons and locals they had forced out of the bar. The young gay patrons of the Stonewall found that they had power in numbers, and with a sudden determination many in the group decided to battle the police. Under a hail of thrown objects, the police retreated into the empty bar, barricaded the doors, and waited for reinforcements. The angry gay men and drag queens outside the bar uprooted parking meters to bash in the doors and attack the police, who were cowering inside.[3]

In the early morning hours of June 28, police reinforcements arrived, and a generalized melee took place outside the bar between police and gay patrons and their respective allies. The next night, the police, who had been surprised to be so outnumbered the first night, returned to the Stonewall in greater numbers to make a statement about who controlled the streets of New York. Gay citizens of Greenwich Village and their allies returned to the Stonewall to meet them, and an even larger second night of rioting ensued. New York's Mattachine Society, which by 1969 consisted of older and more established gay men who were more experienced with being in the closet than with fighting the police, was aghast at the violence and urged "people to please help maintain peaceful and quiet conduct on the streets."[4]

A legend (based on actual events) was born out of Stonewall about gay people fighting back against injustice. In the immediate aftermath of the riots, a more radical gay rights movement started to grow in the U.S. The Gay Liberation Front (GLF) was founded in New York, only to fall apart less than a year later. GLF meetings were chaotic, and the politics of the era was pulling people in many different directions. The GLF was torn apart by the kind of sectarian Left divisions that tended to devour groups in those days: Did the GLF have to recognize (and send money to) the Black Panther Party, vanguard party of African American radical politics? What if the Black Panther Party was hostile to gay rights? What role should women have in the GLF?[5] Some of the women in the GLF broke off and formed the Radicalesbians, but that group was also pulled apart by its internal political divisions.

Marches and Parades

While the GLF and the Radicalesbians soon folded, the memorialization of Stonewall in June Pride parades is the most durable legacy of the Stonewall era. In 1970, activists organized small marches involving perhaps five thousand marchers in New York and a few hundred each in Los Angeles and Chicago. The original New York march to commemorate the one-year anniversary of the Stonewall riots was organized by the Christopher Street Liberation Day Umbrella Committee (as the Stonewall Inn was on Christopher Street), led by Mattachine Society (New York branch) veterans Craig Rodwell and Foster Gunnison.[6]

In both New York and in Los Angeles (organizing under the Christopher Street West name), groups organizing for a 1970 parade were initially denied permits to march. The Los Angeles group sued, and a local judge forced the city to give the gay marchers a permit.[7] Both the Los Angeles and the New York organizers envisioned the 1970 parades as more celebration than protest. The New York parade route was from Greenwich Village north up Sixth Avenue to Central Park. The marches were fun; they gave queer folk an opportunity to express themselves and to be out to each other without having to agree on a particular political agenda. The marchers and organizers initially feared that they might be attacked by hostile onlookers, but those fears proved unfounded. Crowds along the parade routes in New York and Los Angeles in 1970 were a mix of quiet amazement and support.[8] In 1971, with fears of attacks having receded to the background, more people turned out to the New York and Los Angeles parades. Bars and other businesses started sponsoring floats.

Pride parades grew slowly in the 1970s. There was often tension in planning Pride celebrations between people who wanted marchers to hew to a unified political message and people who wanted diverse groups of gay people and their allies to express themselves however they saw fit. There was tension over how much bare-chested nakedness was appropriate for a parade. Over time, as the parades grew, diversity became the governing rule and starched-shirt politicians, gay-friendly church groups, businesses large and small, and radicals all found their place in Pride parades. Straight allies joined the parades in increasing numbers, so that onlookers were able to see not only what a diversity of gay, lesbian, and transgender people looked like but also what a variety of presumably straight people who supported gay rights looked like. By 1989 the New York Pride parade drew more than 200,000 marchers and spectators, and the San Francisco Pride parade drew 300,000 marchers and spectators. The tradition of late June parades spread to cities and towns all over the world, meaning millions of people were involved in gay pride events. As the parades grew in size and drew in a wider and more diverse set of participants and sponsors, they tended to take on a less radical and more inclusive and corporate tone, to the chagrin of some of the more radical organizers and participants. Sociologist Katherine Bruce found that Pride parade participants in the U.S. were generally happy to see corporate support.[9] In any political struggle allies are important, and powerful allies especially so.

In New York City in 2019, for the fiftieth anniversary of Stonewall, the Pride parade was reported to have drawn 4 million spectators, almost a thousand times more people than had been involved in the first parade in 1970. Pride parades spread from New York to other large American cities, and then from large cities to smaller towns, and from the U.S. to the rest of the world. The Pride parade of São Paulo, Brazil, was reported to have drawn about 4 million people in 2011. Madrid, Toronto, Cologne, London, and Rome have all had gay pride marches since 2010 that drew more than a million spectators and marchers. The small college town of Conway, Arkansas (population 60,000) started a Pride parade in 2004. The parades put gay rights and gay, lesbian, trans, and queer people in front of each other and in front of their neighbors in a powerful and increasingly popular way.

Figure 3.1 shows the spread of Pride parades across U.S. cities and towns. There was steady growth from three parades in 1970 to eighty-nine in 2010. Between 2010 and 2012 American public approval of gay rights and same-sex marriage crossed into majority territory for the first time. At the beginning of 2010, only five states had marriage equality: Massachusetts,

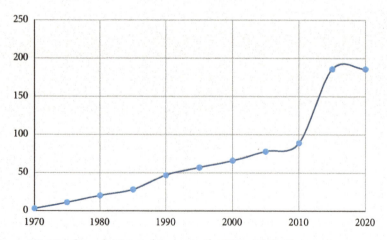

Figure 3.1 Number of cities and towns in the U.S. with Pride parades.
Source: Appendix C1 in Bruce (2016) and most recent years from gaypridecalendar.com.

Connecticut, Iowa, Vermont, and New Hampshire. By the summer of 2015, all fifty states and District of Columbia had marriage equality. Pride parades grew in number in the 1970s and the 1980s in the face of a generally hostile U.S. public, and then doubled in number after 2010, around the time gay rights gained majority support.

Crowd size at a moving event such as a parade, without gates or tickets, is notoriously difficult to measure. Typically, the police and the organizers' estimates for crowd size can vary quite a lot. Figure 3.2 must therefore be viewed as very approximate, and there are missing values where I could not find a press release or news story referencing crowd size. What we see in Figure 3.2 is that the New York Pride parade was typically of modest size (for a city as enormous as New York) through the 1970s and 1980s, when the number of participants and spectators was in the neighborhood of 50,000 to 100,000 each year between 1975 and 1988, with between 100,000 and 300,000 each year from 1989 to 2004, and then a big order of magnitude jump to 2 million spectators in 2015 and 4 million in 2019. In recent years, the Pride parade in San Francisco has drawn more than a million spectators and marchers, which is especially impressive because the city itself has fewer

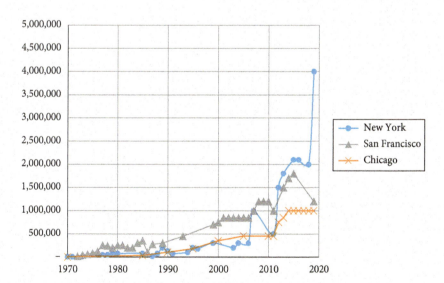

Figure 3.2 The number of Pride marchers and spectators by city and year.

Source: News reports from *The New York Times*, the Associated Press, Chicago Pride, Wikipedia and other sources.

than 900,000 residents. People come to Pride parades from near and far, and many plan their summers around them.

Armstrong and Crage (2006) found that the confrontation between gay patrons and the police at the Stonewall Inn in 1969 was not as unique an event as legend has described it. The Stonewall itself had been raided regularly before June 1969. There were several battles between gay patrons and the police in the same era in other places at a scale similar to what happened at Stonewall. What was different about Stonewall was not the event itself, but the memorialization. Gay rights groups around the U.S. were able to memorialize the events and create and enlarge the memory and legend of Stonewall with an annual march. The radical moment of Stonewall, June 1969, gave birth to an amazing, colorful, and ever-growing series of annual parades that helped to celebrate gay people in their communities. Gay Pride parades put the police to work protecting (and in more recent years, marching under their own rainbow banners) rather than beating their gay fellow citizens.

Marriage and the Ideology of the GLF

The earnest radicalism of the gay rights movement of the Stonewall era provided an important spark for what came later. The ideology of the GLF was self-consciously radical, antiestablishment, and antimarriage. Carl Wittman (1970: 4), whose writings were circulated by the GLF, wrote in his *Gay Manifesto*:

> Traditional marriage is a rotten, oppressive institution. . . . Gay people must stop gauging their self respect by how well they mimic straight marriages. . . . To accept that happiness comes through finding a groovy spouse and settling down, showing the world that "we're just the same as you" is avoiding the real issues and is an expression of self-hatred. . . . We have to define for ourselves a new pluralistic, rolefree social structure.

Wittman's critique of marriage perfectly encapsulated a 1960s activist view that traditional institutions of U.S. society, including heterosexual marriage, were "rotten" and needed to be discarded. The radicals were not wrong to see marriage as a problematic institution. Heterosexual marriage was an old institution in 1970, but one on the verge of significant changes. Among the original purposes of marriage were control of the inheritance of land and control of women by making wives the legal property of their husbands.

Wives were no longer the property of their husbands in the U.S. in the 1960s, but some of the norms and traditions of the patriarchal origins of marriage remained. The institution of marriage is in some ways permanently marked by its patriarchal origins.

For instance, it was not until the 1970s that all married women in the U.S. had the option to keep their own surname. In the 1960s and before, when Barbara Jones married James Smith, he remained James Smith but she became Barbara Smith, or her prior identity was even more erased as she became Mrs. James Smith. Wives taking their husbands' names was a tradition left over from the earlier era when the wife had been the husband's property and when the wife had lost her independent legal identity at marriage. In a 1995 study, more than 95% of American women had taken their husbands' surnames at marriage, even though the law did not require them to do so.[10]

Betty Friedan was busy in the 1960s teaching an audience of mostly White, educated women that their unhappiness in the housewife role was not their fault. She had been born Betty Goldstein and took the surname Friedan when she married Carl Friedan in 1947. Betty and Carl divorced in 1969, but she spent the rest of her life carrying his name around. Friedan's 1963 bestseller, *The Feminine Mystique*, gave birth to second-wave feminism and described the unhappiness of women's role in marriage as due, in part, to educated women's frustrated aspirations to have careers. Influenced by Friedan, married women started streaming into the labor market. Arlie Hochschild, doing research on married couples in the 1970s and early 1980s, found that wives were still frustrated by their access to meaningful work. Even wives with important and high-earning careers found that their husbands expected them to come home after work and do a second shift of housework and child care.[11]

Heterosexual marriage encodes a variety of gendered inequalities. In feminist scholar Jessie Bernard's view, *his* marriage has always been better than *hers*.[12] From the first serious research on American divorce in the 1940s until the present time, about two-thirds of divorces have been requested by the wife, whereas in nonmarital unions breakups tend to be mutual and gender-neutral. Women's predominance in requesting divorce is matched by wives consistently reporting lower marital quality than their husbands do.[13] Married people (including wives) tend to be happier than adults who are not married, but within marriage wives tend to be less satisfied than husbands. Marriage is an institution with a long and complicated history, which simply means that there was plenty of room for feminists, gay rights activists, and others to be critical of the institution of marriage.

Second-wave feminism's critique of marriage (led by Friedan and others) had a deep impact on gay rights activists. Although Friedan was keen to explain that feminism was intended to improve rather than to undermine heterosexual marriage,[14] the feminist movement had shown that marriage was problematic in a number of ways. Gay activists like Wittman saw nothing in the institution of marriage that was worth saving or replicating. Wittman and other gay activists resented gay couples who wanted to marry for what Wittman saw as mimicry of unworthy heterosexual traditions. He thought gay couplehood should involve a new set of rules and traditions, quite apart from the traditional baggage of marriage.

Even though the GLF was antimarriage, ironically the gay rights radicalism of the early 1970s helped to pave the road to marriage equality. The new ideas of groups like the GLF helped more people to think about and come to terms with their own non-heterosexual identities. Some of the people inspired by gay rights eventually would decide, years after the GLF was gone, that not only did they want to marry their same-sex partners, but they were also willing to fight for marriage equality.

Utopian left-wing groups like the GLF had their roots in the radical student movements of the 1960s. By the early 1970s, groups like Students for a Democratic Society had collapsed under the weight of infiltration and disruption by the police, and also due to the extravagant overreaches of their idealistic leaders, according to Elizabeth Armstrong (2002). The gay rights movement in the later 1970s re-formed with a less utopian and less revolutionary message and a more identity-based politics. In Armstrong's terms, gay pride replaced gay power.[15] Within gay pride there would eventually be more room for the pursuit of the specific goal of marriage equality, a goal the GLF had disdained.

Social Science and the Depathologization of Homosexuality

In the 1960s and early 1970s gay activists were not only marching in the streets; they were trying to make their voices heard in the corridors of power. A great deal of the discrimination against gays and lesbians in the past in the U.S. was justified by law and by what passed at the time as scholarship about homosexuality. Up until 1973, the American Psychiatric Association (APA) defined homosexuality as pathological. In the 1960s that definition came under scrutiny from new scholarship and came under attack from newly energized gay activists.

Because gays and lesbians were generally in the closet, most of the homosexuals who psychiatrists saw clinically were in prisons and psychiatric hospitals. Given such a sample, it was no wonder psychiatrists believed that homosexuality was associated with mental illness. The closet kept healthy gays and lesbians hidden from view.

In the 1950s Evelyn Hooker was a researcher in the Psychology Department at the University of California, Los Angeles. Hooker happened to have a former student who was gay, who introduced her to other gays and lesbians who were connected to the Mattachine Society in Los Angeles, and who were therefore out to each other. It was only because of the Mattachine Society that there was a network of gay people in Los Angeles who were out of the closet to each other, who felt safe enough to be recruited into a study by Hooker.[16]

Other researchers had been unable to reach the noninstitutionalized gay population who remained in the closet. Meeting gay men and women who seemed to be socially and psychologically well-adjusted gave Hooker the idea that psychiatry had fundamentally misunderstood the nature of homosexuality. Hooker (1957) gave thirty homosexual men and a comparison sample (matched on age, education, and IQ) of thirty heterosexual men a series of personality tests, including the Rorschach test. The tests were designed to elicit signs not only of pathology but also of femininity, affect, and difficulties in relationships with others. Hooker gave the test results to a panel composed of experts in interpreting psychological personality tests and asked them to identify which of the sixty subjects were homosexual. The expert panel could not identify the homosexual subjects from their test results. Hooker's research was the first important study in the U.S. that showed that homosexuals and heterosexuals were not distinguishable psychologically. Other scholars followed Hooker's lead and reached the same results.[17]

As a result of her novel work with gay men, Hooker was asked to chair a task force on homosexuality at the U.S. National Institute of Mental Health. The task force report recommended decriminalization of sodomy (following the ALI's pioneering recommendation),[18] called for more research on homosexuals outside of institutions (as Hooker herself had done), and allowed that for some homosexuals who desired to change their sexual orientation, therapy with a goal toward conversion to heterosexuality was reasonable. Later research would show that conversion therapy was dangerous and ineffective, and eventually the leading national mental health professions abandoned it, leaving only the antigay religious groups to practice conversion therapy.

In 1968, gay rights activists started appearing at the APA's annual national conferences to denounce psychiatrists who claimed to be able to cure homosexuality. Academic meetings that were usually staid and conservative were thrown into chaos. At the 1971 APA meetings, a gay psychiatrist addressed the audience in disguise. APA members who believed they had never met a gay or lesbian professional person were introduced, quietly, to colleagues who were gay.

Frank Kameny (whom we met in chapter 2 as he was losing his government job and becoming a gay rights activist) and Evelyn Hooker and other scholars, along with gay rights activists outside and inside the APA, all played a role in persuading the APA to change its definition of homosexuality. In 1973 the APA reclassified homosexuality as a normal manifestation of human sexuality and issued a statement deploring all discrimination against gays and lesbians.[19]

Some prominent members of the APA resisted the 1973 reclassification and continued to insist that homosexuality was an illness that could be cured (e.g., see Socarides 1978). But the old guard and their view that homosexuality was a curable pathology became increasingly isolated. From 1973 onward, researchers, politicians, and religious leaders who maintained the old view of homosexuality as a sickness were working against a steadily growing social scientific consensus which increasingly certified the health and normalcy of gays and lesbians and their children. The more researchers were able to find gay and lesbian subjects in venues other than punitive institutions, the more the health and normalcy of gays and lesbians became clear.

In subsequent decades, as new data became available, social science moved definitively away from the old theory that homosexuality was a dangerous illness. Changes in the way social scientists viewed homosexuality did not, however, translate quickly into public opinion liberalization toward gay rights. American public opinion toward gays and lesbians remained uniformly hostile in the 1970s, and then became even more hostile in the 1980s, before attitudes started to liberalize in the 1990s. Conservative politicians and Christian Right leaders would retain and promote the old and discredited theory that homosexuality was a dangerous illness for many decades after the APA officially abandoned it.

The 1973 APA reclassification of homosexuality as normal and healthy had many important ramifications. For example, the U.S. Immigration and Naturalization Service (INS) had been depending on the pathological classification to exclude homosexual immigrants, but after 1973, exclusion was more and more difficult to justify.[20] The APA's reclassification helped to (slowly) open the political opportunity structure for gays and lesbians.

Law and the Definition of Marriage:
The First Same-Sex Marriage Battle

Frank Kameny was an energetic whirlwind, advising gays and lesbians across the U.S. One of his advisees was Jack Baker. Baker and his partner Michael McConnell had met at a series of Halloween parties in Oklahoma in 1966, one of which was broken up by the police. They wanted to marry.

Baker had moved to Minnesota to start law school, and McConnell accepted a job in the University of Minnesota library. Like family law statutes in most states at the time, Minnesota's did not specify that marriage could only be between a man and a woman. The Minnesota legislature had never considered the possibility that same-sex couples might want to marry, but, as Baker and McConnell's case shows, Minnesota's courts were ready to deny marriage licenses to same-sex couples anyway.[21]

Michael McConnell (center) and Jack Baker (right) applying for a wedding license in Minneapolis in 1970. Photo by R. Bertrand Heine for the *Minneapolis Star Tribune*. Copyright Minnesota Historical Society negative number 015051-16, reprinted with permission.

Kameny urged Baker and McConnell to apply for a marriage license and, if denied, to sue.[22] Their request was refused, but their trip to the county clerk's office made the local news. When the University of Minnesota regents saw McConnell's picture in the paper, with his male partner, they rescinded their offer of employment.

Because of the loss of his job, McConnell was involved in two different lawsuits: one to try to get his library job back, and the second, with Baker, to be allowed to marry. McConnell won his suit to get his job back in the state trial court, but the University of Minnesota appealed that ruling to the federal Eighth Circuit Court of Appeals, which reversed the lower court ruling. The university argued that McConnell was unqualified to be a librarian because sodomy was illegal in Minnesota, and McConnell's intention to marry Baker demonstrated that he was presumptively guilty of sodomy. McConnell never got his job back.

Baker and McConnell sued Gerald Nelson, the clerk of Hennepin County, to try to force him to grant them a marriage license. They lost that case and appealed to the Minnesota Supreme Court, which treated their request as absurd. The Minnesota Supreme Court's decision in *Baker v. Nelson* (1971) cited the biblical book of Genesis to make the point that marriage had always been understood to mean marriage between a man and a woman and quoted Webster's dictionary, which in the 1966 edition defined marriage as "the state of being united to a person of the opposite sex as husband or wife."

Baker and McConnell then appealed to the U.S. Supreme Court, which, in *Baker v. Nelson* (1972), rejected the appeal with a one-sentence ruling: "Dismissed for want of a substantial federal question." That decision set an important precedent that stood for decades. *Baker v. Nelson* (1972) meant that the U.S. Supreme Court was going to allow states to ban same-sex marriage. American courts were sending same-sex couples a clear message about marriage in the early 1970s: *Don't be ridiculous.* American public opinion was similarly hostile to gay rights in the 1970s, and remained so for decades.

Anita Bryant, the Briggs Campaign in California, and Harvey Milk's Strategy of Coming Out

The visibility of even a few out-of-the-closet gay activists and a few local gay rights victories in the 1970s proved to be irresistible organizing fodder for a rejuvenated Christian Right movement. The Christian Right grew by leaps and bounds in the 1970s by fundraising and organizing around an anti-gay-rights message and in response to women's rights and the possibility of a gender-equality-guaranteeing Equal Rights Amendment, which the Christian Right eventually helped to defeat.[23] Antigay messages were not just a passing proclivity of the Christian Right agenda; they became the *core* of that agenda. No other issue worked as well as antigay messages to mobilize conservative evangelical Christians and conservative Catholics to political action and to donate money. The Christian Right is a movement whose antigay credentials were not superficial, but fundamental and deep.[24]

The Christian Right has every right to oppose marriage equality and gay rights, just as other groups have the right to support marriage equality and gay rights. If the Christian Right's campaigns against gay rights had been entirely based on biblical arguments, I would not criticize them. The Christian Right, however, relentlessly and falsely claimed that social science research supported their arguments that gays and lesbians were bad parents, that homosexuality was a correctable disease, that gay people preyed on children, and that same-sex marriage would lead to an end of civilization. Social science is evidence-based, and therefore claims about social science are falsifiable. My disagreements with the Christian Right are disagreements over social science.

In the 1970s, Anita Bryant, a gospel singer, television personality, and spokesperson for Florida Orange Juice, became an icon of the Christian Right by campaigning against gay rights. The commissioners of Miami Dade County, Florida, passed an ordinance in 1977 that protected gays and lesbians from discrimination in housing, employment, and public accommodations. Bryant described the ordinance this way: "Moral character no longer counts. . . . All government jobs, even the most sensitive must be thrown open to homosexuals, pimps, prostitutes and every other . . . unnatural sexual libertine."[25]

The campaign against the Dade County antidiscrimination ordinance called itself "Save Our Children" because, they argued, the ordinance would necessarily subject Dade County's children to harassment and predation by gay teachers and other adults. Dade County's children needed to be saved, according to Bryant, by overturning the ordinance. The Save Our Children campaign falsely claimed, in a full-page newspaper ad, that homosexuals wanted to abolish laws governing the age of sexual consent.[26] The county agreed to allow voters to decide the fate of the ordinance and scheduled a referendum.

Reverend Jerry Falwell, at the time a rising Christian Right star, told a Save Our Children rally in the days before the Dade County referendum, "Homosexuality is a perversion. . . . It will bring this nation to an end. . . . Homosexuals do not reproduce, they recruit. . . . I want to tell you we are dealing with a vile and vicious and vulgar gang. They'd kill you as quick as look at you."[27] The claim that homosexuals "don't reproduce, they recruit" was often repeated by Bryant.

In June 1977, the voters of Dade County overturned their antidiscrimination ordinance by 69.3 to 30.6%, giving Bryant a resounding victory and demonstrating how powerfully persuasive antigay tropes were in the 1970s. Referenda overturning local gay rights measures followed in St. Paul, Minnesota, Eugene, Oregon, and Wichita, Kansas. A wave of antigay ballot measures led to an upsurge of violent attacks and killings of gays and lesbians, including in San Francisco.[28] The success of local antigay ballot measures helped inspire a national upsurge in Christian Right organizing around antigay themes. The Christian Right group Moral Majority was founded in 1979 by Jerry Falwell and Paul Weyrich. The Moral Majority thrived for about ten years with direct-mail marketing stoking fears of gay rights and feminism.

In 1978, the antigay movement was brought to California by a conservative politician named John Briggs. The Briggs Initiative was broader and more far-reaching than Dade County's Save Our Children campaign. The Briggs Initiative proposed to fire public school teachers in California who could be shown to be homosexual or whose words or deeds were supportive of homosexuality. Like Save Our Children, the Briggs Initiative was based on the premise that any contact with homosexuals was harmful to children. It was an attack not only on gay rights and on the right of employment for gays and lesbians, but it was also an attack on free speech. Early polling led supporters of the Briggs Initiative to believe they would win by a wide margin because Bryant's anti-gay-rights campaign had been scoring victories across the U.S.

In San Francisco, newly elected city supervisor Harvey Milk, one of the first out-of-the-closet gay elected officials in U.S. history, was constructing a strategy to defeat the Briggs Initiative:

Even if we lose, having the debate moves us forward, just by requiring people to think about the issue [gay rights]. The more they think about it, the more progress we make. And we have to get everyone to come out of their closets. . . . If we all come out, we will win. Once people understand that they have gay friends and family members and coworkers and neighbors, they won't fear [us], they won't hate us, and they won't vote against us. That's how we win. Everyone must come out.[29]

In 1978, few gay and lesbian Americans were out of the closet, so Milk's strategy was radical. Being in the closet made gays and lesbians unable to defend themselves against the kind of falsehoods that the Briggs Initiative was based on. Briggs had said, "Everybody knows that homosexuals are child molesters. Not all of them, but most of them. I mean, that's why they are in the teaching profession."[30] Tellingly, however, when he debated Milk on local television, Briggs was unable to cite any scientific research showing that homosexuals were more likely than heterosexuals to molest children. Milk and his allies had research at their disposal showing that homosexuals were no more likely than heterosexuals to molest children. Bryant had been no better than Briggs when it came to command over facts and research. When pressed on policy questions, she would resort to quoting the Bible and singing hymns.[31]

Milk and other gay rights supporters organized a statewide door-to-door campaign against the Briggs Initiative, which included many activists explaining to their neighbors that they were gay and how the Briggs Initiative would affect them.[32] Gay and lesbian activists handed out cards that read:

> The purpose of this card is to make you aware of the fact that you ride with, talk to, eat with, and see gay people every day. I hope that the time you spent with me has helped you to realize that we are people just like you.
>
> Please vote no on Proposition 6 (The Briggs Initiative) on November 7, because it directly affects human rights, particularly mine as a gay person.[33]

In the television debate, Milk countered the claim that gay and lesbian teachers would recruit children to homosexuality: "I was born of heterosexual parents. I was taught by heterosexual teachers, in a fiercely heterosexual society, with television ads and newspaper ads fiercely heterosexual. A society that puts down homosexuality. And why am I a homosexual, if I am affected by role models? I should have been a heterosexual."[34] California's heterosexual voters in 1978 did not know what made people gay and lesbian. Harvey Milk, a successful out-of-the-closet gay man, was in a unique position to explain it. It was not role models or recruitment that made him gay: he explained that it was simply in his nature to be gay.

Milk demonstrated that gay people were nothing to be afraid of. By winning the debate with Briggs, by being reasonable, thoughtful, and funny, and by wearing his gay identity proudly, Harvey Milk was demonstrating the positive political power of coming out.[35] Coming out enabled gay political leaders to undermine and discredit the conservative frames of gays and lesbians as sick and dangerous.

One of the main claims of the Christian Right in the 1970s and for decades after was that gays and lesbians could be readily cured by conversion therapy. Ex-gays and ex-lesbians were regularly presented to Christian Right audiences as evidence that homosexuality was not an inborn or a stable identity.[36] The Christian Right was carrying forward ideas about the pathology of homosexuality that had lost credibility within professional circles. Subsequent research has shown that some people experience their sexual identity as fixed from their earliest self-awareness, while others experience fluid sexual identity and gender attraction in young adulthood. For some people sexual identity fluidity extends into adulthood.[37]

Across the U.S. population, sexual identity is more fluid over the life course on average than racial identity. One study of a nationally representative sample showed that over seven years of young adulthood (when sexual orientation is most subject to change), 91% of self-identified gay men and 73% of self-identified lesbian women had stable gay identities.[38] The fluidity of sexual identity is greater for women than for men. Racial identity can also be fluid, but the frequency of racial identity change is much lower, more like 2% over the entire life course for change between Black and White identities.[39]

While some people experience identity change between straight and gay identities, the Christian Right's claim that *all* gays and lesbians could be readily converted to heterosexuality turned out to be a sham. Sexual identity fluidity within some individuals and over the life course does not imply that individuals have control over whom they are attracted to. The reality of sexual fluidity within some individuals also does not imply that interventions (such as conversion therapy) to change the objects of a person's attraction are safe or effective. Many gay people, especially young gay people put into conversion therapy by their parents, faced a kind of coercive therapy intended to make them disgusted at their own natural desires, i.e., disgusted at themselves. These kinds of coercive therapies caused real harm to some people. The American Psychological Association established a task force to examine whether conversion therapy was effective, and whether it harmed the people who were subjected to it. Following the task force's recommendations, the American Psychological Association officially rejected conversion therapy in 2009.[40]

In the dictionary definition, an "immutable" trait is a trait that cannot be changed. Yet personal characteristics, including race, gender, religion, physical appearance, sexual identity, and nationality, are all changeable to some degree. In American law, an immutable personal trait is not necessarily a trait that can *never* be changed but rather a trait that is resistant to change, or more precisely a trait "so central to a person's identity that it would be abhorrent for government to penalize a person for refusing to change, regardless of how easy that change might be physically."[41] By this broader legal definition of immutability, homosexuality is immutable, as are gender, religion, race, physical appearance, and nationality.[42]

As straight people began to learn that sexual identity is resistant to change and reasonably stable over time, this knowledge helped to dispel the misleading falsehood that children of a gay teacher would be converted to homosexuality by simply being in the teacher's presence. Harvey Milk, one of the few out-of-the-closet gay political leaders of his era, used his personal story to allay fears and dispel falsehoods about the supposed transmissibility of homosexuality. He pointed out that most gay people had had nothing but straight role models.

The Briggs Initiative was opposed by not only the Democratic governor of California, Jerry Brown, but also by California's most popular conservative politician, Republican ex-governor and future president Ronald Reagan. A week before Election Day in 1978, Reagan wrote in a newspaper editorial:

> Although statistics are not kept nationally, informed observers usually put the percentage of child molesting cases by homosexuals at well under 10 percent. The overwhelming majority of such cases are committed by heterosexual males against young females. As to the "role model" argument, a woman writing to the editor of a Southern California newspaper said it all: "If teachers had such power over children, I would have been a nun years ago."
>
> Whatever else it is, homosexuality is not a contagious disease like the measles. Prevailing scientific opinion is that an individual's sexuality is determined at a very early age and that a child's teachers do not really influence this.[43]

Regan was promulgating a view of sexual identity's innateness and resistance to change that was quite consistent with Milk's explanation.

In the campaign against the Briggs Initiative, Milk and his allies leveraged an allegiance with the labor movement that Milk had won through his support of the Teamsters' union boycott against Coors beer. He had been able to get all the gay bars of San Francisco to stop serving Coors, and Coors subsequently gave in to the Teamsters' demands. The Briggs Initiative was fundamentally antiteacher, so the teachers' unions were vigorously opposed to it. Milk's political credit with the Teamsters helped bring other unions on board to oppose the Initiative, and the unions in turn helped provide venues in rural California for out-of-the-closet activists to appear and make anti-Briggs presentations.[44]

On Election Day in 1978, California voters rejected the Briggs Initiative by 58.4 to 41.6%. The surprisingly lopsided defeat was the only statewide referendum victory for gay rights of its era. It was a triumph for Milk and for his political philosophy of promoting out-of-the-closet political engagement.

Milk did not live long enough to savor his victory or to expand on his strategy of out-of-the-closet political engagement. Three weeks after he led California to defeat the Briggs Initiative, he and San Francisco mayor (and Milk ally) George Moscone were assassinated by bitter conservative former San Francisco supervisor Dan White.

White shot both Mayor Moscone and then Milk in the head at point-blank range. At White's trial, however, the prosecution was not vigorous and the jury was sympathetic to him. White was an army veteran and a former fireman and policeman, and though he appeared to have some mental health issues, he represented a traditional White ethnic and socially conservative constituency in San Francisco that Milk and the gay men of the Castro neighborhood were competing with politically. White was acquitted of murder and convicted only of manslaughter, a lesser crime. His acquittal on murder charges led to an impromptu, angry, and violent riot in the Castro, Milk's old San Francisco neighborhood and one of America's gay meccas. White was sentenced to seven years but served only five and later committed suicide.[45]

Milk had been planning a national gay rights march in Washington, D.C., when he was murdered. The march took place without him in October 1979. About 100,000 marchers participated, far more than in any earlier national gay rights demonstration in the U.S.[46]

Lessons from the 1970s

The defeat of the Briggs Initiative taught gay and lesbian activists that out-of-the-closet engagement was capable of changing straight people's minds. Harvey Milk was the most prominent out-of-the-closet American politician in 1978. His political leadership inspired citizens, activists, and teachers to come out of the closet and campaign against the Briggs Initiative in rural places and in conservative districts where out-of-the-closet gays and lesbians had never been seen in public before. His out-of-the-closet political engagement was a winning strategy in California in 1978 in part because of his special charisma and his (then) rare status as an out-of-the-closet elected official.

Pride parades in the 1970s gave gay and lesbian people a day's worth of experience about what it was like to be out of the closet and proud. Most of the parades were very small by today's standards, and not all of the gay and lesbian participants were out to their families or coworkers. The effect of gay pride marches on crowds of observers could not approach the powerful effect of coming out to one's own friends and family; nonetheless, people reported experiencing something thrilling when they marched down the street in a celebratory throng of similarly identified people. Gays and lesbians in the U.S. had not had opportunities before to feel the strength and power in their own numbers.

The defeat of the Briggs Initiative was one of the few gay rights political victories of the 1970s. Gay rights activists won the battle in part because of a successful out-of-the-closet political campaign by Harvey Milk and his allies, but the victory was also due to the Briggs Initiative's own faulty political strategy. The Initiative was a massive political overreach that failed to secure support from the most important conservative leaders in California. The Briggs Initiative was an example of what social movement scholar William Gamson (1990) has referred to as a movement with displacing goals because it sought to take away rights such as rights to employment and rights to (constitutionally protected) free speech that an established group of teachers already enjoyed. Gamson found that groups with displacing goals were dramatically less likely to be successful than groups with more moderate, nondisplacing goals.

Unlike the Briggs Initiative, the marriage equality movement when it was later created (and when the political opportunity structure was open enough to allow it a fair hearing) had the advantage of being nondisplacing. Granting same-sex couples the right to marry did not take away anyone else's right to marry. The states already had offices and procedures and forms to enable couples to marry. Aside from rewording some of the forms and printing a few extra marriage licenses, there were no costs to states and counties for allowing same-sex marriage. Gay rights activists learned hard lessons from every defeat of the 1970s and the 1980s, and they certainly learned lessons from their victory over the Briggs Initiative.

Activists and scholars (including Evelyn Hooker) working together pushed the APA to reclassify homosexuality in 1973. The APA's reclassification of homosexuality was the second occasion in U.S. history (after Kinsey and the ALI's 1962 model penal code suggested the decriminalization of sodomy) when research about gays and lesbians helped to build a new scholarly consensus to liberalize U.S. national immigration policy toward gay people. The reclassification created an important precedent for how scholarly research and scholarly societies could influence public policy relating to gay rights. By the 1970s, scholarly societies like the APA and elite professional groups like the ALI were well ahead of public opinion on gay rights issues. Their more liberal attitude on gay rights formed a wedge that started to pry open the door that kept gay and lesbian adults from enjoying full citizenship rights in the U.S.

Despite some progress in the political opportunity structure for gays and lesbians, the courts' emphatic rejection of McConnell and Baker's Minnesota marriage application was a clear sign that marriage equality in the early 1970s in the U.S. was a distant and remote goal. It would take more than two decades after McConnell and Baker's defeat for courts in the U.S. to start to take same-sex marriage plaintiffs seriously.

The way scholars view the gay rights activism of the 1970s is the final lesson to consider here. The surge of activism in the 1970s and the focus of gay rights scholarship on Stonewall and its immediate aftermath have provided a misleading lesson to scholars about the timing of when gay and lesbian people in the U.S. came out of the closet en masse. Some scholars and historians have assumed that the 1970s was the period when the majority of gay people in the U.S. came out of the closet because the gay rights vanguard was active in the 1970s. Social movement scholarship tends to focus on organizations and movement leaders because both leave a documentary trail. One ought not to assume that the vanguard gay rights organizations of the 1970s were representative of the wider population of gay and lesbian people. Within small activist circles in the 1970s, gay rights activists were out to each other. A few, such as Harvey Milk, were out to everyone and were at least locally famous.

Inside the confines of gay activist circles, it might have seemed that everyone was out. Outside those small circles, hardly anyone was out.

Consider the number of out-of-the-closet gay elected officials. At the time of his election as San Francisco city supervisor in 1977, Milk was not the first out-of-the closet gay elected official in the U.S., but he was *almost* the first; there had been maybe five earlier.[47] There are about 300,000 elected officials in the U.S., including city and county elected officials and disregarding school boards and special districts.[48] Even if only 2% of those elected officials were gay or lesbian, that would mean that in the 1970s United States, there were perhaps six thousand gay or lesbian elected officials, of whom only five were out of the closet, meaning, as a very rough estimate, more than 99% of the gay and lesbian elected officials in the U.S. were closeted in the 1970s.

Bayard Rustin was among the many influential gay political figures in the 1970s in the U.S. who were at least partly in the closet. Rustin was an important civil rights tactician and an advisor to activists and to leaders around the world. He was a celebrated speaker on subjects relating to peace, nonviolence, nuclear disarmament, race, civil rights, social change, and electoral politics. His fearlessness was legendary; he had suffered beatings at the hands of White racists and been incarcerated several times. Rustin's friends knew him to be gay, but he never spoke publicly about his homosexuality until the late 1980s, near the very end of his life.[49] Men of Rustin's generation (he was born in 1912) had been taught not to speak of such things.

The overwhelmingly closeted status of gay politicians in the U.S. in the 1970s is one way to understand how few of America's gays and lesbians were out of the closet in that time. The timing of when they came out is important. I return to this subject in my discussion of the 1990s, when the evidence shows that gay and lesbian Americans were coming out of the closet in large numbers and when attitudes toward gay rights started to rapidly liberalize.

4

The 1980s

AIDS

The AIDS crisis broke into the national consciousness in 1981, when the first devastating HIV infections were reported. Gay men were one of the groups that were especially victimized by the virus, and they realized that their legal disabilities, including the inability to marry their life partner, left them all too often without the medical access, healthcare surrogacy, inheritance rights, and other legal rights they needed. Gay men were forced, in the midst of the extreme crisis of AIDS, to organize themselves politically.[1]

The administration of President Ronald Reagan ignored AIDS for years. Jerry Falwell, Christian Right leader of the group Moral Majority, said of gay men and AIDS in 1983, "When you violate moral, health and hygiene laws, you reap the whirlwind. . . . You cannot shake your fist in God's face and get away with it."[2] For the Christian Right, AIDS was an opportunity to scapegoat gay men and to reinforce the old falsehoods that homosexuality was pathological and dangerous.

AIDS and the Reagan administration's inattention demonstrated to gay men that they needed to come out of the closet in order to do the political organizing and fundraising that the AIDS epidemic demanded of them.[3] The early years of the AIDS crisis, 1981–1988, did not make Americans more tolerant of gay rights; rather, it was a time of intensified fear and intolerance of gays. In 1980, 74% of Americans said gay sex was "always wrong"; in 1988, 77% said gay sex was "always wrong."

AIDS outed many gay men, including Rock Hudson in 1985. "Rock Hudson" was a stage name for Roy Scherer, who was marketed by Hollywood in the 1950s as a heterosexual leading man with dreamy good looks. If manly Rock Hudson was gay, then anyone could be gay.

Andrew Sullivan (1996: 124) wrote:

Early gay rights campaigners had once claimed that much of their argument would be won if only all homosexuals had some visible characteristic,

The Rainbow after the Storm. Michael J. Rosenfeld, Oxford University Press. © Oxford University Press 2022.
DOI: 10.1093/oso/9780197600436.003.0004

like purple hair. Well, AIDS gave gay men purple lesions and pneumocystis and cryptosporidiosis, and any number of horrifying and debilitating and invisible infections. Suddenly, the funny uncle at Thanksgiving was sick; and it was obvious why and how. And then he was dead, and what had once been easily avoided became a moment for candor to begin to break out. HIV acted as an unprecedented catalyst for the collapse of the norms of public discussion of homosexuality. It made the subject not merely una-voidable; it made it necessary. And it made hypocrisy unsustainable. The public-private compact between heterosexuals and homosexuals had to be renegotiated.

AIDS, which was killing thousands of American gay men every year in the 1980s in painful and debilitating ways, created a crisis. Out of the crisis emerged a more militant gay activist movement led by groups like ACT UP and Queer Nation, reviving radical gay rights politics that had been mostly dormant since the demise of the Gay Liberation Front in the early 1970s. ACT UP was founded in New York in 1987 by Larry Kramer. Queer Nation was founded in New York in 1990.

Outing and the Reign of *OutWeek*

Among the new radical voices of the late 1980s was Michelangelo Signorile, star writer for the New York–based *OutWeek* magazine, which published from 1989 to 1991. In Signorile's March 18, 1990, column, he outed the re-cently deceased and closeted Malcolm Forbes, scion of a prominent conser-vative family, as a gay playboy.

Forbes and his publicists would arrange for him to be photographed in the company of actresses, and then they would plant stories in the gossip columns about Forbes's romantic association with them. Even gossip columnists who had reason to know that Forbes was gay participated in the charade, thereby maintaining Forbes's closet.

Forbes's friends and associates included many conservative politicians and pundits with homophobic records. For Signorile, Forbes's cheerful association with homophobes made him a traitor to gay people in their time of crisis. The fight against AIDS was a political war. Signorile was naming the traitors, and outing them. Outing was controversial among gay rights leaders, and it was not obvious how outing Forbes would benefit gay rights or AIDS victims.[4] Signorile argued that gay people needed to know, for their own survival and self-respect, that some prominent people were also gay.

Because the closet was such a central institution in gay life for so long, gays and lesbians had become accustomed to keeping each other's secrets. The AIDS epidemic created exceptions to the blanket of privacy and secrecy. Signorile believed that outing some prominent gay people would induce other closeted gay people to come out on their own.[5] Accompanying his article outing Forbes, *OutWeek* ran an editorial:

> So we say this to the youth of our tribe: There are idols you aren't allowed to dream of. There are thousands of paragons you aren't allowed to know. There are lesbian movie stars and gay sports stars and famous gay writers and gay politicians and lesbian and gay geniuses. They are ours and, like them, Malcolm Forbes was ours. And in your name and for your futures we claim them all.[6]

OutWeek magazine folded in June 1991. Two months later, having moved to the gay magazine the *Advocate*, Signorile outed one of the U.S. military's chief public relations officers, Pete Wilson. The military had a policy at that time of not allowing gay men to serve, yet military leaders knew Wilson was gay and he remained their spokesman. The ban on gay soldiers started to lose credibility.

Soon after the public outings, gay and lesbian Americans started coming out of the closet in larger numbers. The outing of important people changed the calculus of the safety of the closet. Historically, the closet had been the only safe place for gay people, but the outing of public people made the closet seem suddenly less safe. Other gay people in the public eye came out on their own, to avoid being outed. The new climate of outness among people in the public eye made it easier for gays and lesbians not in the public eye to come out.

The Trend of States Decriminalizing Sodomy

Meanwhile, and without a lot of attention or fanfare, states had been decriminalizing sodomy. Between the ALI's 1962 model penal code and the mid-1980s, twenty-five states had dropped their bans against sodomy, through

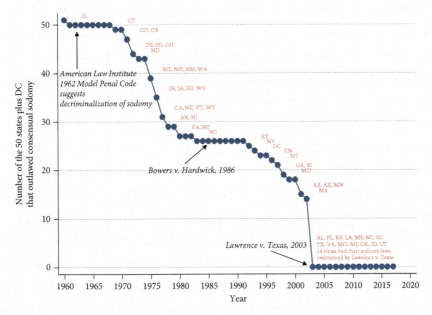

Figure 4.1 The decline in the number of U.S. states with bans against consensual sodomy. States listed as their bans were removed.

Source: Data on the end of sodomy laws in each state from the Appendix in Eskridge (2008).

either legislative or state judicial action. Figure 4.1 shows the decline in the number of states that retained sodomy bans in their criminal codes. In 1986, only twenty-five states, including Georgia, still had their criminal bans on sodomy in place. The decriminalization trend was strong. The sodomy laws had always been a fundamental barrier to gay people coming out of the closet and claiming their rights. To some in the gay rights legal community, the state-by-state erosion of the sodomy laws indicated that a U.S. Supreme Court challenge to the remaining sodomy laws was in order. But the challenge proved to be premature.

Bowers v. Hardwick (1986)

Michael Hardwick was a bartender at a gay bar in Atlanta in the mid-1980s. He had received a $50 ticket for drinking beer in public, gone to the courthouse, and paid his fine. Officer Keith Torrick obtained a warrant to arrest Hardwick, based on the false premise that he had failed to pay his fine. When

Torrick showed up at Hardwick's door with a warrant, someone let him in to the apartment. The officer went to the back bedroom and there found Hardwick in bed having sex with another man. The officer arrested both Hardwick and the other man under Georgia's sodomy law. Torrick allowed Hardwick and his partner to dress, handcuffed them together, and took them to the police station, where Hardwick's alleged offense of sodomy was gratuitously announced to all.

The penalty in Georgia for sodomy was between one and twenty years in prison. Atlanta's district attorney, however, refused to prosecute Hardwick. Two lawyers from the American Civil Liberties Union convinced Hardwick to sue Georgia in federal court to try to overturn the state's sodomy law. Hardwick lost in the district court, but won his appeal in the 11th Circuit Federal Court of Appeals.[7] Georgia's attorney general Michael Bowers appealed to the U.S. Supreme Court, which granted *Cert* and heard the case.

Historically, few people in the U.S. had ever been prosecuted for sodomy. As written, Georgia's sodomy law applied equally to heterosexual couples and gay couples and to married and unmarried couples. In practice, when the sodomy laws were enforced (or threatened to be enforced), the targets were usually gay men. Hardwick was an out-of-the-closet gay man whose out-of-the-closet status had made it all too easy for local law enforcement to put his freedom in jeopardy.

Before California decriminalized sodomy in 1975, San Francisco used to have between two thousand and three thousand felony arrests of gay men for sexual misconduct every year.[8] Many of these charges were based on entrapment by officers. Gay men were keenly aware of how the sodomy statute made them vulnerable to all kinds of other charges the police might levy against them, and they felt rightly freed from a heavy burden when California decriminalized sodomy.[9]

At the initial conference of the Supreme Court justices the vote was 5–4 in favor of Hardwick. Moderate Lewis Powell, a Nixon appointee nearing his retirement from the Court, subsequently changed his mind and swung the majority to Georgia's side.[10] After his retirement, Justice Powell changed his mind again and regretted his vote in *Bowers v. Hardwick*, but then it was too late.[11]

The majority decision in *Bowers v. Hardwick* (1986)[12] gave a full-throated and sweeping endorsement of state sodomy laws:

No connection between family, marriage, or procreation on the one hand and homosexual activity on the other has been demonstrated, either by the Court of Appeals or by respondent [Hardwick]. Moreover, any claim that . . . private sexual conduct between consenting adults is constitutionally insulated from state proscription is unsupportable. . . . [T]he privacy right . . . [does] not reach so far. . . .[13]

Proscriptions against that conduct [sodomy] have ancient roots. . . . Sodomy was a criminal offense at common law and was forbidden by the laws of the original 13 States when they ratified the Bill of Rights. . . . Against this background, to claim that a right to engage in such conduct [sodomy] is "deeply rooted in this Nation's history and tradition" or "implicit in the concept of ordered liberty" is, at best, facetious.[14]

The *Bowers v. Hardwick* decision fell like a hammer on gay rights activists. Thomas Stoddard from the gay rights group Lambda Legal said, "For the Gay rights movement, this is our Dred Scott,"[15] referencing the infamous *Dred Scott v. Sandford* (1857) Supreme Court decision that had endorsed slavery and found that American descendants of slaves kidnapped from Africa were not U.S. citizens and hence had no standing to sue in U.S. federal court.[16] In effect, the *Dred Scott* decision had said that Black people in the U.S. had no rights.

One of the reasons that Justice Powell was unconvinced by the personal rights argument of Michael Hardwick was that, like most people of his generation, Powell believed he had never known a gay or lesbian person. The irony was that at the time, Powell was speaking to his own law clerk who was gay.[17] Powell had chosen closeted gay clerks for his small staff for years. The closet did tremendous damage by hiding the reality of gay and lesbian lives from others who had to make decisions about the value of gay rights. The further irony is that it was partly the sodomy laws, which *Bowers* was about to uphold, that kept gay people hidden in the closet in the first place. The majority decision in *Bowers* treated gay people as an unknown other because the closet kept them unknown.

Gay rights activists mobilized for a march on Washington, D.C. Fifteen months later, in October 1987, more than 500,000 people descended on Washington to demand rights for gays and lesbians and to demand legal recognition of gay and lesbian relationships. Six hundred people were arrested on the steps of the U.S. Supreme Court building protesting against the *Bowers* decision.[18]

Change in the Supreme Court

The retirement of the Supreme Court's swing vote Lewis Powell in 1987 allowed President Reagan to nominate ultraconservative Robert Bork to the high court. However, Bork was not confirmed by the Democratic-controlled U.S. Senate. His defeat did not have much apparent effect on attitudes toward gay rights at the time, but it became important a decade later. Bork had been a steadfast opponent of almost every civil rights victory in the U.S. since the 1940s. He also had a sharply antigay judicial record, but since gays and lesbians had lost almost every U.S. court battle up to that point, his antigay judicial record was not so unusual. After losing his confirmation battle in 1987,[19] Bork continued to be just as implacably hostile to gay rights. Years later Bork (2004) wrote that "the rationale for same-sex marriage would equally support group marriage, incest, or any other imaginable sexual arrangement," a critique of marriage equality known as the slippery slope argument. According to the slippery slope argument, if society's ban on same-sex marriage were lifted, no other social distinctions or legal barriers could be maintained, and therefore society would collapse into chaos, a situation that Bork described as representing a "nuclear" threat to society.

With Bork's defeat, Reagan nominated Douglas Ginsburg, but had to quickly withdraw the nomination when reports of Ginsburg's marijuana use surfaced. Reagan's third choice to fill Powell's seat was Anthony Kennedy, who was confirmed 97–0 in the Senate.

Like Bork, Kennedy had ruled on several cases involving gay rights and, like Bork, had ruled against the gay plaintiffs in every case, so he may not have appeared to be so different from Bork on the issue of gay rights in 1987. Hardly anyone in the top echelons of U.S. political life was actively promoting or even sensitive to gay rights in 1987. However, a close reading of Kennedy's appellate court decisions suggested that, unlike Bork, he was at least capable of considering discrimination against gay people to be problematic. In *Beller v Middendorf* (1980: 811), Kennedy had authored an opinion which upheld the navy's dismissal of gay sailor Beller and others but noted that "regulations which might infringe upon constitutional rights in other contexts may survive scrutiny because of military necessities." In other words, employment discrimination against gay people in the civilian world *might* infringe upon the gay employees' constitutional rights. For U.S. courts in 1980, that sounded almost like progressive thinking about gay rights.

Over the next thirty years, Kennedy's view of gay people and gay rights would evolve, paralleling the liberalization of attitudes toward gay rights in the U.S. as a whole. He would go on to author the majority opinion in four gay rights victories in the Supreme Court: *Romer v. Evans* (1996); *Lawrence v. Texas* (2003), overturning *Bowers v. Hardwick*; *U.S. v. Windsor* (2013), striking down part of the Defense of Marriage Act of 1996; and *Obergefell v. Hodges* (2015), making marriage equality the law across the U.S. Yet at the time of Kennedy's confirmation in 1987, he had a record of no particular distinction on gay rights issues; in fact, the National Gay and Lesbian Task Force was one of the few groups that opposed his confirmation.[20]

Kennedy's nomination to the U.S. Supreme Court, and therefore his eventual enormous impact on gay rights in the U.S., came about as the result of a series of political events and accidents that had nothing to do with gay rights. Had the public not found out that U.S. intelligence agents had sold arms to Iran in order to illegally fund the Nicaraguan Contras (the "Iran-Contra Affair"), the Republicans might not have lost their majority in the U.S. Senate in the elections of 1986.[21] Had the U.S. Senate still had a Republican majority in 1987, Bork (Reagan's first choice) would likely have been confirmed instead of Kennedy.[22] Had Bork been on the Supreme Court instead of Kennedy, the course of gay rights in the U.S. may have been different.[23] Public policy change can depend on seemingly random or unrelated events, and therefore change and the timing of change are both difficult to predict.

Lessons from the 1980s

The AIDS plague wrought devastation on gay men around the world and overturned many preexisting social expectations within the gay community. Fundraising and political engagement that had once seemed like a luxury became a necessity. If people were going to be organized to donate time and money to fight AIDS and to lobby governments to fight AIDS, they had to be out of the closet. In the past it had been a nearly iron-clad rule that gay and lesbian people, knowing the necessity of the closet, would not out each other. In the radical political moment of the emergency of AIDS, the old niceties of respecting everyone's private life no longer applied. The fight against AIDS was a war, and all wars have casualties. The closet was one of them.

The U.S. Supreme Court decision in *Bowers v. Hardwick* was galvanizing because it showed a generation of gay and lesbian people and their allies just how far they still were from being treated as full citizens of the U.S. *Bowers* also showed how much difference a single vote on the Supreme Court could make. *Bowers* was a 5–4 hammer blow against gay rights, with moderate Lewis Powell casting the deciding vote. Powell retired a year later, and Anthony Kennedy took his place.

PART II
ATTITUDES TOWARD GAY RIGHTS BEGIN TO CHANGE

5

The 1990s, Fulcrum of Change: Politics and Culture

On the campaign trail in 1992, Democratic presidential candidate Bill Clinton did something surprising: he spoke out in favor of gay rights, and he promised to repeal the ban on gay people serving in the military. Clinton's promise went unfulfilled during his administration, but the promise itself may have been influential.

In 1992, Clinton attended a fundraising meeting of gay leaders from Los Angeles and told them that he would happily give up his political career if he could find a cure for AIDS. Thousands of copies of Clinton's speech were circulated in the gay community.[1] No main party presidential nominee had ever affirmed gay people and their struggles in that way. His endorsement of gay rights goals surely helped the leaders organize and may also have helped gays and lesbians feel secure enough to come out of the closet in greater numbers.

In his nationally televised speech accepting the Democratic nomination on July 16, Clinton (1992) referred to the gay community explicitly as part of a common America that the Republican Party was seeking to divide:

> The New Covenant is about more than opportunities and responsibilities for you and your families. It's also about our common community. Tonight every one of you knows deep in your heart that we are too divided. It is time to heal America. And so we must say to every American: Look beyond the stereotypes that blind us. We need each other—all of us—we need each other. We don't have a person to waste, and yet for too long politicians have told the most of us that are doing all right that what's really wrong with America is the rest of us—them. Them, the minorities. Them, the liberals. Them, the poor. Them, the homeless. Them, the people with disabilities. Them, the gays. We've gotten to where we've nearly them'ed ourselves to death. Them, and them, and them. But this is America. There is no them. There is only us. One nation, under God, indivisible, with liberty and justice for all.

The Rainbow after the Storm. Michael J. Rosenfeld, Oxford University Press. © Oxford University Press 2022.
DOI: 10.1093/oso/9780197600436.003.0005

The effect of Clinton's embrace of gay people on the biggest stage in American political life was electrifying, according to Jeffrey Schmalz's (1992) reporting in the *New York Times*. Compared to the wall of enthusiastic antigay discrimination that had come from prior administrations, Clinton's pro-gay-rights rhetoric was revolutionary.[2]

The Role of Bill Clinton's 1992 Campaign

Figure 5.1 shows that the first great rise in approval toward gay people occurred around 1992, subsequent to the outings of famous people and coincident with Clinton's first campaign for the presidency. In 1991, 22.6% of Americans told the GSS that sex between two people of the same sex was not "always wrong." In 1993, that number was 33.9%, an increase of more than 11 percentage points in two years, a large and highly statistically significant change. Only 5% of public opinion attitudes measured in the GSS have changed by as much as 0.97 percentage points per year (on average, from first

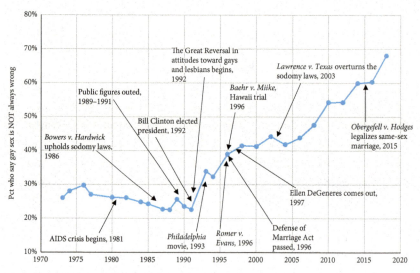

Figure 5.1 The rise in approval of gay rights.

Source: Weighted GSS data about approval of gay sex: "What about the sexual relations between two adults of the same sex?" with potential answers "always wrong," "almost always wrong," "sometimes wrong," and "not wrong at all." All answers except "always wrong" are combined and coded as approval of gay rights.

observation to last). The average rate of change of attitudes in the GSS was 0.34 percentage points per year.

Clinton is not remembered fondly by gay rights activists[3] because of two setbacks during his first term: Don't Ask, Don't Tell (DADT), built on a Defense Department directive issued in December 1993, which forced gay and lesbian military service people into the closet, and the Defense of Marriage Act of 1996. Yet Figure 5.1 shows that Clinton may have had a more liberalizing effect on gay rights attitudes in the U.S. than is usually acknowledged. The correlation in time between his 1992 campaign and the change in attitudes suggests but does not prove that Clinton independently changed Americans' attitudes.

A month after Clinton's July 1992 address accepting the Democratic nomination, conservative commentator and presidential candidate Pat Buchanan spoke to the Republican National Convention, nominating George H. W. Bush as candidate for a second term as president. Buchanan focused on what he referred to as the "culture war," i.e., the war over cultural values, and specifically over gay rights:

> My friends, like many of you last month, I watched that giant masquerade ball up at Madison Square Garden—where 20,000 liberals and radicals came dressed up as moderates and centrists—in the greatest single exhibition of cross-dressing in American political history. . . . Yet a militant leader of the homosexual rights movement could rise at that same convention and say: "Bill Clinton and Al Gore represent the most pro-lesbian and pro-gay ticket in history." And so they do. . . .
>
> My friends, this election is about more than who gets what. It is about who we are. It is about what we believe, and what we stand for as Americans. There is a religious war going on in this country. It is a cultural war, as critical to the kind of nation we shall be as was the Cold War itself, for this war is for the soul of America. And in that struggle for the soul of America, Clinton and Clinton are on the other side, and George Bush is on our side.[4]

Buchanan painted the entire Democratic convention as cross-dressers. Conservative political speech in this era made gay imagery a central trope. Conservatives had become used to leveraging gay images because antigay messages were effective in frightening and mobilizing their evangelical Christian base.

In 1992 Clinton was indeed, as Buchanan claimed, the most gay-positive candidate the U.S. had ever had, by a wide margin. His pro-gay-rights statements represented a change in the U.S. political opportunity structure in favor of gay rights activists. His express support for gay rights made it easier for gays and lesbians to come out of the closet, to organize, and to influence others and may also have made straight Americans more receptive to gay rights.

Clinton's symbolic embrace of gay people undermined the frame of stigma, abnormality, and perversity that American political leaders had previously applied to gays and lesbians.[5] Elite opinion leaders (among whom the president is the most elite and therefore the most influential) can have a powerful effect on public opinion, especially in areas where the public lacks personal experience. Before gays and lesbians in the U.S. had come out of the closet in sufficient numbers to turn the tide of opinion in favor of gay rights, elite opinion was probably the most important influence on Americans' views about gay rights.

As Zaller (1992) notes, there are public policy issues such as the U.S. role in NATO and governmental deficit spending where most citizens have neither personal experience nor firsthand knowledge nor the grasp of historical facts to generate their own opinion. In such cases, citizens necessarily turn to their leaders for direction.

The most critical moment in the relationship between elites and public opinion comes when a formerly solid elite consensus breaks into dissensus. In the late 1960s, for example, elites in the U.S. government, media, and clergy started to criticize the U.S. role in the war in Vietnam. A formerly strict elite consensus in favor of U.S. involvement dissolved into a bitter political debate. As a result of the elite dissensus on the Vietnam War, the public started to hear criticism of the war from elites for the first time.[6] In the space of a few years, public support for the war collapsed, aided by the perception that Lyndon Johnson's (and later Richard Nixon's) rhetoric about the war in Vietnam had been less than truthful.[7]

Clinton's 1992 presidential campaign was a break with the elite consensus on gay rights, but he was able to move public opinion about gay rights only because most people had never heard elites proclaim support for gay rights before. Clinton had no apparent prior history of supporting gay rights as governor of Arkansas,[8] and as a southern White man he was not a classic social issues liberal. Nor did he seem to be the kind of political leader who would naturally espouse pro-gay-rights views. His tough-on-crime policies were more consistent with conservative than liberal politics, and in fact, as president he oversaw an enormous expansion of incarceration in the U.S.[9] He ran on, and enacted, an end to welfare (as a long term commitment to support poor people), thereby overturning one of America's signature social safety net measures first enacted by Franklin Delano Roosevelt. Paradoxically, President Clinton's conservative reputation on some social issues may partly explain why his support of gay rights appears to have been so influential: even if only symbolic, his support was unexpected and therefore harder to anticipate and harder for opponents to defend against.

When Clinton was sworn in as president in January 1993, he had strong Democratic majorities in both the House of Representatives and the Senate. He had assumed that his Democratic allies in Congress would help him overturn the ban on gays serving in the military, but he miscalculated. Conservative congressional Democrats rebelled, and in the military the generals and admirals were, to varying degrees, opposed to Clinton's plan. Even though one survey in 1992 showed that 56% of Americans favored gays being allowed to serve in the military,[10] opponents were much better organized and their outrage was at full boil. Calls opposing the right of gays to serve openly in the military poured into the White House and congressional switchboards.

Military leaders were responding in part to a survey by Northwestern University sociologists Charles Moskos and Laura Miller that showed that men in the U.S. military were overwhelmingly opposed to allowing gays and lesbians to serve.[11] Moskos, the leading sociologist of the U.S. military, endorsed a policy that came to be known as Don't Ask, Don't Tell. DADT was quickly adopted by the military in December 1993 with Clinton's grudging approval, and proved to be disastrous for gay soldiers and sailors. As long as gays remained strictly in the closet they could remain in the military, but as soon as someone found out they were gay they faced the grim prospect of military discharge. Over the life of DADT, from 1994 to 2010, when it was repealed, more than thirteen thousand gay service people were discharged for being gay.

Even though gays and lesbians lost their battle in 1993 to serve openly in the military, the public debate opened the eyes of many straight people. Straight people began to see that gays and lesbians had always been in the military and were facing discrimination while serving their country. Story after story filtered out of gay service people who had won medals for bravery or for extraordinary accomplishments and who had won the admiration of their colleagues, being discharged only because they were gay.[12]

Cross-Generational Evidence of a Shift toward Gay Rights

Figure 5.2 shows GSS data on the percentage of U.S. adults by birth generation who said sexual relations between two adults of the same sex was not "always wrong." The separation between the generations in Figure 5.2 demonstrates a powerful gap in attitudes about gay and lesbian people. The earlier the generation, the more likely Americans were to think that sex between people of the same sex was "always wrong."[13] Conversely, the more recent the birth generation, the more support there is for gay sex and, by extension, for gay rights.

From 1973 to about 1990, with every passing year, the GI generation, the Silent Generation, and the Baby Boomers were becoming more intolerant of gay sex. Even as people from the Silent Generation began to experience mortality and were replaced in adult society by Baby Boomers and then by young

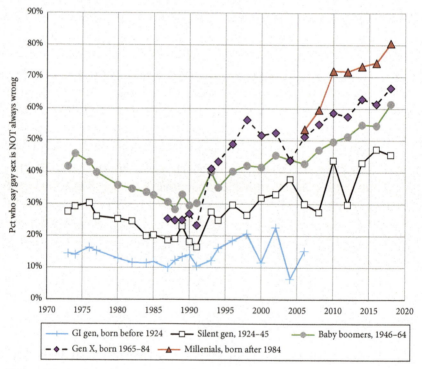

Figure 5.2 Support for gay rights by birth generation.
Source: Weighted data from the GSS.

adults from Generation X, American society was making everyone, regardless of birth generation, more hostile to gay rights.

And then, around 1992, the GSS data record an important transition. Instead of adults within each generation becoming more hostile toward gay rights as they aged, as had been the case in 1973–1990, adults started to become less hostile as they aged. Note how in Figure 5.2 around 1992, the Silent Generation (whose average age was about sixty), the Baby Boomers (average age about forty), and adults from Generation X (average age twenty) all started becoming more supportive of gay rights at the same time.[14] From 1992 to the present this trend in greater tolerance toward gays and lesbians within generations has continued. Figure 5.2's simultaneous changes across the birth generations is classic evidence for historical, or period-specific, effects. From 1992 forward, the historical climate allowed Americans from all generations to become less hostile toward gay rights with each passing year.[15]

Political Polarization

The increasing political distance between social and political groups over time is known as political polarization. Gay rights is one set among many polarizing issues in American politics. Figure 5.3 documents the divergence on gay rights between Americans who identify with the Democratic and Republican parties over time. The divergence after 1992 between Democrats' and Republicans' views of gay rights is another piece of evidence that supports candidate Clinton's impact on gay rights attitudes in the U.S.

In the 1970s and 1980s, Democrats and Republicans were similarly opposed to gay rights, indicated by the overlap in the confidence intervals (the areas around the point estimates) in Figure 5.3. When the confidence intervals overlap, we are not sure that Democrats and Republicans in the U.S. had different views of gay rights.

Coincident with Clinton's 1992 campaign, gay rights started to become a much more politically partisan issue in the U.S., and Democrats' and Republicans' views of gay rights started to diverge. Another interpretation of Figure 5.3 is that after 1992 Americans who supported gay rights were more attracted to the Democratic Party, while Americans who opposed gay rights were more attracted to the Republican Party. As the parties started giving different signals about gay rights after 1992, voters may have changed their

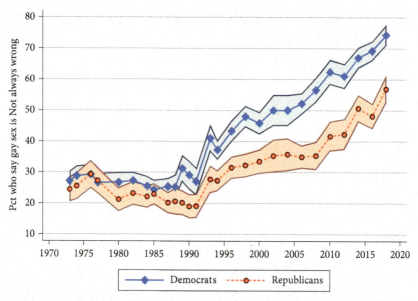

Figure 5.3 Increasing polarization by political party in attitudes toward gay rights.

Source: Weighted GSS data with 95% confidence intervals.

party affiliation in order to be in the party that better fit their view on gay rights.

In 1991 Democrats and Republicans were only 8 percentage points apart in their belief that gay sex was "not always wrong" (19% of Republicans thought so, compared to 27% of Democrats). In 1993, they were 13 percentage points apart. By 2018, they were 17 percentage points apart (57% of Republicans said gay sex was "not always wrong" compared to 74% of Democrats).[16]

On the same question of whether gay sex is "always wrong," biblical literalists have grown further apart from people who think the Bible is an "ancient book of fables, legends, history, and moral precepts recorded by men." Men and women too have grown further apart, as women now support gay rights more than men, whereas in the 1970s there was no gender gap. On the other hand, the gap between people with college degrees and high school dropouts over whether gay sex is "always wrong" has narrowed considerably over time.[17]

Scholars have documented polarization similar to that seen in Figure 5.3 across a wide set of issues. The two main U.S. political parties are getting better at recruiting people along ideological lines, so that there are fewer liberal Republicans and fewer conservative Democrats, and the parties are moving apart ideologically over time on a range of issues.[18] Since 1992 Congress has become dramatically more polarized along party lines than at any time since World War II, meaning there are fewer and fewer times in which Democratic representatives and Republican representatives vote the same way.[19]

Political parties and elected officials have become more polarized since 1992 on many issues, including gay rights. Whether the population of U.S. citizens is more politically polarized than it used to be is more of an open question in political science.[20] There are reasons to think that the diversification and Balkanization of news sources in the internet era has led to a more polarized population, as the news people receive is more tailored to their political affiliations.[21] Ideologically targeted news provides liberals and conservatives with incompatible information about the same events. While the policy preferences of U.S. citizens may not have become more polarized, citizens who identify with each political party increasingly view members of the other party in a negative way.[22]

Residential neighborhoods in the U.S. are becoming more ideologically polarized. Liberals and conservatives have different tolerances for ethnic diversity and seek different kinds of amenities and different proximities to urban downtowns.[23] Ideologically sorted communities lead to more ideologically polarized legislative districts, which in turn lead to more ideologically polarized elected representatives, which then attract more like-minded people to the district. Political polarization at the level of districts and representatives can be a self-reinforcing cycle.

Clinton's 1992 campaign appears to have been one historical event that began to reverse American public opinion about gay rights into a more pro-gay-rights direction. Clinton's pro-gay-rights statements in the campaign did not spring out of a vacuum. He was a famously adept reader of public opinion, so he must have thought that in 1992 the public was ready for gay rights. The gay rights movement was growing but still was relatively small in 1992 compared to its organized opponents. AIDS activism had focused moral attention on the plight of gay men and their partners. Clinton must also have understood that the distinction he was making between himself as a surprising proponent of gay rights and the Republican Party as a staunch institutional opponent of gay rights would make him seem to younger voters to be the candidate of change and hope. Clinton defeated George H. W. Bush in the November 1992 elections.

Clinton's (2004) memoir *My Life* has nothing to say in its more than nine hundred pages about why he decided to support gay rights in the 1992 campaign, or whether he thought that his support of gay rights had any positive effects. On the contrary, his memoir rues the way that DADT and a focus on gay rights issues helped the Republicans take the political wind out of his sails in 1993 and stall the rest of his political agenda. Clinton's memoir also does not mention the executive orders that he signed ending decades of discrimination against gays and lesbians in federal employment.[24] In this chapter I am giving him more credit than he gives himself in his own lengthy memoir for helping to make the U.S. a more gay-tolerant country.

Clinton's influence on gay rights attitudes in the U.S. has been underappreciated even by Clinton himself, because his influence on attitudes toward gay rights emerges only after examination of a long time trend in public opinion data. One needs more than a decade of hindsight and analysis of a very specific kind of trend data on attitudes about gay rights to identify the specific year when those attitudes started changing. In the heat of the moment, or in hindsight without the right data, Clinton's liberalizing impact on American attitudes about gay rights is difficult to appreciate.

Philadelphia, 1993

As American attitudes toward gay rights were beginning their rapid liberalization, and as political leaders such as Bill Clinton were giving gay rights issues more mainstream legitimacy, space opened up in the popular culture for more favorable views of gay people. In December 1993, TriStar Pictures released the movie *Philadelphia*, directed by Jonathan Demme. Demme's previous movie, the Oscar-winning and commercially successful *The Silence of the Lambs* (1991), had been criticized as homophobic by some gay rights activists because it featured a homicidal central character with gay affectations.[25]

Philadelphia stars Tom Hanks as an ambitious and successful gay lawyer with AIDS who is fired by his law firm when they notice Kaposi's sarcoma lesions on his face. No star of Hanks's caliber had ever played a sympathetic gay leading role in a major Hollywood movie before. In the opening scene, we see Hanks's character, Andy Beckett, winning a case against another local attorney played by Denzel Washington. Beckett returns to his firm and receives a promotion. The opening scenes establish Beckett's bona fides as a lawyer.

The honorable and self-confident Beckett is a world apart from the evil and pitiable gay characters Hollywood had generally portrayed in the past.[26]

The partners in the firm don't know Beckett is gay until they see the lesions on his face. He has been outed by AIDS. After being fired, Beckett decides to sue the firm for wrongful termination but cannot find a lawyer to take his case. Eventually Washington's character, Joe Miller, agrees to represent Beckett, despite Miller's own homophobia. Part of the journey of the movie is Miller overcoming homophobia through interaction with the smart and decent Beckett. Beckett and Miller win their case against Beckett's old firm, and Beckett dies at the end of the movie.[27]

Philadelphia opened in just a few cities initially. Praise from critics allowed TriStar to expand to 1,200 theaters in January 1994, when the movie became the number-one box office attraction in the U.S. Hanks was nominated for Best Actor in February, and in March 1994 won the Oscar, his first. In his acceptance speech he thanked his gay high school drama teacher and said a brief prayer for the victims of AIDS.

Ellen Comes Out, 1997

Before the majority of American gays and lesbians could feel safe enough to come out of the closet, there had to be examples of famous people voluntarily coming out and weathering the storm. Actress Ellen DeGeneres came out of the closet as a lesbian in 1997, and then supplied an on-screen coming-out story in her eponymous television show, *Ellen*, in 1997, playing the character Ellen Morgan.

In the coming-out episode, which aired on April 30, 1997, Ellen Morgan is having dinner with her longtime male friend Richard, a television news reporter and potential love interest from out of town. Richard's coworker Susan joins them at the hotel restaurant table. Ellen and Susan flirt a little. Richard is the episode's potential love interest, but Ellen falls for Susan instead.

At the end of the episode, Ellen is at the airport with Susan. She leans over toward Susan and says, "I'm gay," which is overheard by the entire airport since there is a microphone between them at the ticket counter. Everyone turns. Susan gives Ellen a very chaste hug. The coming-out episode ends without consummation or even a kiss between Ellen and Susan. Ellen Morgan's coming out is a desexualized story, and the episode leaves open the possibility that the character is bisexual or asexual rather than exclusively homosexual.

Ellen's coming-out episode was a full hour special and was anticipated by a *Time* magazine cover story on April 14, 1997, wherein Ellen DeGeneres herself came out of the closet. The cover photo showed a smiling DeGeneres in a shapeless black outfit, with the caption "Yep, I'm Gay." The coming-out episode was seen by 42 million viewers, more than double the show's usual audience.

The *Ellen* coming-out episode was followed by a special episode of Oprah's television show in which DeGeneres talked about both her personal coming-out and her character's coming-out. She told Oprah that she decided to come out in part because she was afraid of being outed by others and she wanted to control the news about herself.

The old calculus had always been that the closet was the only safe place for gay and lesbian Americans, which was why they remained in the closet. In the new calculus, being in the closet meant one had a secret that could be exposed by others. Living in the closet became a vulnerability that had to be mitigated by coming out. If mild-mannered, kind, midwestern-nice Ellen DeGeneres could come out of the closet, face down criticism, and live her own life, then others could do it as well.

Ellen DeGeneres became the most famous out gay person in America. Christian Right leader Jerry Falwell referred to her as "Ellen Degenerate" and called on his group, the Moral Majority, to boycott the advertisers on her TV show. The network that aired *Ellen*, ABC, and its parent company, Disney, immediately came under fire from conservatives. Both Chrysler and J.C. Penney refused to advertise on the coming-out episode, though J.C. Penney later reestablished its advertising relationship with DeGeneres.[28]

For some observers of gay and lesbian politics, DeGeneres's television coming out was too timid.[29] She was self-consciously apolitical and admitted that she "never felt like [she] belonged to the gay community."[30] For politically moderate Americans, DeGeneres was the ideal person to convey the idea that homosexuals were normal, just like themselves. *Ellen* carefully anticipated the kinds of discomforts and objections that heterosexual Americans might have to homosexuality, to gay rights, and to having their friends come out as gay. The show placed heterosexual characters in positions to overcome these discomforts and objections. *Ellen* pulled its audience toward more acceptance of gay rights slowly and gently.

Ellen had a story arc of coming out and then being an out-of-the-closet gay person from the end of the show's season 4 in the spring of 1997 through the end of season 5 in the summer of 1998. In the episode after the coming-out episode, Ellen Morgan comes out to her parents. They are alarmed, surprised, and angry. She tells them, "You always wanted me to be open and honest," and her mother responds, "Oh no, honey, that's what you wanted. We were always very happy keeping our feelings bottled up."[31] It seems as if her parents will not come around, but once they see her being verbally attacked by a homophobe, they rally to her defense and are supportive and loving from that moment forward. Later in season 5, Ellen Morgan asks her father what allowed him to come around to supporting her, and he answers simply, "When you were born, I said I would always love you. And that's a promise. And there is nothing that would ever change that."[32]

After *Ellen*'s season 4 and before season 5, *Newsweek* magazine sponsored a nationally representative phone survey in June 1997, asking, "What is your opinion of TV actress Ellen DeGeneres, and her character, coming out as gay earlier this year? Do you think it was a GOOD THING because it promoted a positive image for gay people, or a BAD THING because it seemed to promote gay lifestyles?" Forty percent of the survey respondents said that DeGeneres's coming out was a *bad* thing, 35% said it was a *good* thing, and the remainder had no opinion. The year 1997 was early in the progression of American attitudes toward more tolerance of gay rights. For Americans who had never thought about gay rights the *Ellen* show was radical, and to some, upsetting.

Newsweek also asked survey subjects what they thought of Disney, the parent company of ABC, and what they thought of television sponsors of the *Ellen* show. Seventy-eight percent of American adults said that it did not make much difference to them whether companies advertised on the *Ellen* show; 15% said they would be less likely to patronize the advertisers, compared to only 3% who said they would be more likely to patronize the advertisers. The *Ellen* show was sailing into a substantial headwind of indifferent or negative public opinion, yet the coming-out theme continued resolutely across two television seasons despite controversy and organized opposition, which is why the *Ellen* show was, in 1997, a pathbreaking show for the public airwaves.

The *Ellen* show and *Philadelphia* were two of the rapidly growing number of popular television shows and Hollywood movies that featured gay characters in the 1990s.[33] The 1998 debut of *Will & Grace* on NBC featured not one but two gay lead characters. Flamboyant and superficial Jack McFarland fit previous Hollywood stereotypes of gay characters, while serious and successful attorney Will Truman fit none of the prior stereotypes. One of the indelible messages of *Will & Grace*, which had an initial run of eight seasons, was that gay people, like straight people, are amazingly diverse.

Research by Jeremiah Garretson has shown that Americans who watched shows and movies that had sympathetic gay characters became substantially more supportive of gay people and gay rights.[34] Popular culture has a broad reach across geographies and populations and is consumed by Democrats and Republicans, by liberal and conservative Americans alike. American popular culture in the 1990s reached and probably changed the minds of Americans both gay and straight.

Lessons from the 1990s

Bill Clinton the politician was famously adept at reading a crowd and at understanding trends. He understood that the crisis of AIDS was shifting the ground underneath a long-standing political consensus in the U.S. that gay people were not entitled to equal rights or equal treatment. Clinton saw gay rights as an opportunity to distinguish himself from a much older and more politically traditional opponent on the 1992 presidential campaign trail, and he seized the opportunity. His advocacy of the right of gays to serve in the military, though unfulfilled while he was in office, corresponds with the historical inflection point in the attitudinal data.

Between 1992 and 1993 attitudes toward gay rights began a sharp and unprecedented liberalizing turn. Americans from every generation started becoming more tolerant of gay rights in 1992. Democrats and Republicans started drifting apart on gay rights after 1992, as Clinton's advocacy made gay rights a partisan political issue in national politics for the first time. President Clinton's advocacy for gay rights opened space in the political opportunity structure. If he could stand up for gay rights and win election to the highest office in the land, the fear of being tarred and feathered for insufficient homophobia was disappearing. Hollywood started to produce more gay-friendly films. Ellen DeGeneres came out and indicated that she had been afraid of being outed. Being out started to seem safer than being in the closet.

The unapologetic presence of popular gay people (DeGeneres) and influential straight people who gave at least the appearance of being allies of gay rights (Clinton, Tom Hanks) helped to shift cultural perceptions that straight Americans had of gay people. The more open political opportunity structure made it easier for gay and lesbian people to decide to come out of the closet. The presence of more out-of-the-closet gay and lesbian people drove further liberalization in attitudes toward gay rights in straight America. The unbroken rise in approval of gay rights in the U.S. that started around 1992 and has continued to the present day is the most remarkable trend in the history of American public opinion.

As some elites in the U.S. started advocating for gay rights, and as gays and lesbians started coming out of the closet in large numbers, and as public opinion was jolted in a more liberal direction on gay rights, the courts started listening to gay and lesbian plaintiffs in ways the courts never had before.

6

The Courts Begin to Appreciate Gay Rights: *Romer* and *Baehr*, 1996

The First Full-Length U.S. Supreme Court Decision Supporting Gay Rights: *Romer v. Evans* (1996)

In the late 1980s several Christian Right organizations, including Focus on the Family's national headquarters, relocated to Colorado Springs, Colorado. Focus on the Family had been founded in California in 1977 by psychologist James Dobson. It grew tremendously in Colorado, becoming the most influential Christian Right group in the U.S., with revenue that would grow to exceed $100 million per year. Focus on the Family spread a core message that Christians should be afraid of gay rights.[1] The more liberal Colorado towns of Denver, Boulder, and Aspen had passed laws that outlawed discrimination based on sexual orientation. In 1992, Christian conservatives in the state collected enough signatures to place Colorado's Amendment 2 on the ballot, which proposed to invalidate any nondiscrimination ordinance in the state that protected gays and lesbians. In their campaign for Amendment 2, Colorado's powerful Christian Right groups claimed that "sexual molestation of children is a large part of many homosexuals' lifestyle—part of the very lifestyle 'gay rights' activists want government to give special class, ethnic status!"[2] In the 1992 election, Clinton won Colorado, but Amendment 2 also passed, by 53 to 47%.

Richard Evans and others sued the governor of Colorado, Roy Romer, in state court to block Amendment 2,[3] and in 1993 Amendment 2 was found to be unconstitutional by Colorado District Court judge H. Jeffrey Bayless. Judge Bayless found that the witnesses in defense of Amendment 2 had provided insufficient evidence for their claims that protecting gay people against discrimination would harm the state of Colorado or its children.[4] The state appealed to the Colorado Supreme Court, which ruled[5] that Amendment 2's fencing-off of gays and lesbians as a special class of people who could not be protected from discrimination was in violation of the

The Rainbow after the Storm. Michael J. Rosenfeld, Oxford University Press. © Oxford University Press 2022.
DOI: 10.1093/oso/9780197600436.003.0006

U.S. Constitution, specifically the guarantee of equal protection under the Fourteenth Amendment. The state of Colorado appealed this decision to the U.S. Supreme Court.

When the U.S. Supreme Court granted *Cert* in February 1995 and agreed to hear Colorado's appeal in *Romer v. Evans*, they "sent a shiver down the spines of every gay-rights attorney in America."[6] Gay rights plaintiffs in Colorado were hoping that the Court would deny *Cert*, finalizing Amendment 2's defeat in the courts. The devastating precedent of *Bowers v. Hardwick* (1986) gave gay rights advocates good reason to be afraid of the U.S. Supreme Court.

The U.S. Supreme Court heard oral arguments in *Romer v. Evans* on October 10, 1995. The oral arguments contained a surprise that turned out to have historic ramifications. Justice Anthony Kennedy, the conservative Catholic, nominated by Reagan and confirmed in 1987, interrupted Colorado's solicitor general with a series of sharp questions.[7] Kennedy wanted to know if the U.S. Supreme Court had ever upheld a state law like Colorado's Amendment 2.

In the five cases dealing with gay plaintiffs facing antigay discrimination that had come before Kennedy in his prior career as a judge in the Ninth (Federal) Circuit Court of Appeals, he had ruled against the plaintiffs every time. His views of gay people and gay rights had clearly evolved by 1995. In the private conference of Supreme Court justices to discuss *Romer v. Evans*, six justices voted to uphold the Colorado Supreme Court's decision striking down Amendment 2. Stevens, the most senior of the six, gave Kennedy the privilege of writing the majority decision.

Kennedy's decision in *Romer v. Evans* (1996: 623–635) put the U.S. Supreme Court behind the idea that gay people were equal to other citizens for the first time:

> One century ago, the first Justice Harlan admonished this Court that the Constitution "neither knows nor tolerates classes among citizens." Unheeded then, those words now are understood to state a commitment to the law's neutrality where the rights of persons are at stake. The Equal Protection Clause enforces this principle and today requires us to hold invalid a provision of Colorado's Constitution....
>
> It is not within our constitutional tradition to enact laws of this sort. Central both to the idea of the rule of law and to our own Constitution's guarantee of equal protection is the principle that government and each of its parts remain open on impartial terms to all who seek its

assistance. . . . Respect for this principle explains why laws singling out a certain class of citizens for disfavored legal status or general hardships are rare. A law declaring that in general it shall be more difficult for one group of citizens than for all others to seek aid from the government is itself a denial of equal protection of the laws in the most literal sense. . . .

We must conclude that Amendment 2 classifies homosexuals not to further a proper legislative end but to make them unequal to everyone else. This Colorado cannot do. A State cannot so deem a class of persons a stranger to its laws. Amendment 2 violates the Equal Protection Clause, and the judgment of the Supreme Court of Colorado is affirmed.[8]

By citing the first Justice Harlan's dissent in *Plessy v. Ferguson* (1896), Kennedy was making an analogy between gay rights and civil rights and comparing the defenders of Colorado's Amendment 2 to the defenders of racial segregation in the nineteenth-century U.S.[9] Gays and lesbians had been in many respects "strangers to the laws" of the United States for decades. Kennedy's decision framed gay people as deserving of equal rights, which was a breakthrough.

Romer v. Evans did not, however, settle the matter of gay rights in the U.S. Although Kennedy's decision in *Romer* did not mention, much less overrule *Bowers*, it did conflict with the *Bowers* decision. Conservative justice Antonin Scalia, in his dissent to *Romer*, argued that if states were allowed to criminalize gay sex, as *Bowers* ruled that states were allowed to do, then gays and lesbians were not the equals of everyone else, and states should not have to treat gays and lesbians as equals. The Colorado legislature had repealed its sodomy law in 1972. Nonetheless, in Scalia's view, Amendment 2 did less to infringe on gay rights than Georgia's sodomy law, upheld as constitutional in *Bowers*. The conflict between *Bowers* and *Romer* would take another Supreme Court decision, *Lawrence v. Texas* (2003), to resolve.

In his *Romer* dissent, Justice Scalia wrote:

In holding that homosexuality cannot be singled out for disfavorable treatment, the Court contradicts a decision, unchallenged here, pronounced only 10 years ago, see *Bowers v. Hardwick*. . . . This court has no business imposing upon all Americans the resolution favored by the elite class from which the Members of this institution are selected, pronouncing that "animosity" toward homosexuality is evil. I vigorously dissent.

In Justice Scalia's view, bias against homosexuals was perfectly reasonable and "animosity" toward homosexuals was not problematic:

> The Court's opinion contains grim, disapproving hints that Coloradans have been guilty of "animus" or "animosity" toward homosexuality, as though that has been established as un-American. Of course it is our moral heritage that one should not hate any human being or class of human beings. But I had thought that one could consider certain conduct reprehensible— murder, for example, or polygamy, or cruelty to animals—and could exhibit even "animus" toward such conduct.[10]

Justice Scalia compared homosexuals to murderers and polygamists and those who would be guilty of cruelty to animals. In his view, gay rights were a form of snobbery unfairly imposed on regular people by an "elite class." He found the *Bowers* decision to be decisive in all matters relating to gays and lesbians. In Scalia's full dissent in *Romer* (only a small portion of which is reprinted above), he cited *Bowers* eleven times.

The day after the *Romer v. Evans* decision was announced, and for the first time since Amendment 2 had passed in 1992, a poll in Colorado showed Amendment 2 opponents outnumbering supporters, 46 to 43%.[11] The influence of Kennedy's decision, his branding of Amendment 2 as biased and unfair, and the finality of Amendment 2's defeat made Amendment 2 suddenly less popular in Colorado than it had previously been. As Justice Kennedy wrote in another context, "[T]he law can be a teacher."[12]

The *Romer* decision, along with more positive depictions of gay people in the movies and the steady decriminalization of sodomy in the states (despite the setback that *Bowers v. Hardwick* represented), the urgency of the AIDS crisis, and the gay rights advocacy of Bill Clinton (despite the setbacks of the Defense of Marriage Act and Don't Ask, Don't Tell), all helped to open up the political opportunity structure for gays and lesbians to come out of the closet. The opening in the political opportunity structure made it easier for gays and lesbians to advocate politically and made it easier for heterosexual Americans to rethink their opposition to gay rights. The opening in the political opportunity structure (along with Justice Kennedy's sharp endorsement of the idea of gay equality in *Romer* on behalf of a Supreme Court majority) made it easier for judges to give new social science studies of gay people the hearing they deserved. As we will see in the 1990s battle over marriage equality in Hawaii, the liberalization of attitudes toward gay rights still had a long way to travel before it would lead to policy victories for marriage equality.

A First Marriage Equality Victory in the Courts: Hawaii

As a five-year-old in Hawaii in 1965, Genora Dancel did not always enjoy school. One day, after her siblings dropped her off at school, she decided not to go in. She sat across the street and watched her schoolmates play in the yard. When school was dismissed, she walked home. The next day she went to school, and the teacher asked her for a note explaining her absence on the previous day. Dancel said there was no note. The teacher sent Dancel to the principal's office. The principal asked Dancel for a note, but Dancel did not have one. The principal pulled down his paddle from the wall and told Dancel she was going to be paddled for misbehavior to teach her a lesson.

Dancel told the principal, "If you hit me, my father will be here tomorrow, and he will hit you right back." There followed several moments of silence. The principal put the paddle away and officially excused her absence for the previous day. Dancel's classmates expected her to be crying when she returned from the principal's office, because every other student had always returned in tears. To their surprise, she reappeared with a confident smile on her face.[13] Self-confidence and persistence are necessary qualities in people who are trying to change the world around them.

In the summer of 1990, Dancel was traveling for work and missing her girlfriend, Ninia Baehr. The two women had been a couple for only a few short months. Baehr was the first serious girlfriend that thirty-year-old Dancel had ever had, the first she had ever considered settling down with. Dancel stopped in a jewelry store and purchased a ring. That night she called Baehr and ask for her hand in marriage, and Baehr said yes without hesitation. When Dancel returned from her business trip, she gave Baehr the ring, and the two set about to find out if they could actually get married in Hawaii or anywhere else. The answer appeared to be no.

In the fall of 1990, Dancel was out to a few friends, and she was out to her parents. She was not out to most of her neighbors or most of her coworkers. There was no protection at her place of work against discrimination based on sexual orientation. Like most gay men and lesbians of her day, she was at least partly in the closet. Baehr was one of the few lesbians Dancel had ever met who was entirely out to everybody she knew. Baehr had been in touch with the local Gay and Lesbian Community Center, whose director, Bill Woods, was trying to get a few gay couples together to try to marry in Hawaii and, if rejected, to sue the state.

Dancel and Baehr were in Woods's office the next day. Dancel remembers, "I had to do what I had to do. I didn't want to be a second class citizen anymore." On December 17, 1990, she and Baehr went to the Honolulu Department of Health to apply for a marriage license. They were denied. Woods had called the media earlier, and several TV reporters were there. One of Dancel's jobs was working as a technician in a Hawaii TV station, so even though she was wearing dark glasses, the reporters recognized her. That day she was transformed from a partly closeted lesbian who lived a quiet, private life into a publicly out lesbian who was one of the faces of a new and controversial social movement for marriage equality.

Dancel's father was excited but concerned for her safety when he saw his daughter's picture in the newspaper. He suspected that his coworkers at the military base were not going to appreciate the news that his daughter was an activist for gay rights. Her mother told her husband to buy several copies of the paper and distribute the story to family and friends because their daughter was going to be famous.

The next day, Dancel went to work with trepidation. Her boss, who happened to also be Baehr's mother, met her at the door of the office, then walked her through the office and stopped at every person's desk to reintroduce Dancel to them. She told each person that if they had anything to say to Dancel, they should say it right now. No one voiced any complaints. At Dancel's other workplace, her coworkers came up to her, one by one, and told her that they respected what she was doing. She discovered that "it was wonderful to be out."

It is not easy to find a good lawyer who is willing to take clients of modest means for a potentially long and uphill battle against the state, where the chance of success is small. Civil rights attorneys and organizations spend much of their effort dissuading people from suing. If plaintiffs take a case to court too early or take a case to an unfavorable venue and lose, that stacks the deck even higher against future plaintiffs. Neither Lambda Legal nor the American Civil Liberties Union initially wanted to take Baehr and Dancel's case against the state of Hawaii. A local Hawaii attorney, Dan Foley, agreed to represent them. Marriage equality pioneer Evan Wolfson was working at Lambda Legal in New York at the time, and he wanted to participate in the Hawaii cases, but the directors of Lambda Legal initially would not allow him to do so.[14]

The main critique in liberal legal circles in the 1990s was that the public was not ready for gay marriage, that the courts and the political system would be fundamentally unreceptive, and that losing the marriage equality fight would leave gays and lesbians worse off than they had been before.[15] Lambda Legal's Paula Ettelbrick had a second, more ideological critique of marriage equality. In her view, *winning* marriage equality would make gay people worse off by further marginalizing the queer people who did not want to marry.[16]

In 1991 Foley filed Baehr and Dancel's marriage equality complaint[17] in Hawaii Circuit Court. The complaint included two other couples as plaintiffs: Patrick Lagon and Joseph Melillo, and Tammy Rodrigues and Antoinette Pregil. Hawaii Circuit Court judge Robert Klein ruled against the plaintiffs, as judges in other jurisdictions had done before. Foley appealed.

The marriage plaintiffs in Hawaii and elsewhere were in a more advantageous situation than most gays and lesbians who had been in court, for one simple reason: the marriage plaintiffs initiated court proceedings on their own terms, without having been dragged into the legal system by the police. Most gays and lesbians who came before courts in the past had already had their reputations tarnished in the eyes of the courts by arrests for "indecent behavior" or "solicitation" or some other trumped-up charge.

In 1993, the Hawaii Supreme Court heard Baehr and Dancel's appeal. For the first time in U.S. legal jurisdiction, a court took gay marriage plaintiffs seriously. In oral arguments, the state of Hawaii's representatives admitted that denial of marriage licenses to same-sex couples was, in fact, discriminatory. But the state claimed it had reasons to justify the differential treatment of same-sex couples. States regularly classify among and treat differently a variety of classes of people: children are treated differently from adults; convicted criminals are treated differently from law-abiding citizens; citizens are treated differently from noncitizens. The state may treat people differently as long as it has defensible reasons for doing so.

The Hawaii Supreme Court remanded the case, i.e., returned the case to the lower court with instructions for a trial. In the trial the state would have to demonstrate that its reasons for treating same-sex couples differently by not allowing them to marry met a strict scrutiny test under Hawaii law.[18] Did the state have a compelling interest in denying marriage licenses to same-sex couples? No state or jurisdiction in the U.S. had had to justify its denial of marriage licenses to same-sex couples in a trial before.

Conservatives in the U.S. Congress realized that if Hawaii legalized the marriage of same-sex couples, which suddenly seemed possible, then any gay couple in the U.S. could marry in Hawaii and be considered legally married everywhere else in the U.S. because states generally recognize marriages from other states.[19] The historic U.S. Supreme Court decision in *Romer* from May 1996 seemed to make a pro-gay-rights decision in Hawaii suddenly more likely.

Representative Bob Barr, Republican of Georgia, introduced the Defense of Marriage Act (DOMA), which passed overwhelmingly in the House of

Representatives and quickly passed in the Senate. DOMA was sitting on President Clinton's desk as the *Baehr v. Miike* trial commenced. DOMA contained two substantive provisions: Section 2 relieved states from recognizing same-sex marriages legally entered into in any other state or jurisdiction; Section 3 stipulated that the federal government would recognize only the marriages of one man to one woman. When I interviewed marriage equality pioneer Evan Wolfson in 2016, more than a year after DOMA had been overruled by the Supreme Court, he was still harboring some resentment that Clinton had signed DOMA. "He didn't have to sign it," Wolfson asserted, but sign it he did.[20]

Genora Dancel and Ninia Baehr, marriage plaintiffs from Hawaii, meeting with reporters in Washington, D.C., to rally opposition to the Defense of Marriage Act, which ultimately passed and was signed into law by President Bill Clinton. AP Photo by Dennis Cook, used with permission.

Social Science Weighs In

Evan Wolfson, one of the marriage equality movement's most important visionaries, foresaw in his prescient law school thesis in 1983 most of the changes that were to follow. Wolfson realized that same-sex couples in committed relationships could change minds and overturn antigay biases that had been dominant for so long. Wolfson (1983: 50) wrote, "If gay lovers, for instance, cannot marry, not only their individual goals and their relationships suffer, but society also loses the chance to see their arrangements and choices as diverse, capable of happiness, and entitled to respect." In 1983, he had difficulty getting any faculty members at Harvard Law School to read his thesis on same-sex marriage because the idea seemed so farfetched at the time.

By 1996, Wolfson was working informally with the Hawaii same-sex marriage plaintiffs' legal team. Preparing for the trial in Hawaii, he called the American Sociological Association (ASA) in Washington, D.C., looking for expertise on the sociology of the family. The ASA had a new committee on the status of LGBT people, headed by Larry Wu, a newly tenured sociology professor at the University of Wisconsin. Wu was also a gay man, out to his colleagues. Hawaii was arguing that recent sociological work by Sara McLanahan and Gary Sandefur (1994) and work by sociologists Andrew Cherlin and Frank Furstenberg on the challenges faced by children raised by single parents would also apply to children raised by same-sex couples because both types of families lacked the presence of parents of both genders and lacked male and female biological parents together. Wu thought Hawaii was misusing the existing research on single-parent families, so he contacted McLanahan, Sandefur, Cherlin, and Furstenberg. All four were unhappy with Hawaii's use of their work, and all four agreed to sign on to an amicus brief with Wu. Wu, McLanahan, Sandefur, Cherlin, and Furstenberg were five of the most prominent American sociologists who studied the family.

Wu made his reputation in sociology and demography by studying unintended fertility. One night, lying beside his boyfriend, he had the insight that same-sex couples cannot have unintended children. All the children of same-sex couples are intended (through adoption, in-vitro fertilization, sperm donation, or custody of children from previous relationships). Intentionality, Wu reasoned, might make same-sex couples better parents. In the amicus brief Wu organized and had submitted to the court, Cherlin et al. (1996) noted that neither the vast literature on heterosexual marriage and divorce nor the then-small literature on same-sex couples and their families provided any reasonable rationale for the state to prevent same-sex couples from marrying.[21] Furthermore, allowing same-sex couples to marry would provide them and their children with important benefits. Over the subsequent years, and with a steadily growing research literature on same-sex couples and their children, a social science consensus on same-sex marriage emerged that was entirely consistent with the short 1996 Hawaii friend-of-the-court brief by Wu, McLanahan, Sandefur, Cherlin, and Furstenberg.

Wolfson asked clinical psychologist David Brodzinsky to come to Hawaii and be a witness in the trial. Brodzinsky had courtroom experience through his work testifying in child custody disputes, which gave him practical trial experience that most social scientists lack. Through his work studying adoption, he had come into contact, both in his clinical practice and in his research, with nontraditional families and had come to understand that the structure of a family was one of many ways that a family might affect children's outcomes. Brodzinsky had seen well-adjusted and neglected children in every kind of family. Hawaii was arguing that only heterosexual married couples could be optimal as parents. Brodzinsky had reason to doubt Hawaii's argument. Wolfson asked Brodzinsky if he was familiar with the research literature on gay and lesbian parents; Brodzinsky promised to educate himself on the subject. After his testimony in *Baehr v. Miike*, Brodzinsky would go on to testify in a series of Florida same-sex couple adoption cases, and then almost two decades later he would testify again in the marriage equality trial *DeBoer v. Snyder* (2014).

Another key witness for the plaintiffs in the Hawaii trial was sociologist Pepper Schwartz.[22] In the 1970s, as an assistant professor at the University of Washington, Schwartz had started a massive interview project that became the landmark book *American Couples* (Blumstein and Schwartz 1983). The project involved twelve thousand questionnaires and three hundred interviews of both straight and gay couples, and was funded by the U.S. National Science Foundation. The surveys and the interviews were collected separately from both partners in each couple, and same-sex couples were oversampled so that the study would have enough to compare to the heterosexual couples.

One of the groundbreaking aspects of *American Couples* was the way it showed that gay couples, lesbian couples, and heterosexual couples (married and unmarried) all had similar sets of goals, similar ranges of interests in commitment, and similar challenges around money, sex, and responsibility. The best-selling book did not say that gay couples and straight couples were exactly alike. The authors found that gay male couples had more consensual nonmonogamy, and lesbian couples had less sex than other couples, for instance.[23] But the core finding of *American Couples* was the similarity of gay couples and heterosexual couples. Blumstein and Schwartz had found that gay couples shared aspirations of commitment and relationship longevity with heterosexual married couples. Whereas Kinsey's famous reports had been about the life course experience and physiology of human sexuality, Blumstein and Schwartz were interested in relationships, with sex as a domain of relationships rather than sex as a subject unto itself.

One of the findings of *American Couples* was that heterosexual cohabiting couples had less stable commitment and lower levels of mutual trust than Blumstein and Schwartz expected them to have. The institution of heterosexual cohabitation was underdeveloped, or in the language of sociologists, underinstitutionalized. Marriage is an institutionalized family form because people come into marriage with a set of expectations about what their own role within marriage should be. Cohabitation is underinstitutionalized because people enter into cohabiting relationships without necessarily knowing what expectations to have or what their role within the relationship is supposed to be. The heterosexual couples who were practicing cohabitation were sometimes at a loss about how to move forward.[24] Because they found that the stability of marriage's long-term commitment gave couples important emotional benefits, Blumstein and Schwartz tentatively endorsed marriage equality for same-sex couples, which was a politically forward position to take in 1983.[25] Schwartz learned from the *American Couples* project that cohabitation might not be the perfect substitute for marriage that her feminist leanings had led her to suspect it should be. As a result of her own research, she decided to marry her long-term romantic partner.

Schwartz's research collaborator Philip Blumstein died of AIDS in 1991. By 1996, Schwartz had testified in several cases relating to gay rights. When Wolfson called her, she knew she had to go to Hawaii to testify in the *Baehr* same-sex marriage trial. Schwartz had started the *American Couples* project twenty years earlier. In 1996 she thought that the possibility of marriage equality in the U.S. was still quite remote, but she thought the cause of marriage equality was worth fighting for. Schwartz had a rare talent for not only doing important social science but also for being able to explain social science to the public. Being an effective communicator is a vital skill for an expert witness.

The Trial

Despite headwinds from DOMA potentially limiting its impact on marriage equality nationwide, the trial of *Baehr v. Miike* (1996) in Hawaii Circuit Court before Judge Kevin Chang was historic.[26] The trial was covered live by Court TV, a cable television network available in millions of American homes. The defendant, Hawaii, had the burden of showing that there was a compelling state interest in denying marriage licenses to same-sex couples. Hawaii called witnesses, several of whom (Kyle Pruett and David Eggebeen) admitted that same-sex couples could and did raise children effectively and that marriage rights would potentially benefit same-sex couples and their children. Another defense witness, Dr. Richard Williams, expressed the view that research relied on by the plaintiffs' witnesses was fundamentally flawed, but Judge Chang found Williams to be "not persuasive or believable because of his expressed bias against the social sciences" and because "Dr. Williams believes that there is no scientific proof that evolution occurred." Expert witnesses who deny evolution and who claim not to believe in social science at all are not likely to carry much weight in court as credible social scientists themselves.

In stark contrast to the low credibility the judge assigned to the arguments and the witnesses for the defense, Chang evaluated witnesses for the plaintiffs, including Brodzinsky and Schwartz, as highly credible. In his decision, Judge Chang ruled, "The sexual orientation of parents is not in and of itself an indicator of parental fitness." Also, "Defendant [the state of Hawaii] has failed to establish a causal link between allowing same-sex marriage and adverse effects on the optimal development of children." Furthermore:

> In Hawaii, and elsewhere, people marry for a variety of reasons including, but not limited to the following: (1) having or raising children; (2) stability and commitment; (3) emotional closeness; (4) intimacy and monogamy; (5) the establishment of a framework for a long-term relationship; (6) personal significance; (7) recognition by society; and (8) certain legal and economic protections, benefits, and obligations....
>
> In Hawaii, and elsewhere, gay men and lesbian women share this same mix of reasons for wanting to be able to marry.[27]

In the trial of *Baehr v. Miike*, the plaintiffs (i.e., same-sex couples seeking to marry) prevailed. In the battle of experts, the plaintiffs' experts prevailed.

The *Baehr* trial established a fundamental legal and scientific precedent that marriage equality was supported by the empirical social science that was available at the time. Judge Chang's decision reflected an understanding that gay people could form romantic unions and commit to relationships the same way that heterosexual couples did, following the fundamental finding of Blumstein and Schwartz's *American Couples*. Judge Chang ordered the state of Hawaii to marry same-sex couples; however, his decision was stayed (held from going into effect)[28] pending an appeal by the state. Plaintiff Antoinette Pregil recalls thinking that Chang's decision meant that she had won.[29] Events proved her optimism to be premature.

The Referendum

In 1997, the Hawaii legislature put a referendum on the ballot for 1998 to enable the Hawaii legislature to block marriage equality.[30] After winning a historic victory in court, the plaintiffs had to go on the road and try to win again, this time in the broad court of public opinion. Even in liberal, multiracial, and mostly secular Hawaii, 1998 was too early to convince a majority to support marriage equality. Antoinette Pregil remembers traveling with her partner, Tammy Rodrigues, to a church to do outreach and finding that the church was an antigay bastion. "Those church folks were really mean. It was kind of scary to be famous," Pregil recalls, "because you had no idea whether anyone you met was for you or against you." Her own father disowned her during this time, but she had been estranged from her family of origin before. She had never done political work, but her partner, though shy in person, was a more experienced public speaker. Pregil remembers Rodrigues meeting public hostility with strength, and this made Pregil love her even more. "Tammy fought the whole world in order to marry me. Who does that? That is amazing."

By this time, Genora Dancel and Ninia Baehr had moved to Baltimore. In 1997 they broke up, but both remained active in the struggle for marriage equality. Hawaii's anti-marriage-equality "Save Traditional Marriage" campaign received heavy support from the Catholic Church, the Church of Latter Day Saints, a local affiliate of Focus on the Family, a coalition of business leaders, and the Hawaii Christian Coalition.[31] In November 1998 Hawaii voters passed a constitutional amendment allowing the state legislature to exclude same-sex couples from marriage in Hawaii by 69 to 31%. The voters of Hawaii had overturned the *Baehr v. Miike* decision.

The Hawaii legislature would reverse itself in 2013, when the governor signed a marriage equality bill. Marriage equality thus came to Hawaii seventeen years after the *Baehr v. Miike* trial and twenty-three years after Baehr, Dancel, Rodrigues, and Pregil had walked into the Honolulu Department of Health requesting marriage licenses. In 2013, Baehr and Dancel were with different partners; Rodrigues and Pregil were still together.

Lessons of *Romer* and *Baehr*

When gay people appeared in court in the U.S. before the 1990s, the courts had not been required to take them seriously. Many people, especially gay men, were simply processed in local courts for offenses like solicitation that derived from the illegality of gay sex. If gay sex was illegal, as it still was in many states, gay people's claims to equal citizenship were not likely to receive a fair hearing. Gay plaintiffs in civil cases often fared just as poorly. One justice in the Minnesota Supreme Court actually stood up and turned his back on lawyers representing same-sex marriage plaintiffs Baker and McConnell in 1971.[32] Justice White's majority decision in *Bowers v. Hardwick* in 1986 expressed a fundamental disdain for the idea that the law should treat gay people as the equals of straight people, as if the very idea of equality of gay and straight people was preposterous.

Because U.S. courts had never had to take gay defendants or gay plaintiffs seriously, it was not obvious how gay rights issues would be adjudicated if and when they ever *were* taken seriously. Kennedy's majority decision in *Romer v. Evans* showed for the first time from the nation's highest court in an affirmative way that gay people were entitled to be treated as the equals of straight people. If gay people had to be treated as equal citizens, then a variety of discriminatory policies and assumptions were on the chopping block. The constitutional assumptions behind a variety of antigay discriminatory policies were going to turn out to be grossly insufficient once they were examined closely.

Just as the flimsy constitutional bases for antigay discrimination had escaped scrutiny for decades, so too had the scientific and pseudo-scientific background for antigay policies escaped official scrutiny for decades. Social science had been making tremendous strides in understanding same-sex couples and their children in the 1970s, 1980s, and 1990s, but U.S. courts had rarely been forced to listen to the social science. Instead antigay policies were backed by sham science, prejudice, and faulty assumptions. The *Baehr v. Miike* trial in 1996 put the defenders of same-sex marriage bans on the witness stand and showed them to be either unconvincing or charlatans. The empirical social science foundation on which antigay policies had been made and justified turned out, on close examination, to be vacant. If you held it up to the light, you could see right through it.

The *Baehr* and *Romer* decisions had enormous implications, undermining the constitutional and empirical credibility of policies that discriminated against gays and lesbians. Still, most antigay policies remained in place for some time. Hawaii's ban on same-sex marriage remained in place for seventeen years after the *Baehr* trial. The credibility of the same-sex marriage ban, however, was already fatally compromised, like a house whose wooden beams had been shown to be rotten. It still looked like a house from the outside, but it was ready to fall over if pushed.

The Hawaii referendum taught marriage equality activists an important practical lesson. In order for marriage equality to prevail, winning in the courts was not enough. Marriage equality was not going to be achieved unless marriage equality could win in state legislatures. Marriage equality was not going to win in state legislatures or elsewhere without majority public support. Public support would insulate marriage equality gains against an inevitable short-term political backlash. From the perspective of the late 1990s, when public support for marriage equality in the U.S. was not even at 25%, it was daunting indeed to imagine how the marriage equality movement might win a majority of the public over to their cause.

The GSS first asked about marriage equality in 1988. Since so few Americans supported marriage equality at that time, the GSS did not field the marriage equality question again until 2004. Figure 6.1 shows the thirty-nine state referenda on marriage equality that took place in the U.S., from Alaska and Hawaii in 1998, which were decisive defeats for marriage equality, to the 2012 referenda in four states that were victories for marriage equality. The blue line indicates the national trend in support of marriage equality. The radically increasing support in popular opinion was the changing background context that turned a long series of referendum defeats into victories for marriage equality in 2012.

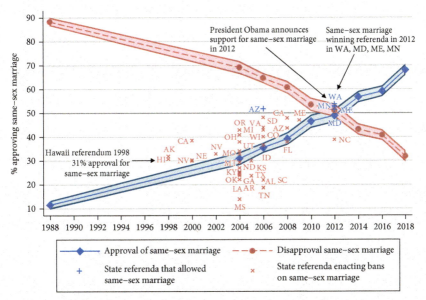

Figure 6.1 Approval and disapproval of same-sex marriage in U.S. public opinion, with state-level referenda results by percentage approving.

Source: Weighted national public opinion data from the General Social Survey (GSS) with 95% confidence intervals. State referenda results indicated next to each state's two letter abbreviation. Data on referenda results are from Ballotpedia (2019).

By the mid-1990s, approval of gay rights and approval of marriage equality in the U.S. had been growing rapidly, but this liberalization in attitudes had not yet made a policy difference. As long as marriage equality approval nationwide remained below 40%, even politically liberal states like Hawaii were going to have a difficult time sustaining any gains toward marriage equality.

7

Coming Out of the Closet and Its Influence, 1985–2013

Intergroup Contact Theory

Gordon Allport was one of the mid-twentieth-century's most prominent academic psychologists. Allport's (1954) book *The Nature of Prejudice* argued that racial integration could overcome individual racial bias. According to Allport, personal interaction between individuals from different groups should lead to a diminution of bias between the groups. American society in 1954 was mired in a long history of racial segregation. The U.S. Supreme Court was about to make the first bold step into racial integration with the landmark decision *Brown v. Board of Education* (1954), which intended to integrate America's public schools. The *Brown* decision was built in part on the social science of people like Allport (a subject I return to in chapter 18). The U.S. Supreme Court and social scientists were concerned about whether school integration would work. Would integration be a viable public policy, or would White backlash against Blacks and against the Supreme Court make an already difficult situation worse?

Allport's book made clear that intergroup contact was not a panacea for eliminating bias. The ability of intergroup contact to erode bias depended, in Allport's view, very strongly on the circumstances. Allport noted that in studies of racially integrated housing, and racially integrated barracks in the army where Whites and Blacks presumably had equal status, Whites and Blacks tended to see each other as equals. On the other hand, where Whites had contact only with Blacks who were servants or people who held lower status than themselves, such contact would reinforce White biases against Blacks. Intergroup contact could diminish or heighten bias, depending on the circumstances.

A difficult question for Allport and for intergroup contact theory was the question of cause and effect. If Whites in integrated housing were observed to have less bias toward Blacks, was that a sign that integration had caused

The Rainbow after the Storm. Michael J. Rosenfeld, Oxford University Press. © Oxford University Press 2022.
DOI: 10.1093/oso/9780197600436.003.0007

bias to decline, or was it an indication that in the 1940s only White people who were already unusually open-minded about race would move into integrated housing in the first place? In 1954 Allport lacked the kind of data that might have helped him unpack the cause and effect between integration and lower levels of individual bias. In the decades after his seminal work, new research on intergroup contact theory has shown that intergroup contact is not only associated with but can actually cause a diminution of bias within individuals.[1]

Although intergroup contact theory was introduced in the U.S. with racial bias and racial integration in mind, ironically racial bias turns out to be especially resistant to intergroup contact for a simple reason: an individual's race is usually identifiable by sight. Before one gets close enough to have a conversation with someone from another race, their racial identity has already triggered whatever preexisting biases one has because race is conspicuous. Once one's biases are triggered, everything the other person says is filtered through the potentially prejudicial biases one already possesses. The vast majority of Americans hold unconscious biases that prime them to view racial minorities more negatively.[2] Intergroup contact is less effective at dispelling prejudice between racial minorities because people enter into interactions with identifiable others by viewing the others through a potentially prejudiced frame.[3]

Contact with sexual minority individuals is more effective at dispelling prejudice than is contact with other kinds of minorities[4] because sexual minorities are generally decategorized (i.e., unidentifiable as minorities) at first contact. Sexual identity is concealable, which is why it is possible for gay people to be in the closet in the first place. First conversations between straight and gay Americans generally take place without being filtered through either party's implicit biases. Additionally, gay and lesbian people usually come from heterosexual families of origin, which gives them the opportunity to come out to their heterosexual parents, who should already love them. It is much less common for Black youth to have White parents.

Personal experience is more persuasive than any kind of secondhand information.[5] For example, when Americans think about industrial policy, they think about their own workplace rather than workplaces in general. The economy is abstract, but your place of work is a concrete reality that you interact with almost every day. As social movement theorist William Gamson (1992) noted, even on an issue as abstract as nuclear power, which most Americans have no personal connection to and little knowledge about, people personalize abstract questions and use their own experience to try to answer them. Is nuclear power safe? Americans think about maintenance problems or safety issues at their own workplaces to answer this question. Is the maintenance on my factory's boiler always up to date? If not, then the nuclear power plant is probably not safe either. Personal experience is the touchstone people use to understand the complicated world around them.[6]

Intergroup contact theory does not imply that interactions with others are necessarily positive. Knowing someone who turns out to be gay or lesbian is not an instant recipe for holding all gays and lesbians in high regard.[7] Personal contact with a gay or lesbian friend, coworker, or family member does, however, bring one's prior beliefs about gays and lesbians into useful contrast with one's personally experienced reality. If the only thing you have ever heard about gays and lesbians is that they are abnormal and dangerous, and your personal experience tells you otherwise, the previous belief will start to lose credibility because it does not square with your experience.[8]

Newsweek Data

The next few sections examine nationally representative survey data from *Newsweek* which included questions about whether respondents had gay or lesbian friends, gay or lesbian coworkers, or gay or lesbian family members.[9] The *Newsweek* data allow for an analysis of the timing of when gays and lesbians came out of the closet in the U.S. The data also allow for an examination of the potential effect of gays and lesbians coming out of the closet on American attitudes about same-sex marriage. Questions about whether Americans had gay or lesbian friends, coworkers, or family members were either not included or else not asked early enough in the other surveys that American researchers most often use.[10] The closet is understudied among scholars who do quantitative analyses of public opinion and gay rights in the U.S. because the attitude surveys that American scholars use most failed to include the relevant questions early enough.[11]

Exodus from the Closet in the 1990s

Figure 7.1 documents the sharp rise in the percentage of Americans who reported having a gay or lesbian friend or acquaintance from 1985 to 2008. In

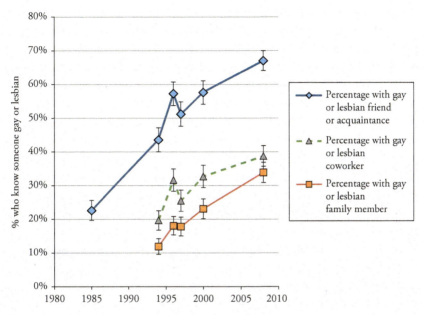

Figure 7.1 Percentage of Americans who know someone who is gay or lesbian.
Source: Rosenfeld (2017), using weighted *Newsweek* data 1985–2008, with 95% confidence intervals.

1985, 22.6% of American adults said they had a gay or lesbian friend or acquaintance. In 2008, that number rose to 67.0%. The percentage of American
adults who reported having a gay or lesbian coworker or family member rose
with a similar slope after 1994. (*Newsweek* did not ask about coworkers or
family members until 1994.)[12]

The dramatic rise in 1985–2008 in the percentage of Americans who
knew someone who was gay or lesbian is due to gays and lesbians coming
out to their friends, coworkers, and families during the 1990s. The timing
of this mass coming-out is crucial, as it helps to explain the sharp liberalization in American attitudes toward gay rights that occurred at the same
time. In Steven Seidman's (2002) life course interviews with gay and lesbian
Americans, he found that regardless of when people were born and how they
grew up, most were coming out of their closets in the 1990s.

There had in the past been a small number of gay activists who were out to
everyone they knew. Frank Kameny was out of the closet in the 1950s. There
were gay rights activists in the 1970s who were out and proud. Harvey Milk
was a rare out-of-the-closet gay politician in the 1970s. But swaying public
opinion took more than the leaders and the activists to come out; it took a

mass exodus from the closet by gays, lesbians, and queer people in all corners of American society. The data show that the mass exodus from the closet did not occur until the 1990s.

Figure 7.2 shows the association between knowing someone who was gay or lesbian and support for same-sex marriage.[13] Looking at the left side of each pair of columns in Figure 7.2, we see that support for marriage equality was 23 percentage points higher for Americans who had a gay or lesbian friend, compared to Americans who did not. Support for marriage equality was 14 percentage points higher for Americans who had a gay or lesbian coworker (compared to not having a gay or lesbian coworker), and support for marriage equality was 17 percentage points higher for Americans with gay or lesbian family members (compared to Americans with no known gay or lesbian family members).

Without controlling for other factors, the three associations between knowing someone gay or lesbian and support for marriage equality were all highly significant, which one can see in Figure 7.2 by the way the whiskers

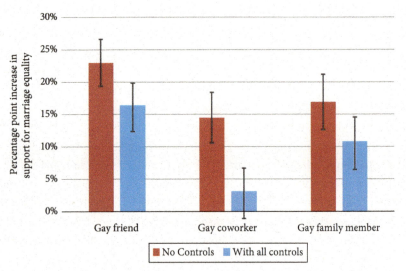

Figure 7.2 The effect of knowing someone gay or lesbian on the probability of supporting marriage equality.

Source: Newsweek Princeton Research Polls from 1994, 1996, 2000, and 2008, weighted. Results are from Ordinary Least Squares linear regressions. Weighted and unweighted logistic regressions yield a similar substantive result, see Rosenfeld (2017). Question wording: "Do you think there should or should NOT be legally sanctioned gay marriages?" and "Do you have a friend or acquaintance who is gay or lesbian." Full set of controls include all 3 types of gay friends/coworkers/family members, plus birth generation, age, region of the U.S., political party affiliation, education, race, and gender.

of the columns, representing the confidence intervals of each measurement, do not come close to 0% in five of the six columns.[14] This means that we are as *certain* as we can be that there was a real association (not only in the *Newsweek* data but also in the U.S. as a whole) between having gay friends (and having gay coworkers and having gay family members) and supporting same-sex marriage.

The red columns on the left of each pair show only that there was a strong correlation between knowing someone who was gay or lesbian and supporting marriage equality. This correlation could have been spurious or misleading if, for instance, the people who had gay or lesbian friends were only the people who already supported marriage equality and gay rights. If gay and lesbian people came out only to those who were already supporters of gay rights, then coming out would not have moved anyone new to support marriage equality.

To begin to understand if having gay friends (or gay coworkers or gay family members) was actually causing people to become more supportive of same-sex marriage than they otherwise would have been, I used regression analysis to control for other predictors of support for marriage equality, and then determined if the coefficients for having gay friends, coworkers, or family members remained positive and statistically significant. The blue columns on the right side of each pair of columns represent the additional support for marriage equality from knowing someone gay or lesbian *after* accounting for all the other factors in the *Newsweek* data that were known to be associated with support for marriage equality.

The shaded columns representing values "with all controls" would be zero if Americans who had gay friends (or gay family members) and who supported marriage equality were only the coastal liberals who would have been expected to support marriage equality in the first place. The fact that the measures with controls were significantly greater than zero means that knowing gay people was predictive of support for marriage equality for a broad population of Americans beyond those who might have been expected to support gay rights in the first place.

The models with all controls account for factors known to predict support for gay rights that were included in the *Newsweek* surveys. The predictors of support for marriage equality in the *Newsweek* data were entirely consistent with predictors of support for marriage equality from other data sets. Millennials and people from Generation X were 36 percentage points more likely to support marriage equality than Americans born in 1945 or before.

Republicans were least supportive of marriage equality; residents of the U.S. Northeast were sharply more supportive of marriage equality than were residents of the South; women were more supportive of marriage equality than were men; and so on. Previous research shows that tolerance of gay rights is associated with women, with having a college degree, with not being an evangelical Christian or a biblical literalist, with being urban, with living in the Northeast or the Pacific Coast of the U.S., with more recent birth generations, with being old enough to have moved away from home, with more recent survey years, with having fewer than five siblings, and with not being a Republican.[15]

Americans with a gay or lesbian friend were 16 percentage points more likely to be a supporter of marriage equality, *after* accounting for all the other things known to predict support for gay rights. If an individual were otherwise expected to have a 35% chance of supporting marriage equality, then adding a gay or lesbian friend would increase the predicted chance of supporting marriage equality to 35% + 16% = 51%.

To be an engine of social change, a predictor of marriage equality approval would have to change over time.[16] Knowing someone who is gay or lesbian *has* been an engine of social change because the proportion of Americans who know someone gay or lesbian has changed dramatically over time. Birth generation is the other important social change engine for marriage equality. Every year in the U.S., people from the GI Generation and the Silent Generation pass away from old age and are replaced by adults from more recent generations. This process is known to demographers as cohort replacement. Cohort replacement ensures that the percentage of American adults who are from the gay-tolerant post-1980 birth generations is steadily increasing.

GSS Longitudinal Data

The *Newsweek* data are limited because each survey subject was interviewed only once. It is easier to get a grasp on causal explanations for changes when the same subjects can be followed over time.[17] The GSS started in 2006 reinterviewing some of the same survey subjects every two years. The GSS also introduced in 2006 questions about whether subjects had gay acquaintances. Daniel DellaPosta (2018) studied the GSS data in order to see whether the people who said they had gay acquaintances in 2006 were more likely to become new supporters of marriage equality by 2010, and he found that they were.

Even though DellaPosta reported fewer than two hundred heterosexual survey subjects who answered the gay acquaintanceship question in the 2006 GSS and who also answered the marriage equality question in 2006 and in 2010, he found a significant effect of having gay acquaintances on becoming a supporter of marriage equality. Support for marriage equality rose from 45 to 61% over those four years for those who had gay acquaintances in 2006. Support for marriage equality went down during the same period among subjects who did not have a gay acquaintance in 2006.

Pew Data

The Pew Center for the People & the Press routinely does some of the most interesting and creative polling and produce some of the most thoughtful writing about public opinion trends in the U.S. In a March 2013 survey Pew asked respondents if they supported same-sex marriage and if they had changed their mind about same-sex marriage, and if so, why. When Pew asked subjects *why* they had changed their minds, they let respondents say whatever came to mind. Such open-ended questions are important because they do not limit respondents to a particular short set of answers the survey researchers have thought to suggest.[18] The Pew Research Center (2013) data provide a unique window into why people changed their minds about same-sex marriage, in their own words.

According to the Pew survey, and extrapolating from the nationally representative survey sample to the population of 242 million American adults, there were 223 million American adults with an opinion about same-sex marriage.[19] Of these, a narrow majority of 118 million supported same-sex marriage, of whom 33 million had changed their mind to support same-sex marriage.

The number-one reason given by subjects in the Pew survey for why they had become more supportive of same-sex marriage over time was knowing someone who was gay. Roughly a third of the subjects who became more supportive mentioned having a gay friend, relative, or coworker in their brief explanations. It is unusual for an open-ended question to have so many answers that coincide because open-ended questions allow respondents to say anything at all, and some respondents give nonsensical answers. The Pew data suggest that 10.5 million Americans became more supportive of same-sex marriage due to directly knowing someone who was gay or lesbian.

Among the different individual responses in the Pew survey, people offered the following explanations for how knowing someone gay or lesbian had led them to become more supportive of same-sex marriage. Some described how finding out that a coworker they really admired was gay or lesbian changed them:

> I'm retired military and several of the most dependable and absolutely wonderful people I've ever known were gay, as I found out later. And they were great and did their job. Very competent at what they did.

Some respondents had a family member come out to them:

> Because my daughter is gay.
>
> Have a family member who is homosexual and I understand more about it than I did when younger.
>
> My brother admitted to being gay. That's all.
>
> I changed my mind because I was being ignorant and stupid. And I have family members in my family that are [gay]. You got to learn to love them for who they are.
>
> My sister is a lesbian and I love my sister incredibly!
>
> I have seen the struggle in my own family.

Others respondents were influenced by their friends:

> Lived close to a gay community. Have friends that are gay. Helps me relate to what they are dealing with.
>
> Found out I had a friend in that situation.
>
> Good friend[s] who have children who are gay and want to get married.
>
> We have lots of married same-sex friends.
>
> Gay friends.
>
> Because of gay friends.
>
> "Known a great many gay people who are living together and are happy.
>
> My best friend from high school is a gay man and he deserves the same rights. They are in a committed relationship.

> Being around it a lot. My best friend's mom is gay and I have a gay friend.
>
> Gotten older, wiser, and met more people and have many gay friends.
>
> I come from a very conservative background, when I was growing up. Now that I'm older my best friend is gay and I would like to see her have the same rights as I do.

Some respondents gave the kind of answer that would have made Gordon Allport, the father of intergroup contact theory, proud. These individuals explained in brief general terms and in their own words how social change works:

> Being exposed to more individuals and realizing that they have the same rights as anybody else. Also, some of the recent rulings.
>
> Personal interaction with people.
>
> Knowing people [who are gay or lesbian]. . . . I disfavor it [same-sex marriage] in theory, but when I see it I can't be against it.

When people were asked why they came to change their mind and support same-sex marriage, one answer dominated all others: they knew someone who was gay or lesbian, and knowing that person changed their mind.[20] Gay rights activists and social theorists have long surmised that gay people coming out of the closet could liberalize American public opinion toward gay rights. Analysis of the *Newsweek* and Pew data demonstrates that gays and lesbians coming out of the closet was the driving force for one of the most dramatic social changes in American history.

"I became more tolerant" was the second most popular explanation in the Pew data for becoming more supportive of same-sex marriage over time. Presumably some of the unspecified individual increases in tolerance were due to unreported personal interactions with gays and lesbians. Other subjects may have been influenced by a realistic sense that society was becoming more tolerant of gay rights, without being able to identify the reasons why.

A small number of Pew survey subjects (corresponding to well under a million adult Americans) who became more favorable about same-sex marriage over time mentioned that gays and lesbians were "born that way" as the reason for changing their mind. Of those who offered this as their reason for becoming more supportive of marriage equality over time, two-fifths mentioned knowing someone who was gay or lesbian. Consider the respondent who said, "I work with people who are gay. I found out close friends are gay. I believe they are born that way. That's it." Even the answers that rest on the biological determinacy of homosexuality tend to rely on personal experience with specific gay friends.

A substantial number of Pew survey subjects mentioned knowing someone who was gay or lesbian as the reason they became more supportive of same-sex marriage compared to zero who mentioned being influenced by political or entertainment elites such as former president Bill Clinton or television star Ellen DeGeneres. The Pew data reveal the power of personal experience over indirect experience or theoretical knowledge of the world.[21] The elites undoubtedly have an influence on public opinion, but the influence is indirect. Elites who came out of the closet or who supported gay rights may have influenced closeted gays and lesbians to come out, who then influenced their friends and neighbors and family members to become more supportive of gay rights.

The Pew data show that Americans who changed their minds to become more supportive of same-sex marriage were mostly not affiliated with the Democratic Party: 12 million political independents liberalized on same-sex marriage, followed by 10.6 million Democrats, 7.2 million Republicans, and 3 million politically unaffiliated people. According to Pew, among the Americans who became more liberal toward same-sex marriage specifically because they knew someone who was gay, there were 4.5 million political independents, 3.5 million Democrats, and 1.8 million Republicans. Liberalization toward gay rights may have affected Democrats more often than Republicans, but people from both main U.S. political parties experienced liberalization. In addition, liberalization toward same-sex marriage was experienced by born-again Christians and evangelical Christians, as well as by liberal Christians, Jews, and nonbelievers. Conservatives, evangelical Christians, and Republicans liberalized at lower rates than atheists and Democrats, but there were individuals in every group who experienced liberalization toward same-sex marriage.[22]

DellaPosta (2018) found that having a gay acquaintance was even more influential (in leading to support of marriage equality) on the attitudes of Americans who were *not* likely to support gay rights than on the attitudes of Americans who were likely already to support gay rights.[23] Knowing a good person who is gay or lesbian is even more surprising and influential to someone who did not expect gay people to be good people. As one subject in the Pew study said, "I disfavor it [same-sex marriage] in theory, but when I see it I can't be against it."

Few Signs of Anti-Gay-Rights Backlash

In contrast to the dynamism of pro-same-sex-marriage opinions, opposition to same-sex marriage found relatively few new converts. Opposition began in the early days of the marriage equality movement by fielding a large base of support but had trouble winning new people. While 33 million Americans were changing their minds to support same-sex marriage, a much smaller number, approximately 4.6 million, were changing their minds in the opposite direction, to become more opposed to same-sex marriage, according to the Pew data.

Several reported becoming more opposed to same-sex marriage because of new religious experiences. One person objected to the media's coverage of gay rights: "Media has beaten everybody down about it [same-sex marriage]. Media has made it an over-discussed topic. I throw my hands up in the air, oppose it more than I did before."

Christian Right leaders have long believed and hoped that if gay rights gains occurred, those gains would lead to an angry backlash.[24] Conservative politicians in the U.S. have used White backlash against civil rights and back-lash against Black political leaders effectively to mobilize White voters for decades. The available data, however, show only a modest trickle of people being repelled by gay rights gains to become more personally opposed to gay rights. Americans' attitudes about gay rights have not yet shown substantial evidence of the kind of backlash that Christian Right leaders were hoping for, the kind of backlash that would turn previously undecided Americans against gay rights. A later chapter takes up the question of why gay rights inspire less new opposition than, for example, civil rights. For now, the Pew data offer a simple answer: "It does not affect me" and "As long as they don't bother me, they can do what they want." In other words, heterosexuals understood that same-sex marriage cost them nothing.

Coming out of the closet, a process that is unique to gays and lesbians, is the key to explaining how attitudes toward gays and lesbians changed so much, and so quickly. Person-to-person contact is especially effective at dispelling prejudice against people from sexual minorities. In the 1990s there was a sharp rise in the percentage of Americans who reported knowing someone who was gay or lesbian. Having a gay or lesbian friend, family member, or co-worker appears to have been a powerful factor in moving Americans toward more acceptance of gay rights.

8

Public Opinion Change and the Uniqueness of Gay Rights

In this chapter I describe survey data evidence about how attitudes toward gay rights have changed more and more rapidly than any other kind of attitude in the history of American public opinion. Most American public opinions are stable over time, owing to several factors. The transition to adulthood tends to crystalize attitudes within the individual, meaning that on most core issues individuals have consistent attitudes over their adult lives.[1] The tendency for attitudes to be stable over time helps to explain why so few people accurately predicted the speed with which Americans would come to accept marriage equality. Within the general stability of American attitudes, the pace of liberalizing attitudes toward same-sex marriage stands out as a stunning outlier.

In 1988, only 11.6% of Americans thought same-sex couples should have the legal right to marry. In 2018, the approval rate was 68.1%, an increase of more than 56 percentage points.[2] In contrast, attitudes toward abortion rights reflect the more typical pattern of stability over time. In 1972, 48.9% of Americans thought a poor woman should have access to legal abortion if she could not afford more children, compared to 48.7% who thought abortion should be legal under the same circumstances in 2018. It is only by examining the data across all recorded attitudes in the U.S. that one can see how unusual the liberalization in attitudes toward marriage equality has been.

The Data

In this chapter I analyze data from the GSS 1972–2018 cumulative file.[3] The GSS data are the cornerstone of most social science studies of attitudes in the U.S., though most of those studies examine just a few attitudes at a time. In order to see the big picture, we need to examine and plot *all* of the GSS attitude variables. The GSS cumulative file has 504 different attitude variables

The Rainbow after the Storm. Michael J. Rosenfeld, Oxford University Press. © Oxford University Press 2022.
DOI: 10.1093/oso/9780197600436.003.0008

that were asked at least three times over a span of at least ten years. Each attitude variable represents the average of the answers of thousands of different people. The text for the GSS same-sex marriage question[4] (available in 1988–2018) reads, "Do you agree or disagree: Homosexual Couples should have the right to marry one another." Valid responses were 1 (strongly agree), 2 (agree), 3 (neither agree nor disagree), 4 (disagree), and 5 (strongly disagree).[5]

Table 8.1 shows that the average attitude measured in the GSS changed 8.55 percentage points in approval from first measurement to last. The mean slope for GSS variables was 0.34 percentage points change per year. The average rate of change of 0.34 percentage points per year across all attitudes is a remarkably slow rate of change. This means that if you wanted to see even a 3-percentage-point change in approval on a typical attitude (in either direction) you would have to wait almost nine years. Public opinion is like a giant ocean liner: to move it even a little takes a great effort. The slow rate of change can sometimes mislead people into thinking that social change is impossible.

Among the different categories of attitudes (gay rights, race, religion, government, abortion, and other), the six gay rights attitudes (two similar

Table 8.1 Summary Data on Extent of Change and Rate of Change in GSS Public Opinion Variables

		Extent of Change	Rate of Change
GSS attitude variables categories	Number of attitude variables averaged in each category	Absolute value percentage point change (end point to end point difference)	Absolute value percentage point change per year
Gay rights	6	39.64	1.07
Race	41	13.75	0.51
Religion	29	9.14	0.36
Government	77	8.42	0.32
Abortion	10	5.39	0.28
Other	341	7.45	0.31
All attitudes mean	504	8.55	0.34
Comparison: attitudes about same-sex marriage		56.44	1.88

Source: Weighted GSS data for attitudes on 504 separate issues, 1972–2018.
Extent of Change uses dichotomous versions of the variables and examines only the first and last year each question was asked, as in the Y Axis of Figure 8.2. Rate of Change uses dichotomous versions of the variables, fitting the best fit line to data from all years using Ordinary Least Squares regressions.

questions about gay sex, one question about marriage equality, and questions about the rights of gay people to teach, to speak in public, and to have their books placed in the library) had the largest average extent of public opinion change, and the fastest rate of change. Ninety-five percent of the 504 GSS attitudes had slopes that corresponded to less change than 0.97 percentage points per year. The six gay rights questions in the GSS changed by an average of 1.07 percentage points per year, meaning the *average* gay rights attitude changed faster than 95% of all attitudes. Approval of same-sex marriage changed by 1.88 percentage points per year, the fastest rate of change of any measured attitude in the history of the GSS. The approval of same-sex marriage, which increased by more than 56 percentage points, was also the single largest extent of change recorded across the 504 attitude variables in the GSS data, measured over more than forty-five years.

Figure 8.1 shows a box plot of GSS attitude variables by attitude category and by extent of change. Note how the six gay rights variables dominate with much greater extent of change than any of the other variable categories.

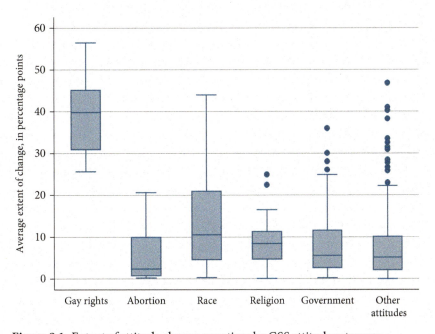

Figure 8.1 Extent of attitude change over time by GSS attitude category.
Source: Weighted GSS data for attitudes on 504 issues divided into 6 categories, 1972–2018. Box plot of extent of change based on dichotomous versions of the variables, fitting the best fit line to data from all years using Ordinary Least Squares regressions (OLS). In the box plot the top of the box is the 75th percentile of each group, the bottom of the box is the 25th percentile, and the line in the middle of the box is the 50th percentile, also known as the median. The dots above the boxes are opinion variables that were distant outliers in extent of change.

Figure 8.2 shows a scatterplot of all 504 GSS attitude variables, indexed by extent of change on the Y axis, and indexed by rate of change on the X axis. The attitudes that changed the fastest and changed the most are found in the upper-right corner. Each of the 504 data points represents the change over time in approval for one GSS question asked over at least ten years to thousands of American adults.[6] Figure 8.2 shows that public opinion toward same-sex marriage is the single biggest outlier both in extent of change (Y axis) and in rate of change (X axis).[7]

The majority of GSS attitude variables are in the lower left corner of Figure 8.2, representing little extent of change and weak rate of change over time.[8] Among the variables which changed most in extent of approval over time are several that document long-term decline in Americans' confidence in fundamental institutions: Congress and the executive branch of the federal

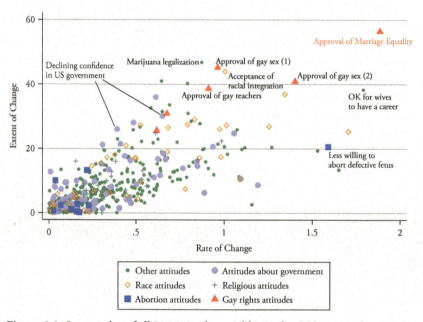

Figure 8.2 Scatter plot of all 504 attitude variables in the GSS to 2018 by extent of change and rate of change.

Source: Weighted data from GSS cumulative file 1972–2018. This figure includes all 504 GSS attitude variables that were asked at least 3 times, with first instance and last instance at least 10 years apart. For this figure, I converted all the GSS attitude variables to dichotomous variables, approve versus disapprove. The X axis is the linear rate of change per year, either approval or disapproval, of the dichotomous version of the variable across all years, from 504 separate OLS regressions. A rate of change of 1 means a change in approval or disapproval of 1 percentage point per year. The Y axis is percentage point change from first observation to last. The GSS asked two questions about approval of gay sex, both of which are among the outliers.

government.[9] Figure 8.2 shows that increased approval for marijuana legalization is an outlier but not as much of an outlier in rate of change as approval of same-sex marriage.[10]

Among the ten abortion attitude variables in Figure 8.2, only one, declining willingness of Americans to abort their own (or their partner's) defective fetus, changed substantially. Between 1990 and 2004, fewer Americans said they would have an abortion if they or their partner was carrying a fetus with a "serious genetic defect." The other abortion questions were about the abortion rights of others, and these hardly changed. The squares representing attitudes toward the abortion rights of others can be found in the crowded lower left corner, along with the multitude of other attitudes that changed little over time.[11]

Marriage Equality as a Vanguard Change That Led to Increased Approval of All Queer Rights

The right-hand panel of Figure 8.3 shows that support for same-sex marriage increased at the same time as support for other gay rights increased,

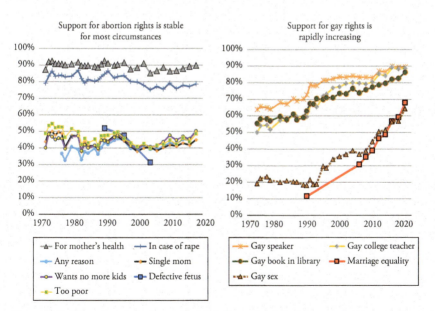

Figure 8.3 Abortion attitudes and gay rights attitudes, time trends compared.
Source: Weighted data from the GSS, see also Rosenfeld (2017).

including the right of gays and lesbians to be teachers, the right to speak publicly, the right of a gay author to have their book available in the library, and an increase in support for gay people to have consensual sex. Data from another source (described later) shows a dramatic increase in support for the right of gays to serve in the military, to adopt children, and to be free from workplace discrimination. Greater acceptance of same-sex marriage has gone hand in hand with greater acceptance of all types of queer rights. Among all the liberalizing changes in attitudes about gay rights, attitudes about marriage equality have changed the most.

Increasing tolerance for gay sex after 1990 made it easier for some of the states that retained their criminal bans on sodomy in the 1980s to overturn the bans, and thirteen states did so in the 1990s and early 2000s. As gay sex became more accepted, state criminalization of sodomy became harder to defend.

Greater tolerance of gay sex means greater tolerance for queer rights in general. Presumably this greater tolerance of gay sex would extend also to greater tolerance for bisexuals, for transgender people, for queer people who did not want to marry, and for other sexual minorities. At the same time as Americans were becoming more comfortable with gay rights, more comfortable with marriage equality, and more comfortable with the idea of gay sex, they were adopting a broader and more inclusive definition of what was meant by the core idea of "family."[12]

Within the gay rights community there has been fierce debate over whether marriage equality gains would improve the status or further marginalize the queer folk who are not inclined to marry or settle down. The argument for further marginalization, coming from the opponents of marriage equality within the gay rights movement and most forcefully expressed by Paula Ettelbrick, was that married gay people would assimilate into mainstream heterosexual society and leave the nonmarried queer people further outside the mainstream, as outlaws. Ettelbrick (1989: 16) wrote, "Ironically, gay marriage, instead of liberating gay sex and sexuality, would further outlaw all gay and lesbian sex which is not performed in a marital context. . . . Lesbians and gay men who do not seek the state's stamp of approval would clearly face increased sexual oppression."

On the other side of the argument, marriage equality advocates like Evan Wolfson (2004) claimed that marriage equality gains would make straight Americans see gay Americans as more like themselves, and that as a result all queer people would enjoy improved status. The broad increase in popular support for queer rights across all questions suggests that Wolfson and the marriage equality advocates were right. Note how in Figure 8.3, Americans became more comfortable with the idea of gay sex (regardless of marital status of the gay people) at the same time (starting around 1992) they were starting to embrace marriage equality.[13]

Not only did approval of marriage equality and approval of gay sex both liberalize at exactly the same time in national data, but approval of marriage equality and approval of gay sex were highly correlated within individuals. Across all waves of GSS data, among individuals who strongly approved of marriage equality, 88% said that gay sex (regardless of marital status) was not wrong at all. Among individuals who strongly opposed marriage equality, only 4% thought that gay sex was not wrong at all. Furthermore, as the marriage equality movement gained ground in the 1990s and 2000s, the correlation in individual attitudes (between support for marriage equality and approval of gay sex) *increased* significantly, as Figure 8.4 shows.[14] The correlation (i.e., the tendency of two variables to move together in the same direction) between the four-category question about approval of gay sex (from "always wrong" to "not wrong at all") and the five-category question about approval of same-sex marriage (from "strongly disagree" to "strongly agree," with a neutral category in the middle)[15] rose from 0.56 in 1988 to 0.68 in 2010 and to 0.74 in 2018. The evidence from the attitude data suggests that

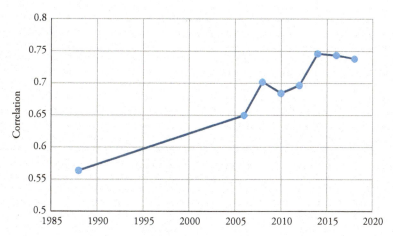

Figure 8.4 Increasing correlation within individuals of support for marriage equality and support for gay sex.

Source: Weighted data from the GSS, 1988–2018.

appreciation for marriage equality strengthened Americans' support for gay sex in general.

To be clear, there is no way to *prove* that changes in one attitude (approval of marriage equality) independently caused changes in the other (approval of gay sex). Both attitudinal changes could be caused by some unmeasured third process. I point out merely that the data that we have on attitudes toward gay sex and attitudes toward marriage equality are more consistent with the view that marriage equality would reduce stigma against all queer people than with the opposing view, that marriage equality would further stigmatize queer people who did not want to marry.

In addition to the direct effects of the marriage equality movement normalizing queer people and gay sex in general, the rising diversity of families in straight America is another reason straight people have arrived at a more tolerant view of gay sex (whether inside or outside of marriage). Straight adults in the U.S. have increasingly chosen to postpone marriage and to forgo some privileges and benefits of marriage in exchange for more freedom and independence.[16] A hundred years ago a woman in the U.S. who was unmarried in her thirties and had a male lover would have been (depending on which community she lived in) something of an outlaw and would potentially have been punished and shunned, so strong was the legal and social prohibition of sex outside of marriage. In the twenty-first-century U.S., the legal and social prohibitions against sex and child-rearing for adult heterosexuals outside of marriage have mostly disappeared. The same thirty-something woman with a boyfriend today might have a hard time finding anyone to disapprove of her choices.

The heterosexual family system in the U.S. has undergone a remarkable broadening and diversifying of forms since the 1960s, with dramatically more divorce, more single parenthood, much later age at first marriage, and more extramarital cohabitation.[17] The diversification of heterosexual family forms and the loosening of family law in the U.S. as it regards marriage, sex, procreation, and birth control[18] have helped straight Americans understand that gay family forms can also be diverse, and that those who do not marry are not necessarily any less deserving of respect than those who do. Just as straight adults accept a certain degree of diversity in straight family forms, so too straight Americans seem to understand that queer families can be diverse as well.

Ettelbrick, an important gay rights movement leader and attorney, worried about how the mobilization for marriage equality might further stigmatize queer people who did not want to marry. By the time marriage equality was approaching majority support in U.S. public opinion, around 2010, straight Americans had mostly accommodated the idea that adults might have sex without being married. Ettelbrick's influential article was written in 1989, predating by decades the successes of the marriage equality movement. Anyone can be forgiven for making mistaken predictions about the future.[19] According to Frank (2017: 357), Ettelbrick softened her view of marriage equality after attending the same-sex weddings of friends; she herself died young, in 2011.

Marriage Equality's Association with Support for Transgender Rights

Another way to think about marriage equality's effect on nonmarital queer rights is to examine the correlation between support for marriage equality and support for the rights of transgender people. Survey data on attitudes toward transgender people in the U.S. is scarce, but the data that do exist show that approval of gay rights is strongly associated with approval of transgender rights. In one nationally representative survey conducted by the Public Religion Research Institute (2011; hereafter PRRI), 81% of Americans agreed ("completely" or "mostly") with the statement "Legal protections that apply to gay and lesbian people should also apply to transgender people." In this same 2011 survey, 58% of Americans reported having a friend or family member who was gay or lesbian, and only 11% reported knowing someone who was transgender.

Despite being unlikely to know any transgender people, Americans in 2011 overwhelmingly believed that transgender people should have equal rights. In another question on the same survey, 89% of respondents agreed ("completely" or "mostly") that transgender people should have the same rights as other Americans. About half of the respondents in the survey supported marriage equality. Among those who favored or strongly favored marriage equality, 97% agreed ("completely" or "mostly") with the statement "Transgender people deserve the same rights and protections as other Americans."

Figure 8.5 shows the very powerful association in the PRRI data between strongly favoring same-sex marriage and completely agreeing that transgender people should have the same rights as any other American.

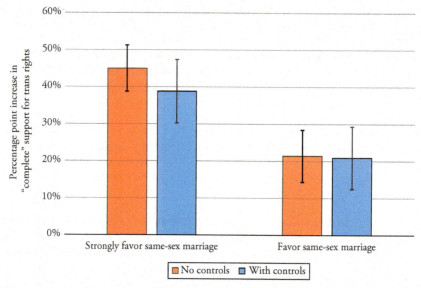

Figure 8.5 Evidence of a powerful association between support for marriage equality and complete support for transgender rights.

Source: PRRI (2011) survey of attitudes toward Transgender Rights, $N = 911$ without controls, and $N = 765$ with controls. Controls include income, education, born again Christian identity, U.S. region, urban/rural/suburban residence, race, political party affiliation, age, and gender. Predicted percentage point increases are compared to subjects who opposed same-sex marriage, from weighted OLS regressions predicting "completely agree" that transgender people deserve the same rights as everyone else, with 95% confidence intervals.

Americans who strongly favored same-sex marriage were 45 percentage points more likely than Americans who opposed same-sex marriage to say that they completely agreed that transgender people should have equal rights. After controlling for all the other factors that predicted support for marriage equality—religious beliefs, gender, age, partisan political identity, income, region, and race—the study subjects who strongly favored marriage equality remained 39 percentage points more likely to completely agree that transgender people deserved equal rights.

While there were many highly significant predictors of support for marriage equality in the PRRI survey from 2011, support for marriage equality was the *only* highly significant predictor of support for transgender rights in the data when all predictors were taken into account. In 2011 in the U.S., marriage equality was a politically charged issue that adults had heard about for years and had had time to form opinions about. Gay and lesbian Americans had been out of the closet for long enough to make an impression on their straight friends and neighbors. In contrast to the long history of political battles over marriage equality and gay rights, transgender people were mostly invisible in 2011 in the U.S., and transgender rights were a new issue that most Americans were not aware of. Because Americans had not heard much about transgender rights in 2011, the usual dimensions of political division (religion, political party affiliation, education, urban versus rural, age, gender, race) were much better at predicting support for marriage equality than they were at predicting support for transgender rights.[20] Americans did not know much about transgender rights in 2011, but if they favored marriage equality they were dramatically more likely to be in complete support of transgender rights.

Figure 8.5 is consistent with (but does not prove) the hypothesis that the marriage equality movement taught U.S. adults to understand and appreciate transgender rights, despite most U.S. adults not believing that they knew any transgender people. Far from undermining the rights of the most marginalized sexual minority groups, the marriage equality movement seems to have helped to normalize rights for all sexual minorities, including the rights of gay people regardless of whether they married, and the rights of transgender people. The American public opinion journey toward greater support of gay rights made it easier for Americans to understand why transgender people should also have rights, despite transgender people being a much smaller and less visible minority group than gays or lesbians were in 2011.

The Gay Rights and Abortion Rights Comparison

Figure 8.3 above shows the time trends in GSS data for approval of abortion rights in the left panel, and approval of gay rights in the right panel. Consistent with what we see in Figures 8.1 and 8.2, the abortion rights questions were all relatively flat or slightly declining in approval over time, except for the GSS question about willingness of respondents to abort their own defective fetus, whose approval rate declined sharply. The slow erosion of support for abortion rights makes an interesting contrast with the fast liberalization of attitudes toward gay rights.

The comparison of abortion rights attitudes and gay rights attitudes is a useful comparison for several reasons. First, the abortion rights issue splits Americans across some of the same political divisions as do gay rights. Republicans, people from the geographic South, religious people, and especially evangelical Christians are among the demographic groups that are much more likely to be opposed to gay rights and also are much more likely to be opposed to abortion rights. Not all of the demographic predictors of gay rights and abortion rights are the same. Women and men support abortion rights in roughly equal proportions, but women support gay rights substantially more than men. Because gay rights have been gaining traction dramatically in the U.S. over time, support for gay rights has a generational dimension: more recent generations are much more supportive of gay rights. The generations are more similar in their views of abortion rights.[21]

If abortion rights and gay rights are similar in the way they divide the American electorate, why have gay rights attitudes liberalized so much while abortion rights attitudes are mostly static? One key difference is that the rapid change in attitudes toward gay rights in the U.S. has been driven by gay and lesbian people coming out of the closet. Women who have had abortions in the U.S. mostly have remained in the closet about their experience, for a variety of reasons.[22] Gay and lesbian people had to come out of the closet to defend themselves; American women have not had to come out of the closet about their abortion experiences.

Another difference between abortion rights and gay rights is the way the Supreme Court imposed change. Both abortion rights with *Roe v. Wade* (1973) and marriage equality with *Obergefell v. Hodges* (2015) were sweeping decisions. When *Roe v. Wade* was decided, all fifty U.S. states had to change their abortion laws to comply. By the time of the *Obergefell v. Hodges* decision, most U.S. states already had marriage equality. Massachusetts, for instance, had had marriage equality in place for more than a decade. The *Obergefell* decision was a more incremental and cautious decision than *Roe* in terms of imposing policy on the states and so may have engendered less political backlash.[23]

Change in Public Opinion Using Data from American National Election Studies

The 1952–2012 cumulative data file for the American National Election Studies (2015; hereafter ANES) is an important supplement to the GSS data, because the ANES data extend further back in time. Both the GSS and the ANES are core long-term American social science projects, funded by the U.S. National Science Foundation, to study American attitudes. The ANES cumulative data file does not include a question about same-sex marriage, but it did include six repeated questions about gay rights. Two were follow-up questions, so there were four different gay rights questions in the ANES cumulative data: Should gays and lesbians be able to adopt children? Did subjects favor or oppose gays in the military? Should there be a law protecting homosexuals from discrimination at work? And there was a general question about feelings toward gay and lesbian people. The ANES includes 187 general attitude variables that were surveyed at least three times over a span of at least ten years.[24]

Table 8.2 shows a pattern for the 187 ANES attitude variables that is similar to the pattern we have already seen in the GSS: as with the GSS data, the gay rights variables in ANES changed more and more rapidly than other variable categories, by both extent and rate of change. Support for laws to protect homosexuals from discrimination at work rose from 54% in 1988 to 77% in 2012. The percentage of American adults who supported gays serving in the military rose from 59% in 1992 to 86% in 2012. The percentage who thought

Table 8.2 Summary Data on Extent of Change and Rate of Change of ANES Public Opinion Variables

		Extent of Change	Rate of Change
ANES variables categories	Number of attitude variables averaged in each category	Absolute value percentage point change end point to end point	Absolute value percentage point change per year
Gay rights	6	28.28	1.21
Abortion	1	4.29	0.11
Race	25	8.19	0.44
Religion	11	6.84	0.28
Government	43	18.70	0.64
Other	101	10.20	0.30
All attitudes mean	187	12.24	0.43
Comparison: GSS attitudes about same-sex marriage		56.44	1.88

Source: Weighted ANES data, 1952–2012.
Extent of Change uses dichotomous versions of the variables and examines only the first and last year that each question was asked, as in the Y Axis of Figure 8.4. Rate of Change uses dichotomous versions of the variables, fitting the best fit line to data from all years, using Ordinary Least Squares regressions.

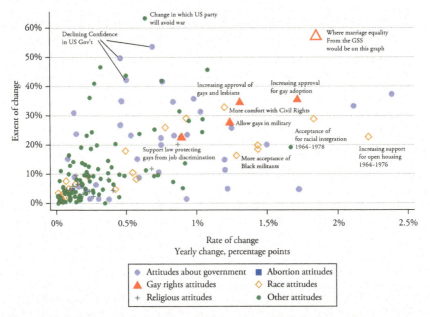

Figure 8.6 Scatter plot of all 187 attitudes from ANES by extent of change and rate of change.

Source: Weighted data from American National Election Studies (ANES) cumulative file 1952–2012. This figure includes all 187 ANES attitude variables that were asked at least 3 times, with first instance and last instance at least 10 years apart. For this graph, all ANES attitude variables were converted to dichotomous variables, approve versus disapprove. The X axis reflects the absolute value of the coefficient for year in 187 separate OLS regressions of each attitude variable on year.

gays and lesbians should be able to adopt children rose from 28% in 1992 to 63% in 2012. When asked to rate gays and lesbians on a 100-degree scale, where 0 represented hostility and 100 represented warmth and friendliness, the percentage of American adults rating gays and lesbians at 50 points or higher (warmer) rose from 34% in 1984 to 73% in 2012.

Figure 8.6 shows a scatter plot of all 187 ANES general attitude variables, plus the marriage equality variable borrowed from the GSS. None of the ANES attitude variables had both a greater rate of change and a greater extent of change than did attitudes toward same-sex marriage.[25] All of the gay rights attitude measures in ANES underwent rapid liberalization.

The Civil Rights Comparison

ANES surveys predate the GSS surveys, so ANES data are useful for comparing gay rights attitude change to earlier attitude change around one of the most important social movement antecedents of gay rights, the civil rights movement of the 1960s. Figure 8.6 indicates several of the ANES civil rights attitude questions whose approval changed decisively over time, particularly in the 1960s. Some changed at a faster rate (X axis) than attitudes toward same-sex marriage, though none of the civil rights attitudes changed as much over time (Y axis) as attitudes toward same-sex marriage. Attitudes toward open housing and whether Whites had the right to exclude Blacks from neighborhoods[26] changed sharply from 1964 to 1976, with Whites becoming more approving (in principle) of integration. In 1968, the first Fair Housing Act was passed. Between 1970 and 1986, Americans became less hostile toward Black militants. And between 1964 and 1992, Americans became more sympathetic to the civil rights movement, as seen by their agreeing less with the statement that the civil rights movement had pushed too fast.

Some race-related public opinions, such as willingness to tolerate integration, changed at historically rapid rates during the civil rights movement and immediately after. In subsequent decades the trends in American public opinion about race and civil rights have been less clear. While support for old-fashioned racism continued to decline, White opposition to government aid to Blacks and opposition to affirmative action in particular increased. There is, in the public opinion record and in the ethnographic record, evidence of a long-simmering White backlash against civil rights.[27]

Lessons from the History of Attitudinal Changes

Consistent with Page and Shapiro's (1992) results from an earlier generation of public opinion data, average support for most public opinion issues in the GSS and the ANES are generally stable over time. In contrast, opinions about same-sex marriage are a fast-changing outlier. No American public opinion has changed more quickly *and* more extensively than have opinions about same-sex marriage. A few civil rights attitudes changed at a faster rate but over a shorter time span.

Even though gay rights and abortion rights are supported and opposed by a similar set of social and demographic groups, approval of gay rights has changed enormously over time, whereas approval for abortion rights in the U.S. has been relatively static over time. The difference in the trajectories of abortion attitudes and gay rights attitudes lends itself to several kinds of explanations that I will return to at the end of the book. The experience of the closet is but one potential explanation: women who have had abortions remain mostly closeted, while gay and lesbian Americans have largely come out of the closet. The uniqueness of the progress of gay rights in American public opinion also suggests that coming out of the closet might not be sufficient by itself to guarantee a rise in public esteem. Racial minority groups have always been out of the closet, but their out-of-the-closet status has not been associated with universal reductions in stigma or improvements in status.

Gay rights attitudes, as a group, changed more and more rapidly than other identifiable groups of attitudes, and all the other attitudes toward gay rights and toward gay people liberalized at the same time. The broad synchronous sweep of liberalization of U.S. public opinion toward gay sex and all manner of gay rights in the post-1992 era is one indication that the social movement for marriage equality has reduced the stigmas faced by all queer people, rather than (as some critics of marriage equality predicted) elevating the stigmas faced by queer people who might not want to marry.

The rising correlation within individuals of approval of marriage equality and approval of gay sex (regardless of marital status) is one piece of evidence to suggest that the marriage equality movement improved the status of all queer people, exactly as the advocates said it would. The fact that individuals who supported marriage equality were so much more likely to support transgender rights (even after accounting for all the other factors associated with support for marriage equality, and even though so few Americans thought they knew a transgender person) is another piece of evidence suggesting that the marriage equality movement raised the status of all queer people.

9

The Early 2000s

American attitudes toward gay rights were starting to liberalize in the 1990s. Gays and lesbians were coming out of their closets in large numbers. However, there still were fundamental legal barriers to equality for gays and lesbians in the U.S. The sodomy laws left intact by *Bowers v. Hardwick* (1986) remained the main barrier.

Lawrence v. Texas, 2003

In the evening of September 17, 1998, in an unincorporated town on the outskirts of Houston, a man named Eubanks called the police and reported falsely that "a N****r was going crazy with a gun" in John Lawrence's apartment, referring to a Black man named Tyron Garner.[1] When the police arrived, they found that Garner was not armed. The police report stated that they found Lawrence and Garner having sex. Dale Carpenter's (2004, 2012) reconstructions of events based on interviews with the people involved cast doubt on whether the police actually observed Lawrence and Garner having sex, or even whether Lawrence and Garner ever had sex with each other. Regardless of what the police actually saw, Lawrence and Garner were gay men, one Black and one White, living in the poor part of town. They were arrested under Texas's sodomy statute, which criminalized sodomy for same-sex couples.

In 1973, Texas had changed its sodomy law to apply only to same-sex couples so heterosexual couples in Texas were free to engage in activities that were illegal for same-sex couples. The arresting officer hauled Lawrence and Garner off to jail, where they spent the night. Lawrence was shoeless and in his underwear.[2]

Texas's sodomy law applied to activities conducted in public and in private but was hardly ever applied to private activity, which was rarely observed by the authorities. Because Lawrence and Garner were the rare adult criminal defendants arrested for private consensual sexual activity, they were, as

The Rainbow after the Storm. Michael J. Rosenfeld, Oxford University Press. © Oxford University Press 2022.
DOI: 10.1093/oso/9780197600436.003.0009

Michael Hardwick had been in Georgia, ideal plaintiffs to challenge the constitutionality of Texas's sodomy law.[3] Gay rights lawyers in Texas quickly learned of Lawrence and Garner, met with them, and convinced them to plead "no contest"[4] and pay the fine. Pleading no contest resulted in a conviction for Lawrence and Garner, who then filed suit to overturn Texas's sodomy law.

Lawrence and Garner lost in the Texas courts, and then appealed to the U.S. Supreme Court, which granted *Cert* and heard Lawrence's appeal.[5] Between 1986, when *Bowers v. Hardwick* was decided, and 2003, when *Lawrence v. Texas* was decided, eleven more states plus the District of Columbia had decriminalized sodomy either through state legislative action or through actions of the state courts. Georgia, the state whose sodomy law was successfully defended in *Bowers*, had their sodomy law overturned by a state supreme court decision in 1998.[6]

In 1986 Justice Powell had claimed that he had never known a gay person (despite some of his own clerks being gay) because so few gay people were out of the closet. By 2003 the situation had changed. A substantial proportion of gay people were out of the closet, and the justices were made aware of the gay and lesbian people in their professional and social circles.[7]

Fourteen states, including Texas, retained laws against sodomy in 2003. We have seen Figure 9.1 before, but now we have arrived at the decisive moment: the 2003 *Lawrence* decision that ended the criminalization of consensual adult sodomy in the U.S.

Courts do not overturn prior decisions lightly. The U.S. Supreme Court regularly overturns decisions of lower courts[8] but rarely reverses itself.[9] Reverence for precedent, i.e., reverence for the accumulated decisions of prior courts, is one of the fundamental principles of the law. The Latin phrase that lawyers sometimes use is *stare decisis*, which means "let the decision stand," in other words, obey the decisions that have come before.

In *Lawrence v. Texas* (2003: 567), Anthony Kennedy's majority decision addressed the *Bowers* precedent directly:

> The laws involved in *Bowers* and here are, to be sure, statutes that purport to do no more than prohibit a particular sexual act. Their penalties and purposes, though, have more far-reaching consequences, touching upon the most private human conduct, sexual behavior, and in the most private of places, the home. The statutes do seek to control a personal relationship that, whether or not entitled to formal recognition in the law, is within the liberty of persons to choose without being punished as criminals.

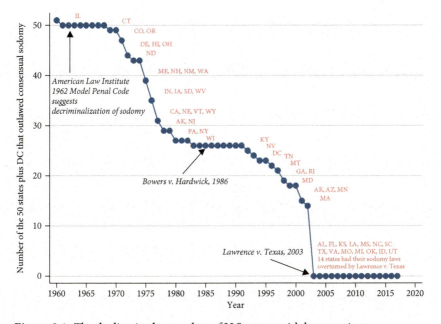

Figure 9.1 The decline in the number of U.S. states with bans against consensual sodomy. States listed as their bans were removed.

Source: Data on the end of sodomy laws in each state from the Appendix in Eskridge (2008).

The phrase "whether or not entitled to formal recognition in the law" was Justice Kennedy's way of indicating that the *Lawrence v. Texas* decision was not going to force states to accept the marriages of same-sex couples. Kennedy continued:

> When sexuality finds overt expression in intimate conduct with another person, the conduct can be but one element in a personal bond that is more enduring. The liberty protected by the Constitution allows homosexual persons the right to make this choice. . . .
>
> The doctrine of *stare decisis* is essential to the respect accorded to the judgments of the Court and to the stability of the law. It is not, however, an inexorable command. . . . The rationale of *Bowers* does not withstand careful analysis. . . . *Bowers* was not correct when it was decided, and it is not correct today. It ought not to remain binding precedent. *Bowers v. Hardwick* should be and now is overruled.[10]

Kennedy's majority decision in *Lawrence v. Texas* swept aside the remaining states' sodomy laws. Justice Scalia was one of the three dissenters to the decision. Scalia wrote:

> Many Americans do not want persons who openly engage in homosexual conduct as partners in their business, as scoutmasters for their children, as teachers in their children's schools, or as boarders in their home. They view this as protecting themselves and their families from a lifestyle that they believe to be immoral and destructive....
>
> [T]he Court says that the present case "does not involve whether the government must give formal recognition to any relationship that homosexual persons seek to enter." Do not believe it. . . . Today's opinion dismantles the structure of constitutional law that has permitted a distinction to be made between heterosexual and homosexual unions, insofar as formal recognition in marriage is concerned. If moral disapprobation of homosexual conduct is 'no legitimate state interest' . . . what justification could there possibly be for denying the benefits of marriage to homosexual couples exercising 'the liberty protected by the Constitution'?[11]

Justice Scalia's dissent claimed that removing the sodomy laws would make gays and lesbians equal citizens with their heterosexual neighbors, and thereby make same-sex marriage inevitable. His intuition was correct. The sodomy laws had placed gays and lesbians under a shadow of illegality, which prevented them from having equal rights. Even though few Americans were ever charged with, much less convicted of criminal sodomy, the sodomy laws were a central tent pole holding up an entire fabric of antigay legal persecutions. Once the tent pole of sodomy criminalization was removed, the whole tent folded up and there was not much police interest left in entrapping gay men with the promise of sex. If gay people were entitled to be treated with dignity and equal rights (as Kennedy's majority decision suggested), then Scalia was right: it was no longer obvious from the perspective of constitutional law why same-sex couples should not have the right to marry. Striking down the sodomy laws freed gay people from one of their last legal burdens and made it possible for them to come out of the closet without fear of criminal prosecution.

As American gay and lesbian adults came out to their friends, neighbors, coworkers, and families in the 1990s and 2000s, public support for gay rights and for marriage equality was steadily growing, though still ran strongly against same-sex marriage. At the time of *Lawrence*, marriage equality across the U.S. was still more than a decade away, and fewer than 30% of Americans supported marriage equality.

A Long Line of Defeats at the Ballot Box for Marriage Equality before 2012

Success did not come to the marriage equality movement overnight. From 1998, when Hawaii held its referendum on same-sex marriage, through 2009, there were thirty-four state referenda on same-sex marriage, and all but one was a defeat for marriage equality.[12] Figure 9.2 revisits the data from a figure in chapter 6, but now we are further along in time, i.e., further right on the X axis. Figure 9.2 shows the results of every state marriage equality referendum, superimposed on the graph of approval versus disapproval of same-sex marriage from the national sample of the GSS.[13]

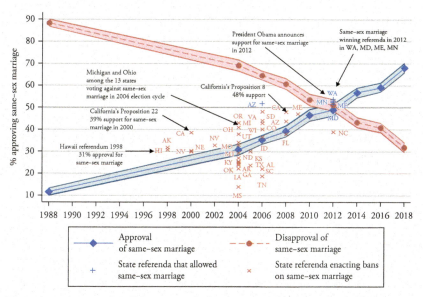

Figure 9.2 Approval and disapproval of same-sex marriage in U.S. public opinion with state-level referenda results by percentage approving same-sex marriage.

Source: Weighted national public opinion data from the General Social Survey (GSS) with 95% confidence intervals. State referenda results indicated next to each state's two letter abbreviation. Data on referenda results are from Ballotpedia (2019).

In 1998, 31% of Hawaiians and a similar percentage of Alaskans voted to legalize same-sex marriage, well below the 50% required to enact marriage equality, so same-sex marriage was disallowed in both states. In Figure 9.2, state referenda below 50% approval are marked with red X's, while state referenda above 50% are marked with blue plus signs.

In 2000, California voters overwhelmingly passed Proposition 22 by 61.4 to 38.6%, enacting a ban on same-sex marriage into California law. In San Francisco, in February 2004, newly elected mayor Gavin Newsom thought that Proposition 22 was inconsistent with California's constitution, so he ordered the city clerk to marry same-sex couples in defiance of Proposition 22. For a few giddy days a line formed around San Francisco's City Hall as thousands of same-sex couples waiting their turn, paid for their marriage licenses, and had their unions blessed by the city clerk. Mayor Newsom worked with San Francisco's National Center for Lesbian Rights to make sure that veteran lesbian activists Del Martin and Phyllis Lyon, who had been together since the 1950s and who had founded the Daughters of Bilitis in San Francisco almost fifty years earlier, were first in line.[14]

Same-sex couples who had never had a serious conversation about marriage and who had never expected to have the opportunity to marry suddenly could marry in San Francisco. As they expected the courts might intervene quickly, couples wanted to marry while they could. Some found that getting married, even without any advance planning, felt more rewarding and important than they had expected it to feel. Being married was more than just a piece of paper. Being married brought a fundamental validation.[15]

Mayor Newsom, however, lacked the authority to change or overturn California law. The California Supreme Court first put a stop to the San Francisco same-sex marriages, and then invalidated the marriages as inconsistent with state law.[16] The court left the question of the constitutionality of Proposition 22 for later.

The summer of 2004 saw a few other towns across the U.S. attempt to seize the mantle of marriage equality and marry same-sex couples in defiance of state laws.[17] As national support for marriage equality was only at 30% in 2004, the Republican Party saw an opportunity to mobilize voters who opposed marriage equality. The Republicans introduced referenda to ban marriage equality in thirteen states.

American voters' opposition to same-sex marriage in 2004 was stoked by the Republican Party and channeled into anti-gay-marriage referenda, which brought conservative voters to the polls and helped reelect President

George W. Bush, a Republican, and defeat his Democratic challenger, John Kerry.[18] Bush's reelection on the back of a national campaign against same-sex marriage seemed to indicate that American voters cared more about defeating same-sex marriage than they cared about traditionally important issues such as the economy or about military and diplomatic failures abroad. Public opinion toward marriage equality had liberalized dramatically, but the starting point had been so low that by 2004 only about 31% of American adults supported marriage equality. The war in Iraq was already seen as a failure by November 2004, but Bush (the war's architect) was reelected nonetheless.

Michigan voters enacted a state constitutional ban against same-sex marriage in 2004, with 41% voting for marriage equality and 59% voting against. Just below Michigan in Figure 9.2 is Ohio, where the ban on same-sex marriage was passed by 62 to 38% that year. The results of the 2004 elections in the U.S. seemed to portend more failure and future defeats for gay rights in the U.S.[19]

"Losing Forward"

In a winner-take-all electoral system like that of the U.S., there is no trophy for second place. If you are one vote short of victory, you are a loser. One of the most difficult things to accomplish in any social movement is to keep activists engaged and enthusiastic in the face of setbacks. At the ballot box, the marriage equality movement experienced several decades of losses in a row, enough losing to create despondency in any group. Even though the losses were becoming narrower over time, they took a toll on the enthusiasm of marriage equality advocates. And yet, despite the cascade of losses, public opinion support for marriage equality was increasing at a historically unprecedented rate.

As Harvey Milk had said about the Briggs Initiative in 1978, "Even if we lose, having the debate moves us forward." This is a strategy that marriage equality pioneer Evan Wolfson, the attorney who founded the marriage equality advocacy organization Freedom to Marry, would later refer to as "losing forward." Milk had known personally about losing forward: he had lost three elections before he was finally elected to the Board of Supervisors of San Francisco in November 1977. With each campaign, he became better known, made more allies, and polished his already formidable political skills.

Because Wolfson understood the concept of losing forward, he was not alarmed by the marriage equality ballot measure defeats of the 1990s and the

2000s. In his view, the states that were banning same-sex marriage had never allowed it anyway, so no public policy change had been enacted. Even in the climate of profound election losses, Wolfson understood the cause of marriage equality was introducing the general public to same-sex couples whose relationships with each other and with their children powerfully demonstrated love and commitment.[20] Demonstrable interpersonal commitment between partners in same-sex unions conveyed a powerful symbolic message about how gays and lesbians shared fundamental values and ideals with their heterosexual neighbors.

Over time, as gay rights organizers and activists went through campaign after campaign, and loss after loss, they gained skills. They learned what worked and what didn't. Each campaign allowed them to build and refine their lists of local donors and supporters. Movements, and people within movements, get better at political campaigns through practice.[21]

Wolfson understood that grassroots work to promote marriage equality was changing American public opinion in a way that would eventually turn the gay rights defeats of the early years into gay rights victories. He believed that marriage equality was such a fundamentally winning proposition that gay rights activists would win converts to their cause with every campaign, and so every political campaign was productive even if the specific campaign was lost. The premise of the "losing forward" strategy was that "forward," i.e., the future, would be more receptive to gay rights than the present and the past had been.[22]

In the 2004 elections, thirteen states reaffirmed or strengthened their states' bans on same-sex marriage. As Wolfson pointed out, however, those thirteen states had never permitted same-sex marriage before, so in a sense nothing substantive had changed. Massachusetts became a marriage equality state in 2004 through judicial action. Wolfson (2005) argued that Massachusetts's adoption of marriage equality (as the first state in the U.S. to do so) would be more politically consequential than the voters' rejection of marriage equality in the thirteen other states.

Weathering the Storm: The Massachusetts Case

In the aftermath of Hawaii, where a state court victory for marriage equality had been overturned in 1998 by a voter referendum that led to a state constitutional ban on same-sex marriage, the marriage equality movement turned its focus to the states that had the most difficult processes for amending and changing their constitutions.[23] The longer it took for a state to try to amend its constitution to ban same-sex marriage, the greater the likelihood that court-imposed marriage equality would have a chance to weather the storm of an initial backlash and become part of normal life.

Massachusetts was one of the states with difficult-to-change constitutions targeted by the marriage equality movement. Activists spent years talking to community groups and lobbying legislators, until they were ready to move forward with a test case.[24] In 2001, Hillary Goodridge and Julie Goodridge, along with several other long-term committed couples, applied for marriage licenses in Massachusetts and were denied. The case wound its way up to the Massachusetts Supreme Court, which ruled in a 4–3 majority in *Goodridge v. Department of Public Health* (2003) that denying marriage licenses to same-sex couples in Massachusetts was unconstitutional.

In 2004, after the Massachusetts Supreme Court ordered the legislature to implement marriage equality at the state level, there followed an extended political battle over the state constitution. Opponents of marriage equality were trying to go through the several-years-long process of amending or changing the Massachusetts constitution to ban same-sex marriage. Meanwhile, starting on May 17, 2004, same-sex couples were getting married in the state nearly every day and showing up on the news, smiling and happy. The local media were naturally attracted to the human interest stories of same-sex couples claiming their rights and demonstrating their love and commitment against a background of political uncertainty.

At the beginning of the battle over marriage equality and the Massachusetts constitution in 2004, opponents of marriage equality in the state had many political and organizational advantages. Outspoken opponents included the Republican governor, Mitt Romney, the Catholic Church (the most influential nongovernmental organization in Massachusetts), President George W. Bush, and a broad array of well-funded religious organizations such as Focus on the Family. Massachusetts Catholic bishops instructed every priest in the state to read a letter from the pulpit calling the *Goodridge* decision "a national tragedy."[25] James Dobson (2004: 42), leader of Focus on the Family, wrote that May 17, 2004, the first day same-sex couples were married in Massachusetts, was "perhaps the worst day for the institution of marriage in the history of the world."

Compared to the enormous power of the organizations arrayed against them, proponents of marriage equality in Massachusetts in 2004 had substantially fewer organizational and political assets. Democratic Senator and presidential nominee John Kerry refused to support marriage equality, calling instead for a civil union "compromise," which the Supreme Court of Massachusetts had already explicitly rejected.[26] Yet despite their organizational and resource limitations, and despite being opposed by the governor and the Catholic Church, advocates of marriage equality in Massachusetts prevailed. Supporters won enough votes in Massachusetts constitutional conventions over three legislative sessions to derail potential constitutional amendments that could have overturned the *Goodridge* decision. The longer the process to attempt to pass an anti-gay-marriage state constitutional amendment in Massachusetts dragged on, the weaker the movement against marriage equality became.

The political position of Massachusetts opponents of same-sex marriage eroded over time for several reasons. First, the support for same-sex marriage was increasing everywhere in the U.S. at a rate that had rarely, if ever, been seen in the history of American popular attitudes. Second, starting in 2004, Massachusetts had actual same-sex married couples in nearly every legislative district. Marriage equality supporters worked diligently to introduce legislators to the same-sex married couples in their districts. Some of the legislators had never talked to an out-of-the-closet gay or lesbian person before. Direct interpersonal contact with these couples and their children helped to sway the views of the legislators.

Opponents of same-sex marriage in Massachusetts also made pilgrimages to the offices of their elected representatives and made a variety of claims that same-sex marriage injured them. But the opponents were unable to demonstrate that they had been harmed in any concrete way by marriage equality because marriage equality is a nondisplacing movement. Opponents expressed variations of the view that same-sex marriage represented a kind of injury to tradition that might upset the balance of the social world, but this kind of injury was very abstract. Same-sex couples and their children had benefited directly and *concretely* from marriage equality in Massachusetts, including through healthcare, inheritance options, tax benefits, and social recognition. The opponents of same-sex marriage had lost none of those benefits.

Same-sex married couples, through their lived examples of familial commitment and devotion, undermined every demeaning stereotype that gays and lesbians in the U.S. had faced. They were making sacrifices for their children, and they were investing long term in each other. They were the kind of respectable upstanding citizens that continue to be the bedrock of any community. One of the objections that came from the left wing of the gay rights movement was that marriage equality presented *too* much of an assimilated and respectable image of gay life. I return to the left critique of marriage equality in a final chapter. From the perspective of the Massachusetts battle over marriage equality in 2004 and in the following years, what we can say for certain is that the respectability of same-sex married couples helped to win over many politically moderate Massachusetts legislators to the then radical idea that same-sex marriage was reasonable, just, and fair. Enough Massachusetts politicians were convinced of the reasonableness of marriage equality that they stuck their political necks out and supported marriage equality in the face of hostile and organized opposition.

The opponents of marriage equality in Massachusetts needed to get fifty of the two hundred state legislators to vote in favor of an anti-marriage-equality measure in two consecutive legislative sessions, in order to put an anti-marriage-equality constitutional amendment before the voters of the state. In January 2007, on the last day of a lame duck legislative session, the opponents garnered sixty-two votes. Democrat (and marriage equality supporter) Deval Patrick was sworn in a few days later as governor, replacing marriage equality opponent Mitt Romney. Four of the sixty-two legislators who were opponents of marriage equality had already lost their seats to marriage equality supporters. The new governor, marriage equality activists, and the newly married couples themselves set about lobbying the remaining fifty-eight legislators who had voted against marriage equality.

When the anti-marriage-equality amendment came up again, in June 2007, the proposal garnered only forty-five votes, five fewer than it needed. Marriage equality has remained the law in Massachusetts, uninterrupted.

The Short-Term Efficacy and Long-Term Failure of Apocalyptic Warnings

A predicted apocalyptic end of the world is one of the cornerstones of evangelical Christian theology. If modernity's corruption was going to lead the world to a fiery end, it was natural within this theology for Christian Right leaders to suggest that same-sex marriage specifically would lead to the end of Western civilization. Televangelist Pat Robertson told his vast audience, "Sodomy, in all history, as far as I can tell, any nation that embraces this so-called 'lifestyle' and legalizes it, celebrates it, protects it is on [sic] the ash can of history. Every single one has gone into decline. There's not one that survived since this happens."[27] Along the same lines, Focus on the Family's Dobson (2004: 18–19) wrote:

> The traditional family and marriage as defined from the dawn of time are among the few institutions that have, in fact, stood the test of time. If we now choose to stand idly by while these institutions are overthrown, the family as it has been known for millennia will be gone. And with its demise will come chaos such as the world has never seen before.

Apocalyptic claims were effective at motivating people in the immediate aftermath of the *Goodridge* ruling because any unexpected social change can make people feel uncertain. And people who feel uncertain are more vulnerable to fear tactics. But as the years went by and same-sex couples married and chaos did not reign and the family system did not end, the air slowly leaked out of the hot air balloon of apocalyptic warnings.

The same pattern of marriage equality gains, short-term political backlash, and then a dissipation of the backlash had been seen in Vermont a few years earlier. The Vermont courts in 1999 were the first to order their state to recognize same-sex unions legally, but with a different name: civil unions.[28] In the initial aftermath of the recognition of same-sex civil unions in Vermont, the opponents of gay rights had all the political momentum, and in the next election their movement "Take Back Vermont" unseated the governor and sixteen pro-civil-union legislators.

Vermont's constitution, like the Massachusetts constitution, took several legislative cycles to change. By the time the next election came around, the new anti-civil-union legislators were themselves turned out of office. Anger at civil unions in Vermont quickly abated when heterosexual Vermonters realized that civil unions cost them nothing.

Apocalyptic warnings can be effective in the short term. If time passes and no sign of the apocalypse is seen, then the apocalyptic message starts to lose its credibility. If you stand on the corner every week, saying that the world will end on the following Tuesday, after a while people may start to view you as a crank.

Proposition 8

In the summer of 2008 the California Supreme Court finally got around to considering the question of whether Proposition 22 (banning same-sex marriage), passed by the voters in 2000, was consistent with California's constitution. The court was returning to a state constitutional question that had been left open since they had struck down the unauthorized San Francisco same-sex marriages from February 2004. The court struck down Proposition 22 (see *In re Marriage Cases* 2008) and made same-sex marriage legal in California. In the summer and fall of 2008, thousands of same-sex California couples married legally. But a storm was looming.

Anticipating the possibility that Proposition 22 would be struck down, opponents of marriage equality had put another same-sex marriage ban on the ballot in 2008. This new measure, if passed, would amend California's constitution to ban same-sex marriage, and thereby make the ban more immune to review by state courts. In the November 2008 elections, Democrat Barack Obama swept into office with a resounding majority in the country as a whole and in California, but California voters also passed Proposition 8 by the narrow margin of 52 to 48%, placing the same-sex marriage ban into California's state constitution.

The passage of Proposition 8 created an awkward and unusual legal discontinuity. The same-sex couples who married in California in the summer of 2008 were legally married as far as the state was concerned, but no subsequent same-sex marriages would be recognized by California as long as Proposition 8 was in force.[29]

PART III

SOCIAL SCIENCE AND
THE COURT BATTLES THAT WON
MARRIAGE EQUALITY

10

Perry and *Windsor*

From *Perry v. Schwarzenegger* (2010) to *Hollingsworth v. Perry* (2013)

National gay rights groups had for a long time been hesitant to sue in the federal courts to try to overturn state laws or state constitutions banning same-sex marriage, lest the case be appealed to the U.S. Supreme Court. In 2009, the national gay rights groups thought the groundwork had not yet been sufficiently established in the states to bring marriage equality before the usually cautious and incremental U.S. Supreme Court.[1] A loss there had the potential to set the marriage equality movement back a decade or longer.

Hollywood mogul Rob Reiner and his pro-gay-rights public relations team (including Chad Griffin, who would go on to lead the Human Rights Campaign) had a more optimistic view. In early 2009, Reiner brought on star liberal attorney David Boies and star conservative attorney Ted Olson to challenge California's Proposition 8 in federal court. The group raised a lot of money, put expensive corporate lawyers on the project, and found plaintiffs Kristin Perry and Sandra Stier, and Paul Katami and Jeffrey Zarrillo. In May 2009 Reiner's team filed the lawsuit, and the case of *Perry v. Schwarzenegger* was born. Judge Vaughn Walker in the Northern District of California called for a trial, the second trial in the history of marriage equality litigation in the U.S.[2]

In the federal case against Proposition 8, California's Republican governor Arnold Schwarzenegger was the first named defendant. Schwarzenegger, however, had become more supportive of marriage equality over time, and he refused to defend Proposition 8 in court. The state's Democratic attorney general Jerry Brown, another named defendant, took the unusual step of joining the case on the plaintiffs' side. Ordinarily, as the chief lawyer of the state, a state attorney general defends any state law or any part of the state constitution that is challenged in court, whether or not they personally approve of the law. Because the governor and the attorney general would not defend Proposition 8, Judge Walker allowed a group of private legal intervenors, led

The Rainbow after the Storm. Michael J. Rosenfeld, Oxford University Press. © Oxford University Press 2022.
DOI: 10.1093/oso/9780197600436.003.0010

by Dennis Hollingsworth and other original supporters of Proposition 8, to defend Proposition 8 in court.

From start to finish, the *Perry v. Schwarzenegger* trial was a full-scale debacle for the defenders of Proposition 8, and an embarrassing defeat for the expert witnesses who were originally listed as potential defense witnesses. Of the six expert witnesses listed by the defendants of Proposition 8, four performed so poorly in their pretrial depositions[3] that the lawyers on their own side would not allow them to testify in open court. The problem for the lawyers defending Proposition 8 was that witnesses who were reasonable and credible were not willing to say, on cross-examination, that same-sex marriage would harm anyone, and the witnesses who were sure that same-sex marriage caused harm were not reasonable or credible.

At the *Perry v. Schwarzenegger* trial, William Tam, one of the architects of the Yes on Proposition 8 campaign, was forced to admit that he had written a document circulated to California churches which claimed that if Proposition 8 was defeated, "one by one, other states would fall into Satan's hand. What will be next? On their agenda list is: legalize having sex with children."[4] The campaign had relied on bias and known falsehoods. Tam had claimed that same-sex marriage would lead to polygamy and incest, and he alleged (falsely) that the legalization of same-sex marriage in the Netherlands had led to the legalization of incest and polygamy there. At the *Perry* trial, Tam was asked to name his source for his claim that same-sex marriage would lead to polygamy and incest; he answered that he had learned the information from "the Internet."[5] [o !]

David Blankenhorn was the star witness for the defense. He was not a professor or a scholar but a popular writer of books about the family. Blankenhorn opposed same-sex marriage, but he admitted at the trial under cross-examination by Boies that "gay marriage would be a victory for the worthy ideals of tolerance and inclusion."[6] His testimony helped the plaintiffs more than the defense. A few years later, Blankenhorn (2012) reversed his position entirely and endorsed same-sex marriage.

In contrast to the witnesses for the defense in *Perry*, the plaintiffs' witnesses included leading academic thinkers with stellar reputations, offering the kind of evidence-based testimony that tends to be persuasive in court. Historian Nancy Cott explained that marriage laws and customs had changed a great deal over time and that the ability to produce children had never been a requirement of marriage in the U.S. She noted that George

Washington, the father of the United States, was sterile but married none-theless. Historian George Chauncey testified about the history of antigay discrimination in the U.S. Social epidemiologist Ilan Meyer testified about how California's discrimination against gay people (by withholding the right to marry) contributed to stigma, stress, and ultimately mental health problems in the gay community. Psychologist Michael Lamb testified about the social science consensus that children raised by same-sex couples have excellent outcomes. Economist Lee Badgett testified that Proposition 8 was costing California money. Political scientist Gary Segura rebutted defense arguments that gays and lesbians were so powerful they needed no legal protections. He showed that gay and lesbian citizens in the U.S. had had their rights diminished more than 140 times by state and local ballot initiatives. Segura had initially resisted being an expert witness in *Perry*, as he had no prior expert witness experience. He eventually relented and would later come to see his participation in *Perry* as one of the proudest moments of his professional career.[7]

Plaintiffs' witness psychologist Letitia Anne Peplau documented the benefits that marriage equality would bring to same-sex couples and their families, and she argued that allowing same-sex couples to marry would strengthen, rather than weaken, the institution of marriage. Psychologist Gregory Herek described the prevailing scholarly consensus that "homosex-uality is a normal expression of human sexuality; the vast majority of gays and lesbians have little or no choice in their sexual orientation; and therapeutic efforts to change an individual's sexual orientation have not been shown to be effective and instead pose a risk of harm to the individual."[8] Whereas the witnesses for the defense were largely discredited in *Perry*, the plaintiffs' expert witnesses emerged with expert testimony that was tested and victorious. Many of the plaintiffs' expert witnesses would go on to submit written testimony in a variety of marriage equality cases over the subsequent three years.

Plaintiffs Perry and Stier testified that they felt demeaned by the Yes on Proposition 8 campaign. They testified about their love and commitment for each other and about the importance of marriage to them.

Ryan Kendall, a lay witness (i.e., not an expert witness or a government official but simply a citizen) for the plaintiffs, testified about the damage that antigay conversion therapy had done to him personally as a young gay man whose parents had rejected him. This last point had personal significance for Judge Walker. It turned out that the judge was a closeted gay man who had subjected himself to a similar kind of therapy when he was young and was trying not to be attracted to other men.

Judge Walker was outed as a gay man after the *Perry* trial had concluded. The Proposition 8 defense legal team asked that his ruling be vacated and the trial redone because, they said, Walker should have recused himself from the case. Proposition 8 proponents appealed to the Ninth Circuit Court of Appeals to have a different judge assigned, but the request was refused. Judges need to recuse themselves when they have a conflict of interest, e.g., if the defendant in the case is a company the judge has invested money in or if the judge's immediate family is involved or if the judge used to be a coworker with a lawyer participating in the case. Black judges hear civil rights cases. Female judges are not forced to recuse themselves from cases about abortion rights. The Ninth Circuit decided that a gay judge could hear a case about gay rights and decide that case impartially.[9]

Judge Walker's *Perry* decision, that Proposition 8 was unconstitutional, was the first federal judicial decision on the constitutionality of bans against same-sex marriage. In his decision, Walker noted that the campaign for Proposition 8 was based on television advertisements that spread falsehoods, including that "denial of marriage to same-sex couples protects children" and "the ideal child-rearing environment requires one male parent and one female parent." He evaluated the plaintiffs' witnesses as highly credible, but he found the defense witnesses to be generally lacking in credibility:

> Proposition 8 singles out gays and lesbians and legitimates their unequal treatment. Proposition 8 perpetuates the stereotype that gays and lesbians are incapable of forming long-term loving relationships and that gays and lesbians are not good parents. . . .
>
> Children raised by gay or lesbian parents are as likely as children raised by heterosexual parents to be healthy, successful, and well-adjusted. The research supporting this conclusion is accepted beyond serious debate in the field of developmental psychology. . . .
>
> The Proposition 8 campaign relied on fears that children exposed to the concept of same-sex marriage may become gay or lesbian. . . . The Proposition 8 campaign relied on stereotypes to show that same-sex relationships are inferior to opposite-sex relationships.[10]

The proponents of Proposition 8 appealed. Judge Walker's trial decision was stayed pending appeal, meaning that Proposition 8 remained in effect until appeals had run their course.[11] As Jerry Brown had succeeded Arnold Schwarzenegger as governor of California, the appeal was named *Perry v. Brown* (2012). The Ninth Circuit Court of Appeals affirmed the trial court decision in favor of the plaintiffs but narrowed Judge Walker's decision in a way that might apply only to California. The defenders of Proposition 8 appealed to the U.S. Supreme Court, which granted *Cert* and agreed to hear the case, then named *Hollingsworth v. Perry* (2013).

President Barack Obama had come out in support of marriage equality in the spring of 2012, and then had been reelected in November 2012. By 2013 the Obama administration's position on marriage equality was consistently positive. One ramification of Obama's support of marriage equality in 2013 was that the solicitor general of the United States, the lawyer who represents the U.S. government before the Supreme Court, wrote a friend-of-the-court brief in support of overturning Proposition 8.

The U.S. Supreme Court decided *Hollingsworth v. Perry* on the narrow grounds that Hollingsworth and the other defendant intervenors did not have standing to make the appeal since they were not official representatives of the state of California. Judge Walker's sweeping trial decision that Proposition 8 was unconstitutional was the controlling decision, so Proposition 8 was struck down.[12]

The *Hollingsworth v. Perry* decision was made public on June 26, 2013. Decisions by the U.S. Supreme Court sometimes do not take effect immediately because time is allowed for rarely used procedural appeals and rehearings. The Ninth Circuit and the attorney general of California, Kamala Harris, however, were ready to move quickly. On June 28, a three judge panel of the Ninth Circuit lifted the stay of Judge Walker's trial decision, which meant Proposition 8 was invalid and same-sex couples could marry in California. That same day in San Francisco's beautiful City Hall, Attorney General Harris presided over the wedding of Kristin Perry and Sandra Stier, with news cameras flashing all around them. Marriage equality had come, finally and permanently, after years of struggle, to California.

Sandy Stier (center) and Kris Perry (right) exchange marriage vows in front of California's attorney general Kamala Harris in San Francisco City Hall, June 28, 2013, two days after the resolution of *Hollingsworth v. Perry* made California a marriage equality state. AP Photo by Marcio Jose Sanchez, used with permission.

U.S. v. Windsor

The U.S. Supreme Court has a long history of trying not to be too far ahead of the states or too far ahead of public opinion, for a variety of reasons, starting with the Supreme Court's reliance on the states and federal government for enforcement of decisions.[13] At the time of the *Hollingsworth v. Perry* decision, same-sex marriage was legal in only twelve states (Connecticut, Delaware, Iowa, Maine, Maryland, Massachusetts, Minnesota, New Hampshire, New York, Rhode Island, Vermont, and Washington) plus the District of Columbia, meaning thirty-eight states, including California, still had bans against same-sex marriage.[14]

Thinking of the states as the laboratories of democracy, the U.S. Supreme Court usually prefers to wait until a majority of the states have adopted a social change before imposing that change on the remaining states. So it was with the watershed *Loving v. Virginia* (1967) decision that invalidated bans on interracial marriage in the seventeen states that still had such bans. And so it had been with the *Lawrence v. Texas* (2003) decision that had invalidated sodomy laws in the fourteen states that still criminalized sodomy.[15] Because thirty-eight states still banned same-sex marriage, the informal Court tradition of respecting the established laws of the majority of states meant that 2013 was too early to impose marriage equality on the remaining states. But the number of states that banned same-sex marriage was about to plunge, so that by 2015, when *Obergefell v. Hodges* was argued in the Court, thirty-six states had marriage equality and only fourteen still banned same-sex marriage.[16]

The second same-sex marriage decision issued by the Court in June 2013 was *U.S. v. Windsor*; it involved a challenge to the federal government's ban on recognizing same-sex married couples, which had been enacted in the Defense of Marriage Act of 1996. Edith Windsor was a widow, whose wife and long-time companion, Thea Spyer, had been diagnosed with multiple sclerosis (MS). In 2007, Spyer was dying of MS, so she and Windsor flew to Canada to get married in order to get their legal arrangements in order and to fulfill a promise to each other that they would one day marry. New York, where the couple lived, did not adopt marriage equality until 2011. The couple had been engaged, they liked to say, since 1967.[17] Windsor was a partly closeted lesbian. She had participated in some gay rights activism over the years but had never told her coworkers she was partnered with a woman.

When Windsor married the dying Spyer in Canada, the marriage was a public act that made the news and made Windsor an out-of-the-closet lesbian to everyone. When Spyer died in 2009, Windsor stood to inherit Spyer's estate, but there was a problem. Spouses in the U.S. generally do not pay estate tax on inheritance from each other, but because of DOMA, the U.S. government did not recognize Spyer and Windsor's Canadian marriage and so treated Spyer and Windsor not as spouses but as strangers. Strangers have to pay estate tax on inheritance. In Windsor's case, the estate tax bill from the federal government amounted to $363,053. The government's lack of recognition of same-sex marriages denied same-sex couples more than a thousand federal benefits and legal remedies and protections, of which tax-free inheritance from spouses was but one. Windsor paid the estate taxes, and then sued the U.S. government to overturn DOMA. Windsor, a petite senior citizen who had been a quiet technology manager at IBM for decades, became, in her eighties, an outspoken activist for marriage equality.

The full name of the case, *Edith Schlain Windsor v. the United States of America* (2012), made Windsor a little nervous, as Windsor herself was quite small and the United States of America was considerably larger. The first important piece of news in the case in the spring of 2012 was that President Obama and U.S. Attorney General Eric Holder had decided not to defend DOMA in court. So the court certified a group of Congress members, the Bipartisan Legislative Advisory Group (BLAG), to defend DOMA.

Roberta Kaplan, lead attorney for Windsor, contacted the same all-star academic cast who had been expert witnesses for the plaintiffs in *Perry v. Schwarzenegger* and asked them to submit amicus briefs for *Windsor*. Because Judge Walker had evaluated these expert witnesses as highly credible and persuasive, their testimony was now even more sought-after. Professor Cott (one of the nation's leading historians of marriage and family life), Professor Chauncey (author of the groundbreaking history *Gay New York*), and Professors Peplau, Segura, and Lamb all submitted amicus briefs. Lamb's work was important in reasserting the scholarly consensus that same-sex couples were raising healthy and well-adjusted children. BLAG did not have any credible experts at their disposal to counter the learned submissions of these professors.

Federal District Judge Barbara Jones decided *Windsor v. U.S.* in plaintiff Windsor's favor. BLAG, the defenders of DOMA, appealed, and Windsor won again in the U.S. Second Circuit Court of Appeals,[18] and then both sides appealed to the U.S. Supreme Court, which granted *Cert* to hear the case, *U.S. v. Windsor* (2013).

Kaplan brought Mary Bonauto of GLAD and Stanford Law professor Pamela Karlan on to Windsor's legal team in preparation for the Supreme Court oral arguments. In their written arguments to the Court, Windsor's legal team reminded the justices of the things Congress had said, on the record, while passing DOMA in 1996. The congressional report on DOMA had specified that refusing federal recognition of same-sex marriage reflected their "moral disapproval of homosexuality." One representative had declared that homosexuality "is based on perversion, that is based on lust." At the oral arguments before the Court on March 27, 2013, liberal justice Elena Kagan asked the lawyer for BLAG if DOMA was an expression of Congress's "moral disapproval of homosexuality." The lawyer had to admit that it was so, and he said, "[I]f that [the animus of the 1996 Congress against homosexuality] is enough to invalidate the statute [DOMA], then you should invalidate the statute." The apparent discriminatory intent of the members of Congress who supported DOMA made it more difficult for the BLAG team to argue that DOMA was an entirely rational and fair policy. Sitting at the counsel table in the Supreme Court, hearing the BLAG lawyer's reply to Justice Kagan, Kaplan thought to herself, "[W]e just won."[19]

Windsor won her case in the U.S. Supreme Court, by 5 to 4. However, the *U.S. v. Windsor* decision struck down only the part of DOMA that related to federal recognition of same-sex marriages legally entered into in the states or in other countries. States that had bans on same-sex marriage were allowed to retain those bans (and were allowed not to recognize same-sex marriages from other states) for the time being because another part of DOMA remained intact. Justice Anthony Kennedy wrote the opinion for the court's majority:

> The history of DOMA's enactment and its own text demonstrate that interference with the equal dignity of same-sex marriages, a dignity conferred by the States in their exercise of sovereign power, was more than an incidental effect of the federal statute. It was its essence. . . .
>
> DOMA's principal effect is to identify a subset of state-sanctioned marriages and make them unequal. . . . This places same-sex couples in an unstable position of being in a second-tier marriage. The differentiation demeans the couple, whose moral and sexual choices the Constitution protects. . . . And it [DOMA] humiliates tens of thousands of children now being raised by same-sex couples. The law in question makes it even more difficult for the children to understand the integrity and closeness of their own family and its concord with the other families in their community and in their daily lives. . . .
>
> The federal statute [DOMA] is invalid, for no legitimate purpose overcomes the purpose and effect to disparage and injure those whom the State, by its marriage laws, sought to protect in personhood and dignity.[20]

Justice Scalia, the Court's most vocal opponent of gay rights, dissented from the majority decision, writing, "By formally declaring anyone opposed to same-sex marriage an enemy of human decency, the majority arms well every challenger to a state law restricting marriage to its traditional definition."[21]

As Scalia had predicted, Kennedy's *U.S. v. Windsor* decision, along with the federal courts' restoration of marriage equality in California, led to a flood of federal court challenges to same-sex marriage bans in the various states. In the immediate aftermath of the *Windsor* decision, with Obama's support for marriage equality and the four marriage equality referenda victories in 2012 in the rearview mirror, and national approval of marriage equality crossing the 50% threshold for the first time, state bans on same-sex marriage started to fall like dominoes.

11

April, Jayne, and Their Children

April DeBoer and Jayne Rowse are two Michigan nurses whose families of origin were White, working class, midwestern, conservative, and downwardly
mobile. April's father was an ex-marine with a difficult temper. In high school
in St. Clair Shores, half an hour northeast of Detroit, April had an idea that
she was attracted to women, but being lesbian was not a practical reality for
anyone she knew at the time. When she was twenty-two, she married a young
man with a motorcycle and a drinking problem. April and her husband were
married for five years, but she was unhappy and saw herself falling into a
pattern of unhappy marriages that she recognized from her extended family
growing up. April's father, who had spent most of his retirement savings on
her wedding, told her that she would be better off walking away from her
husband. Both of her parents helped her pay for the divorce. At age twenty-
nine, April was on her own and looking for a new start in life.

Jayne Rowse was the youngest of six children, raised in the small southern
Indiana town of Ellettsville. Her father was a truck driver who overextended
his trucking business and then had health problems which put his business in
jeopardy. Jayne remembers her family of origin going through difficult times.
As a child, she had pushed some gender boundaries in her small town by
playing Little League baseball with the boys. Young Jayne had relatives who
were prominent in the small town, and they helped to calm the Little League
controversy. By the time she was in high school, Jayne knew she was a lesbian.

Suspicious of Jayne's social life, her father followed her one day to figure
out who she was hanging around with, and then he confronted her. Jayne told
her father she was attracted to women. Her parents were not supportive of her
being a lesbian, and when Jayne went away to college at Indiana University,
her parents refused to pay, so Jayne worked to pay for her own college education, relishing her geographic and social independence.[1]

Jayne was working as a reserve police officer in 1999 when she first met
April, who was then separated from her husband and dating a man, a coworker of Jayne's. April and Jayne were both thinking of getting out of their
current jobs and starting nursing school. They met, flirted a bit, and went

The Rainbow after the Storm. Michael J. Rosenfeld, Oxford University Press. © Oxford University Press 2022.
DOI: 10.1093/oso/9780197600436.003.0011

on a couple of dates, but nothing came of it right away. April started nursing school a year ahead of Jayne. They remained friends through nursing school; April graduated in 2004, and Jayne in 2005. They both got jobs at the same Detroit area hospital, and they became a couple.

In 2006, April moved in with Jayne, who owned her own home in the suburbs outside of Detroit, and they started thinking about children. Jayne had always wanted children, but she and April found the adoption process difficult and expensive. April tried artificial insemination and became pregnant with triplets, but lost the triplets in a miscarriage in 2007. If their artificial insemination plan had produced children, April and Jayne might never have adopted children. If they had never adopted children, they would not have found themselves facing off against the governor and the attorney general of Michigan in federal court in Detroit in 2012.

In February 2008, April and Jayne held a small commitment ceremony with thirty guests inside a handicrafts store run by a friend. April's parents were there, and some of Jayne's relatives drove up from southern Indiana. It was an intimate gathering, with a friend as photographer. April and Jayne considered themselves to be married from that moment forward, but the state of Michigan took a different view.

The Children

By late 2009, April and Jayne had been through several failed attempts at adopting children. One woman was going to let them adopt her child, but changed her mind after the child was born. April and Jayne were scammed out of $5,000 by another woman who claimed to be pregnant but was not. April and Jayne's personal adoption fund had been depleted. They were exhausted. One day in January 2009 they received a phone call from a coworker at the hospital whose family member was seeking to give their child up for adoption. April and Jayne met the mother, and after a thirty-minute conversation the mother told them that they could raise her baby. They brought Nolan home, and in November 2010 Jayne adopted him. Aside from a little bit of acid reflux, Nolan was healthy.

Nolan was adopted by Jayne as a single person rather than by April and Jayne together because Michigan adoption law refers to adoptions being carried out by individual persons or by persons together with their spouse.[2] Because of the Michigan Marriage Amendment of 2004, April and Jayne could not be recognized as married in that state. In Michigan law, April and Jayne were strangers who happened to live together. Nolan was Jayne's child, and if Jayne were to pass away, it would be up to family court to decide who would have custody of him.

Before Jayne adopted Nolan, she and April had had developed a family policy that they were open to taking care of foster children, including children with disabilities. If a foster child needed parents, they would consider adopting the child. "We didn't find them, they found us," Jayne recalls.[3]

Jacob was born at twenty-five weeks (i.e., fifteen weeks premature) in November 2009 in the neonatal intensive care unit where April worked. He weighed 1 pound, 9 ounces. Jacob was born with marijuana, cocaine, opiates, and methadone in his system, and he spent his first weeks hooked up to a ventilator. Then he went into liver failure. Jacob's mother, described in court documents as a "drug addicted prostitute," left the hospital after giving birth and never returned.[4] April used to sit by Jacob in the hospital, put her hand into his incubator, and feel his tiny fingers grasp her finger. She understood that he wanted to know that there was life outside the incubator, something warm and alive to hold onto. The doctors told April that Jacob would probably never live to go home from the hospital, and that if he did leave the hospital he was not likely to survive for long. And even if he did survive, the doctors said, April should expect that he might not be able to walk, speak, or function as normal. April made a promise to tiny neonatal Jacob: if he survived, she would take him home.

Originally the foster agency told April they would select someone else to be Jacob's foster parent, and April had accommodated herself to the idea that she might lose contact with him. But then the foster agency asked Jayne to foster Jacob. April took Jayne to the hospital to see Jacob. He was bronze colored and sickly looking, but when Jayne offered Jacob her hand, he grabbed it, and Jayne started to cry. April knew at that moment that Jacob was meant to be part of her family. The foster agency certified April and Jayne as foster parents to Jacob, so April took Jacob home, just as she had promised to do. Jayne filed papers to adopt Jacob, but his biological mother reappeared, and the adoption process dragged on for two years, until October 2011, when Jayne officially adopted Jacob. April and Jayne invested not only time and love but also occupational therapy, physical therapy, and speech therapy to promote Jacob's development.

Jacob's liver function returned, and he went on to be one of the happiest children April and Jayne had ever met. He went through a lot of physical struggles as an infant and then difficult physical therapy as a toddler, but he never stopped smiling. Despite the dire prognosis the doctors had given when he was struggling to stay alive in the neonatal intensive care unit, Jacob walks, speaks, and has developed normally. He loved preschool. One day April took him back to the hospital to meet the doctor who had originally told her that he would never walk, talk, or feed himself. The doctor looked Jacob up and down, amazed, and said, "There are only two things that could have saved that baby: God and a mother's love. Apparently he had both."

When Jacob first came home to live with April and Jayne, April had just adopted an African American girl named Ryanne. Ryanne started out as a foster child in April and Jayne's home. Her mother had not had any prenatal care, and as an infant she had some motor skill delays. Her foster placement with April and Jayne was supposed to be a temporary arrangement, but when her biological mother left Michigan and her biological father could not be found, April adopted her in 2011.

In both April's and Jayne's families of origin, when they heard talk of Black people, the talk was always negative, so there was no doubt in April's and Jayne's minds about the anti-Black prejudice of their parents and extended families. The only real question was how deep the prejudice went. There had also been no shortage of antigay bias in their families of origin, but April and Jayne had been an out lesbian couple for years, and both sides of the family had come to accept them as a couple. April and Jayne had, through the example of their stable relationship, their self-sufficient finances, and their selfless maturity, served as a positive example to many of their struggling relatives.

As April prepared to adopt Ryanne, she had to consider whether her parents would accept a Black grandchild. Initially, April and Jayne had specified that they would consider adopting only White children because they did not want any child of theirs to face discrimination from within their extended families, but neither woman felt right about racial exclusivity. Both had grown accustomed to living by their own rules. They had had such a difficult time having children that they did not feel right turning any child away, certainly not because of race. Nolan was biracial, but he looked White. Ryanne was very clearly Black. April called her father:

"Look: there is no way you can pass her off for anything but African American. So this is how this is going to happen. You are going to treat her exactly like you treat the rest of them. You are going to put her picture up when she comes over. If you take it down when she leaves, that's your pre-rogative. You will hold her, you will buy her gifts. You will love her. You will never say in front of her that she's your *adopted* grandchild."

"Well, I don't do that now," said April's father.

"This is different," April said. "There is no passing this child off as any-thing other than what she is. And if you can't accept those terms, then you will not be part of any of our lives."

It took him a few months of being around the kids before April's father was ready to pick Ryanne up, but over time he came to love Ryanne. April's mother, by then divorced from April's father, rallied right away to love and support her Black granddaughter.

With three children under two years old, April and Jayne needed a bigger house. In 2010, they bought a house in Hazel Park, a working-class suburb located on the northern border of Detroit, and closer to April's family. Hazel Park seemed to have some diversity, and the house was big enough and not too expensive.

April, Jayne, Nolan, Jacob, and Ryanne were a family in a very modern and nontraditional way: same-sex couple parents raising adopted children of dif-ferent races. Because Michigan law treated April and Jayne as an unmarried couple, they and their children were not legally a family.

The Near-Miss Car Accident

Sometime in 2011, April, Jayne, Nolan, Jacob, and Ryanne were traveling in a van from Ohio back to their home in Michigan. It was a snowy afternoon, and their GPS system had put them on a lonely, two-lane road. Suddenly a truck appeared in their lane, passing the car going the other direction. The road had no shoulder. There was no way to avoid the collision. April and Jayne braced for impact, but at the last moment, instead of hitting them head-on, the truck swerved off the road and came to rest in an empty field. The truck passed so close that the air pushed by the truck shook their van. April and Jayne drove on in shock until they could gather their composure.

When they finally pulled their van over and could have a conversation, they took stock of their situation. If either of them were to pass away, the children could end up in different places because April had no legal rela-tionship to Jacob and Nolan, and Jayne had no legal relationship to Ryanne.

April and Jayne realized that their family was legally fragile, and they needed a remedy.

Michigan attorney Dana Nessel had been posting on online discussion boards for adoptive parents. When April and Jayne met with her in March 2011, she explained how precarious their situation was. Nessel could write guardianship agreements so that April and Jayne could each be the legal guardian of all three children. But even if a judge approved the agreements, guardianships are reviewed every year in Michigan. A future judge could easily revoke the arrangement. Nessel suggested that April and Jayne move to another state with more favorable marriage or adoption laws, or at least buy a second house in another state to establish residency there. But April and Jayne could not afford a second house, and they both had good jobs in Michigan and substantial expenses in taking care of the children.

April and Jayne talked to attorneys from the American Civil Liberties Union of Michigan, who advised them that they could attempt to go to court, renounce the children, and try to readopt them as a couple. There apparently was at least one Michigan judge from the liberal Ann Arbor area who had been willing to allow unmarried couples to jointly adopt children, but it was not clear whether those judgments would stand up to appeal or review.[5] April and Jayne found this advice to be anathema. They were absolutely unwilling to renounce the children, even if renunciation was just a legal technicality. They assumed that renouncing the children would be held against them in any future court proceeding.

The Beginnings of a Lawsuit

The children needed two legal parents instead of one. April and Jayne wanted to cross-adopt their children, but Michigan law prevented them from doing so. The law seemed to allow only married couples to jointly adopt or to adopt each other's children as second parents. April and Jayne were prevented from marrying by the Michigan Marriage Amendment of 2004, a voter referendum that had changed the state constitution to ban same-sex marriage.[6] In January 2012, they and their three children sued Governor Richard Snyder and Attorney General Bill Schuette (in their official capacities) in federal court in Detroit, attempting to overturn Michigan's ban on unmarried couples adopting each other's children. It was important to April and Jayne that their three children were also plaintiffs in the case, as it was the children's need to have two legal parents that was the core of the lawsuit. The case of *DeBoer v. Snyder* was born.[7] Nessel took on assistance from Michigan attorneys Carole Stanyar and Kenneth Mogill and Wayne State law professor Robert Sedler.

Federal lawsuits are expensive and time-consuming undertakings. Ordinarily in U.S. law, each party pays the cost of their own attorneys, but there are exceptions. Federal law allows courts to award attorneys' fees in civil rights cases to lawyers for the prevailing parties.[8] Attorneys can take civil rights[9] clients who cannot afford to pay for complex litigation and, if they prevail in the case, bill the defendants for their lawyers' fees. In the case of *DeBoer v. Snyder*, the state of Michigan would pay the plaintiffs' attorneys on the governor's and attorney general's behalf if and when April and Jayne ultimately prevailed. Before April and Jayne's attorneys could hope to get paid, they needed to fundraise for their own expenses for the four years that it would take to litigate the case to its final conclusion. If April and Jayne lost their case, their attorneys would not be paid.

April and Jayne had been active in foster parent and adoption organizations. However, those organizations were unhappy with how the lawyers' January 2012 complaint described Jacob's biological mother as a "drug-addicted prostitute." In the foster and adoption communities, it is frowned upon to call out biological parents for drug use or for stigmatized behaviors because that might discourage future biological parents from coming forward to put their children up for adoption. That's why, as the *DeBoer v. Snyder* case commenced, April and Jayne lacked institutional allies.

In January 2012, *DeBoer v. Snyder* was a narrow case, dealing only with Michigan's law on second-parent adoption. In the summer of 2012, U.S. District Court Judge Bernard Friedman, who was presiding over the case, suggested in a hearing with both sides' lawyers that Michigan's adoption law was probably consistent with the U.S. Constitution. Friedman added, however, that if the plaintiffs (April and Jayne and their children) wanted to amend their complaint to challenge the constitutionality of the Michigan Marriage Amendment, that case would have better prospects. In September 2012, April and Jayne's attorneys filed an amended complaint, challenging the constitutionality of the Michigan Marriage Amendment.[10]

Once April and Jayne's case became about the constitutionality of the Michigan Marriage Amendment, the case had national implications, and April and Jayne started to be covered by the local news. The children would be sitting in their living room and arguing about something, and someone would say "Mom's on TV again!" and everyone would quiet down. Four-year-old Jacob would see himself on TV and say "Hey, that's me," and then go back to doing whatever he was doing. April and Jayne found that neighbors they had never met would come up to them in a local pizza place, press a few dollars into their hands for their legal expenses, and say "I'm really supporting you. Can I just give you five bucks?" April and Jayne would give the money to Nessel, who was struggling to pay the bills for their legal expenses.

Some people they met out in public were hostile to their marriage-equality lawsuit. April recalls, "Most people don't recognize us unless the ducklings are followed in a row behind us, so I think most people had enough respect, if they disagreed, not to say anything in front of the kids."

Jayne added, "I also think the thing that won more people over was that it was about the kids. That was the issue, and why this was important to us, and . . . that these kids did not have protections of two parents, and what if something happened. . . . You could sympathize with the kids."

April DeBoer, Jayne Rowse, and their three children, Ryanne, Jacob, and Nolan (left to right) in March 2013, eleven months before the *DeBoer v. Snyder* trial. AP Photo by Paul Sancya, used with permission.

Between September 2012 and October 2013, the plaintiffs' attorneys traded motions and responses and countermotions with the Office of the Attorney General of Michigan, Bill Schuette. In October 2013, both sides in *DeBoer v. Snyder* were waiting for a decision from Judge Friedman. Friedman's decision surprised both sides. Instead of deciding the case based only on the legal briefs, he called for a trial to settle the conflicting claims the two sides made about the impact of same-sex marriage on children.

12

On Children's Outcomes

Protecting children is a universal value and an important state interest. When opponents of same-sex marriage argued that the state should prevent same-sex couples from being allowed to marry, protecting the children (from being raised by same-sex couples) was their core rationale. The opponents of same-sex marriage argued that same-sex couples would so harm the children under their care that the state had a compelling interest in preventing the couples from being able to marry and raise children. This chapter reviews one part of the evidence about children's outcomes when raised by same-sex couples, evidence that played a role in the *DeBoer v. Snyder* trial.

The Data: The 2000 U.S. Census Public Use Files

One of the challenges in attempting to study children raised by same-sex couples is that they are a needle-in-a-haystack population.[1] The low rate of children being raised by same-sex couples meant most random surveys, even if they asked the right kind of questions, would not turn up a large enough sample size of children raised by same-sex couples to study meaningfully.

The decennial census in the U.S. is a survey of all Americans. The public use records of the 2000 U.S. census included 5% of the U.S. population, i.e., information on 15 million individuals (stripped of names and other identifying information). This enormous sample size meant that small minority populations, including children raised by same-sex couples, were represented in substantial numbers. If one wants to find a large number of needles in the haystack, one should start with the biggest possible haystack, and that is what the 2000 U.S. census public use files were: the biggest possible population haystack.

For the analysis here, if a child was in the correct grade for their age, they were making good progress in school. If a child was one or more years older than the average age for their grade, they must have been held back to repeat a grade. Being held back in elementary school is strongly associated with later

The Rainbow after the Storm. Michael J. Rosenfeld, Oxford University Press. © Oxford University Press 2022. DOI: 10.1093/oso/9780197600436.003.0012

failure to complete a high school degree, which is in turn strongly associated with a broad array of problems in adulthood. Family stress or dysfunction can contribute to children's lack of readiness for school.[2] Parental education, household income, race, metropolitan residence (i.e., urban versus suburban versus rural), and gender of the child all are associated with children's school performance. We also know that the *quality* of the relationships between the parents and the quality of the relationships between the parents and the children in each household matter to children's performance. There are, unfortunately, no measures of relationship quality in the census data.

Table 12.1, adapted from Rosenfeld (2010), shows the crude differences in the percentage of elementary school children who had ever been held back in school, and whether those differences are statistically significant, before and after controlling for the other factors that we know affect children's school performance.

According to Table 12.1, among the different family types, children being raised by heterosexual married couples had the lowest rate of ever being held back in school, at 6.8%. Children raised by same-sex couples had a higher rate (9.6%). The difference in grade attainment between the children raised by heterosexual married couples and the children raised by same-sex couples was small, 9.6% – 6.8% = 2.8%, meaning the average grade accomplished by the children of the same age in the two family-structure groups differed by less than 3% of one year of school. Because the 2000 U.S. census public use files had such an enormous sample size, even a small difference such as this can be and is statistically significant, meaning we are relatively certain that in the U.S. as a whole, children raised by same-sex couples in the 1990s had slightly worse progress through school compared to children raised by heterosexual married couples.

Quantifying differences is only the beginning of sociological studies of human outcomes. The more important part of analyses is *explaining* observed differences. In the case of the same-sex couples who were raising children in the 1990s, the parents were substantially more likely to have low or modest income and substantially more likely to be from racial minority groups. We know, with complete certainty, that parental socioeconomic status has a strong predictive effect on children's educational progress in the U.S. and elsewhere. Furthermore, the racial gaps in school achievement in the U.S. are well established, of long standing, and pernicious. There is a strong history of racial segregation in the U.S. that builds disadvantages into minority communities and segregates public schools by race.[3]

Table 12.1 What Factors Affect Children's Progress through Primary School?

	% of students held back in grades 1–8	Is the difference in the reference category statistically significant?	Does the difference remain significant after other key factors are accounted for?
Family Type			
Heterosexual married (reference)	6.8	—	—
Same-sex couple	**9.6**	yes	**no**
Single women	11.1	yes	yes
Single men	11.4	yes	yes
Heterosexual cohabit	11.7	yes	yes
Orphanages/group quarters	34.4	yes	yes
Inmates	78.0	yes	yes
Child's Relationship to Householder			
Own child (reference)	7.4	—	—
Adopted child	10.6	yes	yes
Stepchild	13.9	yes	yes
Foster child	20.6	yes	yes
Child's Race			
Asian American	5.8	yes	yes
Non-Hispanic White (reference)	6.8	—	—
Hispanic	9.0	yes	yes
Non-Hispanic Black	12.6	yes	yes
Household Income (US$ 1999)			
>100,000 (reference)	5.3	—	—
50,000–99,999	6.1	yes	yes
25,000–49,999	8.7	yes	yes
<25,000	12.6	yes	yes
Child's Gender			
Female (reference)	6.5	—	—
Male	9.0	yes	yes
Metro Status			
Suburban (reference)	6.0	—	—
Urban	8.6	yes	yes
Rural	10.3	yes	yes
Householder's Education			
BA+ (reference)	4.4	—	—
Some college	6.3	yes	yes
HS degree	8.7	yes	yes
<HS	14.3	yes	yes

Source: Rosenfeld, *Demography*, 2010. U.S. Census 2000 microdata, via IPUMS, percentages reflect census weights. Statistical significance derived from weighted logistic regressions, see Rosenfeld (2010).

All children had been living in the same place with the same parents for at least five years. Children include "natural-born children," stepchildren, adopted children and foster children. The "other key factors" that are controlled for in the last column include parental income, parental education, child race, child disability, child gender, and state of residence. For children in group quarters or prisons, no parental information is known, so their comparison to other children is net of race, disability, gender, and state.

After controlling for household income and race, the 2.8% difference in the grade attainment of the two groups disappeared. The last column of Table 12.1 shows no significant difference between children raised by same-sex couples and children raised by heterosexual married couples, after other factors (including race and family income) have been taken into account.

Heterosexual married parents in the 1990s in the U.S. enjoyed the thousand legal benefits and privileges of marriage as well as the elevated social status that few of the same-sex couple parents enjoyed, since the U.S. government and most states and localities did not recognize same-sex unions then. It is especially interesting that, even without having the legal benefits of marriage to provide for their children, same-sex couples raised their children to have school progress that was statistically indistinguishable from similarly situated children raised by heterosexual married couples.

Progress through School Compared to Children from Other Types of Households

Unmarried heterosexual couples were situated similarly to same-sex couples in the 1990s, as neither family type enjoyed the legal benefits of marriage. Table 12.1 shows that the children raised by same-sex couples were *less* likely to have been held back in school compared to children raised by unmarried heterosexual couples (9.6% compared to 11.7%).

The 9.6% grade retention rate (i.e., the percentage of students who have been held back to repeat a grade) for children raised by same-sex couples was much lower than the 34.4% grade retention rate for children living under the care of the state in orphanages and shelters (in census terminology, "group quarters"), and much lower than the 20.6% rate for foster children. The comparison to foster children and children under the care of the state is important because those are children who are often available for adoption. April DeBoer and Jayne Rowse adopted children who would otherwise have been in foster care or under the care of the state. Children raised by same-sex couples were doing dramatically better in school compared to foster children and children in group quarters.

Among the other predictors of children's progress through school listed in Table 12.1, note that household income had a dramatic effect, as did race (Asian American children had the best progress through school, i.e., the lowest rate of having been held back), metropolitan status (children in the suburbs were most likely to be making good progress through school, while children in rural America were the least likely to be making good progress), and parental education. All of these predictors of children's progress through school remained significant after the other predictors were taken into account (see the last column of Table 12.1).

The Fallacy of the Optimality Standard

In the *DeBoer v. Snyder* trial, described in the next chapter, the expert witnesses who opposed same-sex marriage argued that same-sex couples should be denied the right to marry if it was even *possible* that their children would have worse outcomes compared to children raised by heterosexual married couples.[4] The idea that only the most "optimal" families should enjoy legal rights is advanced by some opponents of same-sex marriage. Michael Wald (2006) has referred to this idea in the context of adoption rights as the Optimality Standard.

If the Optimality Standard were applied broadly to the right to marry in the U.S., then poor people would not be allowed to marry since the children of well-to-do families have (on average) better outcomes. Urban and rural couples would not be allowed to marry, since suburban children have (on average) the best progress through school. Furthermore, White couples and Black couples would not be allowed to marry since Asian children have (on average) better progress through school than White children or Black children. If the Optimality Standard were applied to marriage rights, only high-income suburban Asian people with PhDs would be allowed to marry, since they would be the optimal family in terms of children's school outcomes. No reasonable person has ever suggested that rural people or poor people or White people in the U.S. should be excluded from marriage. We do not apportion rights in the U.S. according to the Optimality Standard.

Far from preventing poor people from marrying as the Optimality Standard would require, the U.S. government has spent hundreds of millions of dollars *encouraging* poor people to marry on the reasonable and fundamentally conservative theory that marriage would increase their couple stability and thereby improve the environment for their children. The U.S. government's marriage promotion programs seem not to have worked,[5] but the resources poured into promoting marriage to poor people demonstrate that marriage is not a right that the U.S. government has sought to withhold from disadvantaged groups.[6]

The irony of the opponents of same-sex marriage making arguments based on the Optimality Standard is that, as Table 12.1 shows, same-sex couples *were* optimal in the 2000 U.S. census data, as their children had progress in school that was just as good as the heterosexual married couples' children of the same race and the same socioeconomic status, even though same-sex couples and their children were at a very substantial disadvantage in legal rights.

13

The *DeBoer v. Snyder* Trial, 2014

In the history of same-sex marriage litigation, there had been scores of cases but only two trials before *DeBoer v. Snyder*: *Baehr v. Miike* (1996) in state court in Hawaii and *Perry v. Schwarzenegger* (2010) in federal court in California. In both the *Baehr* and *Perry* trials, conservative opponents of same-sex marriage had been defeated. Also in both trials, conservatives believed they lost because the states (Hawaii and California) had been insufficiently enthusiastic in their defense of same-sex marriage bans. Another story opponents of gay marriage told themselves was that their side had lost the *Perry* trial because the judge, Vaughn Walker, was gay.[1]

In contrast to *Baehr v. Miike* and *Perry v. Schwarzenegger*, the *DeBoer* trial promised to deliver what conservatives had always wanted but had never been able to obtain: a chance with the cards stacked in their favor to defeat same-sex marriage and to undermine the credibility of mainstream social science. First, Michigan attorney general Bill Schuette was a true conservative. Unlike California's Jerry Brown, Schuette was an opponent of gay rights and an energetic defender of the Michigan Marriage Amendment, which banned same-sex marriage.[2] Second, federal appeals from Michigan go to the Sixth Circuit Court of Appeals, which was one of the nation's more conservative federal appellate circuits in 2014. The Sixth Circuit had placed gay rights issues under the lowest level of scrutiny, the rational basis test, meaning the *DeBoer* trial would be held under ground rules most favorable to the state.

Third, the U.S. district court judge assigned to *DeBoer*, Bernard Friedman, was a White man in his seventies who had been appointed to the bench by Republican president Ronald Reagan. White men born before 1945 were a demographic group whose average support of gay rights was low compared to women and compared to people from more recent generations.[3] Fourth, conservative foundations had spent millions of dollars after the *Perry v. Schwarzenegger* loss to help produce new anti-gay-marriage scholarship. The circumstances of the *DeBoer* trial seemed to give the defendants (the governor and attorney general of Michigan) every possible advantage.

The Rainbow after the Storm. Michael J. Rosenfeld, Oxford University Press. © Oxford University Press 2022.
DOI: 10.1093/oso/9780197600436.003.0013

When Judge Friedman called in October 2013 for a trial, the attorneys for DeBoer and Rowse were stunned. Only about 3% of all civil rights federal cases in the U.S. are resolved through a trial.[4] Although the two sides in *DeBoer* had, through their legal briefs, made contrary claims about whether same-sex marriage would benefit or harm children, the plaintiffs' attorneys did not expect the judge to decide that the social science evidence was materially central to the case. Trials are necessary only when facts that are material to the resolution of the case are in dispute.

None of the plaintiffs' Michigan attorneys were experts in the social science on same-sex couples and their children, the themes around which the trial would turn. Michigan attorneys Carole Stanyar, Kenneth Mogill, and Dana Nessel had ample trial experience; they knew how to examine and cross-examine expert witnesses, how to manage trials, and how to present their cases in court. Their experience, however, was in criminal trials. As the trial excerpts indicate, however, by the time the trial started in February 2014, the local attorneys for DeBoer and Rowse had taught themselves enough of the social science to put the state's witnesses in real difficulty.

The attorney general of Michigan's office was also lacking in experts on social science. Unlike the plaintiffs' attorneys, however, the lawyers from the attorney general's office never educated themselves on the social science issues in question. If they had had a better grasp of social science and a better understanding of their own witnesses' fringe status within social science, they might have made different choices. They could have withheld some of their side's witnesses from appearing in person at the trial, as the defense lawyers had done in *Perry v. Schwarzenegger*.

After Judge Friedman's October 2013 order calling for a trial, Carole Stanyar (lead attorney for plaintiffs DeBoer and Rowse) worried about how to pay for it. Expert witnesses typically charge several hundred dollars per hour for preparation and delivery of their testimony. Unlike the plaintiffs' lawyers' hours, which could eventually be billed to the state if the plaintiffs' side in the case prevailed, payments to the plaintiffs' expert witnesses would have to come out of donations. Furthermore, the plaintiffs' attorneys were going to recover payment for time worked only *if* they prevailed in the case, and appeals might put the final resolution off for years. Because she was working nearly full time on the *DeBoer* case, Stanyar had had to turn away paying clients, and her income declined precipitously. Kenneth Mogill and Dana Nessel both had law partners to help keep some income flowing from their usual paying clients.

Fundraising for the plaintiffs' side in *DeBoer* was slow. With an expensive trial looming, the plaintiffs' side needed cash up front. Stanyar could find only one way to quickly fund the case: she sold her house to front the money for the plaintiffs' legal expenses. Attorney Stanyar was all in. Other attorneys I have talked to could not remember ever hearing of a lawyer who sold their own house to pay for a client's legal expenses. Eventually, Stanyar and the other plaintiffs' attorneys would be paid for their work on the *DeBoer* case, but Stanyar never got her house back.[5]

By calling for a trial, Judge Friedman was doing more than making extra work for the attorneys on both sides of the case. Trials are the vehicle for establishing facts in the legal context. As same-sex marriage cases were winding their way through the courts in dozens of states, and working their way up through the appeals process toward the U.S. Supreme Court, there were areas of fact, social science, and data interpretation that were in dispute. The *DeBoer* trial would help to establish a record that settled the facts about same-sex couples and their children.

The Tension between Local Attorneys and National Civil Rights Organizations

A natural tension exists between the civil rights organizations based at the national level and local attorneys such as Stanyar, Mogill, and Nessel who represent individual plaintiffs in civil rights cases. National civil rights organizations often discourage local attorneys from bringing suit because the organizations are afraid that a loss in any one case will create a precedent that will be a setback for similarly situated plaintiffs across the U.S.[6]

Because Michigan is in the conservative Sixth Circuit, the ACLU believed that even if DeBoer and Rowse won their case at the district court level (which they did), the Sixth Circuit Court of Appeals would be likely to reverse the decision and find in Michigan's favor (which it did). Then the case might go to the U.S. Supreme Court, and the ACLU was of the opinion that, in 2014, it was too early to press for a potentially final decision on marriage equality in the U.S. Supreme Court. A defeat there could potentially set the marriage equality movement back a decade or more. Stanyar remembers hearing a mixture of "It's too soon" and "You will lose it for everybody" and "You don't know what you are doing" from the national civil rights organizations.[7]

Once the trial in *DeBoer v. Snyder* was on the calendar, the local attorneys and the national civil rights organizations had to patch up their differences and work for a common goal. Leslie Cooper of the ACLU joined the plaintiffs' side and contributed specialized knowledge about same-sex couples and social science that the local Michigan attorneys had initially lacked. Mary Bonauto and Vickie Henry of Gay and Lesbian Advocates and Defenders also assisted the local Michigan attorneys.

Expert Witnesses in *DeBoer v. Snyder*

In November 2013, the attorney general of Michigan produced a witness list for their side of the trial; it included Douglas Allen, economist from Simon Fraser University; Joseph Price, economist from Brigham Young University; Loren Marks, child and family studies professor from Louisiana State University; and Mark Regnerus, sociologist from the University of Texas, Austin. Reading through the witnesses' published work, the plaintiffs' attorneys found an article by defense witnesses Allen and Price (Allen, Pakaluk, and Price 2013) in the journal *Demography* criticizing my analysis of census data about progress through school (Rosenfeld 2010), and they found my response to the critics (Rosenfeld 2013). Based on this published exchange, plaintiffs' attorney Mogill emailed me and asked me to be an expert witness for their side in the case. I agreed immediately. I donated my time to the *DeBoer* trial, charging the plaintiffs' attorneys only for reimbursement for my out-of-pocket travel expenses to go to Detroit and testify.

I had two roles to play in the *DeBoer* trial. First, I was to testify about my own research on children raised by same-sex couples; that was the easy part because I was of course familiar with my own research. Second, I was asked to explain the weaknesses of the state's witnesses' arguments, both to the plaintiffs' lawyers and to the judge.

The other experts for the plaintiffs were prominent social scientists with high-profile experience in prior gay rights cases. Historian Nancy Cott had previously testified in the *Perry v. Schwarzenegger* (2010) trial. Cott is the preeminent historian of marriage and the American family. Psychologist David Brodzinsky had testified in the *Baehr v. Miike* (1996) same-sex marriage trial and in several Florida same-sex couple adoption cases. Brodzinsky's combination of clinical experience working with children from all sorts of families and his research on children and adoption made him an especially compelling expert witness. In addition to studying data about children, Brodzinsky had made a career of working directly with children.

Prominent historian George Chauncey had organized historians' amicus briefs in the *Romer v. Evans* (1996) and *Perry v. Schwarzenegger* cases. Gary Gates was the leading demographer of gay and lesbian life in the U.S., and he had been involved in several cases before. Gates had devoted his research to scouring the available data in order to answer fundamental questions about the prevalence of same-sex couples and the number of children being raised by same-sex couples. As this was the first case I had ever been involved with, it was gratifying to be part of a team of scholars with such great academic reputations and important legal experience. We were jointly tasked with defending the social science consensus that being raised by same-sex couples does not impose any disadvantage on children.

The Social Science Consensus on Children Raised by Same-Sex Couples

For the 1996 *Baehr v. Miike* trial in Hawaii, the leading sociologists of the family in the U.S., Andrew Cherlin, Frank Furstenberg, Sara McLanahan, Gary Sandefur, and Lawrence Wu (Cherlin et al. 1996: 3), had reviewed the literature available at the time on same-sex parents and their children and they concluded in an amicus brief, "These findings suggest no systematic differences between gay or lesbian and heterosexual parents in parenting ability, quality of parent-child relationships, stability of home environments or patterns of child rearing. . . . [A]ll available evidence suggests that sexual orientation is irrelevant to an individual's or a couple's ability to establish and maintain optimal home environments for children."

By the time of the *DeBoer v. Snyder* trial in 2014, the scholarly literature on children raised by same-sex couples had expanded considerably. The vast majority of studies had found that children raised by same-sex couples fared well; these were the studies that the scholarly consensus was built upon. There were, however, a few studies that argued the scholarly consensus was wrong and that children raised by same-sex couples were at much higher risk for poor outcomes, potentially as a result of poor parenting. *DeBoer* state witnesses Regnerus, Allen, Price, and Marks were the key contributors to the conservative attack against the scholarly consensus.[8]

President Cecilia Ridgeway of the American Sociological Association (ASA; the professional organization of American sociologists) asked Wendy Manning to do the sociological research for an amicus brief to aid the U.S. Supreme Court in their 2013 deliberations in the *Perry* and *Windsor* same-sex marriage cases. Manning felt honored to be chosen by the ASA, and she also felt the weight of the responsibility of working on a project that might be more consequential than the typical sociology paper.[9]

Manning composed the social science parts of the brief, and the lawyers working with the ASA submitted their brief in February 2013. Manning's own research covered cohabitation, marriage, and parenting. Much of the literature on same-sex couples was new to her. A revised version of the ASA (2013) marriage equality amicus brief, which she researched, was entered into evidence in the *DeBoer* trial. The ASA brief noted, "The clear and consistent consensus in the social science profession is that across a wide range of indicators, children fare just as well when they are raised by same-sex parents when compared to children raised by opposite-sex parents."[10]

The ASA was not alone in its assertion. The American Psychological Association, the American Academy of Pediatrics, the American Medical Association, the American Psychiatric Association, the American Psychoanalytic Association, the National Association of Social Workers, and their local affiliates were all part of the scholarly consensus on same-sex couples and their children. The national organizations of scholars, doctors, and practitioners had joined together to submit an amicus brief in the *U.S. v. Windsor* (2013) case which supported the social science consensus, specifically: "There is no scientific basis for concluding that gay and lesbian parents are any less fit or capable than heterosexual parents, or that their children are any less psychologically healthy and well adjusted" (American Psychological Association et al. 2013: 22).

Thus the witnesses for the state of Michigan were locked in a battle against a broad set of national scholarly and professional associations, each of which had reviewed the literature and endorsed the scholarly consensus on the healthy outcomes of children raised by same-sex couples. In their pre-trial affidavits for *DeBoer*, the state's witnesses criticized the scholarly consensus in a variety of ways. Allen's (2013a) affidavit criticized the consensus as having been based mostly on "soft" measures of outcomes and for using mostly nonrepresentative samples. Regnerus's (2013) affidavit alleged that political correctness had stifled debate on same-sex marriage and children in the social sciences. In *DeBoer* not only was the constitutionality of the 2004

Michigan Marriage Amendment on trial, but the credibility of social science in general was also on trial.

The Curious Graphs of Dr. Allen

Expert affidavits (the witnesses' sworn written testimony) in *DeBoer v. Snyder* were due in Judge Friedman's court in December 2013.[11] The plaintiffs' lawyers subsequently sent me the state's witnesses' affidavits to review. Allen's affidavit contained figures that purported to represent the differences in and the uncertainty of measurement of grade attainment of children raised in different family structures, using data from the U.S. census. I knew the U.S. census data intimately, and when I looked at Allen's figures, I knew they were wrong: not just a little bit wrong, but wrong by a factor of between 10 and 100. It was difficult to imagine how Professor Allen could have generated figures that were so wrong.

When Allen, Pakaluk, and Price (2013) were preparing their critique of my paper in *Demography* which relied on data from the 2000 U.S. census, Joe Price emailed me asking for a copy of the census extract I had used, along with the programs necessary to replicate my published analyses. I sent him the data and the programs, because data sharing is the ideal norm in academia. Data sharing is not only the right thing to do, but it also has practical advantages. If we were going to have a debate, I wanted the debate to be substantive and based on data we had both analyzed. One key advantage of having shared my data with Allen, Pakaluk, and Price is that, just as they could replicate my results, I could replicate their results as well—if their results were based on the data.

The left panel of Figure 13.1 replicates a key figure from Allen's (2013a) pretrial affidavit. The point of Allen's affidavit, and his later testimony in court, was that there was too much uncertainty in the measure of the difference in grade attainment of children raised by same-sex couples in the U.S. census to allow same-sex marriage. The 95% confidence ellipse[12] in Allen's figure seems to show that, at age eight,[13] children raised by same-sex couples could have an average grade attainment of anywhere from one to four years, which is another way of saying that we actually know nothing about the grade attainment of children raised by same-sex couples. Allen argued that if we knew nothing about same-sex couples as parents, we should fear the worst. In fact, because the 2000 U.S. census data files were so enormous, the true

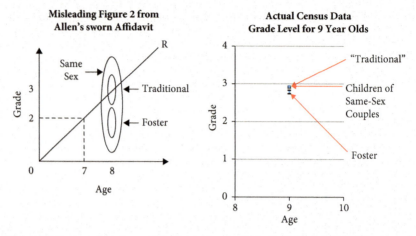

Figure 13.1 A comparison of defense witness Douglas Allen's (2013a) figure, on the left, showing unrealistically large differences and unrealistic uncertainties in grade attainment. On the right: the actual data.

Note: The grade scales are matched, as much as possible. In the right-hand figure, where actual weighted data from the 2000 U.S. census is used, the children of "Traditional" heterosexual married couples cannot be distinguished visibly from the children of same-sex couples because at this scale the points overlap and the 95% confidence intervals are, in fact, narrow because the U.S. census sample size is so large. Note that even at this scale, on the right-hand side (with the actual data) one can see that foster children fall outside the 95% confidence interval of grade for children raised by same-sex couples. The figure on the left is from Allen's affidavit. The data on the right-hand side come from actual census data, as described in Rosenfeld's (2014b) trial testimony slides, with children of "Traditional" heterosexual married families at 6.6% below third grade at age nine, children of same-sex couple families at 8.5% below third grade, and foster children at 21.5% below third grade. In Allen's expert report, he wrote misleadingly (at point #26) "What Rosenfeld actually found is represented in Figure 2."

95% confidence interval for grade attainment of children raised by same-sex couples was not a three-year range but rather one-seventieth as large, a range of 4% of one year.

Figure 13.1 compares Allen's figure, what he described as "what Rosenfeld actually found," to a proper data graph based on the census data of what I actually found, plotted on the same Y-axis scale. As you can see from the right-hand portion of the graph, the children of "traditional" (heterosexual married) families and the children of same-sex married parents were so close in grade attainment that at this scale those two points cannot be distinguished.[14] In Allen's figure, the center of the "traditional" ellipse looks to be at grade 3, and the center of the same-sex ellipse looks to be at approximately grade 2, a difference of a whole year, corresponding to an exaggeration of fifty times the real difference of 2%. In Allen's figure, the foster children are statistically indistinguishable from the children of same-sex couples because the ellipses overlap, whereas in the actual data the foster children performed significantly worse than the biological children raised by same-sex couples.

Studying Allen's graph for a few minutes and running the numbers myself, I came to the rapid conclusion that his figure was not based on the data at all; rather he had drawn the figure freehand. When I called the plaintiffs' attorneys to report that Allen's figures were not based on the data, they were incredulous.

A few weeks later, at Allen's pretrial deposition, plaintiffs' attorney Mogill was asking the questions, and Allen was under oath. The deposition is the opportunity for each side's attorneys to ask the other side's witnesses questions before the trial. One purpose of the deposition is for each side's attorneys to know what questions to ask at cross-examination during the trial and to know before the trial what the answers to those questions will be.[15] Mogill asked Allen if his figures were intended to be precise figures based on the data, and Allen said "No." Mogill then asked Allen if he had so indicated in his sworn affidavit. Allen again said "No."

Credibility is the stock-in-trade of expert witnesses. It is unheard of for an expert witness to admit that key parts of their testimony were not even *meant* to be accurate. Allen could have submitted a supplemental affidavit to correct the record of errors that he had acknowledged in his first affidavit, but the corrected affidavit never arrived. Instead, he presented the *same figures* at the trial, figures that he had already admitted in sworn testimony were not accurate and were not intended to be accurate. He presented figures that exaggerated the uncertainty in grade attained of children raised by same-sex couples by a factor of about 70, and figures which falsely indicated that children raised by same-sex couples did no better in making progress through school than foster children.

At cross-examination at the trial, Mogill asked Allen if the figures were accurate and if the figures were meant to be accurate. Allen answered "No" to both questions, again. Mogill asked Allen if he had written in his report that the figures were not accurate and were not intended to be accurate. The answer was again "No."[16] Allen's justification for his inaccurate figures was that the figures were simply "stylized" and "a metaphor." Judge Friedman's eventual trial decision in *DeBoer v. Snyder* included a pointed criticism of the credibility of all the state's witnesses. No one who was paying attention to the trial proceedings should have been surprised.

One of the odd puzzles about Allen's testimony in *DeBoer* is that he did not *have* to make anything up. He had already published, using the real census data, a critique of my census results relating to the outcomes of children raised by same-sex couples (Allen, Pakaluk, and Price 2013).[17] He had real research at his disposal, but he chose not to use it.

At the trial, Mogill asked Allen if he believed that "the consequence of engaging in homosexual acts means . . . going to hell," and Allen responded, "[I]f it is not repented, yes."

Regnerus's Spurious Comparisons

The highest profile witness for the defense was Mark Regnerus, sociologist from the University of Texas. Regnerus had received a large grant from a conservative foundation and had fielded a nationally representative survey. His New Family Structure Study (NFSS) questionnaire included a detailed family structure calendar, which the adult subjects used to retrospectively report what family structure they had been living in during every year of their childhoods. In terms of data gathering, the NFSS[18] was and remains a valuable social science contribution. How Regnerus interpreted the data, however, was problematic and misleading and created a storm of controversy.

Regnerus's paper had been published in the journal *Social Science Research* (*SSR*). Academic journals rely on a system of peer review which is supposed to be blind (the reviewers, ideally, don't know who the author is, and the author doesn't know who the reviewers are). *SSR* relied on two reviewers for Regnerus's (2012a) initial report on the NFSS data. One reviewer was a funder of Regnerus's NFSS project, and the other had been a paid consultant on the project. *SSR* did not escape their share of blame and criticism for publishing Regnerus's misleading findings: Gary Gates's (2012a) critical letter to the editor of *SSR* had 199 additional scholars as cosigners.[19]

Regnerus defined lesbian mothers as mothers who ever had a girlfriend and gay fathers as fathers who ever had a boyfriend, regardless of whether the same-sex partner ever lived with or even knew the study subject as a child.[20] The vast majority of subjects who were defined by Regnerus as having had gay or lesbian parents never lived in a same-sex couple family. The few who had lived in a same-sex couple family had mostly done so briefly.[21] The NFSS data simply did not have enough subjects who were actually raised by same-sex couples in committed relationships to say anything statistically significant about what the effect of same-sex marriage on children might be.[22]

Childhood Family Transitions and the Life Course

Table 13.1 describes the life course of two typical NFSS subjects whose mothers ever had a girlfriend, and who were categorized by Regnerus as children of lesbian mothers. Case 1 is an eighteen-year-old woman who grew up on public assistance and had seven childhood family transitions. Case 1 was categorized by Regnerus as having had a lesbian mother because her mother had a relationship with a woman at some time. She is similar to the majority of Regnerus's children of "lesbian mothers" and children of "gay fathers" in that they appear to have never lived with a same-sex couple. She lived through two breakups of her mother and father.

When I presented Table 13.1 at the *DeBoer* trial, Judge Friedman asked me how Case 1, the subject who never lived with same-sex couple parents, could have been considered by Regnerus as having been raised by a lesbian mother. I explained that most of the study subjects Regnerus considered to have had lesbian mothers or gay fathers were like Case 1, in that they never lived with same-sex couple parents. The judge nodded his head.

Case 2 of Table 13.1 illustrates one of the fundamental challenges of studying subjects who ever lived in nontraditional families. Before she ever lived with same-sex couple parents, Case 2 lived with married biological parents (a heterosexual couple) for ten years, and then lived through their breakup and the departure from the household of her father. She is typical of children in the NFSS who ever lived with same-sex couples in that she did not start out life living with same-sex couple parents.[23]

The breakup of biological parents has been shown to have at least a modest short-term negative impact on children.[24] Estimates of the effect of same-sex couples on children's outcomes are nearly always confounded by the impact of the prior heterosexual relationship and its breakup. Failing to account for prior family disruptions biases analyses against the nontraditional families that occur after breakup of the biological mother and father.[25]

Family Structure and Family Transitions

In Regnerus's[26] analyses of the NFSS data, he compared the children of "lesbian mothers" and children of "gay fathers" not to all other children but only to children whose heterosexual married parents had been perfectly stable, i.e., children whose parents had always been together and had never broken

Table 13.1 Two Typical Life Course Profiles of Women of "Lesbian Mothers" from NFSS

Case 1	Years spent living with same-sex couple: 0 On public assistance growing up	Case 2	Years spent living with same-sex couple: 2 On public assistance growing up
Age	Status, or family transition	Age	Status, or family transition
At birth	Biological mother and biological father, together	At birth	Biological mother only
age 5	Biological father moves out	age 1	Biological father moves in with biological mother
age 6	Both grandparents move in	age 11	Biological father moves out; mother's girlfriend moves in
age 7	Both grandparents move out	age 13	Subject moves from home of biological mother and mother's girlfriend to biological father's house
age 12	Biological father moves back in with biological mother		
age 14	Biological father moves out again		
Adult outcomes:	Unemployed, receiving public assistance, 12th grade education (no diploma), light smoker, no arrests or convictions, no depression	Adult outcomes:	Employed part time, receiving public assistance, has HS diploma, income less than $15,000, in a good relationship, heavy smoker, no arrests or convictions, no depression
Total family transitions	7	Total family transitions	6
Breakups of heterosexual parenting couples	2	Breakups of heterosexual parenting couples	1

up, even in the years after the subject child had left home. As you can see in Table 13.1, the typical subject in the NFSS data whose mother ever had a girlfriend went through several childhood family transitions. Childhood family transitions have a negative and cumulative impact on children's outcomes.

Early critics of Regnerus (2012a) had argued that his results were biased by his failure to include family transitions as a control in his models.[27] Those critics turned out to be right. All of the negative outcomes that Regnerus associated with the family structure of "lesbian mothers" and "gay fathers" were actually due to childhood family transitions.[28] Figure 13.2 shows the strong linear relationship between the number of childhood family transitions in NFSS subjects and a negative outcome index derived from the outcome variables Regnerus used. Every additional childhood family transition of all types, including not only family breakups but also the arrival in the household of new parental partners, grandparents moving in, and so on, was associated with a steady worsening of children's average outcomes.[29]

Regnerus (2012c) and Allen, Pakaluk, and Price (2013) have argued that same-sex couples are inherently unstable, and that therefore couple instability and family instability are a pathway through which the children of same-sex couples come to have poor outcomes. Take a close look, however, at Case 2 in Table 13.1. Case 2 lived for two years, from age eleven to thirteen, with a same-sex couple, her mother and her mother's girlfriend. At age thirteen, Case 2 moved out of her mother's home and lived with her father

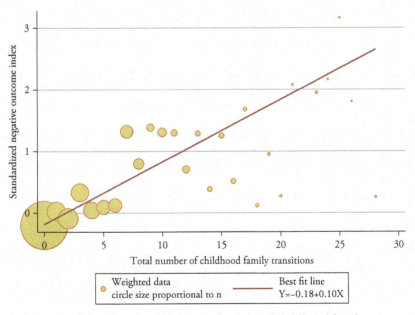

Figure 13.2 Negative outcome index as a function of childhood family transitions.

Source: Reproduced from Rosenfeld (2015) using NFSS data, weighted by "weight4." *N*=2466. The larger the circle, the more cases are represented. Smaller dots mean fewer cases, and less influence over the slope of the line.

instead. Her story is typical of NFSS subjects who ever lived with same-sex couple parents, in that the family upheavals they experienced resulted more often from custody loss by the gay or lesbian couple rather than the breakup of the same-sex parenting partnership.

Although the NFSS data do not provide any clues as to why mothers with same-sex partners so often lost custody of their children, literature on family law documents a strong bias against gay and lesbian parents in judicial custody decisions in the past.[30] A key ingredient in the lower stability of same-sex couple parent families was the law's discrimination against same-sex couples.

Couple Longevity

Research on same-sex couple longevity using data that predated the era of same-sex marriage generally showed that same-sex couples were less stable than heterosexual married couples. Blumstein and Schwartz's (1983) pioneering work, *American Couples,* suggested that heterosexual married couples were the least likely type of couple to have broken up after eighteen months, followed by heterosexual cohabiting couples and gay male couples, while lesbian couples had the highest breakup rate of all couple types.[31]

The witnesses for the state of Michigan in *DeBoer v. Snyder* made repeated attempts to argue, based on the Optimality Standard, that the instability of same-sex couples from the era before marriage equality should have made them ineligible for marriage in the U.S. Whether marriage equality eventually leads same-sex married couples to have higher or lower divorce rates than heterosexual married couples, we will not know for some time. Propensity for higher divorce rates, however, is not a bar to marriage in the U.S. Based on data from the Centers for Disease Control and Prevention's National Survey of Family Growth in 1995,[32] the probability of breakup among heterosexual couples after ten years of marriage was 20% for Asian American couples, 32% for White couples, and 47% for African American couples. Even though Asian American couples had the lowest divorce rate, White and Black couples are still allowed to marry in the U.S. The Optimality Standard, as noted in a previous chapter, has for good reason never been applied to the right to marry in the U.S. Research shows that a marriage-like commitment is associated with improved couple longevity for same-sex couples, just as for heterosexual couples.[33]

State's Witness Regnerus under Cross-Examination

The day before Michigan's star witness Mark Regnerus testified in Detroit in the trial of *DeBoer v. Snyder*,[34] the chairwoman of his department at the University of Texas, Christine L. Williams issued a statement disavowing his testimony and highlighting how his professional credibility had fallen among his own colleagues:

> Like all faculty Dr. Regnerus has the right to pursue his areas of research and express his point of view. However, Dr. Regnerus' opinions are his own. They do not reflect the views of the sociology department of the University of Texas at Austin. Nor do they reflect the views of the American Sociological Association which takes the position that the conclusions he draws from his study of gay parenting are fundamentally flawed on conceptual and methodological grounds and that findings from Dr. Regnerus' work have been cited inappropriately in efforts to diminish the civil rights and legitimacy of LBGTQ partners and their families. We encourage society as a whole to evaluate his claims.

In Regnerus's (2012a: 766) first report using the NFSS data, he had written, "As scholars of same-sex parenting aptly note, same-sex couples have and will continue to raise children. . . . This study is intended to neither undermine nor affirm any legal rights concerning such." Plaintiffs' attorney Leslie Cooper from the ACLU national office, in her cross-examination of Regnerus, pointed out to him that he was doing exactly what he wrote in his 2012 report that he would *not* do, i.e., to use his paper as evidence to undermine the legal rights of same-sex couple parents.[35] Cooper quoted sociologist Paul Amato, who had been a paid consultant on Regnerus's NFSS project and one of the two reviewers for Regnerus's paper. Amato, who had assisted Regnerus with his work, wrote that "given these cautious early statements it is exasperating to see Regnerus later cite his own study as evidence against same-sex marriage."

Marks, Witness for the State of Michigan, under Cross-Examination

Loren Marks's testimony at trial criticized the convenience sample and small sample studies that made up part of the social science consensus on same-sex couples and children. Marks was, interestingly, criticizing the literature on same-sex couples and their children for relying on methods that he himself specialized in. At cross-examination, plaintiffs' attorney Stanyar asked Marks what kind of research he did, and his answer was "qualitative research." Marks had done some convenience sample research on Muslim families, which (similar to children raised by same-sex couples) are difficult to make a nationally representative sample of because of their small numbers in the U.S. Stanyar asked Marks if *any* of his own research met the gold standard of research as he defined it, i.e., nationally representative and with a large sample of every relevant population. He answered, "No." Then she asked him if any other kinds of research, i.e., other than nationally representative and large samples, ever contributed to the development of social science. He answered, "I certainly hope so or I wasted an awful lot of my time."[36]

Price, Witness for the State of Michigan, under Cross-Examination

In defense witness Joseph Price's (2013: 17) pretrial affidavit, he had written, "There are three important mechanisms that provide a reasonable explanation for why children being raised by same-sex couples have worse outcomes than children being raised by a married heterosexual couple. These mechanisms are parental gender, biological relatedness, and family stability." At cross-examination, plaintiffs' attorney Dana Nessel asked Price how his claims about the ideal environment for children related to actual policy implications for children.

NESSEL: The last thing you indicated was that the ideal environment for children is with their biological mother and father, correct?

PRICE: That's correct.

NESSEL: What do you propose to do with the children of April and Jayne who had biological parents that abandoned or surrendered them at birth? . . . I am asking, what would be the ideal environment for those children who no longer have a biological mother or father? Are you suggesting to the Court that people like April or Jayne who are same-sex couples ought not to be taking that child into their home and raising that child?

PRICE: So the way I phrased my statement was, I believe that the ideal environment for a child is to be raised by a father and a mother. And then

I added a layer that said particularly if they're biologically related to those parents and particularly if they—those parents are married to each other.[37]

NESSEL: Well, not every child has the ability to have that ideal environment, correct?

PRICE: It doesn't change what the ideal environment is.

NESSEL: There are lots of kids in the State of Michigan and in the United States that don't have the opportunity to have that ideal environment, correct?

PRICE: I wouldn't have any information about that.

NESSEL: You don't have any information about that?[38]

Professor Price had omitted from his academic résumé submitted to the court a grant he had received from the conservative Witherspoon Institute. When asked by Nessel why he had omitted the grant, Price conceded, it was because "it might look bad."[39]

The *DeBoer* Decision

The *DeBoer v. Snyder* trial ended with closing arguments on Friday, March 7, 2014. On Friday, March 21, Judge Friedman issued his decision: "After reviewing the evidence presented at the trial, including the testimony of various expert witnesses . . . the Court concludes that the Michigan Marriage Amendment is unconstitutional and will enjoin[40] its enforcement."

Friedman's view of the witnesses for the state of Michigan was not positive: "The Court finds Regnerus's testimony entirely unbelievable and not worthy of serious consideration. The evidence adduced at trial demonstrated that his 2012 'study' was hastily concocted at the behest of a third-party funder." And as for the other defense witnesses:

The Court was unable to accord the testimony of Marks, Price, and Allen any significant weight. Marks's testimony is largely unbelievable. . . . They, along with Regnerus, clearly represent a fringe viewpoint that is rejected by the vast majority of their colleagues across a variety of social science fields. . . .[41]

The common flaw of the Regnerus and Allen studies was the failure to account for the fact that many of the subjects who were raised in same-sex households experienced prior incidents of family instability (e.g., divorce or separation) or were initially placed in the foster care system.

Judge Friedman understood that the defendants' argument that same-sex couples should be denied marriage rights if they or their children had sub-optimal outcomes was not consistent with how marriage policy is applied to other groups:

> [T]he state defendants' position suffers from a glaring inconsistency. Even assuming that children raised by same-sex couples fare worse than children raised by heterosexual married couples, the state defendants fail to explain why Michigan law does not similarly exclude certain classes of heterosexual couples from marrying whose children persistently have had "sub-optimal" developmental outcomes. . . .
>
> As [plaintiffs' witness Gary] Gates testified, there are thousands of same-sex couples currently raising thousands of children in Michigan, and these numbers have steadily increased over the past 20 years. Prohibiting gays and lesbians from marrying does not stop them from forming families and raising children. Nor does prohibiting same-sex marriage increase the number of heterosexual marriages or the number of children raised by het-erosexual parents. . . .
>
> Accordingly, IT IS HEREBY DECLARED that Article I § 25 of the Michigan Constitution and its implementing statutes are unconstitu-tional because they violate the Equal Protection Clause of the Fourteenth Amendment to the United States Constitution.[42]

Hearing from the court that the decision would be released on March 21, Nessel invited the press to come to April DeBoer and Jayne Rowse's house. The cameras were rolling as Nessel read the last paragraph of Judge Friedman's decision and the plaintiffs learned that Friedman had decided in their favor. With their children scampering about, nervous about all the strangers in their kitchen, April and Jayne started to cry.

Aftermath of the *DeBoer* Decision

The first ramification of the *DeBoer* decision was that same-sex couples could immediately marry in Michigan, starting on March 21, 2014, because Judge Friedman had not accompanied his ruling with a stay. The purpose of a stay is to put the ruling on hold until appeals in higher courts have been decided. Until a stay was issued by a higher court, same-sex couples could marry in

Michigan, but until the appeals were finished, the issue of same-sex marriage in Michigan would remain unresolved. Michigan announced that it would appeal the ruling. On Saturday afternoon, March 22, 2014, one day after Judge Friedman had issued his trial decision, the Sixth Circuit Court of Appeals stayed the decision, meaning Michigan's ban on same-sex marriages was reinstated after a one-day hiatus during which approximately three hundred same-sex couples in Michigan obtained licenses and married.[43]

The legal status of the Michigan same-sex couples married on March 21 and 22, 2014, was not clear until the couples who were married in that one-day window sued to be recognized as married in Michigan, and won.[44] DeBoer and Rowse themselves decided that they would not seek a marriage license until the case was finally settled. They had been through enough uncertainty already.

For the battle over the social science consensus on same-sex couples and their children, the *DeBoer* trial decision was more like a final decision. The trial had a powerful and immediate effect on the way other courts in other jurisdictions assessed the social science evidence about same-sex couples and their children. Appellate courts can reverse a trial court's judgment about the law or about the constitution, as the Sixth Circuit would soon do to Judge Friedman's decision, before being itself reversed by the U.S. Supreme Court. Appellate courts only rarely overturn the trial court's finding of facts, and appellate courts only rarely overturn the trial court's conclusion about the credibility of the witnesses. The trial judge hears the witnesses in person and can ask them questions, whereas the appellate judges do not hear in person from the witnesses. Judge Friedman's scathing criticism of the credibility of all the defense witnesses served to disqualify them, and their arguments, everywhere in the U.S.[45]

In November 2014, the Sixth Circuit Court of Appeals reversed (in a 2–1 decision) Judge Friedman's *DeBoer v. Snyder* trial decision. The reversal came on constitutional rather than evidentiary or social science grounds. The Sixth Circuit majority decision, while overturning the *DeBoer* trial decision, accepted the social science consensus about same-sex couples and their children, ratified in *DeBoer*:

> Over time, marriage has come to serve another value—to solemnize relationships characterized by love, affection, and commitment. Gay couples, no less than straight couples, are capable of sharing such relationships. And gay couples, no less than straight couples, are capable of

raising children and providing stable families for them. The quality of such relationships, and the capacity to raise children within them, turns not on sexual orientation but on individual choices and individual commitment.[46]

The *DeBoer* trial vindicated a social science consensus that had been under consistent attack from conservatives. The witnesses for the state of Michigan tried to frame their loss as an example of anti-Christian bias in the U.S. After being judged as lacking in credibility, defense witness Allen told the press that he wanted to "fight back, and to stand up for the principles of academic freedom, the freedom of expression, and the freedom of religion."[47]

For DeBoer and Rowse and their children, the decision was just another step in a four-year legal journey. First, they had to endure the Sixth Circuit reversal. Their legal journey would not end until after the *Obergefell v. Hodges* Supreme Court decision in June 2015 finally made same-sex marriage legal in all fifty U.S. states.

DeBoer v. Snyder would have substantial political aftereffects in Michigan. Plaintiffs' attorney Nessel achieved a degree of fame in the state for her work and as a spokesperson for the marriage equality movement. Four and a half years after the trial, in 2018, Nessel ran as the Democratic nominee for the office of Michigan attorney general and won, replacing same-sex marriage opponent Bill Schuette. Schuette, who was term-limited out of the attorney general's office, ran as the Republican candidate for governor of Michigan in 2018. He was soundly defeated by Democrat Gretchen Whitmer. On election night in 2018, Nessel spoke to a crowd of supporters: "And for all of you out there that can't handle the fact that I'm about to become the first openly gay person to hold statewide office [in Michigan]," and then she kissed on her wife, Alanna Maguire. A moment later, Nessel called DeBoer and Rowse up to the stage to honor the two women whose legal struggles had started it all.[48]

14

Obergefell v. Hodges, 2015

In 1992, Jim Obergefell was twenty-six years old. He had just met John Arthur and had fallen in love. Falling in love with Arthur fixed something in Obergefell's mind about who he was. He returned to Sandusky, Ohio, to tell his father something that he had been meaning to tell him for years: that he was gay. His father responded, "All I have ever wanted was for you to be happy."[1]

John Arthur had an undiagnosed medical problem, and by 2011 he was having trouble walking and his symptoms were getting worse. That year he was diagnosed with amyotrophic lateral sclerosis (ALS), also known as Lou Gehrig's disease. ALS is a degenerative neurological disease for which there is no cure or effective treatment. People with ALS often end up suffocating because of their lack of muscle and lack of neurological capacity to breathe.

Obergefell and Arthur had always planned to get married, but Ohio was one of the states that had voted for a same-sex marriage ban in 2004. Obergefell and Arthur were hopeful that one of the Supreme Court cases that was awaiting decision in 2013 would make marriage equality the law everywhere in the U.S. Unfortunately, both *Hollingsworth* and *Windsor* resulted in narrower victories for marriage equality, leaving Ohio's ban on same-sex marriage intact. With Arthur already unable to walk and able to breathe only with difficulty, Obergefell arranged for a special medical flight to Maryland, where same-sex marriage was legal. The two married on the plane at the airport in Maryland on July 11, 2013.

From the official Ohio perspective, Obergefell and Arthur had never married because the state constitution (after the 2004 state referendum) specifically stated that Ohio would not recognize same-sex marriages from any jurisdiction. Arthur's death certificate was therefore going to list Arthur as single, with no surviving spouse. For Obergefell, who had loved Arthur in sickness and in health, the prospect of being left off his husband's death certificate was a bitter indignity. In the fall of 2013, Cincinnati civil rights attorney Al Gerhardstein convinced an initially reluctant Obergefell to sue in federal court to force Ohio to list him as surviving spouse on Arthur's

The Rainbow after the Storm. Michael J. Rosenfeld, Oxford University Press. © Oxford University Press 2022.
DOI: 10.1093/oso/9780197600436.003.0014

expected death certificate. The case was *Obergefell v. Wymyslo* (2013), with Theodore Wymyslo, director of the Ohio Department of Public Health, sued in his official capacity as the chief executive of the office that issued Ohio's death certificates.

In *Obergefell v. Wymyslo*, the city attorney for Cincinnati took Obergefell's side. Their support was especially meaningful for Obergefell because he had always thought of his hometown as a conservative city that was hostile to gay rights. U.S. District Court Judge Timothy Black wasted little time in finding for the plaintiffs Obergefell and Arthur. John Arthur died in Cincinnati from complications of ALS on October 22, 2013.

In *Obergefell v. Wymyslo* (2013: 975), Judge Black took issue with the way that the primary sponsor of Ohio's 2004 anti-same-sex-marriage amendment, the group Citizens for Community Values (CCV), had spread falsehoods about gays and lesbians:

> CCV sent letters to school boards and superintendents in Ohio warning them, erroneously, that they would face criminal and daunting civil liability if they took measures to protect lesbian and gay students from violence and harassment. In one of CCV's campaign publications, the organization misled Ohio voters about the need for the amendment, stating that marriage equality advocates sought to eliminate age requirements for marriage, advocated polygamy, and sought elimination of kinship limitations so that incestuous marriages could occur. CCV warned Ohio employers that "sexual relationships between members of the same sex expose gays, lesbians, and bisexuals to extreme risks of sexually transmitted diseases, physical injuries, mental disorders and even a shortened life span." The television and media campaign in support of the amendment contained misleading statements, such as . . . "every major social science study tells us time and time again: families are stronger with a wife and a husband; children do better with a mother and a father."

Judge Black's decision in favor of same-sex couples in Ohio was one of many U.S. federal court decisions in 2013 and 2014 that found the various state bans against same-sex marriage unconstitutional.[2]

The dramatic change in public support for gay rights altered the political opportunity structure in a way that made it easier for Judge Black in 2013 to overturn a state ban on recognizing same-sex marriages that had been passed by voters in 2004 by a 62 to 38% margin. In 2004, U.S. public support for marriage equality was at about 31%, putting Ohio's 38% support for marriage equality above the national rate but still well below the 50% threshold (see Figure 9.2). By December 2013, when Judge Black issued his decision in *Obergefell v. Wymyslo*, U.S. support for marriage equality had risen to about 54%. If Ohio's support for marriage equality continued to be higher than the national average, then support for marriage equality in Ohio was probably near 60% in December 2013. Any policy that has strong majority public support is reasonably well insulated against backlash and opposition, no matter how motivated its opponents are.

Although the background of increasing public approval of marriage equality undoubtedly was part of the context within which judges made marriage equality decisions in the post-*Windsor* era, judicial decisions rarely cite or acknowledge public opinion. Federal judges have lifetime appointments in part to isolate them from public opinion, but they might care about it nonetheless. Judge Black's decision made no reference to polling data or survey results, but he did make a passing and oblique parenthetical reference to the fact that opinion in Ohio seemed to have changed: "[T]he question is presented whether a state can do what the federal government cannot—i.e. discriminate against same-sex couples . . . simply because the majority of the voters don't like homosexuality (or at least didn't in 2004)."[3]

We do not know how much rapidly changing public opinion may have influenced Black (or other judges who heard same-sex marriage cases in the post-*Windsor* era, including Judge Friedman in the *DeBoer* trial), but we can observe a correlation. The U.S. Supreme Court did not issue a decision on marriage equality until after public support for it had gone well past 50%. In the post-*Windsor* era, and with a majority of U.S. adults supporting marriage equality, judges at every level started to see marriage equality in a more favorable light.

To establish the facts about same-sex couples, Judge Black relied heavily on the social science consensus on same-sex couples and their children. His decision in *Obergefell v. Wymyslo* repeatedly cited the ratification of the scholarly consensus on same-sex couples and their children from the *Perry v. Schwarzenegger* trial in 2010 as justification for his rejection of the anti-marriage-equality arguments of the CCV. The plaintiffs' attorneys in *Obergefell* had presented written testimony from historian George Chauncey, psychologist Letitia Anne Peplau, and political scientist Gary Segura, all veterans of the *Perry* trial. Ohio's defense in *Obergefell* had no effective counter to such scholarly power.

As Justice Scalia's dissent in *U.S. v. Windsor* had predicted, once the U.S. Supreme Court had struck down the federal government ban on recognizing same-sex marriages, it was a short step for federal judges to strike down the various state bans. The *Windsor* decision had profoundly undermined the legal credibility of same-sex marriage bans in the U.S. In the years 2013–2015, all over the U.S., federal judges were hearing challenges to state bans against marriage equality and finding the bans to be unconstitutional.

The state of Ohio appealed Black's ruling to the Sixth Circuit Court of Appeals. By then, Richard Hodges had replaced Theodore Wymyslo as the director of Ohio's Department of Public Health, so Obergefell's case was renamed *Obergefell v. Hodges*. In the summer of 2014, Michigan's appeal of Judge Friedman's *DeBoer v. Snyder* trial ruling was consolidated with Ohio's appeal of *Obergefell v. Wymyslo*, and these were consolidated with similar appeals from Tennessee and Kentucky, where federal judges had also struck down state bans on same-sex marriage.

The Marriage Equality Whirlwind of 2013–2015

In the U.S. federal judicial system, there are ninety-four district courts. Appeals from the district courts go up to one of the twelve appellate courts known as circuits. Appeals from the circuit courts go up to the U.S. Supreme Court, which is the final arbiter of the law in the U.S. The Court can choose to hear appeals (i.e., to grant *Cert*) from the lower courts or to refuse to hear the appeal (i.e., deny *Cert*) and let the lower court ruling stand. Figure 14.1 depicts the state-by-state hierarchy of U.S. district courts and appellate circuits.

Figure 14.2 charts the timing of the adoption of marriage equality by the different states, or when states had their bans on same-sex marriage overturned.[4] Of the states that adopted marriage equality earliest, Massachusetts was first, in 2004. There followed Connecticut in 2008, Iowa and Vermont in 2009, New Hampshire and the District of Columbia in 2010, New York in 2011, Maine and Washington in 2012, and Maryland in January 2013. From May 2004 to January 2013, nine states plus D.C. had transitioned to marriage equality, at a pace of roughly one state per year. From January 2013 to June 2015, over two and a half years, the remaining forty-one states would transition to marriage equality.

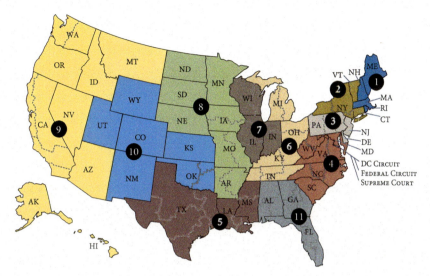

Figure 14.1 Geographic boundaries of U.S. courts of appeals and district courts.
Note: The dotted lines indicate where states are subdivided into smaller districts. The white numbers in black circles indicate appellate districts, or circuits. Source: https://www.uscourts.gov/about-federal-courts/court-role-and-structure.

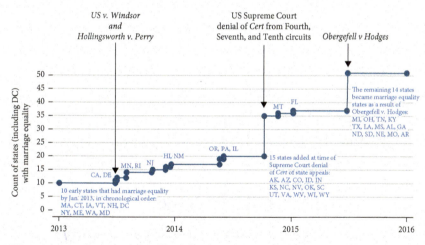

Figure 14.2 2013–2015 timeline of states adopting marriage equality, with three Supreme Court interventions.

The U.S. Supreme Court delivered three major breakthroughs for marriage equality between 2013 and 2015. First was *U.S. v. Windsor* (2013), which struck down §3 of DOMA. The second was the October 2014 denial of *Cert* of state appeals from various appellate circuits. The third was the June 2015 *Obergefell v. Hodges* decision.

In the summer of 2013 the *Hollingsworth v. Perry* Supreme Court decision made California a marriage equality state. By the summer of 2014 Delaware (by state legislative action), Minnesota (through state legislative action and after the defeat of an anti-same-sex-marriage ballot measure in 2012), Rhode Island (through state legislative action), New Jersey (through a state court decision), Hawaii (through state legislative action), New Mexico (through a state court decision), Oregon (through a federal court decision), Pennsylvania (as a result of a federal court decision), and Illinois (through state legislative action) had all become marriage equality states.

On June 25, 2014, the U.S. Court of Appeals for the Tenth Circuit issued its opinion in the Utah same-sex marriage case of *Kitchen v. Herbert*, affirming a district court decision in *Kitchen v. Herbert* (2013) that had struck down Utah's same-sex marriage ban. Utah had been taken by surprise by the rapidity of the district court decision and had not prepared a motion to request that the decision be stayed pending appeal. Because both the district judge and the Tenth Circuit had refused to issue a stay of the district court decision, same-sex couples were marrying on Christmas Eve 2013 in Utah, one of the most conservative and most religious states in the U.S.[5]

Eventually, on January 6, 2014, the U.S. Supreme Court issued a stay, so that same-sex marriages in Utah were temporarily halted. In the seventeen days before then, however, three thousand same-sex couples married in Utah. The mayor of Salt Lake City kept city offices open late to accommodate the crush of couples wanting to marry, and so that he himself could preside over the weddings of same-sex couples. The local news was awash with stories of joyful couples standing in line to marry. Nine months later, when the Court lifted the stay, not only did Utah become a marriage equality state, but attitudes toward gay rights in Utah had softened to the point that the legislature would pass a law protecting gays and lesbians from discrimination in employment and housing and the Church of Latter Day Saints (the church of the Mormons, the predominant religious group in Utah, with a history of supporting anti-gay-rights measures) would support the new antidiscrimination law.[6]

Virginia's same-sex marriage ban was struck down by the federal district court on February 13, 2014, in *Bostic v. Rainey*. When Virginia appealed, the Fourth Circuit decided in *Bostic v. Schaefer* (2014) to uphold the lower court decision, finding Virginia's same-sex marriage ban unconstitutional.

Indiana and Wisconsin had their same-sex marriage bans reversed by their respective U.S. district courts. Both states appealed to the Seventh Circuit, where, at oral arguments, the states' legal representatives faced blistering questions from the judges.[7] The Seventh Circuit's unanimous decision in *Baskin v. Bogan*, issued on September 4, 2014, was written by conservative jurist Richard Posner, who had in the past written skeptically about same-sex marriage (Posner 1992). In *Baskin*, Posner showed how much his personal thinking had changed. The *Baskin v. Bogan* (2014: 662) decision mocked the idea that Indiana and Wisconsin were trying to protect children with their bans on same-sex marriage. Judge Posner had decided that such bans were not only wrong and unconstitutional but ridiculous:

> At oral argument [Indiana's] lawyer was asked whether "Indiana's law is about successfully raising children," and since "you agree same-sex couples can successfully raise children, why shouldn't the ban be lifted as to them?" The lawyer answered that "the assumption is that with opposite sex couples there is very little thought given during the sexual act, sometimes, to whether babies may be a consequence." In other words, Indiana's government thinks straight couples tend to be sexually irresponsible, producing unwanted children by the carload, and so must be pressured (in the form of governmental encouragement of marriage through a combination of sticks and carrots) to marry, but that gay couples, unable as they are to produce children wanted or unwanted are model parents—model citizens really—so have no need for marriage. Heterosexual couples get drunk and pregnant, producing unwanted children; their reward is to be allowed to marry. Homosexual couples do not produce unwanted children; their reward is to be denied the right to marry. Go figure.

Indiana, Wisconsin, Virginia, and Utah all appealed to the U.S. Supreme Court to overturn the various district court and appellate court decisions that had stripped the states of their bans on same-sex marriage. On October 6, 2014, the Court denied *Cert* to this broad set of appeal requests, letting stand the decisions of the Fourth, Tenth, and Seventh Circuit Courts, which meant that in Indiana, Wisconsin, Virginia, and Utah, marriage equality was the law, and stays of the lower court decisions were lifted. Virginia started marrying same-sex couples right away, on October 6. Utah, which had seen same-sex marriages taking place in late December 2013, before the Court imposed a temporary stay, was a marriage equality state once again now that the stay had been lifted and the state's appeals had run out.

Federal appellate court rulings set precedent and define the law for all the states within each appellate court's jurisdiction. By denying *Cert* on the same-sex marriage appeals from states in the Fourth, Seventh, and Tenth Circuits, the U.S. Supreme Court brought marriage equality not only to Indiana, Wisconsin, Virginia, and Utah but also to the other states in the same circuits: Colorado, Kansas, and Wyoming (Tenth Circuit) and West Virginia, North Carolina, and South Carolina (Fourth Circuit). South Carolina dragged its heels for six weeks, from October 6 to November 20, 2014, until the U.S. Supreme Court denied their emergency request for a stay.

In *Latta v. Otter* (2014), the U.S. Court of Appeals for the Ninth Circuit heard appeals from Idaho and Nevada, whose same-sex marriage bans had been successfully challenged in federal district courts. The Ninth Circuit decision in the case, issued on October 7, 2014, upheld the lower court decisions overturning the state bans on same-sex marriage. By the end of October 2014, same-sex marriage was the law in thirty-six states plus the District of Columbia. States were being added in bunches to the marriage equality column.

The *Obergefell v. Hodges* Oral Arguments

As long as *all* the courts of appeals found that same-sex couples had a constitutional right to marry, the U.S. Supreme Court could simply let those decisions stand and postpone having to make a decision themselves on the constitutionality of same-sex marriage. The Sixth Circuit Court of Appeals was the outlier that forced the Supreme Court's hand. On November 6, 2014, the Sixth Circuit's review of *DeBoer v. Snyder* (2014), which included *Obergefell v. Hodges* and the cases from Tennessee and Kentucky, reversed the lower court decisions and reinstated the same-sex marriage bans in Michigan, Ohio, Tennessee, and Kentucky. The U.S. Supreme Court was then faced with a situation in which different appellate courts had reached conflicting conclusions on the same set of constitutionality issues.

The divergent opinions needed to be resolved by a definitive Court opinion on the constitutional right to marriage for same-sex couples. The plaintiffs in the Sixth Circuit cases, including Obergefell from Ohio and DeBoer and Rowse and their children from Michigan, all appealed to the Court, which granted *Cert* on January 16, 2015. The Obergefell legal team submitted their appeal motion first, so the Supreme Court same-sex marriage case took on the name of the Ohio case, *Obergefell v. Hodges*.

The Court divided the *Obergefell* oral arguments into two issues. The main issue was whether states were required to license marriages of same-sex couples; the second was whether states were required to recognize same-sex marriages legally entered into in other states. For each of these two issues, the advocates for marriage equality would have only thirty minutes and only one lawyer to make their case in person before the Court.

Thirty minutes is not a lot of time to make a complicated argument for new constitutional rights and to answer all the questions that the justices might ask. The difficulty in a case such as *Obergefell* is that each of the plaintiffs' groups from the four different states had their own local lawyers, and the national gay rights organizations had a separate set of lawyers. Lawyers who regularly argue cases before the U.S. Supreme Court are a specialized and elite group, comprising a third set of lawyers altogether. The *Obergefell* part 1 oral argument, on the issue of whether the states were obligated to license marriages to same-sex couples, was going to be historic, and only one lawyer was going to argue it. Debate raged over who that one lawyer should be.

Initially, some of the plaintiffs' lawyers in *Obergefell* wanted a lawyer with a lot of Supreme Court experience to argue the case. Among the available lawyers who fit that criterion, none had an established connection to gay rights issues, and all were expensive. The plan of hiring a Supreme Court specialist made sense to the plaintiffs' lawyers from several states, but it did not make sense to DeBoer or Rowse. They were incredulous at the possibility that a straight White man who had never been an advocate for gay rights could be asked to represent the most important gay rights case in the history of the U.S. Supreme Court.

At a planning meeting of lawyers and plaintiffs in the *Obergefell* cases, DeBoer and Rowse made their voices heard. DeBoer said, "How am I supposed to look at my two African American female daughters [by this time the couple had a fourth adopted child living with them, Rylee, born twelve weeks premature, who was their second African American daughter after Ryanne] and tell them I let a straight White male argue the biggest civil rights case in my generation? How am I supposed to do that? I can't."

DeBoer and Rowse wanted one of their private attorneys, Carole Stanyar, to make the oral argument, but Stanyar was a local Michigan attorney not well known to the lawyers from Kentucky, Tennessee, and Ohio. Eventually a compromise was reached. Mary Bonauto, the path-blazing attorney for GLAD, who had been assisting the Michigan plaintiffs' legal team, was chosen. Bonauto had never argued before the U.S. Supreme Court before, but she had a national reputation and had argued the victorious (for marriage equality) *Goodridge v. Department of Public Health* (2003) case before the Massachusetts Supreme Court.[8]

April 28, 2015, was the day set for oral arguments. Bonauto was questioned by Justice Scalia, who kept insisting that if the Supreme Court endorsed marriage equality, American clergy would be forced to preside over the weddings of same-sex couples, and the principle of religious liberty would be violated.

Despite Scalia's claims, clergy in the U.S. have always had the liberty to refuse to preside over the weddings of adults who are otherwise eligible to marry. The U.S. has a system of civil marriage. To be married one needs a license from the government; participation of clergy is optional. The county clerk, as an agent of the government, must provide a marriage license to any eligible couple, including to same-sex couples under a regime of marriage equality. In states that already had marriage equality in 2015, clergy had never been required to preside over same-sex weddings, though many clergy were happy to do so.

After Bonauto's thirty minutes of advocacy for same-sex marriage before the nine justices of the U.S. Supreme Court, U.S. Solicitor General[9] Donald Verrilli was allocated fifteen minutes. Verrilli was in the Court to convey President Obama's view that marriage equality should be the law of the land.[10]

Left to right: plaintiffs Jayne Rowse and April DeBoer and attorneys Carole Stanyar and Mary Bonauto on the steps of the U.S. Supreme Court, April 28, 2015, after the oral arguments in *Obergefell v. Hodges*. AP Photo by Cliff Owen, used with permission.

The *Obergefell v. Hodges* Decision

As the spring of 2015 turned to summer, Americans waited for the Supreme Court's *Obergefell* decision. DeBoer and Rowse started to feel some of the pressure of the situation they had put themselves in. They had started the *DeBoer v. Snyder* lawsuit years earlier as the only route to give their children two legal parents, and they had tried to keep their focus on that simple issue: protecting their children. But now that the country was waiting on a same-sex marriage decision from the U.S. Supreme Court, the couple had to contemplate the possibility of what might happen if the decision went against them. If they lost, not only would they be denied the ability to marry or to cross-adopt their children in Michigan, but hundreds of thousands of other same-sex couples across the U.S. would lose rights. A loss in the U.S. Supreme Court could encourage some of the states that had had marriage equality imposed by the courts to roll back gay rights and eliminate marriage equality. A loss would have had serious negative consequences for gay and lesbian people all over the U.S. As the country waited for the decision, the ramifications of a potential loss weighed heavily on DeBoer and Rowse.

On June 26, 2015, a little after 10:00 a.m. Eastern Time, Justice Anthony Kennedy announced the Court's opinion. Kennedy was speaking for a 5–4 majority. The decision required states to issue marriage licenses to same-sex couples and to recognize same-sex marriages from other jurisdictions, overturning the remaining part of DOMA that had been left intact by Kennedy's *U.S. v. Windsor* (2013) decision. The *Obergefell* Supreme Court decision was the culminating public policy breakthrough of a decades-long marriage equality movement.

Kennedy wrote:

The Constitution promises liberty to all within its reach, a liberty that includes certain specific rights that allow persons, within a lawful realm, to define and express their identity. The petitioners in these cases seek to find that liberty by marrying someone of the same sex and having their marriages deemed lawful on the same terms and conditions as marriages between persons of the opposite sex. . . .

The nature of injustice is that we may not always see it in our own times. The generations that wrote and ratified the Bill of Rights and the Fourteenth Amendment did not presume to know the extent of freedom in all of its dimensions, and so they entrusted to future generations a charter protecting the right of all persons to enjoy liberty as we learn its meaning. . . .

As all parties agree, many same-sex couples provide loving and nurturing homes to their children, whether biological or adopted. And hundreds of thousands of children are presently being raised by such couples [citing an amicus brief by demographer Gary Gates].[11]

Note Justice Kennedy's focus on same-sex couples and their adopted children. The *DeBoer v. Snyder* case raised the issue of children's need to have the protections that only marriage could provide. After his retirement, when he was asked about *Obergefell*, Kennedy returned to the issue of adopted children and their same-sex couple parents, referencing the size of that population from Gary Gates's research.[12] The *Obergefell* decision continued:

Excluding same-sex couples from marriage thus conflicts with a central premise of the right to marry. Without the recognition, stability, and predictability marriage offers, their children suffer the stigma of knowing their families are somehow lesser. They also suffer the significant material costs of being raised by unmarried parents, relegated through no fault of their own to a more difficult and uncertain family life. . . .

The limitation of marriage to opposite-sex couples may long have seemed natural and just, but its inconsistency with the central meaning of the fundamental right to marry is now manifest. . . . *Baker v. Nelson* must be and now is overruled. . . .

No union is more profound than marriage, for it embodies the highest ideals of love, fidelity, devotion, sacrifice, and family. . . . [The plaintiffs'] plea is that they do respect it, respect it so deeply that they seek to find its fulfillment for themselves. Their hope is not to be condemned to live in loneliness, excluded from one of civilization's oldest institutions. They ask for equal dignity in the eyes of the law. The Constitution grants them that right. The judgment of the Court of Appeals for the Sixth Circuit is reversed.[13]

Sitting in the Supreme Court's small gallery, Jim Obergefell sobbed quietly. Back in Ann Arbor, the Michigan plaintiffs and lawyers were sitting in an LGBT community center trying anxiously to figure out if they had won or lost, when attorneys Nessel and Stanyar told them they had won. DeBoer and Rowse had to compose themselves. A television reporter turned on her light, put her microphone in front of Rowse, and asked what she and DeBoer were going to do now. "We have to plan a wedding and adopt some kids," Rowse replied. DeBoer had another reporter's microphone in front of her, and she said, "It really means everything to us that marriages and relationships like ours are going to be recognized, and we are going to be treated equally, and that children of families like ours are no longer going to be discriminated against," and then she started to cry.[14]

A little while later at the LGBT community center in Ann Arbor, a dance party broke out that would last until midnight.

Baker v. Nelson (1972), the one-sentence Court ruling that had dismissed an early marriage equality appeal from Minnesota "for want of a substantial federal question," and which had been a thorn in the side of gay rights advocates for more than forty years, was overturned in the *Obergefell* decision.

In Cincinnati, Jim Obergefell's hometown, the mayor presided over five weddings of same-sex couples in a downtown park. Later that day, Obergefell took a congratulatory phone call from President Obama. At night the White House was lit up in rainbow colors.

A Wedding and Adoptions

On August 22, 2015, at a banquet hall in Southfield, Michigan, April DeBoer was wearing a flowing white wedding dress and Jayne Rowse was wearing a black tuxedo and a red vest. Their children too were all dressed up. Unlike their first wedding, in 2008, which had been a small, informal, and legally unrecognized event, their second wedding was big, official, and newsworthy. A local congresswoman was in attendance; her husband had been cared for in the hospital by Rowse. Television cameras were recording. Lights and microphones were everywhere. Two hundred fifty guests were in attendance. Presiding over the wedding was U.S. District Court Judge Bernard Friedman, who had presided over the *DeBoer v. Snyder* trial and whose decision had led to the overturning of Michigan's same-sex marriage ban. Friedman reported that DeBoer and Rowse had given him two instructions: "involve the children, and it has to be quick."[15]

DeBoer was halfway through her vows when her son Jacob indicated that he needed a bathroom break, and DeBoer's father was called to escort him. Their children took vows, taking DeBoer and Rowse as their legal mothers and promising to love them forever. Then Judge Friedman addressed DeBoer and Rowse:

> By the power vested in me, and most important by the love that the two of you have for each other, and the love that the two of you have for your children . . . and for the commitment that the two of you have made to each other . . . By the power vested in me by the state constitution, and by the United States Constitution, I hereby pronounce you lawfully wedded spouses.

Attorneys Stanyar, Nessel, Mogill, and Bonauto and law professor Sedler were in attendance and signed the marriage license as witnesses. Five-year-old Jacob, who had started his life in the neonatal intensive care unit, ran into the crowd to give his teacher a hug, and then started looking for cake.

Judge Bernard Friedman, who presided over the *DeBoer v. Snyder* trial in 2014, reading wedding vows to Jayne Rowse, April DeBoer, and their children in Southfield, Michigan, August 22, 2015. Photo by Tanya Moutzalias of the *Ann Arbor News*-MLive.com Detroit via AP, used with permission.

On November 5, 2015, April DeBoer and Jayne Rowse, along with their children, were in the Michigan courtroom of Judge Karen McDonald for the purpose of cross-adoption. This legal ceremony had been DeBoer and Rowse's sole purpose from the beginning. All four children raised their right hands. Judge McDonald asked DeBoer, "Do you understand that if your request is granted here today, you will be legally responsible for the support and maintenance of Jacob and Nolan [who had been initially adopted by Rowse] including food, clothing, shelter, education, and medical care?"[16]

"Yes I do," DeBoer responded.

"Do you understand that you will be legally undertaking their intellectual, spiritual, and moral guidance?"

"Yes I do."

"Do you understand that if your request is granted, you will be the parent in all respects, just as if you were their birth parent?"

"Yes I do. . . ."

"Do you understand that if your request is granted, you will be called upon to provide love, affection, and encouragement?"

Attorney Dana Nessel shows Ryanne DeBoer-Rowse her adoption certificate after the adoption ceremony in Oakland County Circuit Court, November 5, 2015. Nessel was elected attorney general of Michigan in 2018. AP Photo by Carlos Osorio, used with permission.

"Yes I do."

"Do you understand that there may be certain great or little inconveniences over the years of parenting?" (At this point there was laughter in the courtroom.)

"Yes I do."

"Is there any reason, either physically or mentally, that you cannot assume these responsibilities?"

"No there is not."

"Do you have any hesitations or reservations whatsoever?"

"None at all."

"The court finds that granting the petition for adoption is in the best interests of Jacob and Nolan, and from this day forward, you are their parent."[17]

PART IV

THE BROADER IMPLICATIONS
OF MARRIAGE EQUALITY

15

Authenticity, Respectability, and the Desire for Marriage

The victory of marriage equality requires a reckoning with the arguments of those who have opposed (and continue to oppose) same-sex marriage and gay rights. Conservative politicians and religious leaders who staked their reputations on opposition to marriage equality sustained a series of profound defeats as marriage equality rose in popularity, won victories in the courts, and then became the law of the U.S. The rapid liberalization in public support for marriage equality in the 1990s and the 2000s (breaking through the majority threshold around 2012) withdrew the public support from those who thought that frightening people about gay marriage would always be a pathway to popularity and political success.

Conservative academics whose research was intended to prove that gay couples were inadequate parents saw their work disregarded by their colleagues and marginalized by their professional organizations. When the academics who were actively working with Christian Right groups to oppose marriage equality testified in court, they saw their reputations tarnished, their shoddy research picked apart, and their faulty premises laid bare.

On the other side of the political spectrum, left-wing critics of marriage equality also saw their arguments undermined by events and by the passage of time. I do not mean to create a false equivalency here between the right-wing and the left-wing critics of marriage equality. The right-wing critics often were spreading known falsehoods and therefore were often *not* operating in good faith. The left-wing critics *were* operating in good faith as far as I can tell. They wanted to see a more radical change in American family forms. They were not wrong for wanting radical change, but they simply overestimated how many gay and lesbian Americans shared their transformative vision.

Despite operating in good faith, the left-wing critics of marriage equality managed to get some important predictions and interpretations of events quite wrong. It is especially ironic that the left-wing critics, most all of whom

The Rainbow after the Storm. Michael J. Rosenfeld, Oxford University Press. © Oxford University Press 2022.
DOI: 10.1093/oso/9780197600436.003.0015

supported gay rights in principle, would have failed to understand the revolutionary potential of marriage equality. The left critique of marriage equality predominated within the gay rights movement and in the academic literature about gay rights right up to (and sometimes even after) the triumph of marriage equality in the U.S.[1] To the extent that the academic record is misleading, correction is needed.

Some gay rights activists had practical reservations about whether marriage equality could be a winning issue in the U.S. Given how many state referenda were lost by the supporters of marriage equality from 1998 to 2009, those practical reservations were not inappropriate.[2] The change in American public opinion toward gay rights was most unusual and therefore not easy to predict. Nonetheless, attitudes *did* change, and did so dramatically over the course of more than two decades. Rapid attitude change meant that marriage equality turned out to be a much more practical kind of policy innovation than the left critics had imagined it could be.

Left and progressive critics of marriage equality argued that it would further marginalize the queer people who did not want to marry (Ettelbrick 1989). I showed in chapter 8 that individuals who supported marriage equality were dramatically more likely to support both the right of gay people to have sex (regardless of marriage) and transgender rights. As the marriage equality movement gained traction, the association within individuals between support for marriage equality and support for gay sex increased, in contradiction to predictions of the left critics of marriage equality.

The proponents of marriage equality within the gay rights movement, such as Evan Wolfson, had always maintained that marriage equality would be a pathway to greater inclusion and respect for all queer people, regardless of their marital intentions, and the success of marriage equality has proved Wolfson and the other supporters of marriage equality to have been correct. But *why* was it so? Why was the marriage equality movement so successful at winning heterosexual Americans over to their cause?

Authenticity and Respectability

Let's consider another one of the prominent criticisms of marriage equality from the Left. Quite a few scholars on the Left of the gay rights movement adopted the view that wanting to marry was not an authentic expression of love between same-sex couples, but a kind of mimicry of heterosexuality that was (in the critics' eyes) carefully curated and designed to make gay people *seem* more like straight people than they really were. One such critic, Nancy Polikoff, wrote, "I believe that the desire to marry in the lesbian and gay community is an attempt to mimic the worst of mainstream society, an effort to fit into an inherently problematic institution that betrays the promise of both lesbian and gay liberation and radical feminism."[3] The widespread (and I believe inaccurate) claim that same-sex marriage was a kind of inauthentic mimicry harkened back to Wittman's (1970) *Gay Manifesto* from the heady days of the Gay Liberation Front.[4]

Polikoff argued that gay people were demeaning themselves by pretending they wanted to marry in order to appeal to the dominant heterosexual society. Social movement scholars have a name for this kind of activity: *respectability politics*. The term is often used derisively, as a criticism of people who are assumed to be demeaning themselves (or who are forcibly demeaned) to earn the respect of someone else.

Respect, however, is something that everyone needs. No one gets anywhere in the world without being shown at least some respect, and there is nothing inherently demeaning about demanding it. Respectability can be demeaning when it is imposed on lower-status people by higher-status people. It would have been demeaning for gay rights organizers to force same-sex couples to pretend that they wanted to marry, but that is not at all what happened. A better understanding of the different kinds of respectability politics is one key to understanding why the marriage equality movement was so much more successful than the critics from the Left expected it to be.

In recent years, the term "respectability politics" has been used to criticize moderate or conservative Black leaders. When a school principal punishes students for their culturally specific clothes or ethnic hairstyles, or when Black politicians mock Black youth for wearing saggy pants, those leaders are engaged in a negative kind of top-down respectability politics.[5]

Same-sex marriage (the aspiration for it, and its eventual reality) was not imposed on same-sex couples from above; just the opposite. Same-sex couples marry because of their own desires and needs, just as heterosexual couples do. Marriage equality was a movement that grew up slowly from the grassroots as couples wanted to marry. For a long time marriage equality was resisted not only by politicians but also by some gay rights social movement groups. Grassroots claims for respectability, such as the movement for marriage equality, lack the demeaning aspects of top-down respectability politics. Although the term "respectability politics" usually has a negative connotation, a grassroots respectability politics can be progressive, positive, and empowering. Classic literature has recognized both types of respectability politics (the demeaning top-down variety and the potentially progressive grassroots variety), and it is important to distinguish between the two.[6]

Marriage is an expression of commitment and love that is specific to the two people entering the union, not a mimicry of marriages that have come before. Because same-sex couples had to fight harder to gain entry into the institution of marriage, the accusation that they were mimicking heterosexual couples (who, except for interracial couples prior to 1967, had always had access to marriage) is especially unfair. The urgency and authenticity of same-sex couples' desires to marry, to fight years-long court battles and to suffer the slings and arrows of the negative side of sudden fame and public exposure, but to continue to seek the right to marry, had a powerful effect on the news media and on news consumers everywhere. Anyone who was willing to fight for years for a marriage license must *really* want to be married. The genuine commitment of same-sex couples and their clear affection for each other and for their children was a beacon to anyone who was paying attention.

April DeBoer and Jayne Rowse demonstrated a special kind of commitment not only to each other but also to a group of adopted and foster children they took in, nurtured, and loved. They and their children were fighting in court for basic rights that heterosexual married couples have always taken for granted. Their fierce commitment to their children was the very embodiment of parental love. By embodying and fighting for parental love, they owned the moral high ground in their several-years-long battle with the state of Michigan. There may be nothing in the world quite so powerful or universally respectable as a mother's love for her children.

The opponents of marriage equality claimed that preventing same-sex couples from being able to marry was in the service of protecting the interests of children. In the legal and political contest between DeBoer and Rowse and the state of Michigan and the opponents of marriage equality, it was not difficult to figure out who really had the best interests of the children at heart. Nothing the state or the conservative scholars they hired as experts could say was able to convince open-minded people in the public that DeBoer and Rowse's children did not deserve to have two legal parents.

The Popularity of Marriage among Gay People

Before marriage equality succeeded, some on the Left of the gay rights movement were skeptical about whether their gay and lesbian constituents really
wanted to marry. If there was little demand for marriage among same-sex
couples, why spend precious resources fighting for marriage equality?
Research suggested that gays and lesbians had diverse opinions about marriage and may not have seen marriage equality as a priority issue.[7] As historian George Chauncey pointed out, if a person knows they cannot have
something, they tend to suppress wanting it.[8] Gay couples had been limiting
their aspirations to marry when they thought marriage was impossible; once
marriage was available to them, however, many gay people voted with their
feet and their hearts to get married.

By the middle of 2017, two years after *Obergefell*, there were approximately
1.3 million people in same-sex marriages in the U.S., representing more than
a fifth of all same-sex couples in the country. While same-sex couples were
still much more likely to be in nonmarital unions than were heterosexual
couples, same-sex couples had only had nationwide access to legal marriage for two years, whereas heterosexual society had had a many-centuries-
long head start in organizing itself and its relationship aspirations around
marriage.[9]

Some critics of marriage equality in the gay rights movement and in the
academy assumed that if same-sex couples had a choice, they would (or
should) choose civil unions or domestic partnerships (the new partnership
forms) over marriage. With several years of marriage equality history behind
us, and with marriage and domestic partnerships both available in some
states, it is now clear that same-sex couples have chosen marriage over domestic partnerships for a simple reason: marriage confers a full set of rights
and well-understood social and governmental recognition, whereas domestic partnerships are a lesser substitute, separate and unequal.[10]

Beginning in January 2000, California offered same-sex couples (and
older heterosexual couples) the ability to register as domestic partners.
Domestic partnerships gave couples rights that were expanded over time. By
2012 California afforded domestic partners the same rights within the state
as married couples. California domestic partnerships did not necessarily
carry any weight outside of California, and the federal government was free
to ignore domestic partnerships as long as DOMA remained in force.

In addition to the legal limitations, the new institution of domestic partnership lacked the social status and recognition of marriage. Everyone understood what it meant to be married, whereas the social meaning of a domestic partnership was not as clear. Without the ability to marry in California (except for the brief window in the last half of 2008, after the state supreme court struck down the state's ban on marriage equality and before Proposition 8 reinstated the ban), domestic partnerships were popular. In the thirteen and a half years between January 2000 and June 2013, about fifty thousand same-sex couples in California registered their domestic partnerships. This large number of couples who filed for domestic partnerships (in the absence of the ability to marry) led some scholars to believe erroneously that gays and lesbians would prefer domestic partnership over the more traditional institution of marriage.

Once marriage equality in California was a settled fact (subsequent to *Hollingsworth v. Perry* at the end of June 2013), the number of same-sex couples requesting domestic partnerships in California declined by 60%.[11] In the eighteen months after the *Hollingsworth* decision made California a marriage equality state, there were approximately 28,000 California same-sex couples who got married and approximately 1,300 who filed for domestic partnerships.[12] When given a choice, same-sex couples were choosing marriage over domestic partnership by a ratio of about 20 to 1. Left-wing critics of marriage equality simply underestimated how popular marriage would be in gay and lesbian communities.

Marriage Can Be Radical

Although marriage is a traditional institution beloved by conservatives, same-sex couples who have chosen to marry were not necessarily making a conservative or politically retrograde statement. There is a transformative aspect to same-sex marriage that the left critics of marriage equality overlooked. It is true that heterosexual marriage is built on a set of traditions and (mostly male-centered) expectations that go back centuries. However, leaders of the religious Right who venerate marriage were among the most tenacious opponents of same-sex marriage because they saw it for what it was: a quietly radical act. Same-sex marriage was quietly radical because it sought to end heterosexual exclusivity in one of society's central institutions.[13] Every time a man refers to his partner as his husband, or a woman refers to the woman standing next to her as her wife, a history of gendered assumptions and expectations are turned around a little in a more gay-friendly direction; the earth shifts a bit.[14]

Sociologist Mignon Moore (2018) described the feeling of discomfort but also of radical challenge to preexisting norms she experienced bringing her wife and their children to the Black Pentecostal church in New York that she was raised in, and where her uncle was the pastor. The religious tradition of the church is fundamentally hostile to homosexuality. The other parishioners may have believed that same-sex marriage is against God's will, but those parishioners also knew and respected Moore and her extended family and have known them for decades. Moore's family is a living contrast to a religious ideology that might demonize same-sex couples. She described her participation in the church as a married queer woman not as assimilation or conformity but as a revolutionary way to make others in the community adjust their actions to accommodate themselves to the reality of her LGBTQ family. In her time in the Pentecostal church as an openly gay woman with a wife and children, she had not heard any homophobic comments. The assumption is that the other parishioners had to rethink their views on homosexuality, or at least had to learn to hold their tongues.

Other peoples' rights matter. Moore also argues that other people's rights should be important to you regardless of whether the specific right applies to you. For instance, we should care about public investment in education whether or not we have children. Likewise, marriage equality benefits people whether or not they want to marry because greater rights for some (that do not infringe meaningfully on the rights of others) yield greater rights and greater well-being for all.

Same-sex marriage is both quietly radical and avowedly mainstream. The mainstream part of marriage, the invocation of traditional symbols and the embrace of the ideals of commitment and love, helped straight America see gay America as sharing a common set of ideals with themselves. Once straight America started seeing gay America as having a common set of ideals with themselves, straight Americans started to have more respect for gay rights in general.

The marriage equality movement was a movement for respect as well as for rights. Gay and lesbian people won respect by seeking and advocating for marriage. Although the term "respectability politics" usually has a negative connotation because people assume that the demand for respectability is pushed down to lower-status people from higher-status people, grassroots respectability politics (the progressive kind of respectability politics) helped to liberalize American attitudes toward gay people. The victory of marriage equality is evidence that grassroots respectability politics can succeed. The grassroots form of respectability politics deserves more respect than it has received.

16

Many Closets

Because of the rapid and unprecedented success of gay rights and marriage equality in the U.S., the metaphor of coming out has been widely adopted by other causes and groups. This chapter examines *other* groups and movements that might benefit or have benefited when individuals come out of their different closets. There are many closets. Humans keep, and sometimes are forced to keep, a multitude of secrets.

There are many reasons to think that the coming-out strategy is a broadly useful one. First, individuals have some control over what they share with others about themselves. People can try to dissuade you, but no one can stop you from coming out. Second, coming out is self-affirming, and therefore empowering.

The trajectory of gay rights history demonstrates that one-to-one interaction between individuals and their friends and families can profoundly change how the friends and family members think. When friends and family members across the country are learning the same new things at the same time, national public opinion can shift, as it did in the U.S. with respect to gay rights in the 1990s and 2000s. Public opinion shifts can lead to dramatic policy change. The coming-out strategy makes it seem that social change begins in one's own back yard, with one's own friends and family. Perhaps all social change begins with one's own friends and family, in an exaggerated form of the old aphorism that "all politics are local."

On the other hand, gays and lesbians have some qualities that seem to make coming out of the closet uniquely powerful for them. It may be a little short-sighted to think that people with other kinds of (hidden) identities can elevate their group's standing with the same strategy. Several elements contributed to the special ability of gays and lesbians to leverage coming out into a successful marriage equality movement in the U.S.

1. Gays and lesbians were ubiquitous and integrated with every community.

The Rainbow after the Storm. Michael J. Rosenfeld, Oxford University Press. © Oxford University Press 2022.
DOI: 10.1093/oso/9780197600436.003.0016

2. Gays and lesbians, being from every type of American family, were not at a socioeconomic disadvantage in interactions with others. When gays and lesbians came out of the closet, they could do so as socioeconomic equals. Intergroup contact theory specifies that contact between equals is more likely to dispel prejudice than contact with social subordinates.

3. Homosexuality is a central identity, which meant that gays and lesbians had a strong incentive to come out, knowing that they would benefit in the future from improvements to gay rights.

4. Homosexuality is at least somewhat concealable. Because gays and lesbians were not identifiable at initial meeting, they were not necessarily viewed through the biased filters that are often unconsciously applied when people first meet someone from an identifiable minority group.

5. Marriage equality is nondisplacing, meaning that same-sex couples gained marriage rights in the U.S. without displacing anyone else's marriage rights. No one lost the right to marry when same-sex couples gained the right to marry, and marriage equality imposed no costs on anyone. Because marriage equality imposed no costs on anyone, marriage equality was more difficult to oppose.

6. To the extent that opponents of gay rights relied on falsehoods, they were vulnerable to being undermined by encounters with the truth in the form of actual same-sex couples and real research. For persecuted minorities the truth can be a powerful weapon.

With this outline in mind I now turn to examine other groups who have tried, some more successfully than others, to follow the same strategy.

Undocumented Immigrants

In June 2016, Larissa Martinez, valedictorian of McKinney Boyd High School in Texas, was giving her speech to the assembled students and families at her graduation ceremony. Martinez had been accepted to Yale University, one of the most selective American universities. In her valedictory speech, she revealed that she was an undocumented immigrant. Her revelation may have made a powerful impression on some of her classmates, because she was the opposite of what anti-immigrant rhetoric leads one to expect undocumented immigrants would be like.[1] Opponents of immigration in the U.S. paint immigrants as lazy and prone to crime. The charge of laziness is easy to dispel, as immigrants often work dirty and dangerous jobs that U.S. natives would not take at any salary. The claim that immigrants in the U.S. are prone to criminality has also been dispelled and discredited.[2] U.S. natives commit violent crimes at higher rates than do immigrants. Martinez seized a rare and powerful opportunity to challenge anti-immigrant stereotypes in her community. Most undocumented immigrants do not have a valedictory speech as a platform in which to come out of the closet as undocumented.

Undocumented immigrants in the U.S. are a closeted minority, and documentary status is a central identity for them.[3] The ability of undocumented immigrants to emerge from the closet is sharply constrained, however, by the threat of deportation. Furthermore, undocumented immigrants are highly segregated by geography, by race and ethnicity, by language, and by socioeconomic status from people born in the U.S. The segregation along several dimensions between undocumented immigrants and U.S. natives means that (quite distinct from the situation faced by gays and lesbians) even if undocumented immigrants came out of the closet in large numbers, their ability to interact with and influence the wider American society would be limited.[4]

Most undocumented immigrants in the U.S. hold low-status positions, and therefore are unable to interact with U.S. natives from a position of equality. Without equality of status, interpersonal contact is much less likely to erode bias.[5] Therefore, a strategy of coming out of the closet does not hold a great deal of promise for undocumented immigrants in the U.S.

Women Who Have Had Abortions

As I noted in chapter 8, the abortion issue and the gay rights issue split the U.S. electorate along similar lines: Republicans, religious people, and southerners are more likely than other Americans to oppose both abortion rights and gay rights. Despite the fact that abortion rights and gay rights divide the U.S. electorate along some similar lines, approval of gay rights has risen dramatically over time, whereas approval of abortion rights has mostly been stagnant. One reason for the striking difference in public opinion is that gays and lesbians have come out of the closet, but women's abortion experiences have remained in the closet.

The *Roe v. Wade* (1973) Supreme Court decision legalized elective abortion in the first trimester of pregnancy, and in the second trimester to save the mother's health. The endorsement of abortion rights in *Roe* should have made abortion rights more normative and therefore more popular in the U.S., but that has not happened.[6] Support for abortion rights grew in the U.S. between 1972 and 1973. After 1973, approval of abortion rights has eroded somewhat.

Nearly half of American adults do not believe they know someone who has had an abortion. Miscarriage is less common than abortion in the U.S., but Americans are much more likely to say they know someone who has had a miscarriage than they are to say they know someone who has had an abortion.[7] If more women who have had abortions disclosed their abortion history to friends and family members, the public perception of abortion rights could potentially be liberalized.

Abortion rights activist Amelia Bonow asked women to come out of the closet and share their abortion experiences under the Twitter hashtag #Shoutyourabortion. Thousands of women have revealed their abortion histories and had those disclosures tweeted about, but this number is tiny compared to the approximately 30 million American women who have had abortions.[8]

The idea of destigmatizing abortion by taking abortion experiences out of the closet is not new. In 1972, in the inaugural issue of the American feminist vanguard magazine *Ms.*, fifty-three women[9] outed themselves as having had abortions. For most of those women, their abortions would have been illegal. The article in *Ms.* asked other women to fill out a declaration stating, "I have had an abortion," and to mail that declaration in to the magazine.[10]

Women who have had abortions have advantages in coming out because abortion is now generally legal in the U.S. Unlike undocumented immigrants today, and unlike gays and lesbians in the past (before *Lawrence v. Texas* in 2003 made state sodomy laws unconstitutional) and unlike American women before *Roe v. Wade*, American women today would face no legal jeopardy for disclosing their previously undisclosed abortions. On the other hand, the stigma against abortion in the U.S. remains fierce, especially in conservative and religious communities, and the antiabortion movement includes some violent groups. Women know that outing themselves as having had an abortion would come with risks and reputational costs.

Although abortion rates are much higher among poor women and women of color, abortion is common enough so that women who have had abortions live in every geographic place and are part of every socioeconomic group and every race and ethnic group in the U.S.[11] Similar to gays and lesbians, women who have had abortions are part of every extended family, every large workplace, and every county in America. Being integrated with, rather than segregated from, the mainstream means that women who have had abortions could potentially sway mainstream American opinion about abortion—if the women came out of the closet.

One of the reasons women's abortion histories have remained so closeted is that they are especially difficult for others to uncover. To a certain extent, gays and lesbians who came out of the closet did so because they were forced to; being gay or lesbian was a secret that could be used against them by police and governments.[12] One of the reasons Ellen DeGeneres gave for coming out when she did was that she wanted to do so on her own terms rather than be outed by others. As long as women are not in danger of being outed for having had abortions, their motivation for outing themselves is reduced.

Coming out of the closet represents a classic kind of sociological dilemma. The costs of coming out weigh more heavily on the individuals who are among the first to come out. The benefits, in terms of elevated status for the group, are shared by all within the group, whether or not they individually come out. The more individuals within the group come out, the greater the benefits to the group. This problem of motivating people to come out is a collective action problem, which explains why it can be difficult to motivate people to contribute personal efforts to collective goods.

The collective action problem for women is amplified by the fact that women age out of the childbearing years. Unlike gay and lesbian identity, which most individuals have consistently throughout their adult lives, an individual's potential need for abortion is specific to the childbearing years.

Abortion history is not generally central to a woman's identity. Women who have had abortions tend not think of themselves *primarily* as someone who has had an abortion. Past abortions (and especially long-past abortions) might not provide sufficient motivation for them to out themselves.

Federal law prevents doctors and hospitals from divulging medical histories. A person's sexual identity is not as conspicuous as their race or gender, but sexual identity is substantially more conspicuous than abortion history. Sexual identity is acted out with partners in the present, which is how both the police and gay rights activists in the past discovered who was gay. The possibility of being outed by others was one reason gays and lesbians made the decision to come out and to control their own stories.

Abortion history, in contrast to sexual identity, leaves no discernable marks. Women generally do not have to fear that they will be outed for having had an abortion. For women who have had abortions, that fact is concealable, too concealable for the coming-out strategy to be widely adopted. Women who have had abortions have little incentive to come out of the closet. As long as abortion histories remain mostly closeted, most Americans don't know who among their circle of friends and family has had an abortion.

American adults know women who have had abortions, but they do not *know* that they know. As long as Americans don't know who among their circle has had an abortion, it will be difficult for abortion rights activists to move public opinion toward greater acceptance of abortion rights.

Victims of Sexual Harassment and Sexual Assault

The #MeToo and #TimesUp movements, organized to fight sexual assault and harassment, are excellent examples of what can be accomplished relatively quickly when people come out of the closet. On April 1, 2017, reporters for the *New York Times* broke the story that Bill O'Reilly, right-wing provocateur and television personality, and his employer, Fox News, had over the years paid more than $13 million to settle sexual harassment claims from at least five different women.[13] The reporters later uncovered that O'Reilly had paid an additional victim $32 million, bringing the total value of payouts to more than $45 million. As a condition of payment, each of O'Reilly's victims had been forced to sign legal agreements that promised nondisclosure and nondisparagement. Victims of harassment were put in the closet.

The legally enforced closet made it possible for O'Reilly to harass more people. This same closet also made it possible for his employer, Fox News, to mislead the women harassed by O'Reilly into believing that no one else had complained about harassment from O'Reilly. If each victim believed she was the only victim, she would naturally fear that no one would find her allegation credible.[14]

Harvey Weinstein, like Bill O'Reilly, was a powerful American media mogul. Politically, he was a famous liberal, whereas O'Reilly was a famous conservative—not that their espoused politics seems to have made any difference in their behavior. Weinstein too was credibly accused of assaulting a number women. For years, his crimes were hidden from the public because the victims were paid for their silence, bullied, and threatened.[15]

Actress Rose McGowan claimed that she was raped by Weinstein in 1997, twenty years before the storm of other women's allegations forced him to resign his job in disgrace. McGowan did not press charges because she was advised by lawyers that she was unlikely to win the case. Instead, she alleged that Weinstein and his powerful Hollywood allies punished her, and her career suffered as a result.[16] In 2020 Weinstein was tried in New York and convicted of sexually assaulting Miriam Haley and Jessica Mann.[17]

Larry Nassar was the physician for the U.S. Women's Olympic Gymnastics Team. In the course of performing physical exams on female athletes, Nassar groped and assaulted more than 250 women and girls. He was convicted of child pornography, was convicted of multiple counts of molestation, and was sentenced to a decades-long prison term that will probably mean he will spend the rest of his life in prison.[18] The U.S. Olympic Committee and U.S.A. Gymnastics, the organizations that oversaw America's gymnastics training program, and Michigan State University, where Nassar worked, all demonstrated a much keener interest in keeping the complaints quiet and in protecting their institutions than they ever demonstrated in protecting the girls he assaulted year after year.[19]

Several factors keep serial harassers and abusers in power in a legal climate in the U.S. in which sexual harassment, rape, and sexual assault are all illegal but difficult to prove and therefore difficult to punish. Serial harassers and perpetrators of sexual assault depend on a calculation that victims and survivors will see keeping quiet as in their own best interest. In the past the stigma of being a victim of harassment, rape, or assault was usually so great that social pressure kept the victims quiet. Women who spoke out against a powerful man were likely to face a storm of criticism. Institutions that employed serial harassers and violent abusers could push victims and survivors into the closet, confident of their silence. In an earlier era, when the closet was the only safe place for a victim of harassment or a survivor of assault, it was easy for abusers and harassers to move on to the next victim, sure that the next victim and the previous victim would never know about each other's shared trauma.

In the early 2000s, evidence began to emerge of a decades-long history of cover-ups within the Catholic Church in the U.S. Hundreds of priests molested thousands of children. Reporters for the *Boston Globe* discovered that private legal agreements, payoffs to victims, nondisclosure agreements, and the victims' feelings of shame all shielded priests from the criminal charges they should have faced. Bishops and archbishops allowed priests who had sexually abused children to remain in their jobs for years because the truth about their crimes was hidden.[20] When people in one parish learned about a priest's sexual abuse of children, church leaders quietly moved that priest to another parish, allowing known abusers to find and abuse new victims.[21] The full picture of priestly abuse of children emerged only when reporters and investigators gathered the previously isolated stories, and when survivors and victims emerged from the closet.[22]

The Impact of #MeToo

In the summer and fall of 2017, American women's willingness to come out about their victimization turned the tables on serial harassers and abusers Bill O'Reilly and Harvey Weinstein, both of whom faced a sea of previously suppressed complaints, and both of whom lost their very prominent positions. Weinstein eventually ended up being convicted of sexual assault and is serving time in prison. Two other prominent men in television, Matt Lauer and Charlie Rose, faced credible complaints in 2017 by different women and soon lost their jobs as well. The Twitter #MeToo hashtag, through which women could publicly share their experience of sexual violence, was popularized. The Me Too movement had been created by Black feminist Tarana Burke a decade earlier specifically to counter sexual violence against women. Speaking out about one's personal truth is one way that people can empower themselves and raise the status of similarly situated others. A willingness to speak out and tell one's truth makes it more difficult for others in the same situation to be silenced. In October 2018, the *New York Times* listed 201 powerful men who had lost their jobs because their abusive and harassing behavior had been made public and corroborated through #MeToo.[23]

The #MeToo moment demonstrated something about women's victimization that gay rights activists have always understood: the silence of the closet is profoundly disadvantageous. It is not clear yet whether #MeToo, which had a powerful surge in attention in 2017 in the U.S., will be associated with greater societal support for or greater hostility and suspicion toward the women who make sexual assault and sexual harassment allegations.[24]

Sexual assault and sexual harassment claims are always contested and displacing of the privileges of the alleged perpetrators. If the accuser is believed, the alleged perpetrator may face severe sanctions. Assault and harassment claims inevitably face specific pushback by the accused because of how much is at stake. Even when the accuser is believed, the displacing nature of the accusations and the seriousness of the potential punishments can make people shy away from following through to punish the accused. The movement to raise the status of sexual assault and harassment survivors has faced a generalized backlash on the grounds that the accusations (of which there are many of all types) have gone too far.[25] Displacing movements generally find that their goals are more difficult to achieve.

#MeToo, a displacing social movement in heavily contested terrain, has won spectacular victories in a short period of time. But despite the high-profile victories, it is too soon to tell whether #MeToo will permanently shift American attitudes about sexual harassment. Some accused perpetrators have sailed forward seemingly without consequences.

A month before the 2016 U.S. presidential election, the *Washington Post* obtained a video in which the Republican candidate, Donald Trump, was heard bragging about sexually assaulting women. Trump offered a weak apology for the video and attacked the media for its supposed political correctness. He implied that the women who accused him of sexual assault were liars. A month later, Trump won a 62% majority of the White male vote and 52% of the White female vote for president. He lost the popular vote by 3 million votes because of opposition by minority voters, but he won the state-by-state Electoral College that determines U.S. presidential elections. Trump's victory and his popularity among White women despite bragging about sexual assault and being credibly accused of sexual assault are reminders that people (and especially powerful people) may still get away with sexual assault despite survivors coming out of the closet.[26]

In contrast to the generally self- authenticating and self-referential nature of gay identity, being a sexual assault survivor is a dyadic identity that necessarily implicates someone else with a very different kind of identity: that of perpetrator. In order to be the survivor of a sexual assault, there must be a perpetrator. In the perpetrator's version of events, however, the survivor may be painted as a liar and an opportunist while the perpetrator identifies as the victim of false accusations. Survivor and victim identities generally displace each other.

Most sexual assaults take place without third-party witnesses. Regardless of the level of public sympathy for sexual assault survivors in general, each individual survivor of assault faces a difficult challenge in convincing others to accept the veracity of their version of events. The difficulty of establishing a survivor or victim identity that will be persuasive to others and the potential for alleged perpetrators to win a persuasion contest in the courts or in the court of public opinion remain strong disincentives for survivors to come out of the closet.

On the Broader Applicability of Coming Out

Coming out of the closet is not a panacea. It is certainly *not* true that all forms of bigotry would disappear if everyone were simply honest and open about who they really are. Racial minority groups are already out of the closet, but being out has not helped them much. Racial minorities are socially and physically isolated from White America. Furthermore, since race is associated with phenotype and is usually not concealable, people from racial minority groups are often prejudged, which means their contact with others is filtered through preexisting biases that are difficult to overcome. Undocumented immigrants could all come out of the closet and declare themselves, but their social distance, status disadvantage, and isolation from the American mainstream would probably prevent them from being able to turn public opinion substantially in their favor.

Feminists have been trying for decades to get women to come out of the closet about their abortion histories, without much success. Women who have had abortions are a group whose situation vis-à-vis the mainstream is perhaps most similar to that of gays and lesbians. Women who have had abortions are part of every family, every racial group, and every social stratum. The concealability of abortion history is generally air-tight, so the incentive for women to come out of the closet about their abortion histories has been, up to now, insufficient. As a result, the vast majority of abortion histories in the U.S. are closeted and probably will remain so. Public support for abortion rights will continue to be held down by Americans' unfamiliarity with the abortion histories of their friends and family.

Social observers have noted an increasing belief in the strategy and the metaphor of coming out across many kinds of minority and stigmatized groups, inspired in part by the real gains in gay rights and marriage equality in the U.S.[27] Groups that urge their people to come out of the closet are not wrong to believe that doing so will help them. Survivors of sexual assault have come out of the closet in recent years and have managed to bring some powerful and important perpetrators to justice.

Coming out might not help other groups to reshape public opinion *as much* as it has helped gays and lesbians to reshape public opinion about gay rights, but it might help enough to make a difference. Few groups are as unpopular in the U.S. now as gays and lesbians were in the past, so most groups do not need to climb a public opinion mountain nearly as steep. On most issues where there is more moderation or more evenly divided opinion to begin with, public opinion would not have to be moved nearly so far in order to facilitate a social change. Attitudes toward abortion, for instance, have always been closely divided.[28] A small change in public opinion about abortion rights can lead to a substantial difference in public policies around access to abortion.

17

Displacing and Nondisplacing Movements

Political scientist Gerald Rosenberg (2008) has argued that American courts are uniquely unable to make social change because they lack implementation capacity. The second *Brown v. Board of Education* (1955) Supreme Court decision, a follow-up to the more famous *Brown* decision from the previous year, called for the desegregation of American public schools to be accomplished "with all deliberate speed." As Rosenberg points out, the Supreme Court could not force school desegregation to happen at any speed. The pace of actual desegregation in American public schools after 1955 was not deliberate, but glacial.[1]

School desegregation was a displacing social movement goal, in Gamson's (1990) terms. In order for Black children to attend public schools with White children, the classroom experience of the White children was necessarily going to be impacted. Many White parents in segregated communities in the U.S. were violently opposed to the idea of their children attending school with Black children, not to speak of having their children bused across town. Furthermore, school desegregation required the building of new schools, as the schools the Black children had been attending were inadequate. School desegregation potentially also required the hiring of new teachers and staff. Any social movement goal that requires substantial spending is necessarily displacing because expenditures for one purpose displace spending on other priorities. Resources are finite.

Like school desegregation, abortion rights are displacing. The right of a woman to have an abortion displaces the alleged right of the fetus to be carried to term. Antiabortion activists focus effectively on what they describe as the rights of the fetus to highlight the extent to which abortion rights are displacing.[2] And as was also true of school desegregation, abortion access is not cheap to provide. Doctors, pharmacists, nurses, and clinics require licensing and a place to practice, and all that comes at a cost. Any goal that carries significant costs is necessarily displacing.[3]

Being a nondisplacing movement was one of the great advantages for marriage equality and one of the key reasons for its eventual success in the U.S.

The Rainbow after the Storm. Michael J. Rosenfeld, Oxford University Press. © Oxford University Press 2022.
DOI: 10.1093/oso/9780197600436.003.0017

Unlike civil rights and abortion rights, marriage equality's lack of displace-ment of the rights of others has made it easier to avoid the backlash that has made the implementation of both civil rights and abortion rights much more difficult to achieve.[4]

Masterpiece Cakeshop *and* Miller v. Davis

In 2012, Coloradans Charlie Craig and Dave Mullins were planning to marry. Same-sex marriage was not yet legal in Colorado, but it was legal in other states. Craig and Mullins visited the Masterpiece Cakeshop in Lakewood, Colorado, and asked baker Jack Phillips to make them an appropriate wed-ding cake. Phillips refused, on the ground that he had religious objections to same-sex marriage and that making a wedding cake would require him to be involved in a same-sex wedding in a way that was unacceptable for him. Colorado had amended its antidiscrimination law in 2008 to protect people from discrimination based on sexual orientation, making Colorado one of the U.S. states that was at the time most protective of gay rights. Craig and Mullins filed a complaint with the Colorado Civil Rights Commission, which heard the complaint and found that Phillips had violated the state's nondis-crimination laws. Phillips appealed to the Colorado courts, where he lost, and then he appealed to the U.S. Supreme Court.

In *Masterpiece Cakeshop v. Colorado Civil Rights Commission* (2018), the U.S. Supreme Court decided 7–2 (with a majority decision written by Justice Kennedy) that the Colorado Civil Rights Commission had failed to take Phillips's religious beliefs reasonably into account. The Colorado Civil Rights Commission had undermined its ruling with statements that were hostile toward religion. A more even-handed state commission might have had a ruling against Masterpiece Cakeshop upheld.[5] Phillips's personal objection to same-sex marriage was rooted in his sincerely held religious faith, a faith which the Court found that the Colorado Civil Rights Commission had not taken seriously enough.

The *Masterpiece Cakeshop* decision was a critique of the inadequacies of the process used by the Colorado Civil Rights Commission rather than a vindication of the baker's asserted right not to do business with gay couples. Phillips claimed that the nondiscrimination law in Colorado (rather than marriage equality) had displaced his rights, but the *Masterpiece Cakeshop* decision simply confirmed that he ought to have been given a respectful hearing.

Unlike marriage equality (which is nondisplacing), laws that ban discrimination are displacing. Policies that are displacing can create conflicts between the rights of different parties. The courts have generally found that religious beliefs do not immunize business people from their obligation to treat patrons in a nondiscriminatory way. The *Masterpiece Cakeshop* decision did not find that the baker had the right to refuse service to gay couples.[6]

Religious people have sometimes argued that marriage equality displaces their rights, but these arguments have fallen flat. Consider the case of Kentucky's Kim Davis, clerk of Rowan County. Immediately after the *Obergefell v. Hodges* (2015) decision legalized same-sex marriage across the U.S., the governor of Kentucky issued a procedural order, ordering county clerks in Kentucky to begin marrying same-sex couples. Davis, the elected county clerk, decided that because of her personal religious objection to same-sex marriage, her office would no longer issue marriage licenses to anyone. April Miller and Karen Roberts applied for a marriage license at the Rowan County clerk's office and were denied. They sued Davis in her official capacity in federal court.

Federal District Judge David Bunning quickly issued an order, compelling Davis to issue marriage licenses to same-sex couples and heterosexual couples alike.[7] Judge Bunning found that Davis's sincerely held religious objections to same-sex marriage did not excuse her from performing her official duties or from allowing the official duty of issuing marriage licenses to be performed by other people. Davis appealed Bunning's ruling to the Sixth Circuit, which ruled against her, and then to the Supreme Court, which denied *Cert* on her appeal. Davis believed that marriage equality displaced her rights, but the courts disagreed. When she continued to refuse to issue marriage licenses as ordered by Judge Bunning, she was briefly jailed for contempt of court. Davis's cause was championed by political leaders of the Christian Right, including Republicans Ted Cruz and Mike Huckabee, who painted her as a Christian martyr to gay rights.[8]

Ultimately, Davis went back to work in the clerk's office and started issuing marriage licenses to same-sex couples and to heterosexual couples, as the law required.[9] Because marriage equality was a nondisplacing social change, it was adopted immediately and, with only a few minor hiccups, implemented everywhere in the U.S.[10]

As the *April Miller et al. v. Kim Davis* cases show, there was some local resistance in the South to the implementation of marriage equality, but the resistance did not have practical effect for long. There was some defiant talk by Republican leaders in the politically conservative states of Texas, Louisiana, Mississippi, and Alabama immediately after the *Obergefell* decision, but three days after *Obergefell* most of the elected officials in the South had fallen in line and complied with orders to allow same-sex couples to marry.[11] The contrast is striking between the rapid and mostly unremarkable dispersion of marriage equality and the decades-long and effective resistance in the South to school desegregation. Some of the difference has to do with the nondisplacing nature of the former, contrasted with the displacing nature of the latter intervention.

The Fight to Protect LGBT People from Workplace Discrimination

Unlike marriage equality, nondiscrimination laws are displacing. Antidiscrimination regimes create regulatory infrastructure, the need for education, and private lawsuits to test and enforce the rules. Antidiscrimination laws are expensive, and they infringe, often reasonably and necessarily, on the asserted rights of discriminators. In the 1980s and 1990s, laws banning workplace discrimination against gays and lesbians had much more popular support than did marriage equality.

In 1988, when marriage equality had only 11.6% support, more than 54% of Americans already supported laws protecting gays and lesbians against job discrimination (see Figure 17.1). It was no wonder that many gay rights activists thought that it would be more fruitful to fight for protections against job discrimination. But despite a much lower level of public support (compared to the movement for workplace nondiscrimination), the marriage equality movement had several advantages as a vehicle for social change. First, marriage equality was nondisplacing. Second, marriage equality plaintiffs were able to show straight Americans a side of gay life that they had never seen before; this reflects the advantage of grassroots respectability politics. There was a special symbolism in same-sex couples claiming marriage that had the power to move straight Americans to be more supportive of gay rights. As a result of the advantages of marriage equality, it was achieved

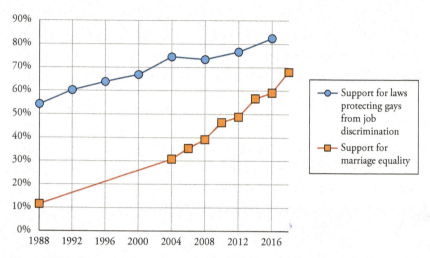

Figure 17.1 Change over time in support for marriage equality and laws protecting gays and lesbians against job discrimination.

Source: Weighted ANES data on support for laws protecting gays and lesbians from job discrimination, and weighted GSS data on support for marriage equality.

nationwide in 2015, while workplace nondiscrimination of gays and lesbians in the U.S. was not achieved until five years later, in 2020.

Before the *Bostock v. Clayton County* (2020) decision, about half of the U.S. states permitted employers to fire employees for no other reason than that they were gay, lesbian, or transgender.[12] That meant that in about half the states, a couple could marry on a Sunday (after *Obergefell* in 2015), have their picture in the paper, and be fired on Monday for being gay.[13] The intolerability of workplace discrimination against gays and lesbians had always been evident to people who believed in gay rights, but marriage equality made the intolerability of workplace discrimination more obvious to others. Marriage equality made gays and lesbians full members of civil society. Full members of civil society ought not to be fired from work for simply being who they are. The achievement of marriage equality helped to erode some of the credibility of defenders of workplace discrimination against gays and lesbians. Although the *Obergefell* decision was about marriage equality, the normative and expressive importance of *Obergefell* had inevitable implications for gay rights in other areas, such as employment.[14]

In *Bostock v. Clayton County*, the post-Kennedy Court ruled, with a 6–3 majority decision written by conservative justice Neil Gorsuch, that Title VII of the Civil Rights Act of 1964, which had made sex discrimination in the workplace illegal, necessarily applied to (and therefore made illegal) workplace discrimination against gays, lesbians, and transgender people. Gay plaintiffs who had been fired from their jobs had been trying for decades after 1964 to convince courts to recognize antigay and anti-transgender discrimination as examples of sex discrimination that would entitle them to protection under the landmark Civil Rights Act of 1964, but for decades the courts had rejected this claim.

The original intent of the 1964 Congress posed a challenge for gay rights plaintiffs. Congress had not intended the Civil Rights Act to protect gay and lesbian people from workplace discrimination. In 1964 sodomy was illegal in every state but one, gay people were subject to many legal persecutions, and transgender people were an invisible minority.

Title VII of the Civil Rights Act of 1964 states, "It shall be an unlawful employment practice for an employer to fail or refuse to hire or to discharge any individual . . . because of such individual's race, color, religion, sex, or national origin." The workplace protections of Title VII apply to all private U.S. employers with at least fifteen employees. By one count, the first thirty federal judges who ruled on the question of whether Title VII's ban on sex-based job discrimination would protect gays and lesbians from job discrimination ruled no.[15]

Members of Congress have attempted on many occasions between 1975 and 2019 to amend Title VII to explicitly ban sexual identity discrimination in the workplace, but those efforts failed.[16] Justice Samuel Alito's dissent in *Bostock* made the point that Congress's attempts to amend Title VII demonstrated that members knew, or at least feared, that Title VII as written did not protect gays and lesbians from job discrimination.

If the Civil Rights Act of 1964 remained (in this one respect) unchanged,[17] and if the dictionary definition of the word "sex" had not changed, and if the courts had established a precedent that gays and lesbians were not protected by Title VII, what did change? First, Congress made other changes to the law regarding discrimination and sexual harassment after 1964. Second, the Supreme Court made other rulings that expanded the kinds of employer behavior that were actionable under Title VII.[18] In one 1989 case,[19] the Court ruled that a straight[20] woman named Ann Hopkins, who was denied a promotion because the leaders of her company thought she was not normatively feminine enough, could sue under Title VII. Hopkins apparently did not look or act womanly enough for her bosses. Legal scholars have noted that gay and lesbian people face exactly this kind of bias and discrimination: failing to accord with someone's gendered norms for how a man or woman should act, live, or appear.

And yet courts had been unwilling to put the pieces together. It was only after the *Obergefell* decision in 2015 that the U.S. circuit courts started to recognize that antigay discrimination was a form of sex discrimination under Title VII.[21] A mere two and a half weeks after the June 26, 2015, *Obergefell* decision was announced, the Obama administration's Equal Employment Opportunity Commission (EEOC) reversed fifty years of policy and made an administrative ruling for the first time that sexual orientation discrimination violated Title VII.[22]

EEOC commissioner Chai Feldblum had long been an advocate for interpreting Title VII to protect LGBT people.[23] By the summer of 2015, Feldblum and staff lawyer Pierce Blue had outlined what a new ruling would look like. Treating antigay discrimination as an example of sex discrimination was not a new idea. The idea that laws prohibiting discrimination based on sex should protect LGBT people from discrimination had been proposed before by marriage equality plaintiffs and had been accepted by some judges in marriage equality cases.[24]

On the other side of the political spectrum, the conservative opponents of the Equal Rights Amendment had argued in the 1970s that equality of the sexes under law would necessarily lead to gay rights and same-sex marriage, which the conservatives knew the country was not yet ready for.[25] In the 1970s, the idea that gender equality would necessarily also include gay rights was used as a bludgeon by conservatives to move public opinion against the ERA. Conservative opponents of the ERA ultimately won their struggle and prevented enough states from ratifying the ERA. Both conservatives and liberals in the U.S. were at least acquainted with the idea that bans on discrimination because of sex might also protect LGBT people.

By 2015 Feldblum had convinced a majority of EEOC commissioners that the time for a reassessment of Title VII had come. The liberalization in public attitudes toward gay rights and the social reality of marriage equality made antigay discrimination in the workplace suddenly less defensible. Courts quickly started to take a fresh look at whether LGBT people should be protected by the language of Title VII.

The Seventh Circuit, taking a cue in part from the EEOC, was the first federal appellate court (in April 2017) to rule that Title VII's ban on discrimination because of sex also protected gays and lesbians. The Second Circuit followed in February 2018, and the Sixth Circuit followed in March

2018.[26] According to Feldblum, U.S. courts had been hesitant to interpret protections "because of sex" in the law as protecting LGBT people because they were afraid of the implications of gender equality for marriage equality. After *Obergefell*, the U.S. already had marriage equality, so that particular concern no longer applied.

Adding to a growing body of law on harassment and discrimination and new Supreme Court precedents, public opinion about gay rights liberalized in a historic way. Social norms around sex and gender changed. Straight people's exposure to gay people increased sharply. Judge Richard Posner's concurrence in the Seventh Circuit case noted, "Nothing has changed more in the decades since the enactment of the statute than attitudes toward sex."[27] Social change, attitude change, and the achievement of marriage equality through the *Obergefell* decision all shifted the landscape for gay rights very substantially.

Gay people came out of the closet in great numbers in the 1990s and 2000s, and suddenly American employers had to consider putting same-sex partners on employee health plans as a way to retain their gay workers. To counter the employers who had fired the gay and transgender plaintiffs in *Bostock*, 206 big American businesses (including General Motors, Bank of America, American Airlines, AT&T, Coca-Cola, Comcast, IBM, Northrop Grumman, Proctor & Gamble, and State Farm) submitted an amicus brief asking the Supreme Court to extend Title VII protections to gay, lesbian, and transgender workers. The 206 prominent companies explicitly endorsed equal treatment for gay, lesbian, and transgender employees in their own corporate networks, and they were not afraid of an expanded interpretation of the Civil Rights Act that would give victims of discrimination new avenues to sue employers.

The great wave of gay people coming out of the closet in the 1990s and 2000s meant that straight employees started to know their gay coworkers. Discrimination against gay and lesbian people was not just an abstract thing anymore for straight people. Discrimination had consequences for people in one's personal circle that made the unfairness of discrimination more obvious and more unacceptable.

Gerald Bostock was a child welfare advocate in Clayton County, Georgia, and by reputation a very good one. Clayton County won awards for Bostock's work. Nevertheless, he was fired when his employer found out that he was participating in a gay softball league. Donald Zarda was a skydiving instructor in New York; he was fired after he told a female client he was gay to allay her fears about being strapped to him during a jump. Aimee Stephens worked at a funeral home in Michigan and was undergoing transition from male to female; Stephens wrote a letter to her employer to explain her transition, and she was fired. Bostock, Zarda, and Stephens all sued, all sought relief under Title VII, and their cases had different trajectories. At the appellate court level, Bostock lost (in the Eleventh Circuit), while Zarda (Second Circuit) and Stephens (Sixth Circuit) won. The divergent decisions required the Supreme Court to resolve the conflict. By the time the Court decided the consolidated case, Zarda and Stephens had passed away.

Gay and lesbian people coming out of the closet helped to shift Americans' attitudes toward gay rights. The marriage equality movement achieved the nondisplacing goal of allowing same-sex couples to marry everywhere in the U.S. Marriage equality went from Supreme Court decision to reality across the U.S. in record time because marriage equality was nondisplacing. The reality that gay people could marry their partners but could still be fired for being gay (in about half of the states, prior to *Bostock*) made workplace discrimination against gays and lesbians seem more outrageous and unfair.

The inclusion of same-sex couples within the institution of marriage helped normalize same-sex couples and, by extension, all queer people. Normalization meant that queer people who were victims of workplace discrimination had their claims taken more seriously in court. Once the courts had to really *hear* the stories of gay and trans people fired only for being gay and trans, and *see* these plaintiffs as being not so different from themselves, it became clear that antigay and antitrans discrimination was (at least in part) a function of sex because of the way the employees' behavior failed to meet normative gendered expectations.[28]

Because of changing attitudes toward gay and transgender people across the whole of U.S. society, plaintiffs like Bostock, Zarda, and Stephens had their claims taken seriously by the courts in a way that previous generations of gay and transgender victims of discrimination had never experienced. Because the courts had to take Bostock's, Zarda's, and Stephens's cases seriously, the courts had to consider *why* employers were discriminating against gay, lesbian, and transgender workers. The Supreme Court majority in *Bostock* decided that if a male employee had a male partner and was fired because of it, but a female employee would not be fired for having a male partner, then antigay discrimination was necessarily about the sex of the employee.[29]

The dissenting opinions in *Bostock* are interesting for the way they distance themselves from outright support of antigay and antitrans discrimination, despite casting their judicial votes against the court's expansion of Title VII. Both Justice Alito's and Justice Brett Kavanaugh's dissents were careful to claim that an end to workplace discrimination against gay people would be welcome, but it was Congress's job to implement the change. In an earlier time Justice Scalia could reflect what he took to be a broad antigay public mood in his dissent in *Lawrence v. Texas* (2003: 602): "Many Americans do not want persons who openly engage in homosexual conduct as partners in their business, as scoutmasters for their children, as teachers in their children's schools, or as boarders in their home. They view this as protecting themselves and their families from a lifestyle that they believe to be immoral and destructive." Justice Kavanaugh's dissent in *Bostock* (2020: 1837) presented a different message, more in keeping with today's public support for gay rights:

[I]t is appropriate to acknowledge the important victory achieved today by gay and lesbian Americans. Millions of gay and lesbian Americans have worked hard for many decades to achieve equal treatment in fact and in law. They have exhibited extraordinary vision, tenacity, and grit—battling often steep odds in the legislative and judicial arenas, not to mention in their daily lives. They have advanced powerful policy arguments and can take pride in today's result. Under the Constitution's separation of powers, however, I believe that it was Congress's role, not this Court's, to amend Title VII.

While both Justices Kavanaugh (in 2020) and Scalia (in 2003) were casting their judicial votes against expansions of gay rights, their expressive messages were quite different. In terms of the expressive meaning of the law, and in terms of the signals sent to those who would discriminate against gays and lesbians, there is a big difference between sympathizing with antigay discrimination, as Scalia did, and sympathizing with gays and lesbians in their quest for rights, as Kavanaugh did. As Justice Alito's dissent in *Bostock* (2020: 1784) noted, "Today, many Americans know individuals who are gay, lesbian, or transgender and want them to be treated with the dignity, consideration, and fairness that everyone deserves."

The passage of time and the change in U.S. public opinion about gay people and gay rights have taken important degrees of credibility away from old-fashioned forms of antigay discrimination. Some kinds of antigay discrimination that were once perfectly acceptable in polite society no longer are. As Justice Alito's dissent in *Obergefell* (2015: 741) noted, "I assume that those who cling to old beliefs will be able to whisper their thoughts in the recesses of their homes, but if they repeat those views in public they will risk being labeled as bigots and treated as such by governments, employers, and schools." Here Alito was bemoaning that changing American attitudes had made bigots out of people who held what decades before were commonly accepted antigay views. His discomfort with the rise of gay rights in public opinion did not prevent him from recognizing that times were indeed changing. The more sympathetic (to gay rights) tone of his *Bostock* dissent five years after *Obergefell* is another sign of the way that liberalizing public opinion on gay rights issues and the reality of marriage equality have shaped judicial views of gay rights.

Alito's dissent in *Bostock* consisted of more than seventeen thousand words, of which the twenty-six words I quoted (about the "dignity, consideration, and fairness that everyone deserves") are but a small part. A substantial part was devoted to listing ways in which the rights of transgender people might potentially displace the rights of others. In Alito's view, the right of transgender people to use the bathroom appropriate for their lived gender identity might displace the right of women to disrobe without genetically male persons in the room; the right of transwomen to play on women's athletic teams might displace the right of biologically female people to have their own athletic competitions; religious schools that want to hire only cisgender teachers might have legal exposure under an expanded Title VII. The issue of whether LGBT rights displace the rights of others and how to resolve the questions where two groups have competing claims will be central issues for years to come. There are many cases working their way through the courts that will test these boundaries.

Although marriage equality was a bitterly contested political issue in the U.S. for more than two decades, once the Supreme Court made marriage equality the law the practical hurdles to marriage equality disappeared amazingly quickly. Within just a few days of the *Obergefell* decision, even in the most conservative parts of the U.S., same-sex couples were marrying. The contrast with school desegregation is striking: more than sixty years after *Brown*, the U.S. still has not achieved school integration by race. The nondisplacing nature of marriage equality was a key advantage that allowed marriage equality to be adopted broadly and rapidly.

The nondisplacing nature of marriage equality also helps to explain why it was achieved before workplace equality, despite the latter having more public support. The *Obergefell* decision led to the rapid implementation of marriage equality across the U.S. because marriage equality is nondisplacing. Opponents of marriage equality had no reasonable grounds to resist once it was the law. The reality of same-sex couples getting married with the blessings of the state had instantaneous ramifications for the way gay people were perceived. Breakthrough progress in the courts on protecting gay, lesbian, and transgender people from workplace discrimination followed quickly. In my view, the order of events is not random or accidental. Marriage equality opened the door for greater appreciation for all kinds of rights for gay and queer people, just as marriage equality advocates had predicted it would.

A greater understanding and acceptance of gay people in popular attitudes and in the law allowed the Supreme Court to see antigay and anti-transgender discrimination as manifestations of sex discrimination. As a result, *Bostock* extended the protections of Title VII to gay, lesbian, and transgender people across the U.S. *Bostock* made job discrimination against gay and transgender people illegal in every part of the U.S. and in every workplace covered by the broadly applicable Civil Rights Act of 1964.[30]

Making antigay and anti-transgender discrimination illegal is a tremendous and historic advance for gay rights, but discrimination against gays and transgender people is not going to disappear anytime soon. The struggle against workplace discrimination is an example of a displacing social change. Displacing social changes usually yield slow progress at best.[31] LGBT people who are victims of workplace discrimination now have a clear path to sue their employers and win. Companies will update their antidiscrimination policies. Human resource departments will put employees through training about how to recognize and avoid antigay and anti-transgender discrimination. Homophobic and transphobic employers and supervisors may still discriminate, but they will have to be more subtle about it. The social acceptability of antigay and anti-transgender discrimination will continue to decline.

Justice Alito's dissent in *Bostock* notes correctly that there are many other federal statutes besides the Civil Rights Act that prohibit discrimination because of sex. Applying the reasoning in *Bostock* to all those other statutes and to all the contexts covered by those statutes will expand protections of LGBT people broadly and consequentially.[32]

18

Social Science in the Courtroom

In the struggle for marriage equality in the U.S., research and scholarship played an important role in helping discredit the falsehoods that have been a bulwark of discrimination against gays and lesbians. The production of scholarly knowledge is a slow process. Scholarly consensus takes time to develop and to be acknowledged even in scholarly circles. The penetration of scholarly truths into public opinion and public policy is even slower. There are usually few chances for true scholarship to compete with the louder, noisier, and more self-assured messages that come from voices who seek to manipulate public opinion. Despite the slowness with which social science knowledge permeates into general discourse, social science is essential for democracy. Without research and knowledge about social, political, and economic choices, the public has little ability to make informed decisions.

The health of same-sex couples and their children and the social scientific consensus about gays and lesbians were ratified in three same-sex marriage trials. The trials put under scrutiny the research of experts on both sides of the marriage equality issue and gave each side opportunities to question the other side's experts, with real people's rights depending on the result and with a judge to decide which side's arguments were more persuasive and credible. The U.S. court system vindicated the social science consensus about same-sex couples and their children and eventually vindicated the rights of same-sex couples.

The landmark *Brown v. Board of Education* (1954) U.S. Supreme Court school desegregation decision was also heavily influenced by social science, specifically the social science consensus that racial segregation in the U.S. was damaging to both Blacks and Whites. In a series of trials in federal and state courts across the country, Thurgood Marshall and other lawyers for the National Association for the Advancement of Colored People Legal Defense Fund put local and national academics on the witness stand to explain to judges why racially segregated schools damaged the psyches of Black children.[1]

The Rainbow after the Storm. Michael J. Rosenfeld, Oxford University Press. © Oxford University Press 2022.
DOI: 10.1093/oso/9780197600436.003.0018

As long as the *Plessy v. Ferguson* (1896) Supreme Court decision endorsing separate but equal accommodations for Blacks and Whites remained in effect, district court judges had their hands tied from striking down segregation in local school systems. If the Black and White schools were equal, or (more commonly) if the states could argue that the segregated schools could be made equal with promised future investments, then the *Plessy* precedent said segregation was constitutional. The school segregation trials built a record of facts and conclusions about the harms of segregation that helped to shape the eventual *Brown* decision overturning *Plessy*.

American psychologist Kenneth B. Clark testified in several of the school segregation trials[2] and would go on to be the first Black president of the American Psychological Association. Clark coauthored a social science statement titled "The Effects of Segregation and the Consequences of Desegregation" that lawyers for the plaintiffs (the Black students who wanted to attend integrated schools) included as an appendix in their brief to the Supreme Court. The Clark, Chein, and Cook ([1952] 2004) appendix documented how segregated schools harmed the aspirations and self-images of Black children, and how segregation taught White children painful lessons about the hypocrisy of their elders. The appendix was approved by American psychologist Gordon Allport (the father of intergroup contact theory), along with social science giants Robert K. Merton, Samuel Stouffer, Arnold Rose, Else Frenkel-Brunswick, Robert Redfield, and two dozen other notable academics.[3]

In defending segregation, the *Plessy v. Ferguson* decision had stated that it was a fallacy to argue that segregation stamped the minority group with a badge of inferiority. By the time of *Brown v. Board* in 1954, social science had produced substantial evidence to the contrary. In the *Brown* decision Chief Justice Warren wrote for a unanimous Court:

> Segregation of white and colored children in public schools has a detrimental effect upon the colored children. The impact is greater when it has the sanction of law.
>
> Whatever may have been the extent of psychological knowledge at the time of *Plessy v. Ferguson*, this finding [of the damage that segregation does] is amply supported by modern authority. Any language in *Plessy v. Ferguson* contrary to this finding is rejected.[4]

The *Brown* decision footnoted social science scholarship from Kenneth Clark, E. Franklin Frazier, and others and cited Swedish economist Gunnar Myrdal's influential book, *An American Dilemma* (Myrdal, Sterner, and Rose 1944), on the corrosive effects of racial segregation. *An American Dilemma* was the culmination of a broad research project, funded by the Carnegie Corporation of New York, involving the input of scores of leading social scientists from across the U.S. *An American Dilemma* was a big, midcentury consensus statement of American social science, reported and explained by a distinguished outsider. The *Brown* decision also cited a paper which showed that 90.4% of American social scientists believed that segregation did psychological harm to minority groups even if facilities were equal, compared to only 2.3% of social scientists who disagreed (the remainder had no opinion).[5] The *Brown* decision, viewed by many as the most important U.S. Supreme Court decision of the twentieth century, was built on a social science consensus.

Like *Brown v. Board*, *Obergefell v. Hodges* was built on a social science consensus. That is not to say that academics are *primarily* responsible for marriage equality in the U.S. Gay and lesbian people coming out of the closet and clamoring for the right to marry were the primary agents of this movement. Their coming out of the closet, expressing their love for each other, and attempting to claim the right to marry helped to liberalize American public opinion toward gay rights.

Social science had an important secondary role in the achievement of marriage equality. Because the social science part of the marriage equality story has rarely been recounted, it is important to credit social science with contributing to this important social change. Some of the academic work that paved the way for gay rights gains was done by people who had a degree of fame outside of academia, such as Alfred Kinsey. Pepper Schwartz and Philip Blumstein's (1983) *American Couples* brought them a degree of fame outside the academy. Scholars such as Larry Wu, Gary Gates, Michael Lamb, David Brodzinsky, Nancy Cott, and Gary Segura may have been less used to the pressure and public attention that comes with participation in important cases, but they all rose to meet their challenges.

Opponents of marriage equality who were used to having their slipshod arguments succeed in the public square found that the courtroom was a less forgiving environment for falsehoods. The three same-sex marriage trials ratified the social science consensus about the health of same-sex couples and their children, which is something that the other branches of

U.S. government were unwilling or unable to do. The U.S. Supreme Court made marriage equality the law of the whole United States.

In the federal courts (district courts, appellate courts, and Supreme Court), judges have lifetime appointments and are therefore well insulated against short-term political backlash that might result from any one decision. State court judges are appointed or elected through a variety of methods, so they are less protected from partisan politics.[6] Judges are more insulated from the winds of partisan politics than are legislators, governors, and presidents, who must face partisan elections every few years. To the extent that U.S. courts are insulated from partisan politics, the court system has been and can continue to be a venue for social science to challenge and to overcome politically expedient propaganda. The courts have the capacity to validate social science and elevate social science consensus into policy. U.S. courts can, not in isolation from but in concert with public opinion, effect social change. It would be very naïve to assume that truth and justice always prevail, but they can and sometimes do.

19

Afterword

A Few Sobering Reminders

It is tempting to end this book on a triumphal note. The achievements of marriage equality and the subsequent banning of antigay job discrimination in the U.S. are remarkable and amazing. And yet, it should be noted, homophobia still exists and the groups that organize to politically promote homophobia remain powerful and numerous in the U.S. Many of the currently unenforceable state bans against same-sex marriage remain in state constitutions, waiting to be enforced if the *Obergefell v. Hodges* (2015) decision were to be overruled by some future Supreme Court. The official platform of the Republican Party that Donald Trump was elected president on in 2016 called for the reversal of *Obergefell*.[1]

The *Obergefell* decision was achieved with the narrowest possible Court majority, 5–4. A change in the composition of the Court in the future could put the decision in jeopardy of being overruled. Justice Kennedy, author of the majority decisions in the four key gay rights victories in the Supreme Court during his career, retired in 2018. Five-to-four Supreme Court decisions on constitutional rights cases are more vulnerable to future reversals than other kinds of Court decisions.[2] On the other hand, the 6–3 decision in *Bostock v. Clayton County* (2020) suggests that there are enough votes for gay rights even in the very conservative current Court, so perhaps *Obergefell* will not be overturned by this Court.

The strong and growing U.S. public support for marriage equality makes it less likely to be reversed. The generation gap in attitudes about gay rights in the U.S., with opponents of gay rights overrepresented among American senior citizens, favors gay rights in the future. With every passing day, mortality decreases the influence on U.S. politics of people born before 1940. Those born after 1990, raised in a climate of greater tolerance and acceptance of gay rights, will increasingly be taking leadership roles in the U.S. A majority of Americans now say they know someone who is gay or lesbian. The fact that the majority of straight Americans know someone who is gay or

The Rainbow after the Storm. Michael J. Rosenfeld, Oxford University Press. © Oxford University Press 2022.
DOI: 10.1093/oso/9780197600436.003.0019

lesbian will make antigay falsehoods less effective in the future than they have been in the past. Between 2016 and 2018, despite the Trump presidency's antigay policies, approval of gay rights and of marriage equality continued to grow at a record pace.

The political victory of marriage equality in the U.S. was abetted by the victory of social science truths about gays and lesbians and their children over falsehoods spread by the Christian Right on the same subjects. The victory of truth over falsehood about gays and lesbians may turn out to have been an unusual victory. It takes a long time and the right alignment of circumstances for the truth to catch up to and overtake a falsehood. In the political arena, falsehoods often have the upper hand.

According to the Pulitzer Prize–winning fact-checking organization PolitiFact (2016), only 16% of candidate Trump's statements during the 2016 presidential campaign were true or mostly true. PolitiFact judged 50% of Hillary Clinton's (Trump's main opponent in the 2016 election for president) statements to be true or mostly true. All politicians stretch the truth from time to time, but Trump set a new low standard. The *Washington Post* documented more than two thousand false statements Trump made in his first year as president.[3] He repeatedly claimed, for instance, that the U.S. had the highest tax burden in the world (not true; the U.S. has a lower tax burden than the average among developed countries), and that the U.S. crime rate was at an all-time high (not true; in fact the crime rate had been falling for decades). President Trump issued falsehoods about immigration and immigration policy, among many other subjects. Despite these falsehoods, or perhaps because of them, Christian Right organizations overwhelmingly supported and evangelical Christians overwhelmingly voted for him.

In the summer of 2017, President Trump made statements about the supposed cost to the military of transgender soldiers to try to justify a ban on transgender people serving in the military, a ban which Christian Right leaders had lobbied for and which Trump announced first on Twitter, and then with a presidential directive. In her decision striking down Trump's ban on transgender soldiers, U.S. District Judge Colleen Kollar-Kotelly noted, "[A]ll of the reasons proffered by the President for excluding transgender individuals from the military in this case were not merely unsupported, but were actually *contradicted* by the studies, conclusions, and judgment of the military itself."[4]

President Trump's tendency to spread falsehoods and his continued popularity among Christian Right and evangelical voters demonstrate how falsehoods can be more powerful, more convincing, and more persuasive in some sectors of the public than the truth. As the president is the most influential person in the U.S., the president's statements can move public opinion, as Bill Clinton's pro-gay-rights statements appear to have moved public opinion in 1992.

Politicians and religious leaders get away with spreading falsehoods because people have an appetite for falsehoods.[5] Fear is a fundamentally effective motivating tool in politics. The fear of the other, the fear of the unknown, the fear of social change, the fear of disorder can easily drown out facts and truth. Everyone is vulnerable to fear and to falsehoods to some degree, but research has shown conservative citizens to be more motivated by and more subject to fear. Conservative and deeply religious citizens are also more dogmatic, less tolerant of ambiguity, and less open to experience. Right-wing citizens have a greater tendency than politically moderate or left-wing citizens to be followers, so they are more inclined to believe in a leader whose statements contradict objective facts.[6] Although dogmatic people are less open to new information, they can change their minds over time, given the right experiences and circumstances. The marriage equality movement proved that not only liberals but also many conservatives, evangelical Christians, and Republicans could become more accepting of gay rights.

The most important lesson of the victory of marriage equality in the U.S. is that any kind of social change is possible. Gay rights were tremendously unpopular in the 1970s in the U.S. Marriage equality had the support of barely more than 10% of U.S. adults in 1988. Marriage equality had to overcome its own unpopularity as well as an entrenched antigay Christian Right social and political movement that had fundamental advantages in money and political access over the gay rights social movement. Even within the gay rights movement, many activists were either skeptical of marriage equality's chance of success or hostile to the goal of marriage equality. Marriage equality was often derided by movement activists as retrograde and bourgeois, as a sellout of the most idealistic aspects of gay rights activism. Yet despite bitter opposition from vastly larger groups on the Right and despite continual criticism from the Left, marriage equality has turned out to be one of the most powerful, transformational, and consequential social changes in recent American history.

If marriage equality can triumph in the U.S. after being as unpopular as it was, then no kind of social change is impossible. Social change takes time and effort. Social change also requires people to believe that change is possible. Regardless of who is in power today or how the prevailing political winds are blowing, you can make change. As Harvey Milk used to say, "You gotta give 'em hope." Take whatever motivational hope you can from the unlikely triumph of marriage equality in the U.S. And then, when the hope has sunk in, put this book down and go out and start working to make the world a better and more just place.

Notes

Chapter 1

1. On the practical objections to marriage equality—that it would not be achieved and would only lead to antigay backlash—see Klarman (2013). Given how many defeats marriage equality suffered in referenda and in the courts in the U.S. before 2012, the practical objection was not unreasonable. In addition to the practical critique, there was an ideological critique of marriage equality from the Left of the gay rights movement. Both critiques are discussed later.
2. A few attitudes measured in the GSS were even more unpopular than same-sex marriage was in 1988: only about 1% of Americans say they personally do not pay enough in federal taxes; only about 3% of American adults say life has no purpose. A more relevant example is American support for laws banning racial intermarriage, which was at 37% in 1972, five years after the laws had been ruled unconstitutional in *Loving v. Virginia* (1967). Support for the laws banning interracial marriage steadily declined over time, but only dropped below 12% for the first time in 1996, twenty-nine years after racial intermarriage had been legal everywhere in the U.S.
3. On the general stability of attitudes, see Alwin and Krosnick (1991) and Page and Shapiro (1992). On the uniqueness of attitudinal change toward gay rights in the U.S., see chapter 8 and Rosenfeld (2017).
4. On the survey data showing when American gays and lesbians came out of the closet, see chapter 7, Rosenfeld (2017), and Garretson (2018).
5. In a civil case, the plaintiff is the party that initiates the lawsuit.
6. The U.S. federal court system has three tiers: district courts, appellate courts, and the U.S. Supreme Court. Each state has its own court system, with trial courts and a state supreme court, and most states have an intermediate appellate court as well. The legality of same-sex marriage was determined by state law and state constitutions (the purview of state courts) but also raised decisive questions of federal law and rights guaranteed by the U.S. Constitution, so that federal courts were eventually and necessarily involved in the battle.
7. See, for example, the following friend-of-the-court briefs presented in the *U.S. v. Windsor* (2013) same-sex marriage case: American Psychological Association et al. (2013) and American Sociological Association (2013).
8. For a discussion of how difficult it is for heterosexuals to give up the unfounded fear that children are vulnerable to exploitation by gays and lesbians, see Goldberg (2010).
9. GSS question on "homosex": "What about sexual relations between two adults of the same sex—do you think it is always wrong, almost always wrong, wrong only sometimes, or not wrong at all?" Possible answers were "always wrong," which is highly

correlated with opposition to gay rights, and three other answers that I combine: "almost always wrong," "wrong only sometimes," and "not wrong at all."

10. On recent gay rights histories that center Stonewall and the GLF, see Faderman (2015), Hirshman (2012), Duberman (1993, 2018), and D'Emilio (1998, 2014).

11. See the literature on political process theory and the theory of political opportunity structure (McAdam, McCarthy, and Zald 1996; McAdam 1982; Meyer and Minkoff 2004) and see the critique of these theories by Goodwin and Jasper (1999).

12. See Gross (1993), Johansson and Percy (1994), and Signorile (2003).

13. On the gay rights movement's disappointments with Clinton, see Vaid (1995). On the influence of Clinton's 1992 campaign on national attitudes toward gay rights, see Wilcox et al. (2007), Schmalz (1992), and Garretson (2018).

14. Approval for marriage equality in the GSS data crossed the 50% threshold around 2012 (see Figure 9.2).

15. On displacing and nondisplacing social movements, see Gamson (1990).

16. See Judge Judith Kaye's dissent in *Hernandez v. Robles* (2006: 391).

17. Figure 8.3, for instance, shows that in the aftermath of the 1973 *Roe v. Wade* decision, support for abortion rights in the U.S. rose by about 5 percentage points, but these gains had mostly disappeared by 1978. There is evidence that gay-positive court decisions led to more gay-friendly public attitudes at least in the short term (Flores and Barclay 2016).

18. For detailed analysis of the inner workings of the gay rights groups in the post-1980 era, see Frank (2017), Fetner (2008), Stone (2012), Vaid (1995), Solomon (2014), Faderman (2015) and Hirshman (2012).

19. The anti-gay-rights groups are Focus on the Family (by far the largest of the groups, with more than $100 million per year of revenue), followed by the American Family Association, the Family Research Council, Concerned Women of America, the Traditional Values Coalition, the National Organization for Marriage, and Eagle Forum. The gay rights groups, from largest to smallest, were the Human Rights Campaign, Lambda Legal, the National Gay and Lesbian Task Force, the National Center for Lesbian Rights, GLAD legal advocates, and Freedom to Marry.

20. The resource advantage of the anti-gay-rights groups means that resource mobilization theory (McCarthy and Zald 1977), which uses fundraising as the main predictor of success, does not explain how the gay rights groups prevailed in the U.S. Funding matters, of course. As the gay rights groups became better funded after 2000, they were able to organize at the local level in a more professional way, and that made a real difference in their ability to win campaigns (Solomon 2014).

21. The figures on same-sex couple and gay, lesbian, and bisexual adult frequency are from the How Couples Meet and Stay Together 2017 data set (Rosenfeld, Thomas, and Hausen 2018). See also an older and more comprehensive survey by Gates (2011), which found about 3.6% of adults in the U.S. were gay, lesbian, or bisexual. See also Gates's (2012b) response to criticism that his estimates were too low.

22. Author's tabulation from weighted GSS data, variable "bible," for 2018.

23. See Herman (1997: 13).

24. For instance, see Leviticus 20:13, King James Version: "If a man also lie with mankind, as he lieth with a woman, both of them have committed an abomination: they shall surely be put to death; and their blood shall be upon them."
25. The Defense of Marriage Act of 1996 had two substantive provisions: the federal government would not recognize same-sex marriages from any jurisdiction; states were not obligated to recognize same-sex marriages from other states.
26. On the interior logic of the opponents of gay rights, see Moon (2004), Dobson (2004), Fetner (2008), Herman (1997), Diamond (1995), and White (2006).
27. On the legal and practical benefits associated with marriage, see Eskridge (1996) and the U.S. Government Accounting Office (1997) "Report to Henry J. Hyde."
28. See *Turner v. Safley* (1987).
29. Opposition and resistance to marriage equality for ideological left reasons were once quite widespread. See D'Emilio (2014, ch. 26, "The Campaign for Marriage: A Dissenting View"), Duggan (2002), Franke (2006), and Bernstein and Taylor (2013). On the different visions of radicals and liberals being a challenge for the gay rights movement, see Gamson (1995) and Frank (2017).
30. See Wolfson (2004) and Stoddard (1989).
31. Quoting Michigan Assistant Attorney General Kristin Heyse on behalf of Governor Richard Snyder, the defendant in *DeBoer v. Snyder* (2014: 40), from her opening statement, trial transcript, February 25: "This case is about one thing, your Honor, the will of the people. The people of the State of Michigan have decided to retain the definition of marriage that encourages what's best of [*sic*] children being raised by both a mom and a dad. They have the authority to address policy questions like this, and they have rational reasons for doing so. Thus, that decision must govern."
32. Quoting Judge Bernard Friedman's decision in *DeBoer v. Snyder*, 973 F. Supp. 2d (2014: 775).

Chapter 2

1. See McAdam (1982).
2. On the Cold War, the Red Scare, the Lavender Scare (the persecution of gay people during the Red Scare), and the connections between the Christian Right and anti-communism, see Johnson (2004), Herman (1997), and Diamond (1995).
3. See Herman (1997: 36).
4. See Chauncey (2004), Klarman (2013), and Kameny (2000).
5. Clinton's 1995 Executive Order #12968 ended discrimination against gays and lesbians in the granting of security clearances, and his 1998 Executive Order #13087 prohibited discrimination in federal employment based on sexual orientation.
6. See Gup (1988).
7. On the historical evidence that Hoover's homophobia was rooted in self-loathing over his own homosexuality, see Potter (2006). Johnson (2004) doubts the credibility of the evidence that Hoover was gay.

8. On the Immigration and Naturalization Service and exclusion of homosexuals from the U.S., see Canaday (2009).

9. See especially Eskridge's (2008: 96) description of California's Atascadero State Hospital.

10. On Harry Hay and the Mattachine Society, and on Del Martin and Phyllis Lyon and the Daughters of Bilitis, see D'Emilio (1998) and Hirshman (2012).

11. On the life of Bayard Rustin, see D'Emilio (2003).

12. See letters to the editor and editor's responses in the June 1959 edition of *The Ladder*.

13. The article pointed out that one extreme interpretation of the obscenity laws would make *ONE* illegal regardless of the magazine's content because homosexual acts were illegal across the U.S. and because *ONE* was therefore a magazine for people whose regular activities were illegal. The author, Eric Julber, rejected that interpretation and noted that as *ONE* was being delivered by the Post Office, the postmaster seemed to have rejected the most extreme view as well.

14. On *ONE*'s battle with the postmaster of Los Angeles, see Murdoch and Price (2001: 27–34); see also the interview with *ONE*'s attorney Eric Julber in the February 1958 edition of *The Ladder*.

15. In the case of *Mutual Film Corporation v. Industrial Commission of Ohio* (1915), the U.S. Supreme Court upheld Ohio's right to impose restrictions on the content of movies shown in the state. The *Mutual Film* decision set the precedent (not reversed until 1952) that movies as commercial activity were not entitled to freedom of speech constitutional protections. Once it was legal for localities and states to enforce their own censorship codes on what movies could be shown based on the movie's content, Hollywood made its own rules to censor itself. The *Burstyn v. Wilson* (1952) Supreme Court decision gave the U.S. film industry its First Amendment protections back, which meant that the need for Hollywood to proactively censor their own movies was reduced.

16. The Hays Code never explicitly defined "impure love." The way the Code was applied, it was clear that "impure love" meant same-sex love and may have covered other non-traditional kinds of love as well.

17. In the 1970s, after the Hays Code was no longer in effect, when gay characters were depicted on television or in the movies as something other than villains or shame-driven suicides, they were often depicted as objects of derision and humiliation, the butt of every joke. The introduction of humor regarding homosexuality, once banned by the Code, proved to be no particular blessing for gays and lesbians. In 1973 the National Gay Task Force wrote to the U.S. movie and television industries and proposed their own, more tolerant set of rules for broadcast and film, the first of which was "Homosexuality is not funny" (Russo 1987: 220).

18. See, for instance, Roberta Kaplan's recollections of being a closeted lesbian in college in the 1980s (Kaplan and Dickey 2015: 25–28).

19. Whereas the Hays Code treated homosexuality as akin to crime, religion received a more favorable treatment:
    1. No film or episode may throw **ridicule** on any religious faith.
    2. **Ministers of religion** in their character as ministers of religion should not be used as comic characters or as villains.
    3. **Ceremonies** of any definite religion should be carefully and respectfully handled. (Motion Picture Association of America, Inc. 1955: 5)

20. See *People of California v. Ferlinghetti* (1957).
21. On *Roth v. U.S.*, see Richards (1974) and Ball (2017).
22. See the Anthony Lewis (January 14, 1958) byline on page 35 of the *New York Times*, "Nudist Magazines Win Mail Rights."
23. In the view of the somewhat salacious biography of Kinsey by Jones (1997), Kinsey was interested in sexology because of his own repressed homosexuality and tendency to masochism.
24. *Sexual Behavior in the Human Male* (Kinsey, Pomeroy, and Martin 1948: 650–651). Academic critics of Kinsey's research noted that the people his team interviewed did not constitute a representative sample of Americans, but a convenience sample of whoever volunteered to be interviewed and whoever was sought out by Kinsey's team. Kinsey had a special interest in gay male interviewees, prisoners, and sex offenders because their life histories brought him novel information. When the leading statisticians of the day were sent to investigate his methods, Kinsey put the three men (William Cochran, Frederick Mosteller, and John Tukey) through his sexual history interview protocol. He convinced the three statisticians that only a face-to-face interview with a trained interviewer could elicit the kind of detailed sexual history he needed. Since mail-out and mail-back survey were insufficient to his task, and since there was no possibility in that era of performing a nationally representative random sample of face-to-face detailed interviews, the statisticians gave grudging and partial approval to Kinsey's nonrepresentative methods.

 In the 1990s, a research team led by Ed Laumann at the University of Chicago fielded a human sexual history survey (implemented face-to-face) to a nationally representative, random sample of Americans. Laumann et al (1994) found a lower rate of homosexuality and same-sex sexual experience than Kinsey had found four decades earlier. Whereas Kinsey had found that 10% of the men in his sample were more or less exclusively homosexual, Laumann et al. (1994: 311) found that 2% of American men identified as homosexual, and 3.1% were attracted only or mostly to other men. Laumann et al.'s estimates from the National Health and Social Life Survey are more consistent with other nationally representative surveys in the U.S. and elsewhere, whereas Kinsey's numbers for the prevalence of male homosexuality are outliers.
25. On Kinsey's role in discrediting the sodomy laws, see Eskridge (2008).
26. For a fuller account of Kameny's story, see Kameny (2000), Murdoch and Price (2001), and Johnson (2004).
27. The petition to a higher court for a review of a lower court decision is a request for a Writ of Certiorari, *Cert* for short. The Supreme Court grants *Cert* in about 2% of all petitions. In cases where the petitioner also requests a waiver of court fees because they are too poor to pay them (e.g., for petitions from inmates), the Court grants *Cert* at an even lower rate. For petitions prepared by lawyers, the Court grants *Cert* at roughly 5% (Supreme Court Press 2018). Four of the nine Supreme Court justices have to agree to hear a case for *Cert* to be granted.
28. See Johnson (2004).
29. See Eskridge (2008: 126).

Chapter 3

1. For classic gay rights histories that place Stonewall at the center of the story, see Duberman (1993, 2018), Faderman (2015), and Hirshman (2012). In D'Emilio's (1998) classic history, Stonewall is the culminating story.

2. In order to have a bar that legally serves patrons, including gay patrons, one needs a liquor license. Like many states' licensing authorities, New York's State Liquor Authority had rules against granting licenses to bars that promoted disorder. Licenses were routinely taken away from bars that served a gay or lesbian clientele, which was seen as disorderly and dangerous to public morals. See Ball (2017), Eskridge (1999), and *Vallerga et al. v. Department of Alcoholic Beverage Control et al.* (1959) from the California Supreme Court.

3. For histories of the events at Stonewall, see D'Emilio (1998) and Duberman (1993).

4. On the Mattachine's response to Stonewall, see Duberman (1993: 207).

5. On the GLF's internal divisions, see Hirshman (2012: 109–114). For a more nostalgic view of the GLF from someone who was part of it, see Duberman (2018).

6. Brenda Howard is sometimes referred to as "the Mother of Pride" (Gonzalez 2019). On the history of Pride parades, see Bruce (2016), and on the first organizers of Pride parades, see Duberman (1993: 270) and Hirshman (2012: 126), and Carter (2004).

7. See Bruce (2016: 46).

8. See Bruce (2016: 56).

9. See Bruce (2016: 123).

10. For the 1970s as the era when the last laws requiring wives to take their husbands' surnames were changed, see Scheuble and Johnson (1993). On the percentage of wives who still take their husbands' surnames, see Johnson and Scheuble (1995), and see Bass (2015) on the pressure applied to married women to change their names.

11. See Hochschild and Machung's (1989) classic ethnography, *The Second Shift*.

12. See Bernard's ([1972] 1982) *The Future of Marriage*.

13. On 1940s American divorces, see Goode (1956). On the more recent gender specificity of who wants divorce and who wants the breakup of nonmarital unions, as well as the consistent trend of wives having lower marital satisfaction than husbands in the U.S., see Rosenfeld (2018).

14. See, e.g., Friedan's ([1963] 1974: ch. 4) extended defense of nineteenth-century first-wave feminists as not the man-hating jezebels they were reputed to be, but rather as attractive heterosexuals, most of whom eventually married.

15. On the divide between radicals and liberals in the women's movement in the 1970s, see Taylor and Rupp (1993).

16. See D'Emilio (1998: 73–74).

17. For summaries of subsequent psychological studies of homosexual and heterosexual psychology, see Gonsiorek (1982, 1991).

18. See Hooker et al. (1969).

19. On the history of how the APA changed its definition of homosexuality in 1973, see Kameny (2000) and Bayer (1987).

20. See Canaday (2009).

21. In 1997, the Minnesota legislature rewrote the state marriage code to specify that only heterosexual couples could marry. In 2012, Minnesotans voted down an attempt to change the state constitution to exclude same-sex couples from marriage. In 2013, the legislature reversed its 1997 action and passed, and the governor signed, a bill bringing marriage equality to Minnesota.

22. Details of the Baker and McConnell story are from Murdoch and Price (2001) and McConnell, Baker, and Karwoski (2016). McConnell's legal name was James Michael McConnell, and Baker's legal name was Richard John Baker.

23. The proposed Equal Rights Amendment (ERA) to the U.S. Constitution (which would have guaranteed gender equality under the law) was approved by the U.S. House of Representatives in 1971 and by the Senate in 1972. The ERA needed the approval of thirty-eight state legislatures, but ended up three states short.

24. On the centrality of antigay messaging to the Christian Right movement of the 1980s, 1990s, and 2000s, see Cahill (2007), Chauncey (2004), Diamond (1995), Fetner (2008), and Herman (1997), and from within the Christian Right movement, see Dobson (2004), Sprigg (2004), Viefhues-Bailey (2010), and White (2006).

25. See Fejes (2008: 113).

26. See Fejes (2008: 123).

27. See Fejes (2008: 134).

28. See Shilts (1982) and Fejes (2008).

29. Quoted in Jones (2016: 135).

30. Quoted in Reagan's (1978) editorial against the Briggs Initiative, from the *Los Angeles Herald-Examiner*.

31. See Fejes (2008: 122).

32. See, e.g., Hollibaugh's (1979) account of campaigning against the Briggs Initiative in rural and conservative parts of California as an out-of-the-closet lesbian.

33. From the Paula Lichtenberg papers in the GLBT Historical Society, San Francisco, quoted in Khalil (2012: 123).

34. See Epstein's (1984) documentary *The Times of Harvey Milk*.

35. On the life and times of Harvey Milk, see Jones (2016), Epstein (1984), and Shilts (1982), and for a dramatized version, see the Gus Van Sant (2008) film *Milk*.

36. On the presentation of ex-gays to Christian audiences, see White (2006). See Dobson (2004) and Sprigg (2004) for Christian Right claims about the malleability of homosexuality.

37. For the purposes of marriage equality, it should not matter what a person's sexual identity is. Some bisexual people have had only different-sex partners; some people with same-sex partners do not claim gay or lesbian identities.

38. See Savin-Williams, Joyner, and Rieger's (2012: fig. 1) study of gay young adults comparing Waves 3 and 4 of the National Longitudinal Study of Adolescent Health. See also Diamond and Rosky's (2016) review of the literature on sexual identity immutability.

39. On racial fluidity, see Saperstein and Penner (2012). On the ambivalence within the gay community about whether sexual identity is immutable or not, see D'Emilio (2002).

40. On the American Psychological Association's reasoning for banning conversion therapy, see Anton (2010).

41. See Judge Norris's concurring opinion in *Watkins v. U.S. Army* (1989: 726).

42. Using the broader legal definition of immutability, Justice Anthony Kennedy referred to homosexuality as immutable in the *Obergefell* (2015: 658) decision.

43. According to Faderman (2015: 382), Reagan had initially intended to support the Briggs Initiative, but gay rights activist David Mixner managed to convince Reagan that if students were able to get teachers fired based only on an allegation that the teacher had said something that could be construed as pro-homosexual, the teachers would lose their authority and the education system would fall into chaos. Reagan wanted to support the classroom authority of teachers, so he turned against the Briggs Initiative.

44. On the grassroots, door-to-door campaign strategy of out-of-the-closet activists opposing the Briggs Initiative, see Khalil (2012) and Hollibaugh (1979).

45. On Harvey Milk, see Jones (2016). For the Dan White murder trial, see Shilts (1982).

46. There had been bigger marches in the U.S. organized around gay themes. The 1978 Gay Freedom Parade in San Francisco on June 25 (commemorating Stonewall and mobilizing people against the Briggs Initiative) attracted a reported 350,000 marchers.

47. See a brief list of 1970s out gay elected officials in Jones (2016: 131). These include Ann Arbor, Michigan, City Councilperson Nancy Wechsler, Ann Arbor City Councilperson Kathy Kozachenko, Massachusetts State Representative Elaine Noble, and Michigan State Senator Allan Spear.

48. On the number of elected officials in the U.S., see Lawless (2012: 33).

49. On Rustin's late-in-life coming-out, see D'Emilio (2003: ch. 20).

Chapter 4

1. See Chauncey (2004) and Shilts ([1987] 2000).

2. Quoted in Vaid (1995: 327).

3. See Schmalz (1992), Chauncey (2004), and Sullivan (1996).

4. See Gross (1993) and Johansson and Percy (1994).

5. See, e.g., the manifesto in Signorile (2003: 363–368).

6. Unsigned editorial, *OutWeek* (1990).

7. Even though Hardwick had not been charged, much less convicted, of sodomy, the courts decided he had standing to sue because he was a potential subject of future arrest for sodomy and had already been arrested once. See *Hardwick v. Bowers* (1985).

8. Sexual misconduct in the law covers a much broader range of activities than sodomy. Von Drak (1976) points out that even after the 1975 changes in California law making sex between consenting same-sex couples in private legal, solicitation for gay sex in public was still illegal. The decriminalization of sodomy, however, seems to have drastically reduced police arrests for the offense of solicitation.

9. See Jones (2016: 95).

10. On Justice Powell's reversal in the lead-up to the *Bowers* decision, see Murdoch and Price (2001), details confirmed by the author's interview with Pamela Karlan, who was clerking for Justice Brennan in 1986.

11. See Murdoch and Price (2001: 335).

12. *Bowers v. Hardwick* (1986) was the second full-length, signed, U.S. Supreme Court decision relating to gay rights, after *Boutilier v. INS* (1967). In *Boutilier*, the Court endorsed the right of the INS to deport and exclude from U.S. citizenship a Canadian citizen, Clive Boutilier, who had been arrested in New York on a sodomy charge and had admitted to the INS in his interview that he was a man who had had sex with men before. The Supreme Court decided *Boutilier* in favor of the INS, by a vote of 6–3, and Boutilier was deported.

13. The U.S. Supreme Court first recognized privacy rights in *Griswold v. Connecticut* (1965), finding that Connecticut's ban on birth control unconstitutionally infringed on the privacy right of heterosexual married couples. The *Bowers v. Hardwick* decision showed that the Court was not yet ready to extend privacy rights to gay couples. Before *Griswold*, a dissent by Justice John Marshall Harlan II in *Poe v. Ullman* (1961) (an earlier challenge to Connecticut's birth control ban) had outlined an argument for recognition of privacy rights as constitutionally protected. Privacy rights arise from a liberal view of the U.S. Constitution, namely the Living Constitution perspective, which argues that our understanding and interpretation of the Constitution has to change with time and as society changes (Tribe 1978, 1992).

14. Quoting from the *Bowers v. Hardwick* (1986: 191–194). The conservative legal principle of Original Intent, arguing that the Constitution must be interpreted only as it was interpreted when it was first written, was central to the *Bowers* decision.

15. Quoted in Murdoch and Price (2001: 332).

16. The *Dred Scott* decision is widely viewed as the worst decision in the history of the U.S. Supreme Court. See, for instance, McCloskey and Levinson (2016). *Dred Scott v. Sandford* (1857) was a 7–2 decision, written by Chief Justice Roger Taney, with five White slaveholding justices among the seven who supported the majority opinion.

17. See Murdoch and Price (2001: 273).

18. See reporting in the *New York Times* by Williams (1987), and see Polikoff (2008: 55).

19. On the Bork nomination and hearings, see Gitenstein (1992).

20. On the gay rights groups and Kennedy's confirmation, see Gitenstein (1992: 319).

21. Sara Diamond (1995) notes that Christian Right groups were enthusiastic supporters of the anticommunist policies of the Republican Party. Fundraising to support the (anticommunist) Nicaraguan Contras was popular in Christian Right circles after Congress had banned U.S. government funds to the support the Contras.

22. See Gittenstein (1992).

23. See Mogill (2015). Bork died in 2012. Barack Obama was president in 2012 and would have nominated Bork's successor if Bork served until his death.

Chapter 5

1. See reporting in the *New York Times* by Schmalz (1992).
2. See reporting in the *New York Times* by Schmalz (1992) and research supporting Clinton's impact on American attitudes toward gay rights by Wilcox et al. (2007) and Garretson (2018). On the earnest attempts of Clinton to repeal the ban on gays serving in the military, see Faderman (2015). Faderman notes that George McGovern's reputation for being willing to support a pro-gay-rights plank at the 1972 Democratic National Convention has been overstated. It is also important to note that while McGovern was running for president twenty years before Clinton, the polling data suggest that U.S. public opinion toward gay rights was no more hostile in 1972 than it was in 1992; see Figure 5.1.
3. For instance, see Vaid (1995).
4. See Buchanan (1992).
5. Frame alignment theory (Benford and Snow 2000) helps to explain why a change in language from a national leader could have shifted the way Americans thought about gay rights.
6. See Zaller (1992).
7. Falsehoods about the Vietnam War included the misrepresentation that U.S. warships had been attacked in the Tonkin Gulf in 1964 and repeated claims that the U.S. was winning the war. The Vietnam War may have started out as an abstract idea for Americans, but over the course of the war more than 2.5 million Americans did military service in Vietnam, and 57,000 Americans died. For those soldiers, and their families and friends, elite American opinion that supported the war did not always square with the soldiers' own firsthand experience. Unlike gay rights, the war in Vietnam itself changed over time, so that it was not the same war in 1964 as it was in 1968 or 1972. When the situation itself changes, public opinion would be expected to change as well, as Zaller (1992) points out.
8. See reporting in the *New York Times* by Schmalz (1992).
9. On Clinton and mass incarceration, see Alexander (2010).
10. From weighted data from the American National Election Study of 1992. The proportion supporting allowing gays and lesbians to serve openly in the military rose to 85% by 2012.
11. For results of the Moskos and Miller survey, see the discussion in chapter 7 of the RAND (National Defense Research Institute 1993) report on gays in the military prepared for Secretary of Defense Les Aspin.
12. For examples, see Shilts (1993).
13. The attitudinal difference between generations (or what demographers refer to as birth cohorts) visible in Figure 5.2 means that cohort replacement can and did contribute to societywide attitudinal change toward gay rights (Andersen and Fetner 2008), even without individuals changing their attitudes (Rosenfeld 2007; Ryder 1965). Cohort replacement is an important factor in liberalization of American attitudes toward gay rights; however, Baunach (2011) has estimated that less than half of the recorded liberalization is due to cohort replacement.

14. The first few years when a birth generation appears in the GSS data for a given survey year, there are too few respondents and the average attitudes are measured with too much error. I trim the plot to reflect survey years with at least one hundred respondents from the specified birth generation.

15. When Generation X youth turned eighteen and were first captured in the GSS in the late 1980s and early 1990s, there followed a sharp liberalization of their cohort's attitudes about gay people. A generation later, when the Millennials started turning eighteen and were first captured in the GSS, their cohort also demonstrated a sharp liberalization of attitudes toward gay people as they aged from eighteen to twenty-two. Going away to college (for those who are privileged to do so) and traveling outside the orbit of one's family of origin exposes young people to a more diverse set of others and (through the experience of independence) builds appreciation for the privacy rights of others (Rosenfeld 2007).

16. In the post-1996 era, Democratic congressional representatives became more consistently supportive of gay rights; see Garretson (2018: 118).

17. Taking the 2010–2016 GSS samples together, 64% of Americans with BAs supported marriage equality, compared to 46% of those with high school diplomas, and 39% who did not finish high school. In the same period, 56.4% of women supported marriage equality, compared to 50.5% of men. Among adults who thought the Bible was a book of fables, 80.3% supported marriage equality, while 27.4% of Americans who thought the Bible was the word of God supported marriage equality. Americans from the Silent Generation had 38% support for marriage equality, Baby Boomers 48%, adults from Generation X 57%, and Millennials 71%. Democrats had 64% support for marriage equality, while Republicans had 38% support. Whites had majority support for marriage equality (56%), while Blacks opposed marriage equality (only 43% support).

18. On divergence over time between the average voters of the Democratic and Republican parties, see Iyengar, Sood, and Lelkes (2012) and Baldassarri and Gelman (2008), but see also Evans (2003).

19. On polarization in congressional votes since World War II, see Benkler, Faris, and Roberts (2018: 296).

20. On the debate in political science over whether voters in the U.S. are more polarized than they used to be, see a brief summary in Benkler, Faris, and Roberts (2018: ch. 10), and see the debate between Fiorina, Abrams, and Pope (2008) and Abramowitz and Saunders (2008). See also Iyengar, Sood, and Lelkes (2012), Baldassarri and Gelman (2008), Park (2018), and Evans (2003).

21. On the way the internet reinforces Balkanized and polarized news, see Adamic and Glance (2005).

22. On the growing hostility between Democratic and Republican citizens, see Iyengar, Sood, and Lelkes (2012).

23. On the political clustering of communities in the U.S., see Bishop (2008).

24. See Clinton's executive orders 13087 (on equal employment) and 12968 (on nondiscrimination based on sexual orientation in the granting of security clearances), and

see Frank Kameny's (2000) history of Eisenhower executive orders that Clinton's orders overturned.

25. *The Silence of the Lambs* had been criticized by Michelangelo Signorile and by Larry Kramer as being homophobic for the gay inflections of the movie's central villain (Signorile 2003).

26. On the depiction of gay characters in Hollywood, see Russo (1987).

27. Screen writer Jan Oxenberg points out in the movie *Celluloid Closet* (Epstein and Friedman 1995; loosely based on the book by Russo 1987), that Andrew Beckett dying (of AIDS) at the end of *Philadelphia* was consistent with the outcomes of gay characters in Hollywood movies from the past.

28. See Hubert (1999).

29. See Hubert (1999).

30. See Handy (1997).

31. *Ellen*, Season 4, Episode 24, "Hello Muddah, Hello Faddah" (Junger 1997).

32. *Ellen*, Season 5, Episode 13, "The Funeral" (Junger 1998).

33. For instance, the 1985 movie *My Beautiful Laundrette*, the 1996 move *The Birdcage*, 1999's *Boys Don't Cry*, and 1992's *The Crying Game*. There were also movies from the 1990s that leaned on old tropes about closeted gay characters who were self-hating and dangerous; see 1999's *The Talented Mr. Ripley* and *American Beauty*.

34. See Garretson (2018: ch. 6). Garretson relies thoughtfully on panel data from the American National Election Studies that determined TV watching habits by asking questions about specific characters from the shows and followed respondents' attitudes toward gay rights from 1992 to 1996. See also Schiappa, Gregg, and Hewes (2006).

Chapter 6

1. On Focus on the Family's obsession with opposition to marriage equality, see White (2006), Cahill (2007), and Viefhues-Bailey (2010). Focus on the Family's James Dobson (2004: 79) wrote, "Congress and the state legislatures must pass a Federal Marriage Amendment to define this historic institution exclusively as being between one man and one woman. That is the passion of my heart at this stage of my life."

2. See Murdoch and Price (2001: 454).

3. Even though Governor Romer was a Democrat and a supporter of gay rights, he was being sued in his official capacity as the chief executive of Colorado, and it was his administration's job to defend Amendment 2, which the voters of Colorado had endorsed. The attorney general of Colorado was Republican Gale Norton.

4. See the Colorado District Court Decision in *Evans v. Romer* (1993), 92-CV-7223.

5. See *Evans v. Romer* (1994).

6. See Murdoch and Price (2001: 460).

7. For audio and text of the oral arguments in *Romer v. Evans*, see the archive at Oyez. org (IIT Chicago-Kent College of Law n.d.).

8. Whereas the Colorado courts had evaluated Amendment 2 on a strict scrutiny standard, Kennedy applied the rational basis test, which is the lowest level of scrutiny and the test most favorable to the state. The victory in *Romer v. Evans* left gay rights with less protection (from future laws in other jurisdictions that might infringe gay rights) than they could have had if strict scrutiny or heightened scrutiny had been applied. On the other hand, the *Romer* decision seemed to expand the ways in which laws burdening gay rights could be found unconstitutional with respect to the Equal Protection Clause of the Fourteenth Amendment and through the rational basis test (Wilson 1997). The *Bostock v. Clayton County* (2020) decision seems to set a precedent that future gay rights claims will trigger heightened or strict scrutiny.

9. Justice Harlan was the lone dissenting opinion in *Plessy v. Ferguson* (1896), a 7–1 Supreme Court decision that endorsed racial segregation and gave official approval to "separate but equal." U.S. governmental endorsement of segregation remained in place until *Brown v. Board of Education* (1954). See Levine (2013) and Kluger ([1975] 2004).

10. From Scalia's dissent in *Romer* (1996: 636–644).

11. See Murdoch and Price (2001: 481).

12. See Kennedy's decision in *Alabama v. Garrett* (2001). On the expressive function of the law, see also Sunstein (1996) and Ryo (2017). For empirical evidence of the (at least short-term) effect of court decisions on American attitudes about marriage equality, see Flores and Barclay (2016).

13. The story of Genora Dancel and Ninia Baehr is from the author's phone interview with Dancel on August 19, 2016, and the journalistic account by Tani (2015).

14. On the internal debates between Wolfson and the leaders of Lambda Legal, see Solomon (2014), Cole (2016), and Frank (2017).

15. See Cole (2016) and Klarman (2013).

16. See Ettelbrick (1989).

17. A civil complaint initiates a lawsuit.

18. See *Baehr v. Lewin* (1993). U.S. law recognizes three levels of scrutiny. The lowest level is the rational basis level of review, which is the default level of scrutiny, requiring a law or governmental activity only to serve a legitimate governmental interest and to be based on some empirical reality (see Ball 2014). The rational basis test accords the existing law a strong presumption of validity, according to Kennedy (see *Heller v. Doe* 1993). Strict scrutiny is a more stringent test because the law or governmental activity has been found to trespass against a legally protected class, such as racial minorities or veterans. When the Hawaii Supreme Court sent the *Baehr* case back to the trial court with instructions that the case was to be tried on a strict scrutiny basis (for potentially trespassing against people's rights by gender), the court was establishing a ground rule for the trial that was most favorable to the plaintiffs and least favorable to the state. Between the rational basis test and strict scrutiny, some courts recognize an intermediate level of scrutiny.

19. The relevant part of the U.S. Constitution is the Full Faith and Credit Clause of Article IV, Section 1: "Full faith and credit shall be given in each state to the public acts, records, and judicial proceedings of every other state. And the Congress may

by general Laws prescribe the Manner in which such Acts, Records and Proceedings shall be proved, and the Effect thereof."

20. Quoted from the author's interview with Wolfson, August 2, 2016. DOMA was introduced in the House of Representatives by Bob Barr on May 7, 1996. It was passed by the House 342–67 on July 12, and then passed by the Senate 85–14 on September 10. As the House and Senate votes were well in excess of the two-thirds majority needed to override a presidential veto, DOMA would have become law whether Clinton signed it or not.

21. The Cherlin et al. (1996) amicus brief was one of thirteen filed in *Baehr v. Miike*; eight on the side of the plaintiffs and five on the side of the state. See Coolidge (2000: note 78).

22. Schwartz's given name was Judith, but in her middle school in Chicago there were several Judy Schwartzes. Pepper was the name she chose to stand out from the others, and the name stuck.

23. Schwartz is sometimes credited with introducing the phrase "lesbian bed death" to describe the low rate of genital sexual relations in lesbian couples surveyed in *American Couples*, but the phrase does not appear in the book, and Schwartz does not remember using it.

24. On the challenges of romantic unions in heterosexual remarriages, a different kind of post-1970 underinstitutionalized heterosexual union form, see Cherlin (1978).

25. See Blumstein and Schwartz (1983: 323).

26. John C. Lewin was replaced by Lawrence Miike as director of the Department of Health of Hawaii, so the case was renamed *Baehr v. Miike*.

27. Quoted from the *Baehr v. Miike* trial decision (1996: 13).

28. A stayed decision does not go into effect until the stay is lifted. In *Baehr v. Miike*, the stay was never lifted because Hawaii's constitutional amendment limiting marriage to one man and one woman went into effect.

29. Pregil's perspective is from the author's phone interview with her on August 8, 2016.

30. There had been an earlier, failed attempt to call a constitutional convention in Hawaii for the purpose of writing the ban on same-sex marriage directly into the Hawaii Constitution (see Coolidge 1997). The referendum wording was "The legislature shall have the power to reserve marriage to opposite-sex couples."

31. See Hull (2001) and Coolidge (2000).

32. See Klarman (2013: 19).

Chapter 7

1. See Pettigrew and Tropp (2006).

2. The implicit association test shows that Whites take much longer to associate positive qualities with a Black name or face, because the positive association with Blacks runs counter to their unconscious biases. See Greenwald, McGhee, and Schwartz (1998).

3. On the subject of how gender frames our interactions, see Ridgeway (2011).

4. See Pettigrew and Tropp (2006).

5. Frame alignment theory (Benford and Snow 2000; Gamson 1992) emphasizes the special power of interpersonal contact and personal experience to make social movement frames resonant and convincing.

6. Personal experience is very convincing, but it is not always accurate. Personal experience is not a good guide to the danger of global climate change, for example, because global climate change is occurring at a much slower pace than the daily and seasonal changes in the weather. Climate change denial is strong in the U.S. in part because the apocalyptic warnings about how climate change might affect the world do not entirely square with personal experience of the weather seeming consistent from year to year (Feinberg and Willer 2011).

7. On the potentially ambivalent effect of coming out of the closet, i.e., the way in which coming out can have a positive or negative effect, see Hart-Brinson (2016) and Ocobock (2013).

8. Herek and Glunt (1993) found that the one-to-one interpersonal contact between friends or family members that "let you know that they were homosexual" was key in explaining liberalization in attitudes toward gay men.

9. See Newsweek (1985, 1994, 1996, 1997, 2000, 2008).

10. In 2006, the GSS fielded a module of questions about whether subjects had gay friends, family, or coworkers, but these questions were not repeated in subsequent years. The American National Election Studies cumulative data file, which I discuss in the next chapter, did not include questions about gay friends or family members.

11. Garretson (2018) used the Newsweek survey data about respondents who had gay or lesbian family, friends, or coworkers and arrived at conclusions similar to mine.

12. Figure 7.1 shows a spike in the percentage of Americans who had a gay or lesbian friend in 1996, followed by a drop to 1997, before increasing again to 2000 and to 2008. The apparent spike in 1996 may be due to random chance or perhaps inconsistencies in question order. Newsweek surveys were less consistent across years than the GSS.

13. The wording from the Newsweek surveys about marriage equality was "Do you think there should or should NOT be legally sanctioned gay marriages?" For more detailed analysis of the Newsweek data on the association between knowing someone gay or lesbian and support for same-sex marriage, see Rosenfeld (2017).

14. The confidence intervals are 95%. The only nonsignificant association in Figure 7.2 was that between gay coworkers and support for marriage equality, including all controls. The t-statistic for no-controls association between gay friends and marriage equality was 12.64, degrees of freedom were 2788, and the associated P value was 1.18×10^{-35}.

15. See Baunach (2011, 2012), Loftus (2001), and Rosenfeld (2007).

16. Alternatively, a predictor's association with the outcome (approval of marriage equality) could change dramatically over time.

17. Surveys that have a repeated structure but have different subjects in each repetition are known as cross-sectional surveys. Surveys that follow the same subjects over time are known as longitudinal surveys, or panel surveys.

18. Survey questions that give respondents a specific set of options to choose from are known as closed-ended questions.

19. The Pew Research Center (2013) study had 1,501 adult subjects, an approximately 1-in-161,000 sample of the U.S. adult population, which at the time was 242 million.

20. Intergroup contact did not function as efficiently in improving relations between Blacks and Whites, for several reasons. First, there was segregation. Blacks and Whites were usually in different families. White people rarely had Black children or Black siblings. Second, because of the identifiability and conspicuousness of race, White people rarely had the opportunity to discover that someone was Black after getting to know them.

21. Literature on political canvassing shows that face-to-face canvassing is dramatically more effective than phone calls or mailings at getting people to vote (Gerber and Green 2000). Phone calls and mailings are cheaper than in-person canvassing, so the effectiveness per dollar is a tricky calculation. There is the famous case of LaCour's field experiment (LaCour and Green 2014), wherein LaCour claimed that lobbying people in person on marriage equality in California had a dramatic effect on their views of marriage equality. LaCour's data were later shown to have been faked, and the LaCour and Green article was retracted. Broockman and Kalla (2016), who had discovered the discrepancies in LaCour's data, ran their own field experiment and showed a positive effect of canvassing on subjects warmth toward (but not support of rights for) transgender people.

22. For another example, see Moon's (2004: 61–62) description of a woman named Jackie who attended the Evangelical Missionary Methodist Church. When asked why Jackie did not view homosexuality as sinful, while many of her co-congregants did, Jackie explained, "I have a brother who's gay. I'm sure that's obviously colored all of my views."

23. On the increasing geographic dispersion of gays and lesbians in the U.S. to the suburbs and the rural areas, i.e., to places outside of the traditional urban gay Meccas like New York and San Francisco, see Rosenfeld and Kim (2005), Rosenfeld (2007), and Ghaziani (2014). On the geography of gays and lesbians in the U.S., see Black et al. (2000) and Gates and Ost (2004). On the lives of gays and lesbians in the rural (and generally conservative) parts of the U.S., see Kazyak (2011).

24. See Dobson (2004) and Sprigg (2004).

Chapter 8

1. See Alwin and Krosnick (1991).

2. I use "percentage point change" rather than "percentage change." An attitude that changed from 3 to 6% approval would have increased approval by 100%, but only by 3 percentage points. I use the language of percentage point change because, from a policy perspective, change from 3% support to 6% support is irrelevant, but change from 40% support to 55% support (smaller percentage change but bigger percentage point change) is potentially revolutionary.

3. See Smith et al. (2019). The GSS is a repeated cross-sectional data set of face-to-face (and recently also online) nationally representative surveys of U.S. residents eighteen and older, with response rates of 61% and above. I rely on the cross-sectional GSS data, rather than on the GSS panel data which began in 2006, because I am interested in attitudinal changes from before 2006. Cross-sectional surveys interview different people with each survey wave. Panel data, also known as longitudinal data, follows the same survey subjects over time and across survey waves. For more detail about the GSS and ANES data and the methods used to analyze the data through 2016, see Rosenfeld (2017). The face-to-face methodology of the GSS used to be considered a gold standard for interview methods; it certainly is the most expensive interview method (phone calls, internet surveys, and mail-out-mail-back surveys are all much cheaper to implement). Paik and Sanchagrin (2013), however, found that the human interviewers could get tired and take short cuts that could lead to biased survey results in face-to-face surveys like the GSS.

4. The GSS same-sex marriage question has the variable name "marhomo." Unfortunately, all of the GSS variables relating to gay rights questions have short variable names containing the word fragment "homo."

5. To be consistent with previous literature, when reducing the data to a simple "agree versus disagree" dichotomy, I counted "strongly agree" and "agree" as approval of same-sex marriage, and I counted "neither agree nor disagree," "disagree," and "strongly disagree" together as disapproval. If I dropped the people who answered "neither agree nor disagree," the apparent change in same-sex marriage approval over time would be even greater.

6. There are other methods of measuring change over time that would take all the variables' categories into account rather than reducing all variables to dichotomous approval/disapproval. The different methods of measuring change over time all yield the same substantive results (see Rosenfeld 2017). Both the Y axis and the X axis of Figure 8.2 are absolute values, so it does not matter whether the change over time was toward more approval or less; every change is recorded as positive.

7. In Rosenfeld (2017) I used an earlier version of the GSS data through survey year 2016. Since attitudes toward same-sex marriage liberalized dramatically between 2016 and 2018, the outlier status of same-sex marriage is even clearer now than it was before.

8. The extent of change and rate of change measures I employ here are measures of sustained change in one direction, and therefore understate the change in variables whose change during one period was reversed during a later period.

9. On the declining trust in the U.S. government, see Chanley, Rudolph, and Rahn (2000) and Smith (2012). The Supreme Court is missing from the list of institutions that Americans trust dramatically less than they used to. The GSS question about confidence in the Supreme Court (GSS variable "conjudge") showed only a slight decline in confidence over time. In 2016, 19.4% of Americans had "hardly any" confidence in the Supreme Court, compared to 52.6% who had hardly any confidence in Congress and 42.2% who had hardly any confidence in the executive branch of the federal government.

10. GSS variable "grass" wording: "Do you think the use of marijuana should be made legal or not?" with answers "legal" or "not legal." Approval of marijuana legalization in the U.S. increased in the 1970s but declined in the 1980s, before increasing sharply after 1990.

11. Evans (2003) noted that American attitudes about abortion had become more polarized, i.e., the variance of the abortion attitude variables increased over time, a finding which does not contradict my finding that the average support for abortion rights has been remarkably flat over time. On the relative stability of abortion attitudes over time, see Wilcox and Carr (2010).

12. On the expanding popular definitions of family in the U.S., and on the places for queer people within the expanding definition, see Powell et al. (2010).

13. The gay sex variable in Figure 8.3 is derived from the same GSS variable for attitudes toward gay sex (variable name "homosex") that we have seen in Figures 1.1 and 5.1. The variable has four outcomes: "always wrong," "almost always wrong," "sometimes wrong," and "not wrong at all." In Figure 8.3, approval is defined as the last two categories for consistency with the other variables, whereas in Figures 1.1 and 5.1 approval includes also the second category, "almost always wrong," because the first category, "always wrong," is the outlier in terms of predicting hostility toward gay rights.

14. Before 2010, among subjects in the GSS who strongly supported marriage equality, 81% thought gay sex was "not wrong at all," and after 2010 the percentage rose to 89% (from the author's tabulation of weighted GSS data variables "marhomo" and "homosex" through survey year 2018). Regression analysis (not shown here) shows that the association between approval of marriage equality and approval of gay sex was significantly increasing over time.

15. GSS variable "marhomo" was originally coded with smaller values representing agreement and larger values representing disagreement with marriage equality. For Figure 8.4 I reverse-coded "marhomo" so higher values would correspond with more approval, consistent with the coding for "homosex," so that positive correlation indicates the higher likelihood of approving of one if a subject approves of the other.

16. For a view of the single life, see Klinenberg (2012). For a view of singlehood in the U.S. that emphasizes some of the ways in which straight single people face discrimination, see DePaulo (2006). For a historical view of the independent life stage, see Rosenfeld (2007).

17. See Rosenfeld (2007), Cherlin (1992, 2009), Acs et al. (2013), and Rosenfeld and Roesler (2019).

18. On the history of heterosexual marriage as an institution, see Cott (2000). On the birth control revolution of the 1960s and 1970s, see Goldin and Katz (2002).

19. For other arguments against marriage and marriage equality in the same vein as Ettelbrick (1989), from the Left of the gay rights movement but published much later, see D'Emilio (2014: ch. 26, "The Campaign for Marriage: A Dissenting View") and Duberman (2018).

20. In the weighted PRRI (2011) data, the same set of predictors (income, born-again Christian identity, region, age, urban/suburban/rural residence, BA degree, gender, race, and political party identification) explained 38% of the variance in attitudes

toward marriage equality, but only 14% of the variance in attitudes toward transgender rights.

21. On predictors of support for abortion rights in the U.S., see Jelen and Wilcox (2003). On predictors of support for gay rights in the U.S., see Rosenfeld (2007) and Loftus (2001).

22. On secrets and the closeted aspects of the abortion experience, see Cowan (2014).

23. The *Roe v. Wade* (1973) decision appeared to have a short-term positive effect on support for abortion rights. The GSS was first fielded in 1972. Between 1972 and 1973, support for abortion rights increased by about 5 percentage points across the various abortion questions (see the earliest two time points in the abortion questions in Figure 8.3). For one example of supporters of abortion rights who recognize that *Roe* may have been a judicial overreach for its time, see Ginsburg (1992).

24. By limiting the analysis to attitudes that were measured at least three times over a span of at least ten years, I eliminate some rapidly changing variables whose referent was temporal, such as questions about political candidates.

25. Compared to the GSS, the ANES data have both greater average extent of change for attitude variables and a greater average rate of change, in part because the ANES variables are less consistent over time in question wording and answer order than are questions in the GSS. See Rosenfeld (2017).

26. ANES question VCF0819 wording: "Some people say that Negroes should be allowed to live in any part of town they want to. How do you feel? Should Negroes be allowed to live in any part of town they want to, or not?" Valid answers were "White people have a right to keep Negroes out of their neighborhoods if they want to" and "Negroes have a right to live wherever they can afford to, just like anybody else."

27. On White attitudes toward Black people, toward civil rights, and toward affirmative action, and on White backlash, see Bobo et al. (2012) and Hochschild (2016).

Chapter 9

1. For details about the *Lawrence v. Texas* case, see Carpenter (2004, 2012) and Eskridge (2008). Eubanks was charged with making a false report on the same night when Garner and Lawrence were arrested, and Eubanks spent at least two weeks in jail. His motivation for the false report was apparently jealousy.

2. In Carpenter's (2004) view, the arresting officer fabricated the story about observing Lawrence and Garner having sex in order to pin the charge of sodomy on them. Carpenter believes the arrest of Lawrence and Garner is not a story about homosexual love or gay sex criminalized, but rather a story of police abuse and malfeasance (enabled by the sodomy laws), victimizing gay men.

3. The unusual circumstance of being arrested in one's own home for sodomy has led some to surmise that the *Lawrence* case was a kind of sting operation to entice the police to make an arrest so that the Texas sodomy law could be challenged in court. Carpenter (2004) considered but rejected the theory. Lawrence and Garner had no

record of participation in gay rights causes. They seem to have hardly known each other; a carefully constructed test case would surely have found a same-sex couple in a committed relationship as the ideal plaintiffs. Additionally, the initial call that Eubanks made to the police about a man "going crazy with a gun" was a kind of police call that could all too easily have resulted in Lawrence and/or Garner (both unarmed) being killed by the police.

4. In a criminal case, pleading "no contest" results in a finding of guilt for the defendants, but it is not a direct admission of guilt. In the case of Lawrence and Garner, the no-contest plea enabled them to avoid testifying about their own version of events, so that the arresting police officer's report was the only report entered into the record. That report was useful to gay rights advocates, because it represented Lawrence and Garner as guilty of sodomy, which enabled the challenge to the sodomy law in Texas.

5. Washington, D.C., litigator Paul Smith made the oral argument at the Supreme Court on behalf of Lawrence and Garner. Smith was a gay man who had been in the closet when he clerked for Justice Powell.

6. The case that overturned Georgia's sodomy law was *Powell v. State* (1998), in which Anthony Powell was accused of rape and sodomy as a result of his having sex with his seventeen-year-old niece. Georgia's sodomy law, you will recall, made no distinction between same-sex and different-sex couples. Powell was acquitted on the charge of rape but convicted on the charge of sodomy. The Supreme Court of Georgia overturned Powell's sodomy conviction and nullified Georgia's sodomy law, on the grounds that if Powell's sex with his niece had not been rape, then it was legally consensual sex, and therefore the sodomy law infringed unconstitutionally on Powell and his niece's privacy. Eskridge (2008) views the Georgia Supreme Court's overturning the state sodomy law in *Powell* as intentionally liberal with respect to gay rights and sodomy.

7. See Karlan (2018: 155).

8. Roughly one in one thousand cases that are decided in the federal appellate courts (the courts that sit below the U.S. Supreme Court) are granted *Cert* for review by the U.S. Supreme Court. Of the roughly sixty appellate court decisions that are heard by the Supreme Court every year, reversal of the appellate court decisions is more frequent than affirmation (Hofer 2010).

9. Spriggs and Hansford (2001) report only ninety-seven reversals of the U.S. Supreme Court between 1946 and 1995. Wikipedia (2017) lists ninety-five overrules in constitutional cases, and an additional twenty-eight overruled statutory cases since the nineteenth century. Of the ninety-five constitutional Supreme Court decisions that were later overruled, the median time from the original case to the overruling case was twenty years. We noted earlier two prior Court decisions that were reversed by later Courts. *Burstyn v. Wilson* (1952) restored the First Amendment protections to the motion picture industry that *Mutual Film v. Industrial Commission of Ohio* (1915) had taken away thirty-seven years earlier. *Brown v. Board of Education* (1954) established that racial segregation in education was unconstitutional, reversing the *Plessy v. Ferguson* (1896) decision that had endorsed the "separate but equal" doctrine fifty-eight years earlier.

10. Quoting from Justice Kennedy's majority decision in *Lawrence v. Texas* (2003: 567, 577–578).

11. Quoting from Justice Scalia's dissent in *Lawrence v. Texas* (2003: 602–605).

12. The lone exception to the string of state referenda losses for marriage equality was the 2006 Arizona referendum, which was written so broadly that it would have stripped rights from many unmarried heterosexual senior citizens and their partners or caretakers. The lone Arizona victory was reversed in 2008, with an anti-gay-marriage referendum that was more narrowly targeted against same-sex couples.

13. The GSS asked the same-sex-marriage legalization question in 1988, and again in 2004 (and regularly thereafter), but between 1988 and 2004 the GSS did not ask the question, so the national trend in same-sex marriage approval and disapproval between 1988 and 2004 in Figure 9.2 should be viewed as very approximate.

14. On the symbolism of San Francisco's 2004 marriages, see Taylor et al. (2009).

15. On the power of marriage to validate couples, see Baumle and Compton (2015) and Rosenfeld (2007: 178–179).

16. See *Lockyer v. City & County of San Francisco* (2004).

17. See reporting in the *New York Times* by Crampton (2004a, 2004b).

18. On the Republicans' use of popular opposition to marriage equality to win the 2004 elections, see Klarman (2013), Rosenberg (2008), Segura (2005), and Lucas (2007). A contrasting view, that the Republican victory was not due to anti-gay-rights turnout, can be found in Lewis (2005).

19. See Segura (2005).

20. See Wolfson and Polaski (2016) and Solomon (2014).

21. See Stone (2012).

22. Evan Wolfson interview by author via Skype, August 2, 2016.

23. See Cole (2016).

24. Details of the Massachusetts marriage equality battles are from Solomon's (2014) *Winning Marriage*, which is an excellent and thoughtful insider account of a victorious political campaign.

25. See Solomon (2014: 13).

26. Same-sex couples with civil unions in Vermont had the same state rights and privileges as heterosexual married couples, but without being able to officially refer to themselves as "married."

27. Pat Robertson, *700 Club*, June 16, 2008, quoted in Goldberg (2010).

28. The case that led to civil unions in Vermont was *Baker v. State* (1999). For the story of the achievement and political aftermath of civil unions in Vermont, see Eskridge (2002), Moats (2004), Klarman (2013), Cole (2016), and Bonauto (2016). Some on the Left in the gay rights movement who opposed marriage equality argued that civil unions and domestic partnerships were better for same-sex couples, since they conveyed most of the rights without any of the historical baggage (Polikoff 2008). Same-sex couples, however, when given the choice of marriage on the one hand, or civil unions or domestic partnerships on the other (in states that offered both), overwhelmingly chose marriage. See chapter 15.

29. See the California Supreme Court's post–Proposition 8 decision, *Strauss v. Horton* (2009).

Chapter 10

1. The *Perry* trial had the effect of delaying the progress of the case and allowing rapid political change to have its effect. When *Perry* was eventually argued in the Supreme Court in March 2013, the political situation for marriage equality had improved dramatically from 2009. By 2013 marriage equality was the majority opinion in the U.S.; four states had endorsed marriage equality in separate referenda in 2012; and President Obama had endorsed marriage equality and gone on to be reelected. And still, as we shall see, *Perry* was decided in the Supreme Court on technicalities over standing, suggesting that in 2013 the Court was still not ready to make a final decision on marriage equality.

2. There were many same-sex marriage court cases, but only three trials. The first trial took place in Hawaii in 1996 (see chapter 6). For the history and background of the ultimately successful federal court battles against Proposition 8, see Becker (2015) and Boies and Olson (2014).

3. The deposition comes after witnesses have submitted their sworn affidavit (written testimony) and precedes the trial. At the deposition, the lawyers from the opposing side have an opportunity to cross-examine the witness in order to explore the witness's expertise and discover potential avenues of questioning for cross-examination at the trial, if the witness should appear to testify at the trial. The deposition transcript can be evidence in the case regardless of whether the case goes to trial.

4. Quoted in Becker (2015: 70).

5. Quoted in Judge Walker's *Perry v. Schwarzenegger* (2010: 937) decision. See also Boies and Olson (2014: 146–147).

6. See Boies and Olson (2014: 167).

7. From the author's phone interview with Segura, August 21, 2019.

8. Quoted in Judge Walker's *Perry v. Schwarzenegger* (2010: 934) decision.

9. This was part of Judge Stephen Reinhardt's opinion in *Perry v. Brown* (2012) in the Ninth Circuit Court. On the broader subject of when judges ought to recuse themselves from a case, see *Caperton v. A. T. Massey Coal* (2009) and commentary by Rotunda (2010). It is worth noting that a lawyer arguing before a Black judge or a woman judge will *know* that the judge is Black or is a woman (and might frame their arguments accordingly), but the defendants in the *Perry* trial may not have known that Judge Walker was gay. If knowing that Walker was gay would have made a difference in the way they argued the case, the defendants' request for a new trial might not have been as unreasonable as the Ninth Circuit judged it to be.

10. Quoted from Judge Walker's *Perry v. Schwarzenegger* decision (2010: 979–980, 990).

11. Lower court decisions are stayed (meaning prevented from taking effect) pending appeal, when the side that lost would lose the benefit of the appeal while waiting for the appeal to be decided. If all the same-sex couples in California who wanted to marry could marry while the appeal of Judge Walker's decision was pending before the Ninth Circuit, and then before the next appeal was pending before the U.S. Supreme Court (an appeals process which took three years), the appeal would have been pointless.

12. The Court's *Hollingsworth v. Perry* decision vacated the Ninth Circuit's decision in *Perry v. Brown* because the Ninth Circuit had allowed Hollingsworth and the defendant-intervenors to appeal Judge Walker's trial decision, but the U.S. Supreme Court had decided that Hollingsworth and the other defendant-intervenors had no standing and therefore were not eligible to appeal.

13. See McCloskey and Levinson (2016).

14. Of the twelve states that had approved same-sex marriage by June 2013, Delaware, Minnesota, and Rhode Island had changed their laws but had not yet started marrying same-sex couples.

15. On the Supreme Court waiting until the majority of states have decided an issue, see Klarman (2013: ix).

16. The U.S. Supreme Court generally does not like to admit that it is guided by the prevailing winds of politics. So, for instance, in Justice Kennedy's majority decision in *Obergefell v. Hodges* (2015: 677), a decision whose timing appears to be carefully sensitive to the national support for marriage equality, he wrote, "It is of no moment whether advocates of same-sex marriage now enjoy or lack momentum in the democratic process."

17. New York did not adopt marriage equality until 2011, but it had recognized same-sex marriages from other jurisdictions starting in 2008. See the discussion in the Second Circuit Court of Appeals, *Windsor v. U.S.* (2012). Spyer and Windsor were therefore legally married in New York, but not legally married in the eyes of the U.S. government, which was owed estate tax. For background on Windsor and Spyer, and on Windsor's (ultimately victorious) court challenge against DOMA, see Kaplan and Dickey (2015) and the documentary film *Edie & Thea: A Very Long Engagement* (Muska and Olafsdóttir 2009).

18. See *Windsor v. U.S.* (2012), Second Circuit Court of Appeals.

19. For the audio of the oral arguments, see Oyez.org (IIT Chicago-Kent College of Law n.d.), and for Roberta Kaplan's internal thought process, see Kaplan and Dickey (2015: 269).

20. Quoted from Justice Kennedy's majority decision in *US v. Windsor* (2013: 770, 772, 775).

21. Quoted from Justice Scalia's dissent in *US v. Windsor* (2013: 800).

Chapter 11

1. On geographic independence and nontraditional unions, see Rosenfeld (2007).

2. See Michigan Code §710.24.

3. Particulars of April and Jayne's story come from my in-person interview with them, on December 15, 2015, along with public records and subsequent email dialogue.

4. See the plaintiffs' amended complaint, Nessel et al. (2012).

5. For a discussion of second-parent adoption and unmarried couple joint adoption in law and in practice in Michigan courts, see Fore (2015).

6. Before the Michigan Marriage Amendment passed in 2004, same-sex marriage was already banned by an earlier statute, signed into law in Michigan in 1995. Before the 1995 law explicitly banned same-sex marriage in the state, precedent and tradition and gendered language in the law were effective (in Michigan as well as elsewhere) at preventing same-sex couples from being recognized as legally married.

7. One cannot sue a U.S. state in federal court because of federalism guarantees to the states embodied in the Eleventh Amendment. One can, however, sue state officials in federal court for their failure to comply with the U.S. Constitution, a use of the federal courts that was codified in U.S. Supreme Court decision *Ex parte Young* (1908; Justice Harlan's dissent, that suing the governor or attorney general in their official capacity was no different from suing the state, notwithstanding). Therefore, the case was *DeBoer v. Snyder* rather than DeBoer v. Michigan.

8. See U.S. Code Title 42 §1988. On the Civil Rights Attorney's Fees Award Act, see Hamilton (1977).

9. The meaning of "civil rights" in this usage is broad: any personal rights guaranteed by law or by the Constitution.

10. The first two defendants in *DeBoer v. Snyder* were Governor Snyder and Attorney General Schuette (in their official capacities). The amended complaint had a third defendant, Republican Clerk Bill Bullard Jr. of Oakland County, Michigan, since it is the clerk's office that issues marriage licenses in Michigan and plaintiffs wanted to compel the clerk to issue a marriage license to them. In November 2012, Democrat Lisa Brown defeated Bullard to become clerk of Oakland County. Brown took the plaintiffs' side in the case and was a friendly witness to the plaintiffs in the February 2014 *DeBoer v. Snyder* trial.

Chapter 12

1. In the past, fewer than one in one thousand children in the U.S. were being raised by same-sex couples. As same-sex couples came out of the closet and sought more openly to raise children, the proportion of U.S. children being raised by same-sex couples rose. In the 2000 U.S. census, about 1 out of every 182 children was living with same-sex couple parents. If we limit the children to those who had lived with same-sex couple parents for at least five years to try to ensure that the children had actually been *raised* by the same-sex couple parents, the numbers go down to about 1 out of every 213 children having been raised by same-sex couple parents.

2. On the later life implications of elementary school grade retention, see Guo, Brooks-Gunn, and Harris (1996) and Brooks-Gunn, Guo, and Furstenberg (1993).

3. On the effects of residential segregation on neighborhoods, see Massey and Denton (1993).

4. See, e.g., the affidavits of the defense witnesses in *DeBoer v. Snyder* (Allen 2013a; Regnerus 2013).

5. On the failure of the U.S. government's "Supporting Healthy Marriage" program to raise marriage rates among poor people, see Lundquist et al. (2014) and Bartlett (2014).

6. In *Turner v. Safley* (1987) the U.S. Supreme Court decided that the right to marriage is so fundamental a right that even convicted prisoners must be allowed to marry, despite the fact that they are deprived of many other rights. In the *Zablocki v. Redhail* (1978) case, the Court decided that states could not block people with unpaid child support bills (a condition especially applicable to poor men) from marriage.

Chapter 13

1. See Becker (2015).

2. The text of the Michigan Marriage Amendment: "To secure and preserve the benefits of marriage for our society and for future generations of children, the union of one man and one woman in marriage shall be the only agreement recognized as a marriage or similar union for any purpose." The amendment was passed in 2004 with 59% support from the voters. It was interpreted by the Michigan Supreme Court as banning not only same-sex marriage but also state recognition of domestic partnerships and domestic partner benefits for same-sex couples (Fore 2015).

3. Fore (2015) notes that Judge Bernard Friedman had a lesbian law clerk, one aspect of Friedman's profile that may have predisposed him to a favorable view of marriage equality.

4. On the outcomes of federal trials, see Kyckelhahn and Cohen (2008). When the material facts of the case are not in dispute, judges render judgment based on the facts as known and based on the legal motion of the prevailing side; this is known as summary judgment.

5. Stanyar and the other plaintiffs' attorneys were paid after the *Obergefell v. Hodges* (2015) Supreme Court decision vindicated the *DeBoer v. Snyder* (2014) trial decision, finally overturning Michigan's same-sex marriage ban and exhausting Michigan's appeals. Carole Stanyar, Dana Nessel, Ken Mogill, Bob Sedler, Mary Bonauto, and Vickie Henry were paid, collectively, about $2 million by the state of Michigan because of the Civil Rights Attorney's Fees Award Act. The attorneys were made financially whole, but Stanyar did not get her house back because another family was living there.

6. See American Civil Liberties Union et al. (2009).

7. Quoted from the author's email exchange with Stanyar (2014–2016). As plaintiffs' attorney Kenneth Mogill (author's email exchange 2013–2016) recalls, the national civil rights organizations' skepticism about the Michigan case was not entirely unwarranted. The plaintiffs did end up losing their appeal in the Sixth Circuit (as the ACLU feared they would). The subsequent appeal to the U.S. Supreme Court, in the *Obergefell v. Hodges* (2015) case, which consolidated four appeals from states in the Sixth Circuit, was won only by the slimmest margin, 5–4. Mogill recalls, "While we were confident that we were doing the right thing in pursuing the [*DeBoer v. Snyder*]

case, it could have turned out that we were wrong. . . . When you eventually win a case 5–4 in the Supreme Court, it's clear that your position was not a slam dunk."

8. See attacks on the scholarly consensus by Regnerus (2012c), Allen (2013a; Allen, Pakaluk, and Price 2013), and Marks (2012).

9. From the author's phone interview with Manning, July 25, 2019.

10. Quoted from the ASA (2013: 3) amicus brief filed in the *DeBoer* case. In addition to describing the social science consensus that children fare as well when raised by same-sex couple parents, the ASA amicus brief called out sociologist (and state's witness) Mark Regnerus's published work as failing to contribute to the debate over children raised by same-sex couples. The ASA brief argued that Regnerus had misclassified lesbian mothers and gay fathers and that Regnerus's (2012a) failure to account for family stability differences undermined his results.

11. The affidavit is the witness's sworn written testimony, outlining the arguments that the witness expects to make and the evidence the witness will rely on in the case.

12. The 95% confidence interval is a statistical way of indicating how much uncertainty there is in a given measure. If we had 100 data sets of the same size, the measure would vary, but we would expect 95 of the 100 measures to be within the 95% confidence interval. The larger the sample size, the more accurate the measure and the smaller the 95% confidence interval should be. Allen's figures overstated the uncertainty of the measures of grade attainment from the U.S. census by factors of between 10 and 100 times.

13. Allen's figure has third grade as the expected grade attainment for eight-year-olds, but this is a year off: nine-year-olds are expected to be in grade 3 when the census is taken in April. The one-year difference is not material to the substance of the graph. The actual data graph on the right side of Figure 13.1 appropriately shows age nine corresponding to grade three.

14. The real data difference in average grade attainment for "own children" (the definition of which excludes adopted, step, or foster children) raised by same-sex couples and "own" children raised by heterosexual married couples was 2% of one year, taking no other factors into account (which is slightly smaller than the 2.8% difference for the same comparison I reported in chapter 12, because here adopted and foster children are not included).

15. The deposition transcript can be evidence in the case whether or not the case goes to trial. Also, the depositions can be much longer and more exploratory than trial cross-examination would be. For instance, I was deposed for a full day before the *DeBoer v. Snyder* trial, but I was cross-examined for only about one hour at the trial.

16. *DeBoer v. Snyder* trial testimony from Thursday, March 6, 2014, from trial transcript starting at page 108.

17. Allen, Pakaluk, and Price (2013) reintroduced into the analyses children who had not lived with the same parents for at least five years, along with adopted and foster children. The authors were obscuring the crucial difference between being *raised by* a same-sex couple, where the parents might conceivably have had a causal effect on the child's outcome, and coming to *live with* a same-sex couple after the fact. Since same-sex couples bring children into their families at later ages and with greater likelihood

of the children having special needs, the intentional confusion between *raised by* and *living with* is a confusion that is prejudicial to same-sex couples in the analyses. Regnerus (2012a) made the same fundamentally misleading error, and Allen (2013b) repeated the same error.

18. See the NFSS data at Regnerus (2012b).

19. At the same time, conservative commentator Ross Douthat (2012) described Regnerus as the voice of reason in the debate over same-sex marriage.

20. NFSS question S7: "From when you were born until age 18 (or until you left home to be on your own), did either of your parents ever have a romantic relationship with someone of the same sex?"

21. Of the 236 lesbian mothers or gay fathers as defined by Regnerus, only 75 were in same-sex unions that the study subjects lived with as children. Among the 75 respondents who had ever lived with same-sex couple parents, the average coresidence with same-sex couple parents was 3.7 years, meaning even for the 75 subjects who ever lived with same-sex couple parents, most of their childhood was spent being raised by family structures other than same-sex couples. Of the childhood years lived by all NFSS subjects in the 1972–2012 period, only 0.11% (weighted average) of the childhood years were lived with same-sex couples. The percentage of children living with same-sex couple parents is lower than the percentage of couples who are same-sex couples (1 to 2% in the most recent censuses) because same-sex couples have fewer children, on average, than heterosexual couples have and because the percentage of children living with same-sex couple parents was substantially lower in the past than it is today.

22. Because of the difficulty of identifying substantial numbers of children raised by same-sex couples in national surveys, most of the previous studies of children raised by same-sex couples have been small convenience sample studies rather than studies drawn from nationally representative samples. There were a few nationally representative sample studies, however, including Potter (2012), Rosenfeld (2010), and Wainright, Russell, and Patterson (2004). Nationally representative sampling starts with all persons in the target universe, and samples randomly from them. Convenience sampling, in contrast, starts with the small target population of interest. If one is trying to obtain a sufficient sample size of a small minority group, such as children raised by same-sex couples, the nationally representative survey must survey or at least screen an enormous number of subjects to achieve a sufficient sample size of the population of interest, which, e.g., Regnerus's nationally representative NFSS was unable to do. Nationally representative surveys also can suffer from the problem of identification error. Imagine that 1% of survey subjects answer questions randomly, without even reading the questions. Any population in the survey whose true percentage was less than 1% might be recorded as having as many false members as true members. Small populations are difficult to identify accurately in representative surveys. See surveys of the literature on children raised by same-sex couples by Meezan and Rauch (2005) and Stacey and Biblarz (2001).

When nationally representative samples are too expensive or otherwise unavailable, scholars use convenience sampling, which starts with subjects in the target population who are easiest to find. Chan, Raboy, and Patterson (1998) studied eighty children whose mothers, lesbian and heterosexual, had become pregnant through sperm donation from one California sperm bank. One advantage of convenience sampling is that in a convenience sample the researcher may have enough information about their subjects to eliminate identification error entirely.

23. Of the seventy-five NFSS subjects who ever lived with same-sex couple parents, only four were living with same-sex couple parents at birth, and the average child's age at first living with same-sex couple parents was eleven years. Single-mother families are formed earlier in children's lives. Fifty-three percent of NFSS subjects who ever lived with single mothers did so before their first birthday, and the average age at first living with a single mother (for subjects who ever lived with a single mother) was 3.8 years.

24. On the effect of parental breakup on children, see Wallerstein and Kelley (1980). But see also Cherlin et al. (1991).

25. The only studies that have measured outcomes for children raised by same-sex couples while avoiding the confounding effect of the breakup of prior heterosexual relationships are the convenience sample studies that relied on samples of mothers who became pregnant through artificial reproductive technology (Brewaeys et al. 1997; Chan, Raboy, and Patterson 1998).

26. Regnerus's original paper was titled "How Different Are the Adult Children of Parents Who Have Same-Sex Relationships" (2012a), and his response to critics was titled "Parental Same-Sex Relationships, Family Instability, and Life Outcomes for Adult Children: Answering Critics of the New Family Structures Study with Additional Analyses" (2012c).

27. Early critics of Regnerus (2012a) include Jim Burroway (2012), Gary Gates (2012a), and Debra Umberson (2012).

28. The only one of Regnerus's associations with gay or lesbian parents that survived reanalysis was that parents who were not exclusively heterosexual had children who were more likely to grow up to be adults who were not exclusively heterosexual (Rosenfeld 2015). For a classic small-sample study of the tendency of children raised by lesbian mothers to be less exclusively heterosexual, see Golombok and Tasker (1996). For a more recent study of young boys in the U.S. raised by lesbians showing less stereotypically male-type play behaviors, see Goldberg and Garcia (2016).

29. Family instability is not, of course, randomly distributed among families. Parents with substance abuse problems, psychological problems, or personality disorders are more likely to have the kind of turbulent family lives that include many family transitions. Because the NFSS data are retrospective, and because little or no information is available in NFSS about how parental characteristics might have influenced the family transitions that subjects experienced as children, the NFSS data have important limitations. The only variable that I could identify in the NFSS data set that was more predictive of later negative outcomes than family transitions was parental welfare dependence (Rosenfeld 2015).

30. On the history of discrimination against same-sex couples in custody disputes, see Wald (2006) and Klarman (2013). For examples of children being taken away from gay or lesbian parents, see *Burns v. Burns* (2002) and *Bottoms v. Bottoms* (1995). For a broader discussion of the difficulties LGBT families faced in the U.S. before *Obergefell*, see Baumle and Compton (2015).

31. See Blumstein and Schwartz (1983: 308). See also Kurdek (1998, 2004), Balsam et al. (2008), Andersson et al. (2006), Kalmijn, Loeve, and Manting (2007), and Ross, Gask, and Berrington (2011). Using the How Couples Meet and Stay Together data (HCMST; Rosenfeld, Thomas, and Falcon 2015), I showed (Rosenfeld 2014a) that same-sex couples who considered themselves to be married had relationship stability similar to heterosexual couples who were legally married, controlling for other important factors such as relationship duration.

32. See Bramlett and Mosher (2002).

33. See Balsam et al. (2008) and Rosenfeld (2014a).

34. Expert witnesses are not supposed to interact with each other directly, or even to hear each other's testimony in court. I have reconstructed the cross-examination of the state's witnesses from the official transcripts of the *DeBoer* trial, which were made public after the trial was over. The trial transcripts can be found at Pacer.gov, or at https://web.stanford.edu/~mrosenfe/DeBoer_docs.htm.

35. *DeBoer v. Snyder* trial transcript, day 6, part 1, page 41.

36. *DeBoer v. Snyder* trial transcript, day 7, part 2, page 46.

37. Opponents of marriage equality have often argued that biological relatedness between parents and children, which heterosexual couples can potentially both have with their common children and which same-sex couple partners cannot both have with their common children, is crucial in positive outcomes for children, and is therefore a reason for the state to preserve marriage for heterosexual couples. The argument for the benefit of biological relatedness does not comport well with all the evidence. See, e.g., Hamilton, Cheng, and Powell's (2007) study showing that adoptive parents invest more in their children than biological parents do.

38. *DeBoer v. Snyder* trial transcript, day 6, part 3, pages 109–110.

39. *DeBoer v. Snyder* trial transcript, day 6, part 3, page 122.

40. From the *DeBoer* (2014: 759) trial decision. By "enjoining" enforcement of the Michigan Marriage Amendment, Judge Friedman ordered the state to stop enforcing the amendment.

41. Quoted from Judge Friedman's *DeBoer* trial decision (2014: 768–770). In contrast to the discrediting of the defense witnesses, Judge Friedman evaluated the plaintiffs' expert witnesses as highly credible, e.g.: "The Court finds Rosenfeld's testimony to be highly credible and gives it great weight." This was the sentence in the *DeBoer* trial decision that my father (a retired attorney himself) liked the best.

42. Quoted from the DeBoer trial decision (2014: 771, 775). The *DeBoer* trial was focused on the social science questions about same-sex couple parents and children. In addition to addressing the social science, Judge Friedman's decision also addressed the wider issue of the constitutionality of the Michigan Marriage Amendment, since the constitutionality question was at the core of both sides' legal arguments, and since the constitutional question (more than the social science questions) were sure to be the focus of the appeals in the Sixth Circuit, and later in the U.S. Supreme Court.

43. The Sixth Circuit's March 22, 2014, stay of Judge Friedman's ruling was legally reasonable because if all the same-sex couples in Michigan could legally marry while the case awaited appeal hearing, then the state's appeal would be moot. If the appealing

side would lose the benefit of the appeal (such as if all same-sex couples could marry while the appeals were pending), then stays are generally granted, but only if the appealing party can demonstrate that they have a chance of winning the appeal.

44. See *Caspar v. Snyder* (2015).

45. Utah's attorney general, whose office had relied on Regnerus's faulty social science in defense of Utah's ban on same-sex marriage (overturned in *Kitchen v. Herbert* 2013), had to reevaluate their own position in light of Judge Friedman's negative appraisal of Regnerus's credibility. On April 9, 2014, Utah's attorney general wrote to the Tenth Circuit Court of Appeals, withdrawing the parts of their argument that had relied on Regnerus: "[T]he Regnerus study cannot be viewed as conclusively establishing that raising a child in a same-sex household produces outcomes that are inferior to those produced by man-woman parenting arrangements."

46. Quoted from the 6th Circuit Appellate decision in *DeBoer v. Snyder* (2014: 405).

47. See Hopper (2014) in Canada's *National Post*.

48. See Gilchrist (2018) in the *Advocate*.

Chapter 14

1. Details about Jim Obergefell's and John Arthur's lives and Obergefell's role as a plaintiff in the same-sex marriage cases are from Cenziper and Obergefell (2016).

2. The one federal district court decision from the post-*Windsor* era that did not favor marriage equality was *Robicheaux v. Caldwell* (2014) in U.S. District Court in Louisiana. See the appendix to the *Obergefell v. Hodges* (2015) decision for a longer list of marriage equality court cases.

3. Quoted from Judge Black's decision in *Obergefell v Wymyslo* (2013: 973–974).

4. The date when same-sex marriage bans were overturned by the courts was followed (sometimes immediately, sometimes more slowly) by the timing of when same-sex couples were allowed to marry without hindrance. See also my discussion later of *Miller v. Davis* (2015) in Kentucky.

5. The Tenth Circuit Court of Appeals refused to issue a stay, on the grounds that it believed Utah's appeal had no chance of succeeding.

6. See Tomsic (2016).

7. See Associated Press (2014).

8. For alternative versions of the discussions around who should argue issue 1 of *Obergefell*, and of how Bonauto came to make the historic oral argument, see Frank (2017: 339–342). See also the film *Love v. Kentucky* (Schuman 2017) for the view of the Kentucky attorneys and plaintiffs who thought the most experienced Supreme Court litigator (regardless of sexual orientation) should make the *Obergefell* oral argument. Both Frank and *Love v. Kentucky* describe the Michigan attorneys and plaintiffs as unwilling to agree to being represented by Supreme Court specialist Jeff Fisher despite Fisher's having bested Michigan attorney Stanyar in a moot court.

9. The solicitor general represents the U.S. government in arguments before the Supreme Court.

10. American courts are institutionally conservative, and deference to executive authority is part of that conservatism. According to Rosenberg (2008: 14), when the U.S. government intervenes in a case, the side it favors wins 70% of the time. John J. Bursch presented the *Obergefell* oral arguments on issue 1 for forty-five minutes on behalf of the states seeking to retain their same-sex marriage bans.

11. Quoted from Justice Kennedy's majority decision in *Obergefell v. Hodges* (2015: 651–668). See Gates's (2015) amicus brief for *Obergefell*. Gates had been found highly credible as a witness in the *DeBoer v. Snyder* trial, which probably amplified his credibility as an authority to Justice Kennedy.

12. See Rubenstein's (2018) interview with Justice Kennedy on Bloomberg.com.

13. Quoted from Justice Kennedy's majority opinion in *Obergefell v. Hodges* (2015: 668–681).

14. See news video feed from MLive (2015).

15. A video of the wedding ceremony can be found on YouTube (cvalner 2015).

16. See reporting and video of the adoption ceremony in the *Detroit Free Press* (Stafford 2015).

17. For more stories of second-parent adoption and its power and importance, see Baumle and Compton (2015).

Chapter 15

1. George Chauncey (2004: 93) wrote about the internal conflicts over marriage equality in 1970s and 1980s: "[S]upport for marriage was a distinctly minority position in the lesbian and gay movement. Although some gay liberationists cheered the Minneapolis [Baker and McConnell; see chapter 3] and Louisville couples on, others criticized them for 'imitating meaningless, bad habits of our oppressors.'" Klarman (2013: 48) notes, "In the early 1990s, the gay community remained deeply divided over whether to pursue gay marriage. Marriage had not been on the gay rights agenda at all in the first half of the 1980s." For a variety of scholarly opinions on marriage equality that privileges the left critiques of marriage equality, see the volume edited by Bernstein and Taylor (2013). For a post-*Obergefell* critique of marriage equality from the Left, see Duberman (2018).

2. On the practical objection to marriage equality as being perceived as having little chance of succeeding and creating a dangerous backlash, see Klarman (2013).

3. See Polikoff (1993: 1536).

4. On the critics of marriage equality who have described it as at least in part an inauthentic mimicry of heterosexual norms, see the classic *Gay Manifesto* by Wittman (1970), Ettelbrick (1989), Franke (2006), Hirshman (2012: 237), and Duberman (2018) and see Taylor et al.'s (2009) description of the 2004 San Francisco same-sex marriages as social action theater and performance. For more on the history of the debate within the gay rights movement over marriage equality, see Frank (2017).

5. On the demeaning side of respectability politics in the Black community, see Harris (2014).

6. See Higginbotham (1993) for a classic description of both the progressive and regressive sides of respectability politics in early twentieth-century Black Christian women.

7. For survey research on the priority American gays and lesbians placed on marriage equality from before most had the opportunity to legally marry, see Egan and Sherrill (2005) and Hull and Ortyl (2013) with survey data from 2007–2008.

8. See Chauncey (2004: 141).

9. For the 1.3 million Americans in same-sex marriages as of 2017, I rely on my own tabulation of weighted data from the 2017 How Couples Meet and Stay Together study (HCMST; Rosenfeld, Thomas, and Hausen 2018) fielded in July 2017. In the HCMST data, 22% of same-sex couples were married, compared to 63% of heterosexual couples. See also a report by Romero (2017) based on survey data from Gallup with similar results, showing 1.1 million married Americans in same-sex marriages in the summer of 2017. The author's tabulation from weighted data from the American Community Survey (a much larger survey than either HCMST or Gallup) showed 1.1 million Americans in married coresident same-sex unions in 2017.

10. For examples of advocacy of domestic partnerships over same-sex marriage, see Polikoff (2008) and Duggan (2002). For a history of domestic partnerships and their relationship to marriage, see NeJaime (2014).

11. The number of same-sex domestic partnerships registered in California dropped from about 195 per month in the six months before the Supreme Court's *Hollingsworth v. Perry* decision in June 2013 to about 77 per month immediately after the decision, a 60% drop overnight.

12. The figure of 28,000 marriages is from weighted data on marriages celebrated in the past twelve months for California residents from the American Community Survey, for 2013, 2014, and half of the 2015 total. The number of registered domestic partnerships for same-sex couples is derived from the author's tabulation of domestic partnerships from a California state database. The California Domestic Partnership Registry does not identify same-sex couples, but same-sex couples can be identified probabilistically by both partners' first names. I merged the California Domestic Partner registry with a database of the gender of first names of all people born in the U.S., derived from a Social Security database, in order to distinguish same-sex couples from different-sex (heterosexual) couples. Different-sex couples were allowed to register domestic partnerships in California in the 2013–2014 period if one partner was at least sixty-two years old. Same-sex couples registered about half of all domestic partnerships in California from July 2013 through December 2014 but accounted for the great majority of domestic partnerships registered in California from January 2000 through June 2013.

13. On the way the Christian Right's tenacious opposition to same-sex marriage helped to illuminate same-sex marriage's a radical side, see Chauncey (2004: chs. 4–5).

14. For an early view of both the radical and the traditional potential of same-sex marriage, see Hunter (1991).

Chapter 16

1. See the news report in Latimer (2016).
2. See, e.g., Hagan and Palloni (1999).
3. The analogy between the closet that undocumented immigrants in the U.S. occupy now and the closet gay and lesbian people occupied in the past has been thoughtfully explored by Eskridge (2015). On the legal disabilities of undocumented status in the U.S. even before the Trump era, see Menjívar and Abrego (2012) and Cunningham-Parmeter (2008).
4. Research by Schachter and Kuk (2019) suggests that contact between immigrants and natives may not lower discrimination against immigrants. U.S. natives who live in immigrant-dense cities have a more positive view of immigrants because the U.S. natives with the most anti-immigrant views have moved away from the areas where immigrants are most commonly found.
5. See Allport (1954) and Pettigrew and Tropp (2006).
6. On the symbolic power of the law, see also Ryo (2017) and Sunstein (1996). The plaintiff in *Roe v. Wade* (1973) was Norma McCorvey, a young Texas woman who had an unwanted pregnancy and wanted an abortion. The fact that the courts allowed McCorvey's name to be hidden behind the pseudonym "Roe" meant that the *Roe v. Wade* decision not only legalized abortion in the U.S. but also contributed to the stigma against abortion by making abortion seem like something that needed to be hidden. Up until 1994, McCorvey was active in the women's rights movement and was working in an abortion clinic in Texas and living as an out-of-the-closet lesbian with her partner, Connie. In 1995, McCorvey had a religious conversion, renounced her lesbian identity, and became active in the antiabortion movement. See McCorvey and Meisler (1994) for McCorvey's story before the religious conversion, and see McCorvey and Thomas (1997) for the postconversion story.
7. See Cowan (2014: appendix B).
8. On the #Shoutyourabortion hashtag, see Vara (2015). According to my reading of the tweets, in the month of January 2018, ninety-four different women had their abortion histories mentioned under the #Shoutyourabortion hashtag (including links to magazine stories about women and abortion). If about 100 women share their abortion stories per month, that would yield about 1,200 disclosed abortion stories per year. More than 600,000 abortions are performed in the U.S. every year (down from more than 1 million in the 1990s). The modest number of 1,200 publicly disclosed abortion stories per year suggests that the vast number of abortion histories remain closeted.
9. The fifty-three women who declared that they had had abortions included Susan Brownmiller, Judy Collins, Nora Ephron, Lillian Hellman, Billie Jean King, Anaïs Nin, Frances Fox Piven, Letty Cottin Pogrebin, Susan Sontag, Gloria Steinem, and Barbara Tuchman.
10. Ms. Magazine repeated the request in 2006 for women to out themselves as having had abortions, and reported receiving "thousands" of affirmations (Rios 2019).
11. On abortion rates in different U.S. groups, see Jones and Jerman (2017).
12. See Chauncey (2004).

13. See the *New York Times* reporting of Steel and Schmidt (2017).

14. See the *New York Times* reporting of Steel et al. (2017).

15. See the *New York Times* reporting by Kantor and Twohey (2017).

16. See reporting in the *Guardian* by Cain (2018).

17. See reporting in the *New York Times* by Ransom (2020).

18. See *New York Times* reporting by Benjamin Hoffman (2017), and later follow-up by Hauser (2018).

19. See *New York Times* reporting by Macur (2018).

20. See *Boston Globe* reporting by Robinson et al. (2002) and the book by Carroll et al. (2015). See also the Pennsylvania Statewide Grand Jury (2018) report on Catholic Church abuse of children in Pennsylvania.

21. See also Freeh Sporkin & Sullivan LLP's (2012) report on Penn State University's cover-up of years of credible allegations against Jerry Sandusky, who was eventually convicted of sexually molesting children in campus facilities.

22. On the way institutions sometimes betray the people they are supposed to protect, which ultimately harms those very institutions also, see Smith and Freyd (2014).

23. See Carlsen et al. (2018) in the *New York Times*.

24. In a comparison of two surveys of American attitudes from late 2017 and late 2018, the *Economist* reported that Americans had become more skeptical of sexual harassment claims and more concerned about false accusations of sexual harassment in 2018 than they had been in 2017. The change toward more skepticism of the Me Too movement in the *Economist* report was driven entirely by Trump supporters. Trump was credibly accused of sexual assault by more than a dozen women, but he denied the specific accusations. See *Economist* (2018), using survey data from YouGov. A separate series of NBC/*Wall Street Journal* polls (2017; 2018a; 2018b) showed no change whatsoever in the percentage of Americans who said that attention to sexual harassment had gone too far.

25. For one critique of the alleged excesses of #MeToo, see Sullivan (2018). On the way the initial focus of #MeToo was broadened from sexual violence to harassment to a variety of other issues, see Garber (2018).

26. On the video of Trump bragging about sexual assault and his weak apology, see Haberman (2016) in the *New York Times*. On the female accusers and Trump's denial of specific stories of assaults, see Twohey and Barbaro (2016) in the *New York Times*. For the race and gender breakdown of the popular vote in the 2016 U.S. presidential election, see data based on exit polls in CNN (2016). The fact that Trump won 52% of the White women's vote is contested, as it seems difficult for some to believe. In the American National Election Studies for 2016, in a sample of 1,053 non-Hispanic White women, the weighted percentage who said they voted for Trump was 52.5%, right in line with what the exit polls showed. A Pew Research Center (2018) study of validated voters showed Trump beat Hillary Clinton among White women in the 2016 election, 47 to 45%. The differing results depend, in part, on whether votes for other candidates (besides Clinton and Trump) are included, and whether or not the category of White women includes Hispanic women.

27. For analysis of a variety of other social movements and identity groups that see identity-claiming and coming out as the path forward, see Saguy (2020).

28. Americans have always been very supportive of abortion rights to save the health of the woman (about 90% support) and if the pregnancy resulted from rape (about 80% support). For women who cannot afford more children, public opinion on abortion rights has been more evenly divided.

Chapter 17

1. According to Rosenberg (2008), there was no progress on school desegregation in the U.S. from 1955 until President Lyndon Johnson made school funding contingent on school desegregation after 1965. By some measures, public school desegregation in the U.S. has never been achieved (see Orfield, Eaton, and Harvard Project on School Desegregation 1996).

2. Fetal ultrasound imaging was pioneered in the 1950s and popularized in the U.S. in the 1970s. The personal experience of seeing one's own potential progeny moving inside the uterus has made some people think of the fetus as more like a living person, which is how the antiabortion movement wants people to think. Many states require women who want to obtain an abortion to be offered an ultrasound of the fetus first, as a way of discouraging abortion. On the history of fetal ultrasound and its impacts, see Nicolson and Fleming (2013). On abortion practice and statistics, see Guttmacher Institute (2018).

3. Some of the costs of providing abortions in the U.S. are due to the unnecessary regulations that abortion opponents have burdened abortion providers with. See *Whole Woman's Health v. Hellerstedt* (2016).

4. Karlan (2018) makes a similar argument, using different terminology. In her view, marriage equality is a nonrivalrous claim, and therefore had an easier path to success, whereas civil rights claims are generally rivalrous and therefore harder to win and subsequently harder to enforce.

5. On the *Masterpiece Cakeshop* decision's general support for antidiscrimination laws and the decision's narrow framing of religious exemptions and the broad protections that should remain for gay people when shopping for services in the marketplace, see NeJaime and Siegel (2018). For a thorough analysis of how U.S. courts have managed religious exemptions to different nondiscrimination laws, see Ball (2017). Liberals tend to see the *Masterpiece Cakeshop* decision as very narrow, but conservatives see the decision as having more sweeping potential to give religious people the right to refuse to do business with gay people or same-sex couples (see Anderson 2018). The courts (and especially the current conservative majority in the Supreme Court) will ultimately decide how the precedent of *Masterpiece Cakeshop* will matter. Gay rights advocates have reasons for apprehension. In the 2021 Supreme Court decision by Justice Roberts in *Fulton v. City of Philadelphia*, which had the endorsement or concurrence of all members of the court, the court decided that Philadelphia did *not* have

the right to exclude Catholic Social Services (CSS) from certification as a foster place-ment agency on the grounds that CSS refused to place children in the homes of same-sex couples (in alleged violation of the city's Fair Practices Ordinance).

6. The distinction between private business (such as the Masterpiece Cakeshop) and state action (such as the work of the clerk of Rowan County, Kentucky) may at first seem stark, but is not. Most businesses, including Masterpiece Cakeshop, are licensed by the state they are in. Being licensed by the state makes a business subject to state regulation and oversight.

7. See *Miller v. Davis* (2015) for the original order, and see the summary of facts in *Miller v. Davis* (2017) when the case had been concluded and the plaintiffs' attorneys fees were considered and awarded.

8. See reporting in the *New York Times* by Rappeport (2015).

9. See reporting in *USA Today* by Loftus (2016), and see the Kim Davis page in *Wikipedia* (2018).

10. The last fourteen state holdouts against marriage equality (Michigan, Ohio, Tennessee, Kentucky, Texas, Louisiana, Mississippi, Alabama, Georgia, North Dakota, South Dakota, Nebraska, Missouri, and Arkansas) were transformed into same-sex mar-riage states by the *Obergefell* decision.

11. See reporting in the *New York Times* by Eckholm and Fernandez (2015). Roy Moore, chief judge of the Supreme Court of Alabama, ordered the state's probate judges to refuse to issue marriage licenses to same-sex couples, but he was suspended from his job in 2016, and same-sex marriages in Alabama resumed (Robertson 2016). Moore ran for an open U.S. Senate seat in Alabama in 2017 and won the Republican nomina-tion but lost the general election to Democrat Doug Jones.

12. See Movement Advancement Project (2019) for a list of states that had banned work-place discrimination against LGBT people before the *Bostock v. Clayton County* decision.

13. See, e.g., Eskridge (2017: 322).

14. On the influence of *Obergefell* on gay rights and Title VII, see Green (2017).

15. See Justice Kavanaugh's dissent in *Bostock* (2020: footnote 9).

16. See Justice Alito's dissent in *Bostock* (2020: footnote 1).

17. Other aspects of the Civil Rights Act of 1964 were expanded or amended by the Civil Rights Act of 1991.

18. See the detailed discussion of Title VII's history in relation to discrimination against gays and lesbians in Eskridge (2017).

19. The case was *Price Waterhouse v. Hopkins* (1989), which was cited in Gorsuch's ma-jority opinion in *Bostock* and discussed by Eskridge (2017) as an important prece-dent for gay and lesbian inclusion under the umbrella of Title VII's protections against sex discrimination. See an earlier discussion of the same issues in Koppelman (1994). Justice Alito's dissent in *Bostock* argued that *Hopkins* was not a precedent that gay and lesbian plaintiffs should be able to rely on because antigay discrimination was not necessarily about gay and lesbian people failing to accord with traditional gender expectations.

20. On Ann Hopkins being a straight woman and why her sexual identity mattered, see Feldblum (2013: 13–15).

21. Three years earlier, in *Macy v. Holder* (2012), the EEOC had ruled that transgender workers in the federal government were protected by Title VII's protections against discrimination because of sex.

22. This was the EEOC's administrative law decision in *Baldwin v. Foxx* (2015), a case about an air traffic controller (Baldwin) who alleged he had been passed over for promotions because he was gay.

23. For Feldblum's history (going back to the early 1990s with the Human Rights Campaign and early drafts of the Employment Non Discrimination Act) with workplace protection for gays and lesbians and the implications of Title VII, see Feldblum (2000).

24. See, e.g., Judge Walker's decision in *Perry v. Schwarzenegger* (2010: 996): "Sexual orientation discrimination can take the form of sex discrimination." See also Judge Marsha Berzon's concurrence in the Ninth Circuit in *Latta v. Otter* (2014) and the Hawaii Supreme Court's decision in *Baehr v. Lewin* (1993).

25. See Eskridge (2017).

26. See *Kimberly Hively v. Ivy Tech Community College of Indiana* (Seventh Circuit, 2017), *Melissa Zarda, Executor of the Estate of Donald Zarda v. Altitude Express* (Second Circuit, 2018), and *Equal Employment Opportunity Commission v. R. G. & G. R. Harris Funeral Homes* (Sixth Circuit, 2018). The Seventh Circuit decision was an *en banc* decision, heard by the entire Seventh Circuit, with an 8–3 majority in support of the finding that antigay discrimination violated Title VII's ban on discrimination because of sex. The *en banc* decision reversed an earlier Seventh Circuit ruling in the *Hively* case, where Hively had lost 2–1.

27. See Judge Posner's concurrence in *Hively* (2017: 354).

28. Justice Gorsuch's majority decision in *Bostock* is an example of seeing LGBT plaintiffs for who they really are because of the way Gorsuch referred to transwoman Aimee Stephens appropriately and repeatedly as "she." Conscious use of the gender pronouns appropriate to a person's lived identity is a way of showing respect. Justice Alito's dissent (see footnotes 58–60), on the other hand, mocked the use of nontraditional and gender-neutral pronouns for trans people and identified the failure to use a person's approved pronoun as a potential way conservatives might be victimized (and their rights displaced) by a new liberal orthodoxy around pronouns.

29. By focusing on and reinterpreting the text of Title VII as "because . . . of sex," Justice Gorsuch's *Bostock* decision was engaged in textual analysis. The judicial theory of textualism centers the words of the statute. Originalism, in contrast, is a judicial theory that centers the intent of the law's drafters. In the case of Title VII, originalism would *not* have yielded a pro-gay-rights result.

30. Title VII applies broadly, but there are some limitations. Private employers with fewer than fifteen employees are exempt. There is a ministerial exemption, so that churches, mosques, and synagogues are permitted to exclude non-coreligionists as ministers.

31. On the slow but measurable and significant effects of the Civil Rights Act on hiring and promotions of women and Black workers in private businesses, see Kalev and Dobbin (2006).

32. By codifying anti-LGBT discrimination as a form of sex discrimination, *Bostock* also sets the precedent that laws or practices that are alleged to discriminate against LGBT

people will face heightened judicial scrutiny because sex discrimination charges invoke a heightened standard of judicial review (as acknowledged in the *Bostock* dissents by both Alito and Kavanaugh). Even in the four gay rights victories of the Kennedy era in the Supreme Court (*Romer, Lawrence, Windsor,* and *Obergefell*), the Court had always evaluated the plaintiffs' claims at the lowest level of scrutiny, the rational basis test. Stricter judicial scrutiny of anti-LGBT laws and practices should make it easier for LGBT plaintiffs in the future to win in court.

Chapter 18

1. See Kluger ([1975] 2004).
2. Part of Clark's testimony included the results of testing Black students with White and Black dolls, to see how much the Black students had internalized a belief that Black people were inferior. Since Clark found Black students across the U.S. to have internalized the inferiority of Black people, it was difficult to discern how much of the internalized inferiority was due to the degree of segregation in their schools (Kluger [1975] 2004).
3. See the reprint of Clark's social science statement in Clark, Chein, and Cook ([1952] 2004).
4. Quoting from the unanimous decision in *Brown* (1954: 494). The first paragraph is Chief Justice Warren quoting from a lower court decision and the second paragraph is Justice Warren's own assessment of how the social science had changed its view of the damage of segregation since *Plessy v. Ferguson* in 1896.
5. See Deutcher, Chein, and Sadigur (1948).
6. See Ballotpedia (n.d.).

Chapter 19

1. See the Republican platform at www.gop.com (Republican National Convention 2016).
2. See Spriggs and Hansford (2001).
3. See reporting in the *Washington Post* (Kessler and Kelly 2018).
4. Italics in original decision. See *Jane Doe 1 et al. v. Trump* (2017) and coverage in the *New York Times* by Phillips (2017).
5. On people's greater appetite for lies than for truth, see Vosoughi, Roy, and Aral (2018).
6. On the political psychology of conservatives, see Jost et al. (2003), leaning heavily on research about right-wing authoritarianism by Altemeyer (1988, 1996, 1998). Altemeyer's research in turn drew heavily on the definition of right-wing authoritarianism developed in Adorno et al ([1950] 1982).

Bibliography

Abbreviations

ACLU	American Civil Liberties Union
AIDS	Acquired Immune Deficiency Syndrome
ALI	American Law Institute
ANES	American National Election Studies
AP	Associated Press
APA	American Psychiatric Association
ASA	American Sociological Association
CNN	Cable News Network
DADT	Don't Ask, Don't Tell
DOMA US	Defense of Marriage Act, 1996
EEOC	Equal Employment Opportunity Commission
ERA	Equal Rights Amendment
GLF	Gay Liberation Front
GSS	General Social Survey
HCMST	How Couples Meet and Stay Together (study)
LGBT	Lesbian, gay, bisexual, and transgender
NCCS	National Center for Charitable Statistics
NFSS	New Family Structures Study
PRRI	Public Religion Research Institute

Interviews

Pierce Blue
David Brodzinsky
Genora Dancel
April DeBoer and Jayne Rowse
Chai Feldblum
Gary Gates
Nan Hunter
Pamela Karlan
Wendy Manning
Kenneth Mogill
Antoinette Pregil
Cecilia Ridgeway
Pepper Schwartz
Gary Segura
Evan Wolfson
Lawrence Wu

Cases

Baehr v. Lewin, 74 Haw 530 (1993). Supreme Court of Hawaii.

Baehr v. Miike, WL 694235 Hawai'i Circuit Court (1996).

Baker v. Nelson, 191 N. W. 2d 185 (1971). Supreme Court of Minnesota.

Baker v. Nelson, 409 U.S. 810 (1972). U.S. Supreme Court.

Baker v. State, 170 Vermont 194 (1999). Supreme Court of Vermont.

Baldwin v. Foxx, Secretary, Department of Transportation, Appeal No. 0120133080 WL 4397641 (2015). EEOC.

Baskin v. Bogan, 766 F. 3d 648 (2014). U.S. Court of Appeals, Seventh Circuit.

Beller v. Middendorf, 632 F. 2d 788 (1980). Court of Appeals, Ninth Circuit.

Board of Trustees of the University of Alabama et al. v. Garrett et al., 531 U.S. 356 (2001). U.S. Supreme Court.

Bostic v. Rainey, 970 F. Supp. 2d 456 (2014). U.S. District Court, Eastern District of Virginia.

Bostic v. Schaefer, 760 F. 3d 352 (2014). U.S. Court of Appeals, Fourth Circuit.

Bostock v. Clayton County, 140 S. Ct. 1731 (2020). U.S. Supreme Court.

Bottoms v. Bottoms, 457 S.E. 2d 102 (1995). Supreme Court of Virginia.

Boutilier v. Immigration and Naturalization Service, 387 U.S. 118 (1967). U.S. Supreme Court.

Bowers v. Hardwick, 478 U.S. 186 (1986). U.S. Supreme Court.

Brown v. Board of Education, 347 U.S. 483 (1954). U.S. Supreme Court.

Brown v. Board of Education, 349 U.S. 294 (1955). U.S. Supreme Court.

Burns v. Burns, 560 SE 2d 47 (2002). Ga. Court of Appeals.

Joseph Burstyn, Inc. v. Wilson, Commissioner of Education of New York, et al., 343 U.S. 495 (1952). U.S. Supreme Court.

People of California v. Lawrence Ferlinghetti (1957). San Francisco Municipal Court.

Caperton v. A. T. Massey Coal, 556 U.S. 868 (2009). U.S. Supreme Court.

Caspar v. Snyder, 77 F. Supp. 3d 616 (2015). U.S. District Court, Eastern District of Michigan.

DeBoer v. Snyder, 937 F. Supp. 2d 757; 12-CV-10285 (2014). U.S. District Court, Eastern District of Michigan.

DeBoer v. Snyder, 772 F.3d 388 (2014). U.S. Court of Appeals, Sixth Circuit.

Dred Scott v. Sandford, 60 U.S. 393 (1857). U.S. Supreme Court.

Equal Employment Opportunity Commission v. R. G. & G. R. Harris Funeral Homes, 884 F.3d 560 (2018). U.S. Court of Appeals, Sixth Circuit.

Evans v. Romer, 92 CV 7223 (1993). Colorado District Court.

Evans v. Romer, 882 P. 2d 1335 (1994). Colorado Supreme Court.

Ex parte Young, 209 U.S. 123 (1908). U.S. Supreme Court.

Fulton v. City of Philadelphia, 593 US ____(2021). U.S. Supreme Court.

Goodridge v. Department of Public Health, 440 Massachusetts 309 (2003). Massachusetts Supreme Court.

Griswold v. Connecticut, 381 U.S. 479 (1965). U.S. Supreme Court.

Hardwick v. Bowers, 760 F.2d 1202 (1985). U.S. Court of Appeals, Eleventh Circuit.

Heller v. Doe, 509 U.S. 312 (1993). U.S. Supreme Court.

Hernandez v. Robles, 7 N.Y. 3d 338 (2006). Court of Appeals of New York.

Kimberly Hively v. Ivy Tech Community College of Indiana, 853 F.3d 339 (2017). U.S. Court of Appeals, Seventh Circuit.

Hollingsworth v. Perry, 570 U.S. 693 (2013). U.S. Supreme Court.

In re Marriage Cases, 76 Cal. Rptr. 3d 683 (2008). Supreme Court of California.

Jane Doe 1 et al. v. Trump; Civ 17-1597 (2017). U.S. District Court, D.C.

Kitchen v. Herbert, 961 F. Supp 2d 1181 (2013). U.S. District Court, Utah.

Kitchen v. Herbert, 755 F. 3d 1193 (2014). U.S. Court of Appeals, Tenth Circuit.

Latta v. Otter, 771 F. 3d 456 (2014). U.S. Court of Appeals, Ninth Circuit.

Lawrence v. Texas, 539 U.S. 558 (2003). U.S. Supreme Court.

Lockyer v. City & County of San Francisco, 17 Cal. Rptr. 3d 225 (2004). Supreme Court of California.

Loving v. Virginia, 388 U.S. 1 (1967). U.S. Supreme Court.

Macy v. Holder, Appeal No. 0120120821 WL 1435995 (2012). EEOC.

Masterpiece Cakeshop v. Colorado Civil Rights Commission, 138 S. Ct. 1719 (2018). U.S. Supreme Court.

April Miller et al. v. Kim Davis, 123 F. Supp. 3d 924 (2015). U.S. District Court, Eastern District of Kentucky, Northern Division.

April Miller et al. v. Kim Davis, 267 F. Supp. 3d 961 (2017). U.S. District Court, Eastern District of Kentucky, Northern Division.

Mutual Film Corporation v. Industrial Commission of Ohio, 236 U.S. 230 (1915). U.S. Supreme Court.

Obergefell v. Hodges, 576 U.S. 644 (2015). U.S. Supreme Court.

Obergefell v. Wymyslo, 962 F. Supp. 2d 968 (2013). U.S. Federal District Court, Southern District of Ohio.

ONE, Incorporated v. Olesen, Postmaster of Los Angeles, 355 U.S. 371 (1958). U.S. Supreme Court.

Perry v. Brown, 671 F.3d 1052 (2012). U.S. Court of Appeals, Ninth Circuit.

Perry v. Schwarzenegger, 704 F. Supp. 2d 921 (2010). U.S. District Court, Northern District of California.

Plessy v. Ferguson, 163 U.S. 537 (1896). U.S. Supreme Court.

Poe v. Ullman, 367 U.S. 497 (1961). U.S. Supreme Court.

Powell v. State, S.E. 2d 18 (1998). Supreme Court of Georgia.

Price Waterhouse v. Hopkins, 490 U.S. 228 (1989). U.S. Supreme Court.

Robicheaux v. Caldwell, 2 F. Supp. 3d 910 (2014). U.S. District Court, Eastern District of Louisiana.

Roe v. Wade, 410 U.S. 113 (1973). U.S. Supreme Court.

Romer v. Evans, 517 U.S. 620 (1996). U.S. Supreme Court.

Roth v. United States, 354 U.S. 476 (1957). U.S. Supreme Court.

Strauss v. Horton, Cal. 4th 364 (2009). Supreme Court of California.

Turner v. Safley, 482 U.S. 78 (1987). U.S. Supreme Court.

United States v. Windsor, 570 U.S. 744 (2013). U.S. Supreme Court.

Vallerga et al. v. Department of Alcoholic Beverage Control et al., 53 Cal 2d 313 (1959). Supreme Court of California.

Watkins v. U.S. Army, 875 F.2d 699 (1989). U.S. Court of Appeals, Ninth Circuit.

Whole Woman's Health v. Hellerstedt, 136 S. Ct. 2292 (2016). U.S. Supreme Court.

Windsor v. United States of America, 833 F. Supp. 2d 394 (2012). U.S. District Court, Southern District of New York.

Windsor v. United States of America, 699 F. 3d 169 (2012). U.S. Court of Appeals, Second Circuit.

Zablocki v. Redhail, 434 U.S. 374 (1978). U.S. Supreme Court.

Melissa Zarda, Executor of the Estate of Donald Zarda v. Altitude Express, 883 F.3d 100 (2018). U.S. Court of Appeals, Second Circuit.

Bibliography

Abramowitz, Alan I., and Kyle L. Saunders. 2008. "Is Polarization a Myth?" *Journal of Politics* 70 (2):542–555.

Acs, Gregory, Kenneth Braswell, Elaine Sorensen, and Margery Austin Turner. 2013. "The Moynihan Report Revisited." Urban Institute. http://www.urban.org/UploadedPDF/412839-The-Moynihan-Report-Revisited.pdf.

Adamic, Lada A., and Natalie Glance. 2005. "The Political Blogosphere and the 2004 U.S. Election: Divided They Blog." *Proceedings of the Third International Workshop on Link Discovery*: 36–43.

Adorno, T. W., Else Frenkel-Brunswik, Daniel J. Levinson, and R. Nevitt Sanford. (1950) 1982. *The Authoritarian Personality*. Abridged edition. New York: Norton.

Alexander, Michelle. 2010. *The New Jim Crow: Mass Incarceration in the Age of Colorblindness*. New York: New Press.

Allen, Douglas W. 2013a. "Expert Witness Report of Douglas W. Allen, Deboer v. Snyder, US District Court, Eastern District of Michigan, Southern Division." Stanford. https://web.stanford.edu/~mrosenfe/DeBoer_affidavits/defense/Allen.pdf.

Allen, Douglas W. 2013b. "High School Graduation Rates among Children of Same-Sex Couples." *Review of Economics of the Household* 11 (4):635–658.

Allen, Douglas W., Catherine Pakaluk, and Joseph Price. 2013. "Nontraditional Families and Childhood Progress through School: A Comment on Rosenfeld." *Demography* 50 (3):955–961.

Allport, Gordon. 1954. *The Nature of Prejudice*. Cambridge, MA: Addison Wesley.

Altemeyer, Bob. 1988. *Enemies of Freedom: Understanding Right-Wing Authoritarianism*. San Francisco, CA: Jossey-Bass.

Altemeyer, Bob. 1996. *The Authoritarian Specter*. Cambridge, MA: Harvard University Press.

Altemeyer, Bob. 1998. "The Other 'Authoritarian Personality.'" Pp. 47–92 in *Advances in Experimental Social Psychology*, edited by M. P. Zanna. New York: Academic Press.

Alwin, Duane F., and Jon A. Krosnick. 1991. "Aging, Cohorts, and the Stability of Sociopolitical Orientations over the Life Span." *American Journal of Sociology* 97 (1):169–195.

American Civil Liberties Union, GLAD, Lambda Legal, National Center for Lesbian Rights, Equality Federation, Freedom to Marry, GLAAD, Human Rights Campaign, and National Gay and Lesbian Task Force. 2009. "Make Change, Not Lawsuits." ACLU, May 27. https://www.aclu.org/files/pdfs/lgbt/make_change_20090527.pdf.

American Law Institute. 1955. "Model Penal Code, Tentative Draft 4, Preliminary Comments." Philadelphia, PA: ALI.

American National Election Studies. 2015. "ANES Time Series Cumulative Data File 1948–2012." www.electionstudies.org.

American Psychological Association, American Academy of Pediatrics, American Medical Association, American Psychiatric Association, American Psychoanalytic Association, California Medical Association, National Association of Social Workers, and New York State Psychological Association. 2013. "Amicus Brief in U.S. v. Windsor, submitted to the U.S. Supreme Court." March 1. https://www.apa.org/about/offices/ogc/amicus/us-windsor.

American Sociological Association. 2013. "Brief of Amicus Curiae American Sociological Association in US v. Windsor." http://www.asanet.org/press/asa_files_amicus_brief_in_same-sex_marriage_cases.cfm.

Andersen, Robert, and Tina Fetner. 2008. "Cohort Differences in Tolerance of Homosexuality: Attitudinal Change in Canada and the United States." *Public Opinion Quarterly* 72 (2):311–330.

Anderson, Ryan T. 2018. "Disagreement Is Not Always Discrimination: On Masterpiece Cakeshop and the Analogy to Interracial Marriage." *Georgetown Journal of Law and Public Policy* 15 (1):123–146.

Andersson, Gunnar, Turid Noack, Ane Seierstad, and Harald Weedon-Fekjær. 2006. "The Demographics of Same-Sex Marriages in Norway and Sweden." *Demography* 43 (1):79–98.

Anton, B. S. 2010. "Proceedings of the American Psychological Association for the Legislative Year 2009: Minutes of the Annual Meeting of the Council of Representatives and Minutes of the Meetings of the Board of Directors." *American Psychologist* 65:385–475.

Armstrong, Elizabeth A. 2002. *Forging Gay Identities: Organizing Sexuality in San Francisco, 1950–1994*. Chicago: University of Chicago Press.

Armstrong, Elizabeth A., and Suzanna M. Crage. 2006. "Movements and Memory: The Making of the Stonewall Myth." *American Sociological Review* 71 (5):724–751.

Associated Press. 2014. "Judges Take Tough Tone at Gay Marriage Hearing." *New York Times*, August 26. https://www.nytimes.com/2014/08/27/us/judges-take-tough-tone-at-gay-marriage-hearing.html.

Baldassarri, Delia, and Andrew Gelman. 2008. "Partisans without Constraint: Political Polarization and Trends in American Public Opinion." *American Journal of Sociology* 114 (2):408–446.

Ball, Carlos A. 2014. *Same-Sex Marriage and Children: A Tale of History, Social Science, and Law*. New York: Oxford University Press.

Ball, Carlos A. 2017. *The First Amendment and LGBT Equality: A Contentious History*. Cambridge, MA: Harvard University Press.

Ballotpedia. 2019. "Marriage and Family on the Ballot." https://ballotpedia.org/Marriage_and_family_on_the_ballot#tab=By_year.

Ballotpedia. n.d. "Judicial Selection in the States." https://ballotpedia.org/Judicial_selection_in_the_states. Accessed July 8, 2021.

Balsam, Kimberly F., Theodore P. Beauchaine, Esther D. Rothblum, and Sondra E. Solomon. 2008. "Three-Year Follow-Up of Same-Sex Couples Who Had Civil Unions in Vermont, Same-Sex Couples Not in Civil Unions, and Heterosexual Married Couples." *Developmental Psychology* 44 (1):102–116.

Bartlett, Tom. 2014. "The Great Mom and Dad Experiment." *Chronicle of Higher Education*, January 20. http://chronicle.com/article/The-Great-Mom-Dad-Experiment/144027/?cid=cr&utm_source=cr&utm_medium=en.

Bass, Brooke Conroy. 2015. "How Couples Negotiate Marital Surname Choice." Unpublished manuscript. https://sociology.stanford.edu/publications/how-couples-negotiate-marital-surname-choice.

Baumle, Amanda K., and D'Lane R. Compton. 2015. *Legalizing LGBT Families: How the Law Shapes Parenthood*. New York: New York University Press.

Baunach, Dawn Michelle. 2011. "Decomposing Trends in Attitudes toward Gay Marriage, 1988–2006." *Social Science Quarterly* 92 (2):346–363.

Baunach, Dawn Michelle. 2012. "Changing Same-Sex Marriage Attitudes in America from 1988 through 2010." *Public Opinion Quarterly* 76 (2):364–378.

Bayer, Ronald. 1987. *Homosexuality and American Psychiatry: The Politics of Diagnosis.* 2nd edition. Princeton, NJ: Princeton University Press.

Becker, Jo. 2015. *Forcing the Spring: Inside the Fight for Marriage Equality.* New York: Penguin Books.

Benford, Robert D., and David A. Snow. 2000. "Framing Processes and Social Movements: An Overview and Assessment." *Annual Review of Sociology* 26:611–639.

Benkler, Yochai, Robert Faris, and Hal Roberts. 2018. *Network Propaganda: Manipulation, Disinformation, and Radicalization in American Politics.* New York: Oxford University Press.

Bernard, Jessie. (1972) 1982. *The Future of Marriage.* New Haven, CT: Yale University Press.

Bernstein, Mary, and Verta Taylor, eds. 2013. *The Marrying Kind? Debating Same-Sex Marriage within the Lesbian and Gay Movement.* Minneapolis: University of Minnesota Press.

Bishop, Bill. 2008. *The Big Sort: Why the Clustering of Like-Minded America Is Tearing Us Apart.* New York: Mariner Books.

Black, Dan, Gary Gates, Seth Sanders, and Lowell Taylor. 2000. "Demographics of the Gay and Lesbian Population in the United States: Evidence from Available Systematic Data Sources." *Demography* 37 (2):139–154.

Blankenhorn, David. 2012. "How My View on Gay Marriage Changed." *New York Times,* June 22. https://www.nytimes.com/2012/06/23/opinion/how-my-view-on-gay-marriage-changed.html.

Blumstein, Philip, and Pepper Schwartz. 1983. *American Couples: Money, Work, Sex.* New York: William Morrow.

Bobo, Lawrence D., Camille Z. Charles, Maria Krysan, and Alicia D. Simmons. 2012. "The Real Record on Racial Attitudes." Pp. 38–83 in *Social Trends in American Life: Findings from the General Social Survey since 1972,* edited by Peter V. Marsden. Princeton, NJ: Princeton University Press.

Boies, David, and Theodore B. Olson. 2014. *Redeeming the Dream: The Case for Marriage Equality.* New York: Viking.

Bonauto, Mary. 2016. "The Litigation: First Judicial Victories in Vermont, Massachusetts, and Connecticut." Pp. 73–89 in *Love Unites Us: Winning the Freedom to Marry in America,* edited by Kevin M. Cathcart and Leslie J. Gabel-Brett. New York: New Press.

Bork, Robert H. 2004. "The Necessary Amendment." *First Things,* August. http://www.firstthings.com/article/2004/08/the-necessary-amendment.

Bramlett, Matthew D., and William D. Mosher. 2002. "Cohabitation, Marriage, Divorce, and Remarriage in the United States." National Center for Health Statistics. http://www.cdc.gov/nchs/data/series/sr_23/sr23_022.pdf.

Brewaeys, A., I. Ponjaert, E. V. Van Hall, and S. Golombok. 1997. "Donor Insemination: Child Development and Family Functioning in Lesbian Mother Families." *Human Reproduction* 12 (6):1349–1359.

Broockman, David, and Joshua Kalla. 2016. "Durably Reducing Transphobia: A Field Experiment on Door-to-Door Canvassing." *Science* 352 (6282):220–224.

Brooks-Gunn, Jeanne, Guang Guo, and Frank F. Furstenberg Jr. 1993. "Who Drops Out of and Who Continues beyond High School? A 20-Year Follow-Up of Black Urban Youth." *Journal of Research on Adolescence* 3 (3):271–294.

Bruce, Katherine McFarland. 2016. *Pride Parades: How a Parade Changed the World.* New York: New York University Press.

Buchanan, Patrick. 1992. "Culture War Speech: Address to the Republican National Convention." August 17. Voices of Democracy. http://voicesofdemocracy.umd.edu/buchanan-culture-war-speech-speech-text/.

Burroway, Jim. 2012. "First Look at Mark Regnerus's Study on Children of Parents in Same-Sex Relationships." *Box Turtle Bulletin,* June 10. http://www.boxturtlebulletin.com/2012/06/10/45512.

Cahill, Sean. 2007. "The Anti-Gay Marriage Movement." Pp. 155–191 in *The Politics of Same-Sex Marriage,* edited by Craig A. Rimmerman and Clyde Wilcox. Chicago: University of Chicago Press.

Cain, Sian. 2018. "Rose McGowan's Memoir Brave Details Alleged Rape by Harvey Weinstein." *Guardian,* January 29. https://www.theguardian.com/film/2018/jan/30/brave-rose-mcgowans-memoir-details-by-harvey-weinstein.

Canaday, Margot. 2009. *The Straight State: Sexuality and Citizenship in Twentieth-Century America.* Princeton, NJ: Princeton University Press.

Carlsen, Audrey, Maya Salam, Claire Cain Miller, Denise Lu, Ash Ngu, Jugal K. Patel, and Zach Wichter. 2018. "#MeToo Brought Down 201 Powerful Men: Nearly Half of Their Replacements Are Women." *New York Times,* October 23. https://www.nytimes.com/interactive/2018/10/23/us/metoo-replacements.html.

Carpenter, Dale. 2004. "The Unknown Past of Lawrence v. Texas." *Michigan Law Review* 102:1464–1527.

Carpenter, Dale. 2012. *Flagrant Conduct: The Story of Lawrence v. Texas.* New York: Norton.

Carroll, Matt, Kevin Cullen, Thomas Farragher, Stephen Kurkjian, Michael Paulson, Sacha Pfeiffer, Michael Rezendes, and Walter V. Robinson. 2015. *Betrayal: Crisis in the Catholic Church.* Revised edition. New York: Little, Brown.

Carter, David. 2004. *Stonewall: The Riots that Sparked the Gay Revolution.* New York: St. Martin's Press.

Cenziper, Debbie, and Jim Obergefell. 2016. *Love Wins: The Lovers and Lawyers Who Fought the Landmark Case for Marriage Equality.* New York: William Morrow.

Chan, Raymond W., Barbara Raboy, and Charlotte J. Patterson. 1998. "Psychosocial Adjustment among Children Conceived via Donor Insemination by Lesbian and Heterosexual Mothers." *Child Development* 69 (2):443–457.

Chanley, Virginia, Thomas J. Rudolph, and Wendy M. Rahn. 2000. "The Origins and Consequences of Public Trust in Government." *Public Opinion Quarterly* 64 (3):239–256.

Chauncey, George. 2004. *Why Marriage? The History Shaping Today's Debate.* New York: Basic Books.

Cherlin, Andrew J., Frank F. Furstenberg Jr., Sara S. McLanahan, Gary D. Sandefur, and Lawrence L. Wu. 1996. "Brief of Amici Curiae in Baehr v. Miike." https://www.lambdalegal.org/in-court/legal-docs/baehr_hi_19961011_amici-marriage-scholars.

Cherlin, Andrew J. 1978. "Remarriage as an Incomplete Institution." *American Journal of Sociology* 84 (3):634–650.

Cherlin, Andrew J. 1992. *Marriage, Divorce, Remarriage.* 2nd edition. Cambridge, MA: Harvard University Press.

Cherlin, Andrew J. 2009. *The Marriage-Go-Round: The State of Marriage and the Family in America Today.* New York: Knopf.

Cherlin, Andrew J., Frank F. Furstenberg Jr., P. Lindsay Chase-Lansdale, Kathleen E. Kiernan, Philip K. Robins, Donna Ruane Morrison, and Julien O. Teitler. 1991. "Longitudinal Studies of Effects of Divorce on Children in Great Britain and the United States." *Science* 252:1386–1389.

Clark, Kenneth B., Isidor Chein, and Stuart W. Cook. (1952) 2004. "The Effects of Segregation and the Consequences of Desegregation: A (September 1952) Social Science Statement in the Brown v. Board of Education of Topeka Supreme Court Case." *American Psychologist* 5 (6):495–501.

Clinton, Bill. 2004. *My Life*. New York: Random House.

Clinton, William J. 1992. "Address Accepting the Presidential Nomination at the Democratic National Convention in New York." July 16. American Presidency Project. https://www.presidency.ucsb.edu/documents/address-accepting-the-presidential-nomination-the-democratic-national-convention-new-york.

CNN. 2016. "Exit Polls." November 23. https://www.cnn.com/election/2016/results/exit-polls.

Cole, David. 2016. *Engines of Liberty: The Power of Citizen Activists to Make Constitutional Law*. New York: Basic Books.

Coolidge, David Orgon. 1997. "Same-Sex Marriage? Baehr v. Miike and the Meaning of Marriage." *South Texas Law Review* 38 (1):1–119.

Coolidge, David Orgon. 2000. "The Hawai'i Marriage Amendment: Its Origins, Meaning, and Fate." *University of Hawai'i Law Review* 22:19–118.

Cott, Nancy F. 2000. *Public Vows: A History of Marriage and the Nation*. Cambridge, MA: Harvard University Press.

Cowan, Sarah K. 2014. "Secrets and Misperceptions: The Creation of Self-Fulfilling Illusions." *Sociological Science* 1:466–492.

Crampton, Thomas. 2004a. "Court Says New Paltz Mayor Can't Hold Gay Weddings." *New York Times*, June 8.

Crampton, Thomas. 2004b. "Issuing Licenses, Quietly, to Couples in Asbury Park." *New York Times*, March 10.

Cunningham-Parmeter, Keith. 2008. "Fear of Discovery: Immigrant Workers and the Fifth Amendment." *Cornell International Law Journal* 41:27–81.

cvalner. 2015. "April DeBoer and Jayne Rowse Wedding 8-22-2015." YouTube, August 27. https://www.youtube.com/watch?v=9kQVXmHz3NU.

DellaPosta, Daniel. 2018. "Gay Acquaintanceship and Attitudes toward Homosexuality: A Conservative Test." *Socius* 4 (1):1–12.

D'Emilio, John. 1998. *Sexual Politics, Sexual Communities: The Making of a Homosexual Minority in the United States 1940–1970*. 2nd edition. Chicago: University of Chicago Press.

D'Emilio, John. 2002. "Born Gay?" Pp. 154–164 in *The World Turned: Essays on Gay History, Politics, and Culture*. Durham, NC: Duke University Press.

D'Emilio, John. 2003. *Lost Prophet: The Life and Times of Bayard Rustin*. New York: Free Press.

D'Emilio, John. 2014. *In a New Century: Essays on Queer History, Politics, and Community Life*. Madison: University of Wisconsin Press.

Demme, Jonathan, dir. 1991. *The Silence of the Lambs*. (Los Angeles, CA: Orion Pictures).

Demme, Jonathan, dir. 1993. *Philadelphia*. (Culver City, CA: TriStar Pictures).

DePaulo, Bella. 2006. *Singled Out: How Singles Are Stereotyped, Stigmatized, and Ignored, and Still Live Happily Ever After*. New York: St. Martin's Press.

Deutscher, Max, Isidor Chein, and Natalie Sadigur. 1948. "The Psychological Effects of Enforced Segregation: A Survey of Social Science Opinion." *Journal of Psychology* 26:259–287.

Diamond, Lisa M., and Clifford J. Rosky. 2016. "Scrutinizing Immutability: Research on Sexual Orientation and U.S. Legal Advocacy for Sexual Minorities." *Journal of Sex Research* 53 (4):363–391.

Diamond, Sara. 1995. *Roads to Dominion: Right-Wing Movement and Political Power in the United States.* New York: Guilford Press.

Dobson, James. 2004. *Marriage Under Fire: Why We Must Win This Battle.* Sisters, OR: Multnomah.

Douglas, Gordon, dir. 1968. *The Detective.* (Century City, CA: 20th Century Fox).

Douthat, Ross. 2012. "Gay Parents and the Marriage Debate." *New York Times,* June 11. http://douthat.blogs.nytimes.com/2012/06/11/gay-parents-and-the-marriage-debate/.

Duberman, Martin. 1993. *Stonewall.* New York: Plume.

Duberman, Martin. 2018. *Has the Gay Movement Failed?* Oakland: University of California Press.

Duggan, Lisa. 2002. "The New Heteronormativity: The Sexual Politics of Neoliberalism." Pp. 175–194 in *Materializing Democracy: Toward a Revitalized Cultural Politics,* edited by Russ Castronovo and Dana D. Nelson. Durham, NC: Duke University Press.

Eckholm, Erik, and Manny Fernandez. 2015. "After Same-Sex Marriage Ruling, Southern States Fall in Line." *New York Times,* June 29. https://www.nytimes.com/2015/06/30/us/after-same-sex-marriage-ruling-southern-states-fall-in-line.html.

Economist. 2018. "#MeToo Polled, Measuring the Backlash: Survey Respondents Have Become More Sceptical about Claims of Sexual Harassment." October 20.

Egan, Patrick J., and Kenneth Sherrill. 2005. "Marriage and the Shifting Priorities of a New Generation of Lesbians and Gays." *PS: Political Science and Politics* 38 (2):229–232.

Epstein, Rob, dir. 1984. *The Times of Harvey Milk.* (TC Films International).

Epstein, Rob, and Jeffrey Friedman, dirs. 1995. *The Celluloid Closet.* (New York: HBO Films).

Eskridge, William N., Jr. 1996. *The Case for Same Sex Marriage: From Sexual Liberty to Civilized Commitment.* New York: Free Press.

Eskridge, William N., Jr. 1999. *Gaylaw: Challenging the Apartheid of the Closet.* Cambridge, MA: Harvard University Press.

Eskridge, William N., Jr. 2002. *Equality Practice: Civil Unions and the Future of Gay Rights.* New York: Routledge.

Eskridge, William N., Jr. 2008. *Dishonorable Passions: Sodomy Laws in America, 1861–2003.* New York: Viking.

Eskridge, William N., Jr. 2015. "Law and the Production of Deceit." Pp. 254–312 in *Deception and Truth-Telling in the American Legal System,* edited by Austin Sarat. New York: Cambridge University Press.

Eskridge, William N., Jr. 2017. "Title VII's Statutory History and the Sex Discrimination Arguments for LGBT Workplace Protections." *Yale Law Journal* 127:322–404.

Ettelbrick, Paula. 1989. "Since When Is Marriage a Path to Liberation." *Out/Look National Gay and Lesbian Quarterly* 6:9–17.

Evans, John H. 2003. "Have Americans' Attitudes Become More Polarized? An Update." *Social Science Quarterly* 84 (1):71–90.

Faderman, Lillian. 2015. *The Gay Revolution: The Story of the Struggle*. New York: Simon & Schuster.

Feinberg, Matthew, and Robb Willer. 2011. "Apocalypse Soon? Dire Messages Reduce Belief in Global Warming by Contradicting Just-World Beliefs." *Psychological Science* 22 (1):34–38.

Fejes, Fred. 2008. *Gay Rights and Moral Panic: The Origins of America's Debate on Homosexuality*. New York: Palgrave Macmillan.

Feldblum, Chai. 2000. "Gay People, Trans People, Women: Is it All about Gender?" *New York Law School Journal of Human Rights* 17 (2):623–702.

Feldblum, Chai. 2013. "Law, Policies in Practice, and Social Norms: Coverage of Transgender Discrimination under Sex Discrimination Law." *Journal of Law in Society* 14 (1):1–28.

Fetner, Tina. 2008. *How the Religious Right Shaped Lesbian and Gay Activism*. Minneapolis: University of Minnesota Press.

Fiorina, Morris P., Samuel A. Abrams, and Jeremy C. Pope. 2008. "Polarization in the American Public: Misconceptions and Misreadings." *Journal of Politics* 70 (2):556–560.

Flores, Andrew R., and Scott Barclay. 2016. "Backlash, Consensus, Legitimacy, or Polarization: The Effect of Same-Sex Marriage Policy on Mass Attitudes." *Political Research Quarterly* 69 (1):43–56.

Fore, Wyatt. 2015. "DeBoer v. Snyder: A Case Study in Litigation and Social Reform." *Michigan Journal of Gender & Law* 22:169–206.

Frank, Nathaniel. 2017. *Awakening: How Gays and Lesbians Brought Marriage Equality to America*. Cambridge, MA: Belknap Press of Harvard University Press.

Franke, Katherine M. 2006. "The Politics of Same-Sex Marriage Politics." *Columbia Journal of Gender and Law* 15 (1):236–248.

Freeh Sporkin & Sullivan LLP. 2012. "Report of the Special Investigative Counsel regarding the Actions of the Pennsylvania State University Related to the Child Sexual Abuse Committed by Gerald A. Sandusky." July 12. https://www.documentcloud.org/documents/396512-report-final-071212.html.

Friedan, Betty. (1963) 1974. *The Feminine Mystique*. Revised edition. New York: Dell.

Gamson, Joshua. 1995. "Must Identity Movements Self-Destruct? A Queer Dilemma." *Social Problems* 42 (3):390–407.

Gamson, William. 1990. *The Strategy of Social Protest*. 2nd edition. Belmont, CA: Wadsworth.

Gamson, William. 1992. *Talking Politics*. Cambridge: Cambridge University Press.

Garber, Megan. 2018. "Is #MeToo Too Big?" *Atlantic*, July 4. https://www.theatlantic.com/entertainment/archive/2018/07/is-metoo-too-big/564275/.

Garretson, Jeremiah J. 2018. *The Path to Gay Rights: How Activism and Coming Out Changed Public Opinion*. New York: New York University Press.

Gates, Gary J. 2011. "How Many People Are Lesbian, Gay, Bisexual and Transgender?" Williams Institute, UCLA School of Law. April. http://williamsinstitute.law.ucla.edu/wp-content/uploads/Gates-How-Many-People-LGBT-Apr-2011.pdf.

Gates, Gary J. 2012a. "Letter to the Editors and Advisory Editors of Social Science Research." *Social Science Research* 41 (6):1350–1351.

Gates, Gary J. 2012b. "LGBT Identity: A Demographer's Perspective." *Loyola of Los Angeles Law Review* 45 (3):693–714.

Gates, Gary J. 2015. "Brief for Gary J. Gates as Amicus Curiae in Support of Petitioners in Obergefell v. Hodges." https://williamsinstitute.law.ucla.edu/research/marriage-and-couples-rights/amicus-briefs-scotus-2015/.

Gates, Gary J., and Jason Ost. 2004. *The Gay and Lesbian Atlas.* Washington, DC: Urban Institute Press.

Gerber, Alan S., and Donald P. Green. 2000. "The Effects of Canvassing, Telephone Calls, and Direct Mail on Voter Turnout: A Field Experiment." *American Political Science Review* 94 (3):653–663.

Ghaziani, Amin. 2014. *There Goes the Gayborhood?* Princeton, NJ: Princeton University Press.

Gilchrist, Tracy E. 2018. "Dana Nessel Kissed Wife before Winning Michigan Attorney General Race." *Advocate*, November 7. https://www.advocate.com/election/2018/11/07/dana-nessel-kissed-wife-winning-michigan-attorney-general-race.

Ginsberg, Allen. 1956. *Howl, and Other Poems.* San Francisco, CA: City Lights Books.

Ginsburg, Ruth Bader. 1992. "Speaking in a Judicial Voice." *New York University Law Review* 67:1185–1209.

Gitenstein, Mark. 1992. *Matters of Principle: An Insider's Account of America's Rejection of Robert Bork's Nomination to the Supreme Court.* New York: Simon & Schuster.

Goldberg, Abbie E., and Randi L. Garcia. 2016. "Gender-Typed Behavior Over Time in Children with Lesbian, Gay, and Heterosexual Parents." *Journal of Family Psychology* 30:854–865.

Goldberg, Suzanne B. 2010. "Sticky Intuitions and the Future of Sexual Orientation Discrimination." *UCLA Law Review* 57:1375–1414.

Goldin, Claudia, and Lawrence F. Katz. 2002. "The Power of the Pill: Oral Contraceptives and Women's Career and Marriage Decisions." *Journal of Political Economy* 110 (4):730–770.

Golombok, Susan, and Fiona Tasker. 1996. "Do Parents Influence the Sexual Orientation of Their Children? Findings from a Longitudinal Study of Lesbian Families." *Developmental Psychology* 32 (1):3–11.

Gonsiorek, John C. 1982. "Results of Psychological Testing on Homosexual Populations." *American Behavioral Scientist* 24 (4):385–396.

Gonsiorek, John C. 1991. "The Empirical Basis for the Demise of the Illness Model of Homosexuality." Pp. 115–136 in *Homosexuality: Research Implications for Public Policy*, edited by John C. Gonsiorek and James D. Weinrich. Beverly Hills, CA: Sage.

Gonzalez, Efrain John. 2019. "Meet 'the Mother of Pride,' the Pioneering Bisexual Activist Brenda Howard." *Them*, June 6. https://www.them.us/story/brenda-howard/amp.

Goode, William J. 1956. *After Divorce.* Glencoe, IL: Free Press.

Goodwin, Jeff, and James M. Jasper. 1999. "Caught in a Winding, Snarling Vine: The Structural Bias of Political Process Theory." *Sociological Forum* 14 (1):27–54.

Green, Matthew W., Jr. 2017. "Same-Sex Sex and Immutable Traits: Why Obergefell v. Hodges Clears a Path to Protecting Gay and Lesbian Employees from Workplace Discrimination under Title VII." *Journal of Gender, Race & Justice* 20:1–52.

Greenwald, Anthony G., Debbie E. McGhee, and Jordan L. K. Schwartz. 1998. "Measuring Individual Differences in Implicit Cognition: The Implicit Association Test." *Journal of Personality and Social Psychology* 74 (6):1464–1480.

Gross, Larry. 1993. *Contested Closets: The Politics and Ethics of Outing.* Minneapolis: University of Minnesota Press.

Guo, Guang, Jeanne Brooks-Gunn, and Kathleen Mullan Harris. 1996. "Parents' Labor Force Attachment and Grade Retention among Urban Black Children." *Sociology of Education* 69 (3):217–236.

Gup, Ted. 1988. "Identifying Homosexuals: What Are the Rules?" *Washington Journalism Review* 10:30–33.

Guttmacher Institute. 2018. "State Laws and Policies: Requirements for Ultrasound." https://www.guttmacher.org/state-policy/explore/requirements-ultrasound.

Haberman, Maggie. 2016. "Donald Trump's Apology That Wasn't." *New York Times*, October 8. https://www.nytimes.com/2016/10/08/us/politics/donald-trump-apology. html.

Hagan, John, and Alberto Palloni. 1999. "Sociological Criminology and the Mythology of Hispanic Immigration and Crime." *Social Problems* 46 (4):617–632.

Hamilton, Laura, Simon Cheng, and Brian Powell. 2007. "Adoptive Parents, Adaptive Parents: Evaluating the Importance of Biological Ties for Parental Investment." *American Sociological Review* 72:95–116.

Hamilton, Scott. 1977. "The Civil Rights Attorneys' Fees Awards Act of 1976." *Washington and Lee Law Review* 34 (1):205–223.

Handy, Bruce. 1997. "He Called Me Ellen Degenerate?" *Time*, April 14.

Harris, Fredrick C. 2014. "The Rise of Respectability Politics." *Dissent* 61 (1):33–37.

Hart-Brinson, Peter. 2016. "The Social Imagination of Homosexuality and the Rise of Same-Sex Marriage in the United States." *Socius* 2:1–17.

Hauser, Christine. 2018. "Larry Nassar Is Sentenced to Another 40 to 125 Years in Prison." *New York Times*, February 5. https://www.nytimes.com/2018/02/05/sports/larry-nassar-sentencing-hearing.html.

Herek, Gregory M., and Eric K. Glunt. 1993. "Interpersonal Contact and Heterosexuals' Attitudes toward Gay Men: Results from a National Survey." *Journal of Sex Research* 30 (3):239–244.

Herman, Didi. 1997. *The Antigay Agenda: Orthodox Vision and the Christian Right*. Chicago: University of Chicago Press.

Higginbotham, Evelyn Brooks. 1993. *Righteous Discontent: The Women's Movement in the Black Baptist Church, 1880–1920*. Cambridge, MA: Harvard University Press.

Hirshman, Linda. 2012. *Victory: The Triumphant Gay Revolution*. New York: Harper Collins.

Hitchcock, Alfred, dir. 1948. *Rope*. (Hollywood, CA: Transatlantic Pictures).

Hitchcock, Alfred, dir. 1951. *Strangers on a Train*. (Hollywood, CA: Transatlantic Pictures).

Hochschild, Arlie. 2016. *Strangers in Their Own Land: Anger and Mourning on the American Right*. New York: New Press.

Hochschild, Arlie, and Anne Machung. 1989. *The Second Shift: Working Parents and the Revolution at Home*. New York: Viking.

Hofer, Roy E. 2010. "Supreme Court Reversal Rates: Evaluating the Federal Courts of Appeals." *Landslide* 2 (3):8–22.

Hoffman, Benjamin. 2017. "Simone Biles Says She, Too, Was Abused by Larry Nassar." *New York Times*, January 15. https://www.nytimes.com/2018/01/15/sports/simone-biles-abuse-team-doctor.html.

Hollibaugh, Amber. 1979. "Sexuality and the State: The Defeat of the Briggs Initiative and Beyond." *Socialist Review* 9 (3):55–72.

Hooker, Evelyn. 1957. "The Adjustment of the Male Overt Homosexual." *Journal of Projective Techniques* 21:17–31.

Hooker, Evelyn, Judd Marmor, Edward Auer, Cleland Ford, Jerome D. Frank, Paul Gebhard, Seward Hiltner, Robert Katz, John Money, Morris Ploscowe, Henry Riecken, Edwin Schur, Anthony Wallace, and Stanton Wheeler. 1969. Final Report of the Task Force on Homosexuality. Edited by U.S. National Institute of Mental Health. Washington, DC: NIMH.

Hopper, Tristin. 2014. "Canadian Economist Never Knew He Would Become Centre of a U.S. Firestorm over His Research on Same-Sex Parenting." *National Post*, March 28. http://news.nationalpost.com/news/canadian-economist-never-knew-he-would-become-centre-of-a-u-s-firestorm-over-his-research-on-same-sex-parenting.

Hubert, Susan J. 1999. "What's Wrong with This Picture? The Politics of Ellen's Coming Out Party." *Journal of Popular Culture* 33 (2):31–36.

Hull, Kathleen E. 2001. "The Political Limits of the Rights Frame: The Case of Same-Sex Marriage in Hawaii." *Sociological Perspectives* 44 (2):207–232.

Hull, Kathleen E., and Timothy A. Ortyl. 2013. "Same-Sex Marriage and Constituent Perceptions of the LGBT Rights Movement." Pp. 67–102 in *The Marrying Kind? Debating Same-Sex Marriage within the Lesbian and Gay Movement*, edited by Mary Bernstein and Verta Taylor. Minneapolis: University of Minnesota Press.

Hunter, Nan D. 1991. "Marriage, Law, and Gender: A Feminist Inquiry." *Law & Sexuality* 1:9–30.

IIT Chicago-Kent College of Law. n.d. "United States v. Windsor." https://www.oyez.org/cases/2012/12-307. Accessed January 6, 2018.

IIT Chicago-Kent College of Law. n.d. "Romer v. Evans." https://www.oyez.org/cases/1995/94-1039. Accessed August 24, 2016.

Iyengar, Shanto, Gaurav Sood, and Yphtach Lelkes. 2012. "Affect, Not Ideology: A Social Identity Perspective on Polarization." *Public Opinion Quarterly* 76 (3):405–431.

Jelen, Ted G, and Clyde Wilcox. 2003. "Causes and Consequences of Public Attitudes toward Abortion: A Review and Research Agenda." *Political Research Quarterly* 56 (4):489–500.

Johansson, Warren, and William A. Percy. 1994. *Outing: Shattering the Conspiracy of Silence*. New York: Harrington Park Press.

Johnson, David K. 2004. *The Lavender Scare: The Cold War Persecution of Gays and Lesbians in the Federal Government*. Chicago: University of Chicago Press.

Johnson, David R., and Laurie K. Scheuble. 1995. "Women's Marital Naming in Two Generations: A National Study." *Journal of Marriage and Family* 57 (3):724–732.

Jones, Cleve. 2016. *When We Rise: My Life in the Movement*. New York: Hachette Books.

Jones, James Howard. 1997. *Alfred Kinsey: A Public/Private Life*. New York: Norton.

Jones, Rachel K., and Jenna Jerman. 2017. "Population Group Abortion Rates and Lifetime Incidence of Abortion: United States, 2008–2014." *American Journal of Public Health* 107 (12):1904–1909.

Jost, John T., Jack Glaser, Arie W. Kruglanski, and Frank J. Sulloway. 2003. "Political Conservatism as Motivated Social Cognition." *Psychological Bulletin* 129 (3):339–375.

Junger, Gil, dir. 1997. *Ellen*. Season 4, episode 24. "Hello Muddah, Hello Faddah." Aired May 7.

Junger, Gil, dir. 1998. *Ellen*. Season 5, episode 13. "The Funeral." Aired January 14.

Kalev, Alexandra, and Frank Dobbin. 2006. "Enforcement of Civil Rights Law in Private Workplaces: The Effects of Compliance Reviews and Lawsuits Over Time." *Law & Social Inquiry* 31 (4):855–903.

Kalmijn, Matthijs, Anneke Loeve, and Dorien Manting. 2007. "Income Dynamics in Couples and the Dissolution of Marriage and Cohabitation." *Demography* 44 (1):159–179.

Kameny, Frank E. 2000. "Government v. Gays: Two Sad Stories with Two Happy Endings, Civil Service Employment and Security Clearances." Pp. 188–207 in *Creating Change: Sexuality, Public Policy, and Civil Rights*, edited by John D'Emilio, William B. Turner, and Urvashi Vaid. New York: St. Martin's Press.

Kameny, Franklin E. 1960. "Petition for a Writ of Certiorari." Kindle. https://read.amazon.com/?asin=B004S7FUM4.

Kantor, Jodi, and Megan Twohey. 2017. "Harvey Weinstein Paid Off Sexual Harassment Accusers for Decades." *New York Times,* October 5. https://www.nytimes.com/2017/10/05/us/harvey-weinstein-harassment-allegations.html.

Kaplan, Roberta, and Lisa Dickey. 2015. *Then Comes Marriage: United States v. Windsor and the Defeat of DOMA*. New York: Norton.

Karlan, Pamela S. 2018. "Just Desserts? Public Accommodations, Religious Accommodations, Racial Equality, and Gay Rights." *Supreme Court Review* 2018:145–177.

Kazyak, Emily. 2011. "Disrupting Cultural Selves: Constructing Gay and Lesbian Identities in Rural Locales." *Qualitative Sociology* 34 (4):561–581.

Kessler, Glenn, and Meg Kelly. 2018. "President Trump Has Made More Than 2,000 False or Misleading Claims over 355 Days." *Washington Post*, January 10. https://www.washingtonpost.com/news/fact-checker/wp/2018/01/10/president-trump-has-made-more-than-2000-false-or-misleading-claims-over-355-days/.

Khalil, Ramy K. 2012. "Harvey Milk and California Proposition 6: How the Gay Liberation Movement Won Two Early Victories." MA thesis, Western Washington University.

Kinsey, Alfred C., Wardell B. Pomeroy, and Clyde E. Martin. 1948. *Sexual Behavior in the Human Male*. Philadelphia, PA: W. B. Saunders.

Kinsey, Alfred C., Wardell B. Pomeroy, Clyde E. Martin, and Paul H. Gebhard. 1953. *Sexual Behavior in the Human Female*. Bloomington: University of Indiana Press.

Klarman, Michael J. 2013. *From the Closet to the Altar: Courts, Backlash, and the Struggle for Same-Sex Marriage*. Oxford: Oxford University Press.

Klinenberg, Eric. 2012. *Going Solo: The Extraordinary Rise and Surprising Appeal of Living Alone*. New York: Penguin Press.

Kluger, Richard. (1975) 2004. *Simple Justice: The History of Brown v. Board of Education and Black America's Struggle for Equality*. New York: Knopf.

Koppelman, Andrew. 1994. "Why Discrimination against Lesbians and Gay Men Is Sex Discrimination." *New York University Law Review* 69 (2):197–287.

Kurdek, Lawrence A. 1998. "Relationship Outcomes and Their Predictors: Longitudinal Evidence from Heterosexual Married, Gay Cohabiting, and Lesbian Cohabiting Couples." *Journal of Marriage and the Family* 60 (3):553–568.

Kurdek, Lawrence A. 2004. "Are Gay and Lesbian Cohabiting Couples Really Different from Heterosexual Married Couples?" *Journal of Marriage and Family* 66 (4):880–900.

Kyckelhahn, Tracey, and Thomas H. Cohen. 2008. "Civil Rights Complaints in U.S. District Courts, 1990–2006."in *Bureau of Justice Statistics Special Report*.

Washington, DC: U.S. Department of Justice. https://bjs.ojp.gov/library/publications/civil-rights-complaints-us-district-courts-1990-2006.

LaCour, Michael J., and Donald P. Green. 2014. "When Contact Changes Minds: An Experiment on Transmission of Support for Gay Equality." *Science* 346 (6215):1366–1369.

Latimer, Brian. 2016. "Yale-Bound Valedictorian Comes Out as Undocumented in Emotional Speech." *NBC News*, June 9. https://www.nbcnews.com/news/latino/yale-bound-valedictorian-comes-out-undocumented-emotional-speech-n589191.

Laumann, Edward O., John H. Gagnon, Robert T. Michael, and Stuart Michaels. 1994. *The Social Organization of Sexuality: Sexual Practices in the United States.* Chicago: University of Chicago Press.

Lawless, Jennifer L. 2012. *Becoming a Candidate: Political Ambition and the Decision to Run for Office.* Cambridge: Cambridge University Press.

Levine, Lawrence C. 2013. "Justice Kennedy's 'Gay Agenda': Romer, Lawrence, and the Struggle for Marriage Equality." *McGeorge Law Review* 44:1–30.

Lewis, Anthony. 1958. "Nudist Magazines Win Mail Rights." *New York Times*, January 14.

Lewis, Gregory B. 2005. "Same-Sex Marriage and the 2004 Presidential Election." *PS: Political Science and Politics* 38 (2):195–199.

Loftus, Jeni. 2001. "America's Liberalization in Attitudes toward Homosexuality, 1973 to 1998." *American Sociological Review* 66:762–782.

Loftus, Tom. 2016. "Judge Dismisses Civil Suits against Kim Davis." *USA Today,* August 20. https://www.usatoday.com/story/news/nation-now/2016/08/20/judge-dismisses-civil-suits-against-kim-davis/89043068/.

Lucas, DeWayne L. 2007. "Same-Sex Marriage in the 2004 Election." Pp. 243–271 in *The Politics of Same-Sex Marriage,* edited by Craig A. Rimmerman and Clyde Wilcox. Chicago: University of Chicago Press.

Lundquist, Erika, JoAnn Hsueh, Amy E. Lowenstein, Kristen Faucetta, Daniel Gubits, Charles Michalopoulos, and Virginia Knox. 2014. "A Family-Strengthening Program for Low-Income Families: Final Impacts from the Supporting Healthy Marriage Evaluation." Washington, DC: U.S. Department of Health and Human Services. http://www.mdrc.org/publication/family-strengthening-program-low-income-families.

Macur, Juliet. 2018. "Who Has USA Gymnastics' Back at This Point? The U.S.O.C. for Some Reason." *New York Times*, January 19. https://www.nytimes.com/2018/01/19/sports/olympics/nassar-gymnastics-raisman.html.

Mankiewicz, Joseph, dir. 1959. *Suddenly, Last Summer.* (Great Britain: Horizon Pictures).

Marks, Loren. 2012. "Same-Sex Parenting and Children's Outcomes: A Closer Examination of the American Psychological Association's Brief on Lesbian and Gay Parenting." *Social Science Research* 41 (4):735–751.

Massey, Douglas S., and Nancy A. Denton. 1993. *American Apartheid: Segregation and the Making of the Underclass.* Cambridge, MA: Harvard University Press.

McAdam, Doug. 1982. *Political Process and the Development of Black Insurgency 1930–1970.* Chicago: University of Chicago Press.

McAdam, Doug, John D. McCarthy, and Mayer N. Zald. 1996. "Opportunities, Mobilizing Structures, and Framing Processes: Toward a Synthetic, Comparative Perspective on Social Movements." Pp. 1–20 in *Comparative Perspectives on Social Movements: Political Opportunities, Mobilizing Structures, and Cultural Framings,* edited by Doug McAdam, John D. McCarthy, and Mayer N. Zald. New York: Cambridge University Press.

McCarthy, John D., and Mayer N. Zald. 1977. "Resource Mobilization and Social Movements: A Partial Theory." *American Journal of Sociology* 82:1212–1241.

McCloskey, Robert G., and Sanford Levinson. 2016. *The American Supreme Court.* 6th edition. Chicago: University of Chicago Press.

McConnell, Michael, Jack Baker, and Gail Langer Karwoski. 2016. *The Wedding Heard 'Round the World: America's First Gay Marriage.* Minneapolis: University of Minnesota Press.

McCorvey, Norma, and Andy Meisler. 1994. *I Am Roe: My Life, Roe v. Wade, and Freedom of Choice.* New York: Harper Collins.

McCorvey, Norma, and Gary Thomas. 1997. *Won by Love: Norma McCorvey, Jane Roe of Roe v. Wade, Speaks Out for the Unborn as She Shares Her New Conviction for Life.* Nashville, TN: Thomas Nelson.

McLanahan, Sara, and Gary Sandefur. 1994. *Growing Up with a Single Parent: What Hurts, What Helps.* Cambridge, MA: Harvard University Press.

Meezan, William, and Jonathan Rauch. 2005. "Gay Marriage, Same-Sex Parenting, and America's Children." *Future of Children* 15 (2):97–115.

Menjívar, Cecilia, and Leisy Abrego. 2012. "Legal Violence in the Lives of Immigrants: How Immigration Enforcement Affects Families, Schools, and Workplaces." Press release. Center for American Progress, December 11. https://www.americanprogress.org/press/release/2012/12/11/47403/release-legal-violence-in-the-lives-of-immigrants/.

Meyer, David S., and Debra C. Minkoff. 2004. "Conceptualizing Political Opportunity Structure." *Social Forces* 82 (4):1457–1492.

MLive. 2015. "April DeBoer and Jayne Rowse Speak after Hearing Supreme Court Decision." YouTube, June 26. https://www.youtube.com/watch?v=MOjZ43ix7V8.

Moats, David. 2004. *Civil Wars: A Battle for Gay Marriage.* Orlando, FL: Harcourt.

Mogill, Kenneth M. 2015. "Obergefell v. Hodges: Marriage and Our Changing Understanding of Discrimination." Paper presented at the meeting of the MCSS Joint Social Studies Conference, Waterford, MI.

Moon, Dawne. 2004. *God, Sex, and Politics: Homosexuality and Everyday Theologies.* Chicago: University of Chicago Press.

Moore, Mignon R. 2018. "Reflections on Marriage Equality as a Vehicle for LGBTQ Political Transformation." Pp. 73–80 in *Queer Families and Relationships after Marriage Equality,* edited by Michael W. Yarbrough, Angela Jones, and Joseph Nicholas DeFilippis. New York: Routledge.

Motion Picture Association of America, Inc. 1955. "A Code to Govern the Making of Motion Pictures: The Reasons Supporting It, and the Resolution for Uniform Interpretation." Washington, DC: Motion Picture Association of America.

Movement Advancement Project. 2019. "Non-Discrimination Laws." https://www.lgbtmap.org/equality-maps/non_discrimination_laws.

Ms. 1972. "We Have Had Abortions." Spring.

Murdoch, Joyce, and Deb Price. 2001. *Courting Justice: Gay Men and Lesbians v. the Supreme Court.* New York: Basic Books.

Muska, Susan, and Gréta Olafsdóttir, dirs. 2009. *Edie & Thea: A Very Long Engagement.* (Philadelphia, PA: Breaking Glass Pictures).

Myrdal, Gunnar, Richard Sterner, and Arnold Rose. 1944. *An American Dilemma: The Negro Problem and Modern Democracy.* New York: Harper.

National Center for Charitable Statistics. 2016. "NCCS Data Web." http://nccsweb.urban.org/.

National Defense Research Institute. 1993. "Sexual Orientation and U.S. Military Personnel Policy: Options and Assessment." Santa Monica, CA: RAND.

NBC News and Wall Street Journal. 2017. "Roper archive #31114771." NY: Roper Center for Public Opinion Research. https://ropercenter.cornell.edu/ipoll/study/31114771.

NBC News and Wall Street Journal. 2018a. "Roper Archive #31114947." Roper Center for Public Opinion Research. https://ropercenter.cornell.edu/ipoll/study/31114947.

NBC News and Wall Street Journal. 2018b. "Roper archive #31115622." Roper Center for Public Opinion Research. https://ropercenter.cornell.edu/ipoll/study/31115622.

NeJaime, Douglas. 2014. "Before Marriage: The Unexplored History of Nonmarital Recognition and Its Relationship to Marriage." *California Law Review* 102 (1):87–172.

NeJaime, Douglas, and Reva Siegel. 2018. "Religious Exemptions and Antidiscrimination Law in Masterpiece Cakeshop." *Yale Law Journal Forum* 128:201–225.

Nessel, Dana M., Carole M. Stanyar, Robert A. Sedler, and Kenneth M. Mogill. 2012. "Plaintiff's Amended Complaint in DeBoer v. Snyder." September 7. https://web.stanford.edu/~mrosenfe/DeBoer_Other/Plaintiffs_amended_complaint_2012.pdf.

Newsweek. 1985. "AIDS." USAIPOSPGONEW1985-85186. Roper Center. ropercenter.cornell.edu.

———. 1994. "Harding, Homophobia, Health Care and Vietnam." USPSRA1994-NW0294. Roper Center. https://ropercenter.cornell.edu

———. 1996. "Gay Rights/ Supreme Court Decision." USPSRA1996-NW96005C. Roper Center. https://ropercenter.cornell.edu

———. 1997. "Gay Rights and Disney." USPSRA1997-NW97009. Roper Center. https://ropercenter.cornell.edu.

———. 2000. "Post Super Tuesday/Gays & Lesbians." USPSRA2000-NW10. Roper Center. https://ropercenter.cornell.edu

———. 2008. "Gay Marriage/President-Elect Obama." USPSRA2008-NW11. Roper Center. https://ropercenter.cornell.edu

Nicolson, Malcolm, and John E. E. Fleming. 2013. *Imaging and Imagining the Fetus.* Baltimore, MD: Johns Hopkins University Press.

Ocobock, Abigail. 2013. "The Power and Limits of Marriage: Married Gay Men's Family Relationships." *Journal of Marriage and Family* 75 (1):191–205.

Orfield, Gary, Susan E. Eaton, and Harvard Project on School Desegregation. 1996. *Dismantling Desegregation: The Quiet Reversal of Brown v. Board of Education.* New York: New Press.

OutWeek magazine. 1990. Unsigned editorial "Claiming Forbes for the Gay Nation," March 18, page 4.

Page, Benjamin I., and Robert Y. Shapiro. 1992. *The Rational Public: Fifty Years of Trends in Americans' Policy Preferences.* Chicago: University of Chicago Press.

Paik, Anthony, and Kenneth Sanchagrin. 2013. "Social Isolation in America: An Artifact." *American Sociological Review* 78 (3):339–360.

Park, Barum. 2018. "How Are We Apart? Continuity and Change in the Structure of Ideological Disagreement in the American Public, 1980–2012." *Social Forces* 96 (4):1757–1784.

Pennsylvania Statewide Grand Jury. 2018. "40th Statewide Investigating Grand Jury Report 1: Interim—Redacted." https://www.attorneygeneral.gov/report/.

Pettigrew, Thomas F., and Linda R. Tropp. 2006. "A Meta-Analytic Test of Intergroup Contact Theory." *Journal of Personality and Social Psychology* 90 (5):751–783.

Pew Research Center. 2013. "March 2013 Political Survey." USPEW2013-03POL. Roper Center. ropercenter.cornell.edu.

Pew Research Center. 2018. "For Most Trump Voters, 'Very Warm' Feelings for Him Endured." August 9. https://www.people-press.org/2018/08/09/an-examination-of-the-2016-electorate-based-on-validated-voters/.

Phillips, Dave. 2017. "Judge Blocks Trump's Ban on Transgender Troops in Military." *New York Times*, October 30. https://www.nytimes.com/2017/10/30/us/military-transgender-ban.html.

Polikoff, Nancy D. 1993. "We Will Get What We Ask For: Why Legalizing Gay and Lesbian Marriage Will Not 'Dismantle the Legal Structure of Gender in Every Marriage.'" *Virginia Law Review* 79 (7):1535–1550.

Polikoff, Nancy D. 2008. *Beyond (Straight and Gay) Marriage: Valuing All Families under the Law*. Boston: Beacon Press.

PolitiFact. 2016. https://www.politifact.com/personalities/donald-trump/ and https://www.politifact.com/personalities/hillary-clinton/ for November, 2016 via the wayback machine, http://archive.org. Accessed January 25, 2018.

Posner, Richard A. 1992. *Sex and Reason*. Cambridge, MA: Harvard University Press.

Potter, Claire Bond. 2006. "Queer Hoover: Sex, Lies, and Political History." *Journal of the History of Sexuality* 15 (3):355–381.

Potter, Daniel. 2012. "Same-Sex Parent Families and Children's Academic Achievement." *Journal of Marriage and Family* 74:556–571.

Powell, Brian, Catherine Bolzendahl, Claudia Geist, and Lala Carr Steelman. 2010. *Counted Out: Same-Sex Relations and Americans' Definitions of Family*. New York: American Sociological Association Rose Series in Sociology and the Russell Sage Foundation.

Price, Joseph. 2013. "Expert Report in DeBoer v. Snyder, U.S. District Court, Eastern District of Michigan Southern Division." December 16. https://web.stanford.edu/~mrosenfe/DeBoer_affidavits/defense/Price.pdf.

Public Religion Research Institute. 2011. "August, 2011 Religion and Politics Tracking Survey." USPRRI2011-08. Roper Center. www.ropercenter.cornell.edu.

Ransom, Jan. 2020. "Harvey Weinstein Is Found Guilty of Sex Crimes in #MeToo Watershed." *New York Times*, February 24. https://www.nytimes.com/2020/02/24/nyregion/harvey-weinstein-trial-rape-verdict.html.

Rappeport, Alan. 2015. "Mike Huckabee (Not Ted Cruz) Captures Spotlight at Kim Davis Event." *New York Times*, September 8. https://www.nytimes.com/politics/first-draft/2015/09/08/mike-huckabee-captures-spotlight-not-ted-cruz-at-kim-davis-event/.

Reagan, Ronald. 1978. "Two Ill-Advised California Trends." *Los Angeles Herald-Examiner*, November 1. https://concurringopinions.com/archives/2010/10/ronald-reagan-and-gay-rights.html.

Regnerus, Mark. 2012a. "How Different Are the Adult Children of Parents Who Have Same-Sex Relationships? Findings from the New Family Structures Study." *Social Science Research* 41:752–770.

Regnerus, Mark. 2012b. "New Family Structures Study (ICPSR 34392)." Interuniversity Consortium for Political and Social Research. http://dx.doi.org/10.3886/ICPSR34392.v1.

Regnerus, Mark. 2012c. "Parental Same-Sex Relationships, Family Instability, and Life Outcomes for Adult Children: Answering Critics of the New Family Structures Study with Additional Analyses." *Social Science Research* 41:1367–1377.

Regnerus, Mark. 2013. "Expert Report in DeBoer v. Snyder." December 20. http://web.stanford.edu/~mrosenfe/DeBoer_affidavits/defense/Regnerus.pdf.

Republican National Convention. 2016. "Republican Party Platform." https://www.gop.com/the-2016-republican-party-platform/.

Richards, David A. J. 1974. "Free Speech and Obscenity Law: Toward a Moral Theory of the First Amendment." *University of Pennsylvania Law Review* 123 (1):45–91.

Ridgeway, Cecilia. 2011. *Framed by Gender: How Gender Inequality Persists in the Modern World*. Oxford: Oxford University Press.

Rios, Carmen. 2019. "We had Abortions—and We're Not Going Back." *Ms. Magazine*. https://msmagazine.com/2019/05/16/we-had-abortions-and-were-not-going-back/.

Robertson, Campbell. 2016. "Roy Moore, Alabama Chief Justice, Suspended over Gay Marriage Order." *New York Times*, September 30. https://www.nytimes.com/2016/10/01/us/roy-moore-alabama-chief-justice.html.

Robinson, Walter V., Matt Carroll, Sacha Pfeiffer, Michael Rezendes, and Stephen Kurkjian. 2002. "Scores of Priests Involved in Sex Abuse Cases." *Boston Globe,* January 31. https://www.bostonglobe.com/news/special-reports/2002/01/31/scores-priests-involved-sex-abuse-cases/kmRm7JtqBdEZ8UF0ucR16L/story.html.

Romero, Adam P. 2017. "1.1 Million LGBT Adults Are Married to Someone of the Same Sex at the Two-Year Anniversary of Obergefell v Hodges." Williams Institute. https://williamsinstitute.law.ucla.edu/wp-content/uploads/Obergefell-2-Year-Marriages.pdf.

Rosenberg, Gerald N. 2008. *The Hollow Hope: Can Courts Bring About Social Change?* 2nd edition. Chicago: University of Chicago Press.

Rosenfeld, Michael J. 2007. *The Age of Independence: Interracial Unions, Same-Sex Unions, and the Changing American Family*. Cambridge, MA: Harvard University Press.

Rosenfeld, Michael J. 2010. "Nontraditional Families and Childhood Progress through School." *Demography* 47 (3):755–775.

Rosenfeld, Michael J. 2013. "Reply to Allen et al." *Demography* 50 (3):963–969.

Rosenfeld, Michael J. 2014a. "Couple Longevity in the Era of Same-Sex Marriage in the US." *Journal of Marriage and Family* 76:905–918.

Rosenfeld, Michael J. 2014b. "Slides for testimony in *DeBoer v. Snyder*." https://web.stanford.edu/~mrosenfe/DeBoer_transcripts/Rosenfeld_trial_slides_final.pptx.

Rosenfeld, Michael J. 2015. "Revisiting the Data from the New Family Structure Study: Taking Family Instability into Account." *Sociological Science* 2:478–501.

Rosenfeld, Michael J. 2017. "Moving a Mountain: The Extraordinary Trajectory of Same-Sex Marriage Approval in the U.S." *Socius* 3:1–22.

Rosenfeld, Michael J. 2018. "Who Wants the Breakup? Gender and Breakup in Heterosexual Couples." Pp. 221–243 in *Social Networks and the Life Course: Integrating the Development of Human Lives and Social Relational Networks*, edited by Duane F. Alwin, Diane Felmlee, and Derek Kreager. Cham, Switzerland: Springer.

Rosenfeld, Michael J., and Byung-Soo Kim. 2005. "The Independence of Young Adults and the Rise of Interracial and Same-Sex Unions." *American Sociological Review* 70 (4):541–562.

Rosenfeld, Michael J., and Katharina Roesler. 2019. "Cohabitation Experience and Cohabitation's Association with Marital Dissolution." *Journal of Marriage and Family* 81 (1):42–58.

Rosenfeld, Michael J., Reuben J. Thomas, and Maja Falcon. 2015. "How Couples Meet and Stay Together." Stanford, CA: Stanford University Libraries. http://data.stanford.edu/hcmst.

Rosenfeld, Michael J., Reuben J. Thomas, and Sonia Hausen. 2018. "How Couples Meet and Stay Together: 2017 Fresh Sample." Stanford, CA: Stanford University Libraries. https://data.stanford.edu/hcmst2017.

Ross, Helen, Karen Gask, and Ann Berrington. 2011. "Civil Partnership Five Years On." *Population Trends* 145 (1):172–202.

Rotunda, Ronald D. 2010. "Judicial Disqualification in the Aftermath of Caperton v. A. T. Massey Coal Co." *Syracuse Law Review* 60:247–278.

Rubenstein, David. 2018. "The David Rubenstein Show: Anthony Kennedy." *Bloomberg*, November 28. https://www.bloomberg.com/news/videos/2018-11-28/the-david-rubenstein-show-anthony-kennedy-video.

Russo, Vito. 1987. *The Celluloid Closet: Homosexuality in the Movies*. Revised edition. New York: Harper & Row.

Ryder, Norman B. 1965. "The Cohort in the Study of Social Change." *American Sociological Review* 30:843–861.

Ryo, Emily. 2017. "On Normative Effects of Immigration Law." *Stanford Journal of Civil Rights and Civil Liberties* 13 (1):95–135.

Saguy, Abigail C. 2020. *Come Out, Come Out, Wherever You Are*. New York: Oxford University Press.

Saperstein, Aliya, and Andrew M. Penner. 2012. "Racial Fluidity and Inequality in the United States." *American Journal of Sociology* 118 (3):676–727.

Savin-Williams, Ritch C., Kara Joyner, and Gerulf Rieger. 2012. "Prevalence and Stability of Self-Reported Sexual Orientation Identity during Young Adulthood." *Archives of Sexual Behavior* 41:103–110.

Schachter, Ariela, and John Kuk. 2019. "A Change of Heart or a Change of Address? The Geographic Sorting of White Americans' Attitudes toward Immigration." Unpublished manuscript.

Scheuble, Laurie K., and David R. Johnson. 1993. "Marital Name Change: Plans and Attitudes of College Students." *Journal of Marriage and Family* 55 (3):747–754.

Schiappa, Edward, Peter B. Gregg, and Dean E. Hewes. 2006. "Can One TV Show Make a Difference? Will & Grace and the Parasocial Contact Hypothesis." *Journal of Homosexuality* 51 (4):15–37.

Schmalz, Jeffrey. 1992. "Gay Politics Goes Mainstream." *New York Times Magazine*, October 11. http://www.nytimes.com/1992/10/11/magazine/gay-politics-goes-mainstream.html.

Schuman, Alex, dir. 2017. *Love v. Kentucky*. (Cleveland, OH: Gravitas Ventures).

Segura, Gary M. 2005. "A Symposium on the Politics of Same-Sex Marriage: An Introduction and Commentary." *PS: Political Science and Politics* 38 (2):189–193.

Seidman, Steven. 2002. *Beyond the Closet: The Transformation of Gay and Lesbian Life*. New York: Routledge.

Shilts, Randy. 1982. *The Mayor of Castro Street: The Life and Times of Harvey Milk*. New York: St. Martin's Press.

Shilts, Randy. (1987) 2000. *And the Band Played On: Politics, People and the AIDS Epidemic*. Stonewall Inn edition. New York: St. Martin's Press.

Shilts, Randy. 1993. *Conduct Unbecoming: Gays and Lesbians in the U.S. Military*. New York: Fawcett Columbine.

Signorile, Michelangelo. 1990. "The Other Side of Malcolm." *OutWeek*, March 18, 40–45. http://www.outweek.net/pdfs/ow_38.pdf.

Signorile, Michelangelo. 2003. *Queer in America: Sex, the Media, and the Closets of Power.* Revised edition. Madison: University of Wisconsin Press.

Smith, Carly Parnitzke, and Jennifer J. Freyd. 2014. "Institutional Betrayal." *American Psychologist* 69 (6):575–587.

Smith, Tom W. 2012. "Trends in Confidence in Institutions, 1973–2006." Pp. 177–211 in *Social Trends in American Life: Findings from the General Social Survey since 1972,* edited by Peter V. Marsden. Princeton, NJ: Princeton University Press.

Smith, Tom W., Michael Davern, Jeremy Freese, and Stephen L. Morgan. 2019. "General Social Surveys 1972–2018." https://gss.norc.org/Get-The-Data.

Socarides, Charles W. 1978. *Homosexuality.* New York: Jason Aronson.

Solomon, Marc. 2014. *Winning Marriage: The Inside Story of How Same-Sex Couples Took on the Politicians and Pundits—and Won.* Lebanon, NH: University Press of New England.

Sprigg, Peter. 2004. *Outrage: How Gay Activists and Liberal Judges Are Trashing Democracy to Redefine Marriage.* Washington, DC: Regnery.

Spriggs, James F., and Thomas G. Hansford. 2001. "Explaining the Overruling of U.S. Supreme Court Precedent." *Journal of Politics* 63 (4):1091–1111.

Stacey, Judith, and Timothy J. Biblarz. 2001. "(How) Does the Sexual Orientation of Parents Matter?" *American Sociological Review* 66 (2):159–183.

Stafford, Katrease. 2015. "DeBoer, Rowse, Formally Adopt Their 5 Children." *Detroit Free Press,* November 5. https://www.freep.com/story/news/local/michigan/oakland/2015/11/05/jayne-rowse-april-deboer-adoption-wedding/75208698/.

Steel, Emily, and Michael S. Schmidt. 2017. "Bill O'Reilly Thrives at Fox News, Even as Harassment Settlements Add Up." *New York Times,* April 1. https://www.nytimes.com/2017/04/01/business/media/bill-oreilly-sexual-harassment-fox-news.html.

Steel, Emily, Michael S. Schmidt, Sarah Stein Kerr, and Barbara Marcolini. 2017. "O'Reilly, Weinstein, and the Culture of Power." *New York Times,* October 24.

Stoddard, Thomas B. 1989. "Why Gay People Should Seek the Right to Marry." *OutLook* 6:8–13.

Stone, Amy. 2012. *Gay Rights at the Ballot Box.* Minneapolis: University of Minnesota Press.

Sullivan, Andrew. 1996. *Virtually Normal: An Argument about Homosexuality.* New York: Vintage Books.

Sullivan, Andrew. 2018. "It's Time to Resist the Excesses of #MeToo." *New York,* January 12. http://nymag.com/intelligencer/2018/01/andrew-sullivan-time-to-resist-excesses-of-metoo.html.

Sunstein, Cass R. 1996. "On the Expressive Function of Law." *University of Pennsylvania Law Review* 144 (5):2021–2053.

Supreme Court Press. 2018. "Success Rate of a Petition for Writ of Certiorari to the Supreme Court." https://supremecourtpress.com/chance_of_success.html.

Tani, Carlyn. 2015. "How Two Hawai'i Women Helped Ignite the National Movement for Same-Sex Marriage." *Honolulu Magazine,* December 17. http://www.honolulumagazine.com/Honolulu-Magazine/December-2015/These-Hawaii-Women-Fought-a-23-year-battle-for-Same-Sex-Marriage/.

Taylor, Verta, Katrina Kimport, Nella Van Dyke, and Ellen Ann Andersen. 2009. "Culture and Mobilization: Tactical Repertoires, Same-Sex Weddings, and the Impact on Gay Activism." *American Sociological Review* 74:865–890.

Taylor, Verta, and Leila J. Rupp. 1993. "Women's Culture and Lesbian Feminist Activism: A Reconsideration of Cultural Feminism." *Signs: Journal of Women in Culture and Society* 19 (1):32–61.

Tomsic, Peggy A. 2016. "The Unlikely Domino: Kitchen v. Herbert." Pp. 227–234 in *Love Unites Us: Winning the Freedom to Marry in America*, edited by Kevin M. Cathcart and Leslie J. Gabel-Brett. New York: New Press.

Tribe, Laurence H. 1978. *American Constitutional Law*. Mineola, NY: Foundation Press.

Tribe, Laurence H. 1992. *Abortion: The Clash of Absolutes*. Revised edition. New York: Norton.

Twohey, Megan, and Michael Barbaro. 2016. "Two Women Say Donald Trump Touched Them Inappropriately." *New York Times*, October 12. https://www.nytimes.com/2016/10/13/us/politics/donald-trump-women.html.

Umberson, Debra. 2012. "Texas Professors Respond to New Research on Gay Parenting." *Huffington Post*, June 26. http://www.huffingtonpost.com/debra-umberson/texas-professors-gay-research_b_1628988.html.

U.S. Government Accounting Office. 1997. "Report to Henry J. Hyde." http://www.gao.gov/assets/230/223674.pdf.

Vaid, Urvashi. 1995. *Virtual Equality: The Mainstreaming of Gay and Lesbian Liberation*. New York: Anchor Books.

Van Sant, Gus, dir. 2008. *Milk*. (Universal City, CA: Focus Features).

Vara, Vauhini. 2015. "Can #Shoutyourabortion Turn Hashtag Activism into a Movement?" *New Yorker*, November 10. http://www.newyorker.com/news/news-desk/can-shoutyourabortion-turn-hashtag-activism-into-a-movement.

Viefhues-Bailey, Ludger H. 2010. *Between a Man and a Woman? Why Conservatives Oppose Same-Sex Marriage*. New York: Columbia University Press.

Von Drak, R. 1976. "Updating California's Sex Code: The Consenting Adults Law." *Criminal Justice Journal* 1:65–78.

Vosoughi, Soroush, Deb Roy, and Sinan Aral. 2018. "The Spread of True and False News Online." *Science* 359:1146–1151.

Wainright, Jennifer L., Stephen T. Russell, and Charlotte J. Patterson. 2004. "Psychosocial Adjustment, School Outcomes, and Romantic Relationships of Adolescents with Same-Sex Parents." *Child Development* 75 (6):1886–1898.

Wald, Michael. 2006. "Adults' Sexual Orientation and State Determinations Regarding Placement of Children." *Family Law Quarterly* 40:385–439.

Wallerstein, Judith S., and Joan Berlin Kelly. 1980. *Surviving the Breakup: How Children and Parents Cope with Divorce*. New York: Basic Books.

White, Mel. 2006. *Religion Gone Bad: The Hidden Dangers of the Christian Right*. New York: Penguin.

Wikipedia. 2017. "List of Overruled United States Supreme Court Decisions." https://en.wikipedia.org/wiki/List_of_overruled_United_States_Supreme_Court_decisions. Accessed January 14, 2018.

Wikipedia. 2018. "Kim Davis." https://en.wikipedia.org/wiki/Kim_Davis. Accessed June 11, 2018.

Wilcox, Clyde, Paul R. Brewer, Shauna Shames, and Celinda Lake. 2007. "If I Bend This far, I Will Break? Public Opinion about Same-Sex Marriage." Pp. 215–242 in *The Politics of Same-Sex Marriage*, edited by Craig A. Rimmerman and Clyde Wilcox. Chicago: University of Chicago Press.

Wilcox, Clyde, and Patrick Carr. 2010. "The Puzzling Case of the Abortion Attitudes of the Millennial Generation." Pp. 123–142 in *Understanding Public Opinion*, edited by Barbara Norrander and Clyde Wilcox. Washington, DC: CQ Press.

Williams, Lena. 1987. "600 in Gay Demonstration Arrested at Supreme Court." *New York Times*, October 14. https://www.nytimes.com/1987/10/14/us/600-in-gay-demonstration-arrested-at-supreme-court.html.

Wilson, William M., III. 1997. "Romer v. Evans: Terminal Silliness or Enlightened Jurisprudence?" *North Carolina Law Review* 75:1891–1941.

Wittman, Carl. 1970. *The Gay Manifesto*. New York: Red Butterfly.

Wolfson, Evan. 1983. "Samesex Marriage and Morality: The Human Rights Vision of the Constitution." Harvard Law School. http://freemarry.3cdn.net/73aab4141a80237ddf_kxm62r3er.pdf.

Wolfson, Evan. 2005. "Marriage Equality and Some Lessons for the Scary Work of Winning." *Tulane Journal of Law and Sexuality* 14:135–147.

Wolfson, Evan. 2004b. *Why Marriage Matters: America, Equality, and Gay People's Right to Marry*. New York: Simon & Schuster.

Wolfson, Evan, and Adam Polaski. 2016. "Movement + Strategy + Campaign: The Freedom to Marry Winning Combination." Pp. 108–119 in *Love Unites Us: Winning the Freedom to Marry in America*, edited by Kevin M. Cathcart and Leslie J. Gabel-Brett. New York: New Press.

Zaller, John R. 1992. *The Nature and Origins of Mass Opinion*. Cambridge: Cambridge University Press.

Index

For the benefit of digital users, indexed terms that span two pages (e.g., 52–53) may, on occasion, appear on only one of those pages.

Tables and figures are indicated by *t* and *f* following the page number